Starting an Online Business

FOR DUMMIES®

6TH EDITION

by Greg Holden

WILEY

Wiley Publishing, Inc.

Starting an Online Business For Dummies®, 6th Edition

Published by
Wiley Publishing, Inc.
111 River Street
Hoboken, NJ 07030-5774

www.wiley.com

Copyright © 2010 by Wiley Publishing, Inc., Indianapolis, Indiana

Published by Wiley Publishing, Inc., Indianapolis, Indiana

Published simultaneously in Canada

For general information on our other products and services, please contact our Customer Care Department within the U.S. at 877-762-2974, outside the U.S. at 317-572-3993, or fax 317-572-4002.

For technical support, please visit www.wiley.com/techsupport.

Wiley also publishes its books in a variety of electronic formats. Some content that appears in print may not be available in electronic books.

Library of Congress Control Number: 2010929413

ISBN-13: 978-0-470-60210-2

Manufactured in the United States of America

10 9 8 7 6 5 4 3

WILEY

About the Author

Greg Holden started a small business called Stylus Media, which is a group of editorial, design, and computer professionals who produce both print and electronic publications. The company gets its name from a recording stylus that reads the traces left on a disk by voices or instruments and translates those signals into electronic data that can be amplified and enjoyed by many. He has been a freelance writer since 1996. He is an avid user of eBay, both as a buyer and seller, and is a blogger.

Greg recently assumed the role of Director of Communications for the Jane Addams College of Social Work at the University of Illinois at Chicago. One of the ways Greg enjoys communicating is through explaining technical subjects in nontechnical language. The first edition of *Starting an Online Business For Dummies* was the ninth of his more than forty-five computer books. He also authored *eBay PowerUser's Bible* for Wiley Publishing. Over the years, Greg has been a regular contributor to CNET and the Web site AuctionBytes (www. auctionbytes.com). He also contributes to *PC World* and the University of Illinois at Chicago alumni magazine. Other projects have included preparing a Web site for a hedge fund management firm with NewCor Group, a group of freelance professionals.

Greg balances his technical expertise and his entrepreneurial experience with his love of literature. He received an M.A. in English from the University of Illinois at Chicago and also writes general interest books, short stories, and poetry.

After graduating from college, Greg became a reporter for his hometown newspaper. Working at the publications office at the University of Chicago was his next job, and it was there that he started to use computers. He discovered, as the technology became available, that he loved desktop publishing (with the Macintosh and LaserWriter) and, later on, the World Wide Web.

Greg loves to travel, but since his two daughters were born, he hasn't been able to get around much. He was able to translate his experiences into a book called *Karma Kids: Answering Everyday Parenting Questions with Buddhist Wisdom.* However, through the Web, he enjoys traveling vicariously and meeting people online. He lives with his family in an old house in Chicago that he has been rehabbing for — well, for many years now. He is a collector of objects such as pens, cameras, radios, and hats. He is always looking for things to take apart so that he can see how they work and fix them up. Many of the same skills prove useful in creating and maintaining Web pages. He is an active member of Jewel Heart, a Tibetan Buddhist meditation and study group based in Ann Arbor, Michigan.

Dedication

To Peggy Lester. Thanks, Mom, for bringing us together.

Acknowledgments

One of the things I like best about this book is that it's a teaching tool that gives me a chance to share my knowledge — small business owner to small business owner — about computers, the Internet, and communicating your message to others in an interactive way. As any businessperson knows, most large-scale projects are a team effort.

While the online business landscape has changed since this book was first published, some basic principles remain the same. One is the fact that the most successful entrepreneurs also tend to be the ones who were the most generous with their time and experience. They taught me that the more helpful you are, the more successful you'll be in return.

I want to thank all those who were profiled as case studies. Thanks go to: John Moen of Graphic Maps; Jeremy G. Alicandri of SimplyVentures.com; Lucky Boyd of MyTexasMusic.com; Mike Holden of lp2cdsolutions; John Counsel of The Profit Clinic; Jeffrey E. Edelheit; Lars Hundley of Clean Air Gardening; Laura Milnor Iverson; Mark Lauer of General Tool and Repair; Doug Laughter of The Silver Connection; John Raddatz of SoftBear Shareware; Skye Ryan-Evans; Kharisma Ryantori; Sarah-Lou Morris of Alfresco; Judy Vorfeld of Office Support Services; Marques Vickers; and Scott Wills. Special recognition also goes to attorney David Adler (www.ecommerceattorney.com) for his assistance with Chapter 16.

I would also like to acknowledge some of my own colleagues who helped prepare and review the text and graphics of this book and who have supported and encouraged me in other lessons of life. And thanks as always to Ann Lindner, whose teaching experience proved invaluable in suggesting ways to make the text more clear.

For editing and technical assignments, I was lucky to be in the capable hands of the folks at Wiley Publishing: my project editor and copy editor Susan Christophersen, and technical editor Joel Elad.

Thanks also to Neil Salkind of Studio B and to Kyle Looper of Wiley Publishing for helping me add this book to the list of those I've authored and, in the process, to broaden my expertise as a writer.

Last but certainly not least, the future is in the hands of the generation of my two daughters, Zosia and Lucy, who allow me to learn from the curiosity and joy with which they approach life.

Publisher's Acknowledgments

We're proud of this book; please send us your comments through our online registration form located at http://dummies.custhelp.com. For other comments, please contact our Customer Care Department within the U.S. at 877-762-2974, outside the U.s. at 317-572-3993, or fax 317-572-4002.

Some of the people who helped bring this book to market include the following:

Acquisitions, Editorial, and Media Development

Project and Copy Editor:
Susan Christophersen
(Previous Edition: Rebecca Senninger, Jennifer Riggs)

Acquisitions Editor: Kyle Looper

Technical Editor: Joel Elad

Editorial Manager: Jodi Jensen

Media Development Manager:
Laura VanWinkle

Editorial Assistant: Leslie Saxman

Sr. Editorial Assistant: Cherie Case

Cartoons: Rich Tennant
(www.the5thwave.com)

Composition Services

Project Coordinator: Sheree Montgomery

Layout and Graphics: Samantha K. Cherolis

Proofreaders: Lauren Mandelbaum,
Bonnie Mikkelson

Indexer: Potomac Indexing, LLC

Publishing and Editorial for Technology Dummies

Richard Swadley, Vice President and Executive Group Publisher

Andy Cummings, Vice President and Publisher

Mary Bednarek, Executive Acquisitions Director

Mary C. Corder, Editorial Director

Publishing for Consumer Dummies

Diane Graves Steele, Vice President and Publisher

Joyce Pepple, Acquisitions Director

Composition Services

Debbie Stailey, Director of Composition Services

Table of Contents

Introduction

You've been thinking about starting your own business for a while now. You heard about the woman whose Julia and Me blog was turned into a book and a popular movie. You've heard about young entrepreneurs who've made billions creating popular Web sites such as Facebook. But you've been slow to jump on the bandwagon. You're a busy person, after all. You have a full-time job, whether it's running your home or working outside your home. Or perhaps you've been laid off or are going through some other life-changing event and are ready to take off in a new direction, but the economic upheavals of recent years leave you understandably reluctant to make a big career change.

Well, I have news for you: *Now* is the perfect time to turn your dream into reality by starting your own online business. More individuals than ever before — regular folks just like you — are making money and enriching their lives by operating businesses online. The clock and your location are no longer limiting factors. Small business owners can now work any time of the night or day in their spare bedrooms, local libraries, or neighborhood coffee shops.

If you like the idea of being in business for yourself but don't have a particular product or service in mind at the moment, relax and keep yourself open for inspiration. Many different kinds of commercial enterprises can hit it big on the Internet. Among the entrepreneurs I interviewed for this book are a woman who sells her own insect repellent; a mapmaker; a woman who provides office services for the medical community; a housewife who sells sweetener and coffee on eBay; a sculptor and painter; a young man who started selling electronics online at age 16; and several folks who create Web pages for other businesses. With the help of this book, you can start a new endeavor and be in charge of your own cyberbusiness, too.

You Can Do It!

What's that? You say you wouldn't know a merchant account, a profit and loss statement, or a clickthrough advertising rate if it came up to you on the street and introduced itself? Don't worry: The Internet (and this book) levels the playing field so that a novice has just as good a chance at succeeding as MBAs who love to throw around business terms at cocktail parties.

The Internet is a pervasive and everyday part of the business landscape these days. Whether you've been in business for 20 years or 20 minutes, the keys to success are the same:

- ✔ **Having a good idea:** If you have something to sell that people have an appetite for, and if your competition is slim, your chances of success are hefty.

- ✔ **Working hard:** When you're your own boss, you can make yourself work harder than any of your former bosses ever could. But if you put in the effort and persist through the inevitable ups and downs, you'll be a winner.

- ✔ **Believing in yourself:** One of the most surprising and useful things I discovered from the online businesspeople I interviewed was that if you believe that you'll succeed, you probably will. Believe in yourself and proceed as though you'll be successful. Together with your good ideas and hard work, your confidence will pay off.

If you're the cautious type who wants to test the waters before you launch your new business on the Internet, let this book lead you gently up the learning curve. After you're online, you can master techniques to improve your presence. This book includes helpful hints for doing market research and reworking your Web site until you get the success you want.

The Water's Still Fine

When I first started revising this new edition in the fall of 2009, I was not surprised to find that many businesses had reduced sales a year after the serious economic crash. I *was* surprised to find that new businesses had started that same year and were doing well. It turns out that *any time* is a good idea to start an online business as long as you have a good idea and a smart business plan.

New resources, many of which didn't exist when I wrote the previous edition, present entrepreneurs with opportunities to market themselves and their products and services. Twitter, Facebook, Google Payments, WordPress — all these Web standards were all either just emerging or hadn't yet come to fruition just a few years ago. Well-known marketplaces such as eBay give businesspeople a solid foundation on which to start a new business. Other well-known Web-based service providers (such as Yahoo!, PayPal, and Amazon.com) give you a way to reach millions of potential customers. Bloggers are an everyday part of the cyberspace landscape, and some are making a regular source of income from their online diaries. Google and Yahoo! are making it easier than ever to gain advertising revenue.

As the Web becomes more of a way of life and broadband Internet connections become widespread around the world, doing business online isn't considered unusual anymore. Still, you may have reasonable concerns about the future of e-commerce for the very entrepreneurs this book seeks to help — individuals who are starting their first businesses on the Web. Your fears will quickly evaporate when you read this book's case studies of my friends and colleagues who do business online. They're either thriving or at least treading water, and they enthusiastically encourage others to jump right in.

"I feel the best time to start an online business is when you are positioned to begin. I do not feel that there is an advantage/disadvantage to waiting for a 'better time' to start," says Mark Cramer, who has run a business called MePage.com for a decade. "The Internet is here to stay, and we have just scratched the surface in terms of potential," says artist Marques Vickers, who has thrived online for the same amount of time. Both provide proof that you can make money online doing just about anything as long as you have the right level of knowledge and enthusiasm.

Where This Book Is Coming From

Online business isn't just for large corporations, or even just for small businesses that already have a storefront in the real world and simply want to supplement their marketability with a Web site.

The Internet is a perfect venue for individuals who want to start their own business, who like using computers, and who believe that cyberspace is the place to do it. You don't need much money to get started, after all. If you already have a computer as well as an Internet connection and can create your own Web pages (something this book helps you with), making the move to your own business Web site may cost only $100 or less. After you're online, the overhead is pretty reasonable, too: You may pay only $10 to $75 per month to a Web hosting service to keep your site online — or nothing, if you sign up with one of the specialty marketplaces that give you a platform for creating Web pages and selling products, and charges a fee only if you make a sale.

With each month that goes by, the number of Internet users increases exponentially. The growth is greatest outside the United States. To be precise, in early 2009, Internet World Stats released data indicating that the number of Internet users worldwide surpassed the 1 billion mark in the previous year and was currently over 1.5 billion. South America posted the fastest growth in the fourth quarter of 2008, with the number of Internet users shooting up 63.2 percent compared with the same period the year before. There are 647 million Internet users in Asia, compared with fewer than 250 million in

North America; the low rate of 17.1 percent of the Asian population that has access to the Internet at home means that "there is much potential for future Internet usage growth in Asia," the report notes. We have long since reached that critical mass where *most* people are using the Internet regularly for everyday shopping and other financial activities. The Internet is already becoming a powerhouse for small businesses.

How to Use This Book

Want to focus on what's new and different in e-commerce? Jump right in to Chapter 1. Looking for an overview of the whole process of going online and be inspired by one man's online business success story? Zip ahead to Chapter 2. Want to find out how to accept credit card payments? Flip ahead to Chapter 7. Feel free to skip back and forth to chapters that interest you. I've made this book into an easy-to-use reference tool that you'll be comfortable with no matter what your level of experience is with computers and networking. You don't have to scour each chapter methodically from beginning to end to find what you want. The Internet doesn't work that way, and neither does this book!

If you're just starting out and need to do some essential business planning, see Chapter 2. If you want to prepare a shopping list of business equipment, see Chapter 3. Chapters 4–9 are all about the essential aspects of creating and operating a successful online business, from organizing and marketing your Web site to providing effective online customer service and security. Chapters 10 and 11 examine the many ways to market your business cost effectively online. Chapters 12–15 explore a variety of marketplaces and services you can exploit, including eBay, Amazon.com, Google, and Facebook. Later chapters get into legal issues and accounting. The fun thing about being online is that continually improving and redoing your presentation is easy. So start where it suits you to do so and come back later for more.

What This Book Assumes about You

This book assumes that you've never been in business before but that you're interested in setting up your own commercial site on the Internet. I also assume that you're familiar with the Internet, have been surfing for a while, and may even have put out some information of your own in the form of a home page.

This book also assumes that you have or are ready to get the following:

- ✔ **A computer and a modem:** Don't worry, Chapters 3 and 4 explain exactly what hardware and software you need.

- ✔ **Instructions on how to think like a businessperson:** I spend a good amount of time in this book encouraging you to set goals, devise strategies to meet those goals, and do the sort of planning that successful businesspeople need to do.

- ✔ **Just enough technical know-how:** You don't have to do it all yourself. Plenty of entrepreneurs decide to partner with someone or hire an expert to perform design and technical work. This book can help you understand your options and give you a basic vocabulary so that you can work productively with the consultants you hire.

What's Where in This Book

This book is divided into six parts. Each part contains chapters that discuss stages in the process of starting an online business.

Part I: Launching Your Online Business

In Part I, I describe what you need to do and how you need to *think* so that you can start your new online business. The first chapter summarizes what's new in e-commerce in case you want to get up to speed right away. Chapter 2 follows the story about how a business started by a graphic artist turned mapmaker has grown into an Internet success story. Subsequent chapters also present case studies profiling other entrepreneurs and describing how they started their online businesses. Within these pages is where I also describe the software that you need to create Web pages and perform essential business tasks, along with any computer upgrades that help your business run more smoothly. You also discover how to choose a Web host and find exciting new ways to make money online.

Part II: Establishing and Organizing Your Online Business

Even if you sell only on eBay or only make money by placing affiliate ads, at some point you need to create a *Web site* — a series of interconnected Web pages that everyone in cyberspace can view with a Web browser. A Web site is a home base where people can find you and what you have to offer. This part explains how to create a compelling and irresistible Web site, one that attracts paying customers around the world and keeps them coming back to make more purchases. This part also includes options for attracting and keeping customers, making your site secure, and updating and improving your online business.

Part III: Building Traffic through Social Networking and More

Some of the most exciting options for starting a business online are ways to build a name for yourself and attract customers to your products and services through word-of-mouth advertising, social networking, and other advertising strategies. In this part, you find out all about those options as well as discover the ins and outs of advertising online. You find how to improve your visibility by optimizing your catalog listings and Web site for search engines such as Google and Bing. Also see how to spread the word on Facebook, Twitter, and your own blog.

Part IV: Expanding beyond Your Own Web Site

You can generate sales revenue without even setting up your own Web site from scratch. Rather than go it alone, you can sign up with one of the many well-established business marketplaces on the Web that enable individuals just like you to create storefronts or sell individual items. In this part, you find out about creating Web sites or storefronts on Google, Amazon, and eBay, among other venues. Many of these sites enable budding businesspeople to conduct a cost-effective and highly targeted form of online advertising called search engine optimization (SEO), which I describe in detail in this part.

Part V: Keeping Your Business Legal and Fiscally Responsible

This part delves into some less-than-sexy but essential activities for any online business. Find out about general security methods designed to make commerce more secure on the Internet. I also discuss copyrights, trademarks, and other legal concerns for anyone wanting to start a company in the increasingly competitive atmosphere of the Internet. Finally, you get an overview of basic accounting practices for online businesses and suggestions for accounting tools that you can use to keep track of your e-commerce activities.

Part VI: The Part of Tens

Filled with tips, cautions, suggestions, and examples, the Part of Tens presents many tidbits of information that you can use to plan and create your own business presence on the Internet, including ten e-commerce marketplaces worth exploring.

Conventions Used in This Book

In this book, I format important bits of information in special ways to make sure that you notice them right away:

- **In This Chapter lists:** Chapters start with a list of the topics that I cover in that chapter. This list represents a table of contents in miniature.

- **Numbered lists:** When you see a numbered list, follow the steps in a specific order to accomplish a given task.

- **Bulleted lists:** Bulleted lists (like this one) indicate things that you can do in any order, or they list related bits of information.

- **Web addresses:** When I describe activities or sites of interest on the World Wide Web, I include the address, or Uniform Resource Locator (URL), in a special typeface like this: `http://www.wiley.com/`. Because the newer versions of popular Web browsers don't require you to enter the entire URL, this book uses the shortened addresses. For example, if you want to connect to the Wiley Publishing site, you can get there by simply entering the following in your browser's Go To or Address box: `www.wiley.com`.

    Don't be surprised if your browser can't find an Internet address you type or if a Web page that's depicted in this book no longer looks the same. Although the sites were current when the book was written, Web addresses (and sites themselves) can be pretty fickle. Try looking for a missing site by using an Internet search engine. Or try shortening the address by deleting everything after the `.com` (or `.org` or `.edu`).

Icons Used in This Book

Starting an Online Business For Dummies, 6th Edition, also uses special graphical elements — *icons* — to get your attention. Here's what they look like and what they mean:

This icon points out some technical details that may be of interest to you. A thorough understanding, however, isn't a prerequisite to grasping the underlying concept. Nontechies are welcome to skip items marked by this icon.

This icon calls your attention to interviews I conducted with online entrepreneurs who provided tips and instructions for running an online business.

This icon flags practical advice about particular software programs or issues of importance to businesses. Look to these tips for help with finding resources quickly, making sales, or improving the quality of your online business site. This icon also alerts you to software programs and other resources that I consider to be especially good, particularly for the novice user.

This icon points out potential pitfalls that can develop into more major problems if you're not careful.

This icon alerts you to facts and figures that are important to keep in mind when you run your online business.

This icon alerts you to find related information elsewhere in the book or in another book altogether.

We're in It Together

Improving communication is the whole point of this book. My goal is to help you express yourself in the dynamic medium of the Internet and to remind you that you're not alone. I'm a businessperson myself, after all. So I hope that you'll let me know what you think about this book by contacting me. Check out the *For Dummies* Web site at www.dummies.com. You're also welcome to contact me directly if you have questions or comments. Visit my personal Web page at www.gregholden.com or send e-mail to me at greg@gregholden.com.

Part I

Launching Your Online Business

The 5th Wave

By Rich Tennant

"Sometimes I feel behind the times. I asked my 11-year old to build a Web site for my business, and he said he would, only after he finishes the one he's building for his ant farm."

In this part . . .

What's all the fuss about starting an online business? In this part, I answer that question with a brief overview of the whole process. Happily, it doesn't need to involve a lot of fuss. The following chapters help you set your online business goals, draw a blueprint for meeting those goals, and explore new ways to market your goods and services.

For those of you who have some familiarity with the subject, I begin with a review of new tools and approaches in the field of e-commerce, including social networking. Just as dentists prepare their drills and carpenters assemble their tools, you need to gather the necessary hardware and software to keep your online business running smoothly. So in this part, I also discuss the business equipment that the online store owner needs and suggest ways that you can meet those needs even on a limited budget.

Let the step-by-step instructions and real-life case studies in this part guide you through the process of starting a successful business online.

Chapter 1

What's New: The Latest Tools and Strategies for Your Online Business

*N*ew technologies are always popping up in the world of online commerce. Things are started on a whim, or just to see whether they'll work at all. When millions of people begin to participate, people think that there must be a way to make money off this opportunity. Companies with money then throw money at the project or buy it outright, and the project becomes more commercial in nature. Finally, average people like you and me pick up on these technologies and add them to our mix. Before long, they become part of the cyberspace landscape.

This scenario is still happening, and anyone who thinks it's too late to make money online has only to look at Facebook, Twitter, and other new venues to see that entrepreneurship is still alive. Keeping up with all the new trends in online commerce is getting harder because it's a constantly moving target. This chapter gives you an overview of some of the many new and exciting ways to conduct e-commerce. If you've heard about e-commerce before and weren't attracted by the thought of creating a Web site and sales catalog, take a look at these innovative options for generating revenue.

New Ways to Spread the Word

When I wrote the first edition of this book back in 1998, you could advertise your online business in a few ways: through a Web site; through postings on online discussion boards; through placing banner ads; and exchanging links to other sites. Now, you can do viral marketing (word-of-mouth advertising) on social networking sites.

Social networking sites are the modern-day equivalent of the town square. When you go to a social networking site, you again strike up a personal relationship with a merchant; after you do, you're that much more likely to buy something from that person. Social networking sites give potential customers another place where they can find you and get to know you. The best-known sites are

- ✔ **Twitter** (www.twitter.com)
- ✔ **Facebook** (www.facebook.com)
- ✔ **MySpace** (www.myspace.com)
- ✔ **Friendster** (www.friendster.com)

If you want to reach a younger generation of consumers, places like Friendster and Facebook are among the best ways to find them. If you sell services that depend on personal contact with a customer, such as a group of musicians that plays for weddings or a wedding planner, people sometimes hire you as much for your personality and personal approach as for your actual work. In these kinds of fields, social networking sites are even more important.

Another networking site, LinkedIn (www.linkedin.com) lets you build a network of business contacts that can get in touch with one another and, they hope, build a community.

Facebooking your business

No, Facebook wasn't started with the idea of business in mind. It is primarily a site where you connect with friends, family, and others on a regular basis. You sign up for a Facebook account and create a page where you post information about yourself and (optionally) a photo. You then make the decision about whether that information is available to the public at large or only to people you invite to see it. That's the nice thing about Facebook, as far as I'm concerned: You control who communicates with you because you "invite" or "approve" them as needed. If you are approached by someone you don't know, you simply decline to approve that person's access.

For me, Facebook is a terrific way to keep in touch with friends I don't see often enough and family members who live far away. Lately, I've been using Facebook to write a story that I share with my Facebook friends. I write an episode of the story on my blog and then announce it via Facebook. One of these announcements is shown in Figure 1-1.

Figure 1-1:
You can use Facebook to keep in touch or promote a story or a cause.

As often happens, this popular online resource has become a place to do business for a few early adopters. With more than 400 million registered users, 50 percent of whom log in every day, it's a natural for businesspeople to advertise themselves and even offer items for sale.

The statistics about Facebook come from the site itself: `www.facebook.com/ press/info.php?statistics`.

A marketplace for artists called ArtFire (`www.artfire.com`) allows its members to display items from their sales catalogs on their Facebook pages. Not only that, but if you shop in one of these Facebook "kiosks," you can make a purchase there without having to go to ArtFire or another site. The utility costs ArtFire members only $12 per month. In Chapter 15, you can read about one enterprising seller who's sold items through Facebook.

MySpace for MyCustomers

MySpace has been around longer than Facebook, but at this writing, it isn't as "hot" as it used to be. That's probably because MySpace functions more or less as a Web hosting site. It allows anyone to create a free Web page and gives anyone in the world access to it. The "friend" concept espoused by

Facebook probably appeals more to young people who want to keep in contact with their nearest and dearest (and block people they don't want to give access to).

Nevertheless, MySpace is still important because of one of the new and exciting principles of doing business online in the twenty-first century. That's the ability to establish multiple presences on the Web. Even better, you can have all those pages and storefronts link to one another. The fact that they link to other Web sites makes them more "valuable" in the eyes of search services such as Google, thereby giving you more exposure through the all-important search marketing services I describe in Chapter 11.

Tweeting for fun and profit

Twitter is a true Internet phenomenon. It distinguishes itself from other social networking sites by limiting users to posting comments that contain no more than 140 characters. Despite this restriction, many businesspeople as well as public figures have latched on to Twitter as a convenient and easy-to-use way to spread the word about anything. That includes senators posting "tweets" about upcoming votes in Congress, Sarah Palin talking about . . . herself, and stars like Ashton Kutcher (Twitter name: aplusk), who at this writing has 4,611,357 people around the world "following" his Twitter posts. Every time he utters a 140-character statement on Twitter, nearly 4.7 million people get the message.

With that kind of platform, anyone can promote him- or herself or a business online. Kutcher, to his credit, regularly promotes social change and peace. But my colleague Ina Steiner, who runs a Web site called EveryPlaceISell, uses Twitter as a platform for sellers. Sellers regularly post "tweets" about sales and promotions. See Chapter 15 for more.

Blogging to build your business

In the late 1990s, Web pages were where it was at as far as e-commerce goes. As of this writing, the blog is the tool of choice for many online entrepreneurs. On the surface, a blog doesn't seem like something that can actually make you money. A *blog* is a Web page, but one that is updated frequently with content to which readers can quickly respond with comments. Many take the form of an online diary: a running commentary that you add to as often as possible — every few days, every day, or perhaps even several times a day.

Blogs do make money, however. When you have a dependable number of viewers, you can generate revenue from your blog by using these methods:

- **Placing ads:** You can use a service such as Blogads (`www.blogads.com`) or Google's AdSense (`adsense.google.com`).

- **Placing affiliate ads:** You sign up for well-known programs that steer potential buyers to Amazon.com or eBay.

- **Building interest in your Web site:** By talking about yourself, your knowledge, or your services, you encourage customers to commit to them.

Creating a blog to support your business is a powerful method to reach potential customers and strengthen connections with current ones. The word-of-mouth marketing that results from successful blog publishing is effective while also being cost-effective: Advertising costs are miniscule compared to a traditional marketing effort.

What's the first step in creating a blog? I usually advocate thinking before clicking. Give at least a few minutes' thought to the kind of blog you want to create. An article titled "How Blogs Can Deliver Business Results" in *Entrepreneur* magazine describes several different types of blogs created by Denali Flavors to promote its Moose Tracks line of ice cream flavors. Each one took a different approach to promoting the same product:

- **Entertainment:** The blog *Moosetopia* is written by the Moose Tracks Moose, the product mascot.

- **Useful advice:** The blog *Free Money Finance* provides something that everyone needs — advice on how to handle their money. The connection to the product is a "sponsored by" Moose Tracks ice cream logo near the top of the blog.

- **Public relations:** Another blog, *Team Moose Tracks,* concerns efforts of the company's cycling team to raise money for an orphanage in Latvia. It reflects positively on the company and the brand.

- **Behind the scenes:** A fourth blog, *Denali Flavors,* takes a look at what goes on in the company.

The article (`www.entrepreneur.com/marketing/marketingideas/article80100-2.html`) reports that site visits went up 25.7 percent after the blogs went online; the company spent less than $700 on all four blogs, too. You can take any or all of these approaches in your own blog, depending on the product you're trying to sell and your available resources. If you're selling a "fun" product, you might decide to take the entertainment approach; if you work for a big company, you might take the behind-the-scenes approach.

After you have a general idea of the approach you want to take, it's time to get started. The first step is to choose your blog host. You don't necessarily have to pay to do this; most of the best-known blog hosts offer hosting for free. They include:

- **Blogger** (www.blogger.com): Blogger doesn't have as many features as other blog utilities, but it's free.

- **WordPress** (www.wordpress.com): WordPress is software you download and install to create and manage your blog. WordPress offers free hosting for blogs and is very popular; find out more in the latest edition of *WordPress For Dummies,* by Lisa Sabin-Wilson (Wiley).

- **TypePad** (www.typepad.com): TypePad has lots of features, but it costs anywhere from $8.95 to $89.95 per month. The Unlimited plan, at$14.95 per month or $149.50 per year, should be sufficient for most online business owners.

- **BlogHarbor** (www.blogharbor.com): Hosting packages start at $8.95 per month; you get security and templates for designing blogs.

Take some time to look at other business blogs and examine how they use type and color. Often, for a purely personal blog, it doesn't matter whether it's carefully designed. But for a blog that has a business purpose, you need to make it look professional.

Next, determine who will do the blogging. You may not want to do it all yourself. If you can gather two or three contributors, you increase the chances that you can post entries on a daily basis, which is important for blogs. That way, if someone needs time off, you'll have backup contributors available.

When you configure your blog, no matter which host you choose, the main features tend to be more or less the same. Figure 1-2 shows the Clean Air Gardening Blog, one of the many blogs created by expert marketer Lars Hundley, whom I profile in the sidebar "Blogs plant seeds, gardening business blooms," later in this chapter. The blog includes some Google AdSense ads to drum up extra revenue; a link for visitors to post comments; categories that organize past blog posts; a chronological archive of posts; and links to other relevant sites, including Hundley's main Clean Air Gardening Web site (www.cleanairgardening.com).

For detailed instructions on how to create a business blog, turn to *Buzz Marketing with Blogs For Dummies,* by Susannah Gardner (published by Wiley).

Figure 1-2:
Make
your blog
attractive,
well orga-
nized, and
interactive.

Perhaps the most difficult aspect of blogging isn't actually creating the blog, but maintaining it. Developing a schedule whereby you publish regular blog posts is important. It's also important to measure how many visits your blog and your business Web site get so that you can measure results. Be sure to do a benchmark test beforehand so that you can judge results afterward. Adjust your site as needed to attract more visitors, but remember to stay "on topic" so that you don't drive away the audience you already have.

Search marketing

Search marketing isn't new, but what's new is the fact that it has obtained a name of its own: Search Engine Optimization (SEO). SEO has spawned a new type of business: a company that helps online businesses market themselves by getting better placement in search results. If your company ends up at or near the top of page 1 of someone's search results on Google, for instance, you're going to get a lot more traffic than a site that only makes it to page 12.

To find out more about SEO and how you can practice it yourself without having to pay a consultant, see Chapter 11.

Blogs plant seeds, gardening business blooms

Lars Hundley is an expert with blogs, photo sharing, and social networking sites to market his products. His Dallas, Texas–based business, Clean Air Gardening (www.cleanairgardening. com), posted sales of $1.5 million in 2006. Sales grew year by year until 2009, when the economy took its toll. "It is the first year that we are not experiencing year-to-year sales growth," says Hundley. But with the optimism that characterizes the successful entrepreneur, he adds: "But every year can't be your best year ever, so I'm optimistic that we'll see growth again in 2010."

Products occasionally receive the attention of traditional media. A few years ago, for example, Clear Air Gardening was mentioned in *The New York Times* as well as on *Good Morning America*.

Lars uses a variety of blogs and online video sites to promote his Clean Air Gardening online business:

- ✔ **Practical Environmentalist** (www.practicalenvironmentalist.com): This blog isn't branded for Clean Air Gardening or directly linked to the company, but it is intended to attract the same kind of environmentally aware person that is its typical customer. This blog is more of a free service than it is a hard-selling kind of blog.

- ✔ **Gardening Gift Guide** (www.gardeninggiftguide.com): This blog is a sort of Gizmodo or Engadget for gardening products. It promotes products from Clean Air Gardening as well as interesting gardening products from other competing sites.

- ✔ **Compost guide** (www.compostguide.com): This blog promotes several different companies. It's designed to generate a lot of composting-related educational information as well as keyword-rich pages and product promotion pages that give Air Gardening a growing body of search engine–friendly composting content over time.

- ✔ **Flash-based video on Clean Air Gardening:** Flash-based video helps sell products. Hundley films the videos with his Canon Powershot S1 digital camera that also shoots video. Then he edits them with his Mac Mini and converts them to Flash so that people can watch them with their Web browser directly on the page. One example is at www.cleanairgardening. com/patdesaustum.html.

- ✔ **Videos on YouTube.com:** Hundley uploads videos so that he doesn't have to pay for the bandwidth. Then he embeds the YouTube video on his product page. That also allows people to find the products on the YouTube site and then click through to Clean Air Gardening. "When we add a video to a Web page, we can increase our conversion rate for that product by up to 20 percent," comments Hundley.

- ✔ **Product and testimonial photos at Flickr:** He puts all his customer testimonial photos on Flickr and links to them from his testimonials page on his Web site. People can access these photos directly on Flickr (www.flickr.com/photos/cleanairgardening). They can then use a link to return to the Clean Air Gardening page.

"If you're thinking about starting your own Internet business, just do it!" says Lars. "Start a small site and do it in your spare time to test the waters. I kept my day job for the first year when I started this business, until it started to take off and make money. Now, 11 years later, it is a multimillion dollar a year company with 14 employees and a large, 14,000-square-foot warehouse and office. You can do it too, if you try!"

New Ways to Accept Payments

When I started writing about e-commerce, the biggest barriers to business were security and trust. Shoppers just didn't trust online merchants. Handing over payment online didn't seem as secure as handing a credit card or cold, hard cash to a clerk in a brick-and-mortar store. All that is a thing of the past, and online payment systems are more secure than ever.

Google Payments

Google is becoming a ubiquitous presence on the Web, and one of the company's most recent forays into e-commerce is its payment service. It's virtually the same as the reigning king of online payments, the service owned by eBay called PayPal (`www.paypal.com`). But Google is a valuable alternative to PayPal, and many shoppers want to see it as an option when it comes time to pay for something online. Find out more about the service in Chapter 7.

Amazon.com Payments

Amazon.com, one of the biggest e-commerce merchants ever, has gained popularity by making it easy for buyers to turn over money for books and other merchandise. Its 1-Click payment system is trademarked, for one thing. Now, Amazon has a slew of payment systems that merchants, developers, and individuals can use. They include:

- **Checkout by Amazon:** This checkout system is designed especially for e-commerce sellers. Because millions of shoppers already have their credit cards numbers and addresses stored with Amazon, you can have those customers buy something from you and pay for it on Amazon.
- **Amazon Simple Pay:** If you sell digital goods such as music, you can add "Buy" buttons to your site. These buttons take buyers to Amazon, where they use their existing Amazon account information to pay you.
- **Amazon Mobile Payments:** If you are an online merchant and you want to give your customers the option of making purchases from their Web-enabled cellphones (a practice that will become more and more popular in the near future), you can use this service to add Amazon's 1-Click payment system to your mobile site.

Amazon.com's payment systems depend on your shoppers already having account information stored on the online retailer's site. Many entrepreneurs feel more comfortable with shoppers paying them through PayPal or another service than with having another merchant handle the transfer of funds. If you want to find out more about Amazon's payment options, however, read about them at `https://payments.amazon.com/sdui/sdui/index.htm`.

Reaching New Sales Venues

The exciting thing about e-commerce in the twenty-first century is that you have so many new ways to conduct it. The core activity is putting your products and services online before a potential audience of millions and attracting the people who are already looking for exactly what you have to offer. The current trend is to have a home base — your Web site — as well as a variety of marketplaces where you can attract customers to a storefront or catalog.

E-commerce works best when you can pop up in multiple locations on the Web. Don't root yourself in one URL and sit there. Just think of the online "empire" you can create: You can have a Web site, a blog, an eBay Store, an Amazon.com aStore, a Squidoo Web page called a "lens," and free Web pages on Microsoft Office Live, Yahoo! GeoCities, MySpace, and probably other outlets that didn't even exist yet when I was writing this chapter. You can use your various online presences to refer to one another; by cross-marketing, you gain more publicity and steer more customers to what you have to offer.

Beyond eBay: Expanding to Amazon.com and more

eBay gives new entrepreneurs a great way to get their feet wet and discover what good customer service is all about. After selling on eBay becomes routine, however, pay close attention to the fees eBay takes out of your PayPal or checking account every month. Moving from eBay to other marketplaces, or to an e-commerce Web site, is a good business decision for many sellers. That doesn't mean you have to abandon eBay altogether. Rather, keep a foothold on eBay and expand your business to new venues.

After you have a product line identified and (optionally) an eBay Store up and running, branch out to sites such as these:

- **iOffer** (www.ioffer.com): This marketplace gives buyers the chance to make an offer for what you have to sell. It includes a software tool called Mr. Grabber that gathers your current eBay sales from eBay and lists them all for you so that you can choose which ones you want to offer to your customers.

- **uBid** (www.ubid.com): This popular and well-traveled marketplace is ideal if you sell computers or other electronics merchandise and want to unload them at a bargain price.

- **Bidz.com** (www.bidz.com): If you are in a hurry and want instant results, list on this site. Your sale can take place in a matter of minutes after you complete the listing; buyers place live bids immediately, and the sale is over almost before you can shout "Sold!"

eBay and Amazon.com are well-established marketplaces. When you branch out and start to look for other places to sell, watch out for the fly-by-night operations. Stay away from sites that ask you for your e-mail address or personal information (such as a credit card number) before you do anything else. You should at least be able to shop and explore the site before you sign up as a seller.

Partnering with a service provider

Many sellers who want to maximize their sales volume to the highest degree possible decide to sign up with high-powered professional business services to help them configure and operate online stores.

Moving from doing all the work yourself to signing up with a service provider is like the difference between having a cleaning service and a specific individual who does your cleaning. If you have an individual, you have to wait until that person can fit you into his or her busy schedule. A cleaning service might cost more, but it's always available, and you might have less stress in the long run.

By signing up with a company, such as ChannelAdvisor (`www.channel advisor.com`) or Infopia (`www.infopia.com`), you not only gain the ability to create an online store but also get help with publicizing it and conducting transactions.

You don't have to be a beginner to align with one of these marketing companies. One of the best online sellers I know, David Yaskulka of Blueberry Boutique (`www.blueberryboutique.net`), signed up with ChannelAdvisor, and he already knows a lot about marketing and selling online.

Moving to brick and mortar

The usual trend for people who want to sell online is that they move from a brick-and-mortar store to an online Web site. In some cases (for instance, in the case of a number of successful eBay sellers I know), business on the Web is so good that they close down their physical presence and focus solely on their online business. Antiques storeowners are the classic example; when a lot of these merchants started selling online and realized they could sell the whole year and reach more potential buyers than they could by "foot traffic," they closed the door and didn't look back.

It's less common for successful online businesspeople to buy or rent space and set up shop at a physical address. But it does happen. In my book *eBay PowerUser's Bible* (Wiley), I profile Kimberly King, who started selling on eBay and eventually opened a brick-and-mortar store where she can sell her wares to the public. Having a "real" store brings lots of advantages:

- ✔ **You drum up more business.** You get more local business, especially from people who bring items to sell on eBay on consignment.

- ✔ **You have space to work and store inventory.** Your family appreciates this because it keeps the clutter out of your home.

- ✔ **You can stick to a schedule and separate work life from family life.** This problem plagues many people who start an online business and find themselves sitting at their computers at 11 p.m. on a Friday night when their family members are in the den playing Monopoly.

Just as often, sellers who find themselves in the lucky position of being awash in inventory and orders purchase warehouses. They get plenty of room for shipping and storage, and they can have offices in their warehouse as well.

When you can choose your location, you get other advantages. The owner of Amazing Keys (www.amazingkeys.com) told me he located his warehouse in North Carolina close to a major airport so that his shipments could get to their destinations that much more quickly.

Expanding to auction sales

If you already have a brick-and-mortar store or successful online business, you have a head start on a successful eBay business. The words "eBay" and "business" don't always go together in many people's minds. But for many ambitious merchants, eBay is a full-time source of income. Sellers who are most likely capable of running a successful full-time business on eBay are ones who already have a source of inventory, a customer base, and a shipping and payment system in place.

Established business owners have less of a learning curve to climb; they solved the all-important question of where to find a steady source of merchandise to sell, and they can do cross marketing. They use their business cards and brochures to promote both their physical store and their online business; they publish the location of their store on their Web site; and their Web site points to their eBay Store and vice versa.

Sharing your work with Flickr

If you're lucky, your products sell themselves. But for some products, photos are a necessity. If you have a big piece of furniture, such as a couch or a rare antique or a work of art, a description that consists solely of words just doesn't cut it. Photos give you a real selling point. Where can you post them online? You can put photos on your own Web site, of course. But the cool and trendy place for them to appear is at the popular photo-sharing site Flickr (www.flickr.com).

Flickr is free and easy to use. I can't think of a better business use for the site than the Clean Air Gardening customer photos, as shown in Figure 1-3. Lars Hundley (whom I profile in the sidebar earlier in this chapter) invites his customers to submit photos of the products they've purchased, such as push reel lawn mowers and weathervanes.

Figure 1-3:
Use photo sharing sites to publish photos of your products in action.

Google's world of business resources

In the past year or two, Google dramatically expanded its business services. Google has so many options for small business owners that I devote a whole chapter (Chapter 14) to hosting, calendars, e-mail, and many other useful tools for business owners.

A useful service for anyone wanting to take the pulse of Web surfers in general and online shoppers in particular is Google Trends (www.google.com/trends). This is a collection of searches done on Google's Web site. If you enter "online business" in the Google Trend's search box and click Search Trends, you get the results shown in Figure 1-4, which are decidedly unlike any search results you've probably seen from Google.

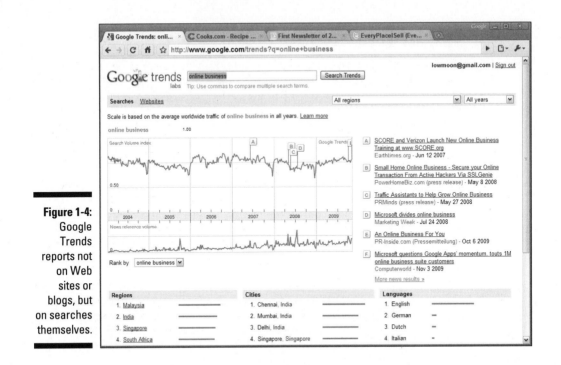

Figure 1-4:
Google
Trends
reports not
on Web
sites or
blogs, but
on searches
themselves.

The graphs on the left tell you how many times your phrase or keyword
appeared on Google in recent years. The headlines on the right point you to
news reports and press releases that use the search term. Often, they point
to significant events and reports that have come out recently. After you know
what people are searching for, you can identify products to sell (see Chapter 9),
or you can choose keywords that help you place ads on Google AdWords or
other search marketing sites (see Chapter 11).

Technologies You Need to Exploit

You can create an online business in some obvious ways. You obtain a
domain name, which lets you have an address like www.mybusiness.com;
you start a Web site; you create a sales catalog. These basics are still the
same, and they are still important, but new ways to market yourself as an
online seller are appearing. Pay attention to those that have been around for
a few years and that you don't necessarily know about, such as RSS and the
other options I describe in this section.

Feeding your site with RSS

Half the battle with an online business is simply making yourself available to the people who choose to find out more about you. I'm a fan of the radio program *Le Show*, for instance (`www.harryshearer.com/news/leShow.php`). At the end of every broadcast, the host, Harry Shearer, lists the different formats in which the program is distributed: via public radio, the Internet, satellite radio, and shortwave radio. Why stick with one format when going through just a little more effort can multiply your audience dramatically?

To some extent, making your online business available is a matter of putting your sales catalog and your Web site contents in a form that people can read. Lots of people put out an RSS feed of their Web site along with the conventional pages created in HyperText Markup Language (HTML), eXtensible Markup Language (XML), Hypertext Preprocessor (PHP), or another markup language.

HTML, XML, and *PHP* are languages used to format or process information that appears on Web pages. *RSS* is a technology used to format content as an XML file so that an RSS reader can display it. You don't need to know any of these techy-sounding languages to use them; you only have to use the right applications that do the formatting or programming "in the background" for you.

Setting up site feeds

As is true of many ways of publishing content online, you don't have to be a programmer to make use of RSS. You do, however, have to meet one important requirement: You need to make a commitment to actually update your content on a regular basis. The whole point behind RSS is that it gives consumers of information a way to automatically view new comments put out by bloggers or other publishers without having to open the Web sites of those publishers on a regular basis. If you don't update your content, all those RSS feeders won't retrieve it.

After you commit to being a periodic publisher, and after you have a text file you want to convert, you can go on to the next step: converting it to RSS format. You have several options:

- ✔ **Built-in software:** If you use a blogging tool, such as WordPress (`http://wordpress.org`) or Blogger (`www.blogger.com`), you can use the built-in syndication software. Blogger supports Atom, a different type of syndication format; see the upcoming section about Atom.

✔ **Standalone program:** You can use a standalone, Web-based syndication program such as RSS Channel Editor (`www.webreference.com/cgi-bin/perl/rssedit.pl`). Figure 1-5 shows the form for RSS Channel Editor that you fill out; then it quickly builds your file. You simply make a link to the file you want to convert, and the program "fetches" it for you. Use RSS Channel Editor only if you plan to create RSS feeds on a regular basis and don't want to install and maintain a standalone application on your system.

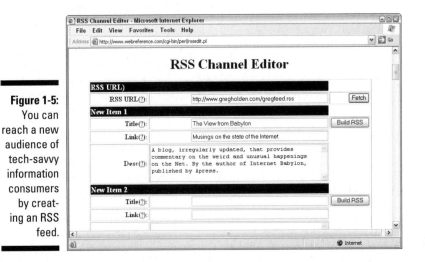

Figure 1-5:
You can reach a new audience of tech-savvy information consumers by creating an RSS feed.

No matter what option you choose, you end up with a file that you upload to your server space on your Web site. You then need to make a link to the file on one of your Web pages and publicize the link so that people find out about it. After you get the system worked out, it becomes easier to update as well as repost your files and reach a wider audience than you ever could otherwise.

Validate your RSS file to make sure that it's in a form that news aggregators can read. An RSS file is comprised of XML commands, which need to be free of errors. Use an application such as Userland RSS Validator (`rss.scripting.com/`) to make sure that your file is correctly formatted.

Atom

Atom is a syndication tool that doesn't use RSS. Instead, it's an alternative to RSS. If you use the popular blogging tool Blogger, you automatically create a feed of your blog in Atom format. Blogger claims that Atom is superior to RSS because it feeds content to not only news aggregators but also Web sites and even hand-held devices.

RSS: Not really simple, but still effective

RSS stands for *Really Simple Syndication*. Frankly, the name is misleading. If your head tends to reel when you think about JavaScript, PHP, XML, DHTML, and the many alphabet-soup types of Web page languages, RSS just adds a new level of complication. RSS is a new language that leads to a method for distributing words and images on the Web. The system works like this:

1. You get some content in the form of an RSS file. You have two options to obtain the content: You convert some of your own to RSS or you obtain someone else's RSS file.

2. You post the file on your Web server.

3. You validate the XML to make sure that news aggregators can read it correctly.

4. You publicize your RSS feed in the directories that specialize in RSS listings.

5. Users around the Web use programs called news aggregators, or feed readers, to subscribe to your feed. The feed reader checks automatically to see whether the RSS file has new content since the last time it checked. If it does, the reader downloads the feed so that the end-user can read it.

6. You keep your file fresh by updating it regularly so that news aggregators continue to retrieve it for your audience.

After you wrap your mind around that scenario, you have to absorb another fact: RSS isn't a single format. Rather, there's a whole family of RSS format standards. They carry version numbers like 0.91, version 1.0, and version 2.0. Some publishers favor one variety, some another. You don't need to pick the latest and greatest standard; just pick the one you're comfortable with. News aggregators come in lots of options, including FeedDeomon, NewsGator, and many others.

Should you climb the RSS learning curve and become a news feed publisher? If you produce content that you intend to update on a regular basis, the answer is yes. RSS is the wave of the future and will only grow more popular. Most of the software you use to create feeds or aggregate them is absolutely free, so your only expense is the usual sweat equity — something you get used to expending very quickly when you become an online entrepreneur.

Feedster: A search engine for RSS feeds

Feedster is a search engine for blogs, podcasts, and other RSS feeds and is a good place to get an overview of the syndication world. When you visit the Feedster Web site (`www.feedster.com`), shown in Figure 1-6, you begin to get an idea of what RSS syndication and site feeds are all about. Behind the technical jargon, RSS syndication is about a new way to access information. Rather than turn solely to traditional information providers, such as newspapers and news radio, busy consumers can select what they're interested in and gather it in a single interface, where they can read it at their leisure (provided, of course, that they have the leisure to read it). Many of those feeds come from newspapers and other traditional news providers, who are generating their own RSS feeds. It's great for small business owners like you who can talk up your products and services or just expound on your expertise in a particular area and find new potential customers.

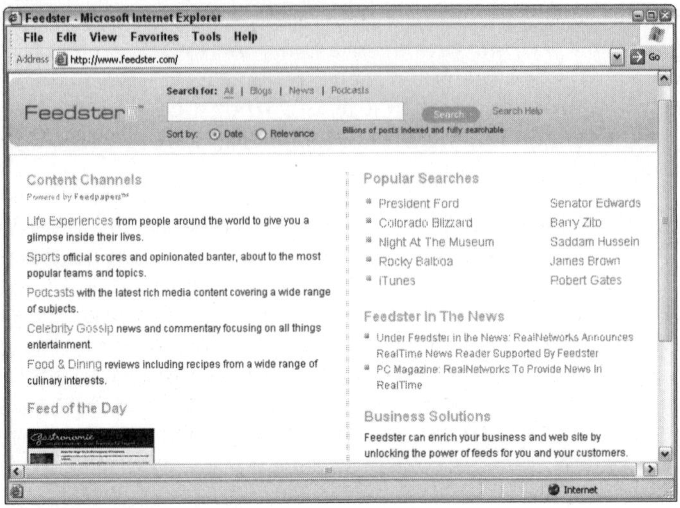

Figure 1-6:
Feedster
and other
RSS directo-
ries provide
a new way
to access
information.

FeedBurner and other RSS syndicators

FeedBurner (www.feedburner.com) calls itself a "feed management provider." It not only turns (or *burns,* to use the correct term) your blog into an
RSS file but also helps promote it. When you create a feed, you post an XML
or RSS logo on your blog that lets others know they can subscribe.

After you "burn" your feed with FeedBurner or another tool, you publicize it
by using a directory of such feeds. Look into Syndic8 (www.syndic8.com),
which is free to use.

After you have a site feed set up, you can use it to list your products on
Google Base. Find out more about this useful resource in Chapter 14.

Connecting with new customers: VoIP

It's so easy to fall into predictable "do and don't" patterns with regard to
using technology. Do: You use a computer for computing. Don't: You don't
use a palm device or a TV. Do: You use an iPod for listening to digital music.
Don't: You don't listen to music on a cellphone.

The same applies to talking with people over long distances. You do use
a telephone or cellphone to call someone across the country or overseas.
You don't use tin cans, Morse code, ham radio, or your computer. But wait

a minute. Sure, Morse code and ham radio aren't popular or convenient anymore, but what's wrong with using a computer for talking to people by carrying on voice conversations? For an increasing number of individuals around the world, the answer is "Nothing at all." When it comes to making phone calls on your computer, look into the most popular software in the field, Skype (www.skype.com).

Skype uses a form of communication called Voice over Internet Protocol (VoIP). It allows you to talk to someone else with your voice through your computer, using a microphone. When you talk on a land line, you connect with someone else over the cable owned and maintained by the phone company. But the DSL (Digital Subscriber Line) connections that bring relatively high-speed Internet to my home (and possibly to yours) can carry both voice and data signals; in fact, they share the same line. If you can use the same cable to talk over the phone, you can certainly talk over your computer, too.

That's what Skype is all about. You connect a microphone to your computer and talk to someone else who has Skype software. If you have a relatively new laptop, you likely have a built-in microphone and perhaps a webcam as well. With a webcam, you can talk to people "face to face" (if the person on the other end has a webcam as well). You can, for example, see and talk with your son who's overseas for a semester abroad — and do all this for pennies, or absolutely free if you both talk on your computers. As an entrepreneur, this also means that you can connect with colleagues and clients all over the world without ever leaving your home.

Skype is hardly the only Voice over IP service around, though. Vonage (www.vonage.com) is also very popular. I mention Skype because it gives you immediate, personal access to your customers, especially those on eBay. If you sell on eBay and someone has a question about one of your auctions, he or she can talk to you if you both have Skype, for instance.

Voice over IP can also help your business's bottom line. My own ISP, Speakeasy (www.speakeasy.net) offers residential VoIP service for about $40 a month, and combined broadband Internet plus VoIP for $83 a month. Compare that to what you're paying now for your landline and your Internet access, and you can save quite a bit (for me, the difference is about $80 per month).

There are some potential downsides to consider with VoIP: You have to buy special phones; you have to realize that if your Internet connection goes down for some reason, your phones stop working; and if your connection is slow due to weather or heavy usage by others in your area, your voice signal might suffer. On the other hand, it can replace your landline while saving your fledgling business lots of money as well.

Chapter 2

Opening Your Own Online Business in Ten Easy Steps

The concept of starting a business online has been around since the 1990s. These days, opening a storefront or a sales channel on the Internet is not the least unusual. In fact, you have lots of success stories to emulate and be inspired by. Also, new software and services are continually developed to make creating Web pages and transacting business online easier than ever. But after you leap a few not-so-high technological hurdles, the basic steps for starting a successful online business haven't really changed. Those steps are well within the reach of individuals like you and me who have no prior business experience.

Online businesses are affected by economic downturns just as offline operations are. But in good times or bad, you can still thrive. All you need is a good idea, a bit of startup money, some computer equipment, and a little help from your friends.

One of my goals in this book is to be one of those friends — someone who provides you with the right advice and support to get your business online and make it a success. In this chapter, I give you a step-by-step overview of the entire process of starting an online business.

Step 1: Identify a Need

"The best of anything hasn't been done yet," says John Moen, the successful e-businessperson I profile in this chapter. "The Web isn't over. Someday someone will invent a better Wal-Mart, and there will be a bigger and better store. As the technology changes, someone will create a business online that makes people say, 'Holy cow, that's cool.'"

In fact, when I was working on this chapter, I found a new kind of online service: RIVworks (www.rivworks.com). RIV stands for Rich Interactive Video, and RIVworks lets small businesses affordably add video clips to their Web sites. It gives businesspeople the chance to choose and schedule video greetings from a prerecorded library. As a result, businesses get more compelling Web sites, and RIVworks gets monthly fees from subscribers to its service. It's an e-commerce win-win.

E-commerce and the Web have been around for nearly 15 years now. But new products and ways to sell them are identified all the time. Think of the things that didn't exist when the first Web sites were created: blogs, Twitter, search ads, podcasts, RSS feeds, MP3s, YouTube, DVDs, and eBay. Consider my brother Mike: For the last couple of years, he has operated his own online business — lp2cdsolutions, Inc. Business has remained steady through both the good years and the slow ones because, like many entrepreneurs, he reached a simple conclusion: "If I want this product so much, I bet a lot of other people do, too." What he wanted was to convert his scratchy old records to clean and repackaged CDs. He spent thousands of dollars on computer hardware and software, and he got really good at audio restoration. Now he's making a modest but steady extra income and putting his technical talents to good use. Will he succeed because he has me to help him? I don't think success is guaranteed. It depends on you — your energy, dedication, and enthusiasm.

Your first job, accordingly, is to get in touch with your *market* (the people who'll be buying your stuff or using your services) and determine how you can best meet that market's needs and demands. After all, you can't expect Web surfers to patronize your online business unless you identify services or items that they really need.

Getting to know the marketplace

The Internet is a worldwide, interconnected network of computers to which people can connect either from work or home, and through which people can communicate via e-mail, receive information from the Web, and buy and sell items with credit cards or by other methods.

A hotbed of commerce

Statistically, the Internet continues to be a hotbed of commerce — and it just keeps becoming more accepted among consumers in general. Listen to what the experts are saying:

- **Forrester Research** (`www.forrester.com`) says U.S. online retail sales reached $175 billion in 2007 and are projected to grow to $229 billion by 2013. B2C e-commerce grows consistently by double-digit rates each year, and even though that rate is expected to slow to 9 percent in 2012 and 8 percent in 2013, according to Forrester, at least it's growing. By contrast, the National Retail Federation forecasts that traditional retail sales will grow more slowly — a 2.5 percent increase in 2010.

- **Statistics Canada** (`www.statcan.ca`), the Canadian government's central statistical agency, reports that e-commerce sales in Canada in 2007 amounted to $12.8 billion, and consumers placed 69.9 million orders online during the year. These sales figure represented a 61 percent increase from 2005.

- **The U.S. Department of Commerce** (`http://www census.gov/mrts/www/data/html/09Q1.html`) reports that e-commerce sales in the United States reached $31.7 billion in the first quarter of 2009. Although this was a 17.7 percent decrease compared to the first quarter of 2008, it was a slight increase from the previous quarter, and a continuation of the steady upward trend that e-commerce sales in the U.S. have posted since 2000.

- **eMarketer** (`http://www.emarketer.com/Report.aspx?code=emarketer_2000527`) reports In the UK, e-commerce has been relatively immune to the economic slowdown thanks to the many factors that make e-commerce attractive to shoppers who are eager to save time and money. These include fuel savings, convenience, and easy and quick ways to do comparison shopping. Other countries show a booming online business environment:According to tech Crunchies (`www.techcrunchies.com`), Thailand's e-commerce business was expected to grow 40 percent in 2009 over the previous year, and German e-commerce nearly tripled from 2003 to 2008.

Many people decide to start an online business with little more than a casual knowledge of the Internet. But when you decide to get serious about going online with a commercial endeavor, it pays to get to know the environment in which you plan to be working.

One of your first steps is finding out what it means to do business online and determining the best ways for you to fit into the exploding field of e-commerce. For example, you need to realize that the Internet is a personal place; customers are active, not passive, in the way they absorb information; and the Internet was established within a culture of people sharing information freely and helping one another. For another, you need to know that although the marketplace continues to grow during this second decade of the twenty-first century, most of the new growth is expected to come from experienced online shoppers rather than people who are making their first purchases online. That means you need to address the needs of experienced shoppers who are becoming more demanding of Web-based merchants.

Some of the best places to find out about the culture of the Internet are blogs, social networking sites such as Facebook, chat rooms, and sites such as Twitter where individuals gather and exchange brief messages online. Visiting discussion forums devoted to topics that interest you can be especially helpful, and you're likely to end up participating. Also visit commerce Web sites (such as eBay, Amazon.com, or other online marketplaces) and take note of ideas and approaches that you may want to use.

"Cee-ing" what's out there

The more information you have about the "four Cs" of the online world, the more likely you are to succeed in doing business online:

- **Competitors:** Familiarize yourself with other online businesses that already do what you want to do. Don't let their presence intimidate you. You're going to find a different and better way to do what they already do.

- **Customers:** Investigate the various kinds of customers who shop online and who might visit your site.

- **Culture:** Explore the special language and style that people use when they communicate.

- **Content:** Although Web sites have become far more visually interesting over the years, what truly distinguishes them and keeps customers coming back is their content. Useful information attracts repeat visitors, which leads to increased sales.

When you take a look around the Internet, notice the kinds of goods and services that tend to sell in the increasingly crowded, occasionally disorganized, and sometimes complex online world. The products that sell best in cyberspace include four Cs:

- **Cheap:** Online items tend to be sold at a discount — at least, that's what shoppers expect.

- **Customized:** Anything that's hard to find, personalized, or unique sells well online.

- **Convenient:** Shoppers look for items that are easier to buy online than at a "real" store, such as a rare book that you can order in minutes from Amazon.com (www.amazon.com) or an electronic greeting card that you can send online in seconds (www.greeting-cards.com).

- **Compelling:** Consumers go online to quickly read news stories that are available by subscription, such as newspapers and magazines; content that is exciting and eye-catching or that exists online only, such as homemade video on YouTube (www.youtube.com); or blogs (a term derived from *Web logs*).

Mapmaker locates his online niche

John Moen didn't know a thing about computer graphics when he first started his online business, Graphic Maps, in 1995. He didn't know how to write *HyperText Markup Language* (HTML), the set of instructions used to create Web pages. (Not too many people in 1995 did.) But he did know a lot about maps. And he heard that setting up shop on the Web was "the thing to do." He scraped together $300 in startup costs, found out how to create some simple Web pages without any photos (only maps and other graphics), and went online.

At first, business was slow. "I remember saying to my wife, 'You know what? We had ten page views yesterday.'" The Graphic Maps site (www.graphicmaps.com) was averaging about 30 page views per day when Moen decided to do something that many beginners may find counterproductive, even silly: He started giving away his work for free. He created some free art (called *clip art*) and made it available for people to copy. And he didn't stop there: He began giving away his knowledge of geography. He answered questions submitted to him by schoolchildren and teachers.

Soon, his site was getting 1,000 visits a day. Today, he reports, "We are so busy, we literally can't keep up with the demand for custom maps. Almost 95 percent of our business leads come from the Web, and that includes many international companies and Web sites. Web page traffic has grown to more than 3 million hits per month, and banner advertising now pays very well."

John now has a half dozen or so employees, receives many custom orders for more than $10,000, and has done business with numerous Fortune 500 companies. To promote his site, John gives away free maps to nonprofit organizations, operates a daily geography contest with a $100 prize to the first person with the correct answer, and answers e-mail promptly. "I feel strongly that the secret on the Web is to provide a solution for a problem, and for the most part, do it free," he suggests. "If the service is high quality, and people get what they want . . . they will tell their friends, and all will beat a path to your URL, and then, and only then, will you be able to sell your products to the world, in a way you never imagined was possible."

Moen created a second site called WorldAtlas. com (www.worldatlas.com) that is devoted to geography. That site generates revenue from pop-up and banner ads that other companies place there because so many people visit. "It is not unusual to have 20 million impressions on that site and hundreds of thousands of geography questions a month from teachers and students who need an answer to a geography question," says Moen.

When asked how he can spare the time to answer questions for free when he has so much paying business available, he responds: "How can you not? I normally work 12-hour and sometimes 16- or 18-hour days. If some little kid, some student, comes home from school, and says, 'Grandpa, I need to find out what's the tallest mountain in North America,' and he does a search on Google that directs him to go to WorldAtlas.com, we will try to answer that question."

His advice for beginning entrepreneurs: "Find your niche and do it well. Don't try to compete with larger companies. For instance, I can't compete with Microsoft or Rand McNally, but I don't try to. Our map site, GraphicMaps.com, is one of the few custom map sites on the Web. There is no software yet available today that will do automatic mapping for a client. If you need a map for a wedding or for your office, we can make you one. I fill some needs that they don't fill, and I learned long ago how to drive business to my site by offering something for free. The fact is that if you have good ideas and you search for clients, you can still do well on the Web."

Visit one of the tried-and-true indexes to the Internet, such as Yahoo! (www.yahoo.com) or the search services Google (www.google.com) or Bing (www.bing.com). Enter a word or phrase in the site's home page search box that describes the kinds of goods or services you want to provide online. Press Enter, and you'll find out how many existing businesses already do what you want to do. Better yet, determine what they *don't* do and set a goal of meeting that specialized need yourself.

Figuring out how to do it better

After you take a look at what's already out there, you want to find ways to make your business stand out from the crowd. Direct your energies toward making your site unique in some way and providing products or services that others don't offer. Offerings that set your online business apart from the rest can be as tangible as half-price sales, contests, seasonal sales, or freebies. They can also involve making your business site higher in quality than the others. Maybe you can just provide better or more personalized customer service than anyone else.

What if you can't find other online businesses doing what you want to do? Lucky you! In e-commerce, being first often means getting a head start and being more successful than latecomers, even if they have more resources than you do. (Just ask Jeff Bezos and others who founded the online bookstore Amazon.com.) Don't be afraid to try something new and outlandish. It just might work!

Step 2: Determine What You Have to Offer

Business is all about identifying customers' needs and figuring out exactly what goods or services you'll provide to meet those needs. It's the same both online and off. (Often, you perform this step before or at the same time that you scope out what the business needs are and figure out how you can position yourself to meet those needs, as I explain in the earlier section, "Step 1: Identify a Need.")

To determine what you have to offer, make a list of all the items you have to put up for sale or all the services that you plan to provide to your customers. Next, decide not only what goods or services you can provide online but also where to obtain them. Will you create sale items yourself? Will you purchase them from another supplier? Jot down your ideas on paper and keep them close at hand while you develop your business plan.

The Internet is a personal, highly interactive medium. Be as specific as possible with what you plan to do online. Don't try to do everything; the medium favors businesses that do one thing well. The more specific your business, the more personal the level of service you can provide to your customers.

Step 3: Come Up with a Cyberbusiness Plan

The process of setting goals and objectives and then designing strategies for attaining them is essential when starting a new business. What you end up with is a *business plan*. A good business plan applies not only to the startup phase but also to a business's day-to-day operation. It can also be instrumental in helping a small business obtain a bank loan.

To set specific goals for your new business, ask yourself these questions:

- ✔ Why do you want to start a business?
- ✔ Why do you want to start it online?
- ✔ What would *you* want to buy online?
- ✔ What would make you buy it?

These questions may seem simple. But many businesspeople never take the time to answer them — to their detriment. And only *you* can answer these questions for yourself. Make sure that you have a clear idea of where you're going so that you can commit to making your venture successful over the long haul. (See Chapter 3 for more on setting goals and envisioning your business.)

To carry your plan into your daily operations, observe these suggestions:

- ✔ Write a brief description of your company and what you hope to accomplish with it.
- ✔ Draw up a marketing strategy. (See Chapter 10 for tips.)
- ✔ Keep track of your finances. (See Chapter 17 for specifics.)

Consider using specialized software to help you prepare your business plan. Programs such as Business Plan Pro by Palo Alto Software (www.palo-alto. com) lead you through the process by asking you a series of questions to identify what you want to do. The Standard version of the program retails for $99.95.

If you set aside part of your home for business purposes, you may be eligible for tax deductions. Exactly how much you may get to deduct depends on how much space you use and whether it is completely dedicated to the business. (You can't work in a corner of the kitchen but then deduct the kitchen, for example.) You can depreciate your computers and other business equipment, too. On the other hand, your municipality may require you to obtain a license if you operate a business in a residential area; check with your local authorities to make sure that you're on the up and up. You can find out more about tax and legal issues, including local licensing requirements, in Chapters 16 and 17 of this book.

Go to my Web site (`www.gregholden.com/busplan.doc`) to download a sample business plan created by business consultant Jeffrey Edelheit.

Step 4: Assemble Your Hardware and Software

One of the great advantages of opening a store on the Internet rather than on Main Street is money — or rather, the lack of it. Rather than rent a space and set up furniture and fixtures, you can buy a domain name, sign up with a hosting service, create some Web pages, and get started with an investment of only a few hundred dollars or perhaps even less.

In addition to your virtual storefront, you also have to find a real place to do your business. You don't necessarily have to rent a warehouse or other large space. Many online entrepreneurs use a home office or perhaps a corner in a room where computers, books, and other business-related equipment reside.

Finding a host for your Web site

Although doing business online means that you don't have to rent space in a mall or open a real, physical store, you do have to set up a virtual space for your online business. The most common way to do so is by creating a Web site and finding a company to host it. In cyberspace, your landlord is a Web hosting service. A *Web host* is a company that, for a fee, makes your site available 24 hours a day by maintaining it on a special computer — a Web *server*.

A Web host can be as large and well known as America Online, which gives all its customers a place to create and publish their own Web pages. Some Web sites, such as Microsoft Office Live (`officelive.microsoft.com`), and Tripod (`www.tripod.lycos.com`), act as hosting services and provide easy-to-use Web site creation tools as well. When my brother decided to create his Web site, he signed up with a company called Webmasters.com, which charges him about $14.95 per month. Webmasters offers many features, including the form shown in Figure 2-1, that enables you to create a simple Web page without having to type any HTML.

Figure 2-1:
Take the time to choose an affordable Web host that makes it easy for you to create and maintain your site.

In addition, the company that gives you access to the Internet — your Internet service provider (ISP) — may also publish your Web pages. Make sure that your host has a fast connection to the Internet and can handle the large numbers of simultaneous visits, or *hits,* that your Web site is sure to get eventually. You can find a detailed description of Web hosting options in Chapter 4.

Assembling the equipment you need

Think of all the equipment you *don't* need when you set up shop online. You don't need shelving, a cash register, a parking lot, electricity, fire protection systems, a burglar alarm . . . the list goes on and on. You may need some of those for your home, but you don't need to purchase them especially for your online business.

For doing business online, your most important piece of equipment is your computer. Other hardware, such as scanners, digital cameras, and printers are essential, too. Make sure that your computer equipment is up to snuff because you're going to spend a lot of time online: answering e-mail, checking orders, revising your Web site, and marketing your product. Expect to spend anywhere between $800 and $5,000 for equipment if you don't have any to begin with.

Keeping track of your inventory

It's easy to overlook stocking inventory and setting up systems for processing orders when you're just starting out. But as Lucky Boyd, an entrepreneur who started MyTexasMusic.com and other Web sites, pointed out to me, make sure that you have a "big vision" early in the process of creating your site. In his case, it meant having a site that could handle lots of visitors and make purchasing easy for them. In other cases, it might mean having sufficient inventory to meet demand.

Having too many items for sale is preferable to not having enough. "We operated on a low budget in the beginning, and we didn't have the inventory that people wanted," one entrepreneur commented. "People online get impatient if they have to wait for things too long. Make sure you have the goods you advertise. Plan to be successful." Cofounder Jinele Boyd adds that they treat every order with urgency and make an effort to ship the same day the order arrives — or no longer than 36 hours after receiving it. "We also hand-write a note inside every box," she says. "We get e-mails and calls all the time from people telling us how amazed they were that a 'real person' handled their order and took the time to hand-address the boxes."

Many online businesses keep track of their inventory (and thus fulfill orders quickly) by using a database that's connected to their Web site. When someone orders a product from the Web site, that order is recorded automatically in the database, which then produces an order for replacement stock. Lucky and his staff originally used a version of Microsoft Excel with database functions to track inventory. They've since moved to a PHP/SQL system. "We still ship the same day, and we never have something for sale on the site that's not in stock. Customers hate to add something to their cart only to find that it's out of stock."

In this kind of arrangement, the database serves as a so-called *back end* or *back office* to the Web-based storefront. This is a sophisticated arrangement that's not for beginners. However, if orders and inventory get to be too much for you to handle, consider hiring a Web developer to set up such a system for you.

Other "back end" features such as packing and shipping are just as important. Boyd coped with increases in shipping costs by raising shipping costs to his customers by 14 cents on the first item and just 1 cent on all additional items — thus encouraging increased sales. He also found a lighter box that cut shipping charges by 17 cents per order. "It really pays to research the little things," he says. "They add up quickly."

Remember that online shoppers are expecting a higher level of customer service. You don't want substandard equipment to slow down responses and performance. It pays to shop wisely and get the best setup you can afford upfront so that you don't have to purchase upgrades later on. (For more suggestions on buying business hardware and software, see Chapter 3.)

Choosing business software

For the most part, the programs you need in order to operate an online business are the same as the software you use to surf the Internet. You do, however, need to have a wider variety of tools than you would use for simple information gathering.

Because you're going to be in the business of information *providing* now, as well as information gathering, you need programs such as the following:

- ✔ **A Web page editor:** These programs, which you may also hear called *Web page creation tools* or *Web page authoring tools,* make it easy for you to format text, add images, and design Web pages without having to master HTML.

- ✔ **Graphics software:** If you decide to create your business Web site yourself rather than find someone to do it for you, you need a program that can help you draw or edit images to include on your site.

- ✔ **Storefront software:** You can purchase software that leads you through the process of creating a full-fledged online business and getting your pages on the Web.

- ✔ **RSS feed software:** RSS (Real Simple Syndication) is a way of formatting Web content in the form of an eXtensible Markup Language (XML) file so it can be read quickly and easily by people who subscribe to it. You can find instructions on how to create an RSS feed and a list of feed creation tools at www.rss-specifications.com/create-rss-feed.htm.

- ✔ **Accounting programs:** You can write your expenses and income on a sheet of paper. But it's far more efficient to use software that acts as a spreadsheet, helps you with billing, and even calculates sales tax.

Some businesspeople (such as Judy Vorfeld, whom I profile in Chapter 5) prefer blog software rather than a full-blown Web editor to create their Web site's content. I also use the software provided by Google's free service Blogger to create content for my personal Web site (www.gregholden.com).

Step 5: Find People to Help You

Conducting online business does involve relatively new technologies, but they aren't impossible to figure out. In fact, the technology is becoming more accessible all the time. Many people who start online businesses find out how to create Web pages and promote their companies by reading books, attending classes, or networking with friends and colleagues. Of course, just because you *can* do it all doesn't mean that you have to. Often, you're better off hiring help, either to advise you in areas where you aren't as strong or simply to help you tackle the growing workload — and help your business grow at the same time.

Hiring technical experts

Spending some money upfront to hire professionals who can point you in the right direction can help you maintain an effective Web presence for years to come. Many businesspeople who usually work alone (myself included) hire knowledgeable individuals to do design or programming work that they would find impossible to tackle otherwise. You'll find many technical experts eager to help you, for a reasonable price, at the freelance marketplace Elance (www.elanceonline.com).

Don't be reluctant to hire professional help to get your business online. The Web is full of development firms that perform several related functions: providing customers with Web access, helping to create Web sites, and hosting sites on their servers. The expense for such services may be considerable at first. The programming involved in setting up databases, creating purchasing systems, and programming Web pages can run over $10,000 for particularly extensive Web sites, but they can pay off in the long term. Choose a designer carefully and check out sites he or she has done before. Tell the designer your plan for the organization and content and spell out clearly what you want each page to do. Another area where you may want to find help is in networking and computer maintenance. Know how to do troubleshooting and find out how to keep your computers running. Find out if you have a computer expert in your neighborhood who is available on short notice.

If you do find a business partner, make sure that the person's abilities balance your own. If you're great at sales and public relations, for example, find a writer or Web page designer to partner with.

Gathering your team members

Many entrepreneurial businesses are family affairs. A successful eBay business, Maxwell Street Market (www.maxwellstreetmarket.com), is run by a husband-and-wife team as well as family members and neighbors: The husband does the buying; the wife prepares sales descriptions; the others help with packing and shipping. John Moen found some retired teachers to help answer the geography questions that come into his WorldAtlas.com site. The convenience of the Internet means that these geography experts can log on to the site's e-mail inbox from their respective homes and answer questions quickly. (For more about John Moen and his Web site, see the sidebar "Mapmaker locates his online niche," earlier in this chapter.)

Early on, when you have plenty of time to do planning, you probably won't feel a pressing need to hire others to help you. Many people wait to seek help when they have a deadline to meet or are in a financial crunch. Waiting to seek help is okay — as long as you realize that you *will* need help, sooner or later.

Of course, you don't have to hire family and friends, but you must find people who are reliable and can make a long-term commitment to your project. Keep these things in mind:

- ✔ Pick someone who already exhibits experience with computers and the Internet.

- ✔ Always review a résumé, get at least three references, and ask for samples of the candidate's work.

- ✔ Pick someone who responds promptly and courteously and provides the talents you need.

- ✔ If your only contact is by phone and e-mail, references are even more important.

Step 6: Construct a Web Site

Although you can make a living buying and selling full time on eBay, a Web site is still likely to be the focus of your online business. Fortunately, Web sites are becoming easier to create. You don't have to know a line of HTML in order to create an effective Web page. Chapter 5 walks you through the specific tasks involved in organizing and designing Web pages. Chapter 5 also gives you tips on making your Web pages content rich and interactive.

Make your business easy to find online. Pick a Web address (otherwise known as a *URL,* or Uniform Resource Locator) that's easy to remember. You can purchase a short domain-name alias, such as `www.company.com`, to replace a longer one like `www.internetprovider.com/~username/companyname/index.html`. If the ideal dot-com (`.com`) name isn't available, you can choose one of the newer domain suffixes such as `.biz`. See Chapter 4 for more information on domain name aliases.

If the perfect domain name for your business is already taken, consider adding a short, easy-to-remember prefix or suffix to your existing company name. For example, if your company name is something common, such as Housing Services, try fairly recognizable names such as `housing.com` and `housingservices.com`. That way, the Web address is still easy to recall and associate with your business. Or create a "cyber" name that's related to your real name; the Art Institute of Chicago can't use `www.artinstitute.edu` because it's already taken by a group of Art Institutes to which it belongs. So the Art Institute of Chicago created the short abbreviation `www.artic.edu` — that I, for one, find easy to remember.

Spellings that differ from the common English, such as `niteline.com`, are difficult for people to remember — and people who only hear the name spoken won't know how to type it in or search for it properly. Also avoid hyphens in your domain name, (such as in `WBX-TV-Bozo@somestation.com`,) because, again, their placement isn't obvious.

Make your site content-rich

The textual component of a Web site is what attracts visitors and keeps them coming back on a regular basis. The more useful information and compelling content you provide, the more visits your site will receive. I'm talking about words, headings, or images that induce visitors to interact with your site in some way. You can make your content compelling in a number of ways:

✔ Provide a call to action, such as Click Here! or Buy Now!

✔ Explain how the reader benefits by clicking a link and exploring your site. ("Visit our News and Specials page to find out how to win 500 frequent flyer miles.")

✔ Briefly and concisely summarize your business and its mission.

✔ Scan or use a digital camera to capture images of your sale items (or of the services you provide) as I describe in Chapter 5 and post them on a Web page called Products.

Don't forget the personal touch when connecting with your customers' needs. People who shop online don't get to meet their merchants in person, so anything you can tell about yourself helps to personalize the process and put your visitors at ease. For example, one of Lucky Boyd's primary goals for his MyTexasMusic.com site is to encourage people to become members so they're more likely to visit on a regular basis. His photos of music fans (see Figure 2-2) personalize the site and remind visitors that they're members of a community of music lovers. Let your cybervisitors know that they're dealing with real people, not remote machines and computer programs.

Figure 2-2: Personalize your business to connect with customers online.

Peeking in on other businesses' Web sites — to pick up ideas and see how they handle similar issues — is a natural practice. In cyberspace, you can visit plenty of businesses that are comparable to yours from the comfort of your home office, and the trip takes only minutes.

Establishing a graphic identity

When you start your first business on the Web, you have to do a certain amount of convincing. You need to convince customers that you're competent and professional. One factor that helps build trust is a graphic identity. A site with an identity looks a certain way. For example, take a look at Figure 2-3 as well as Figure 2-4, later in this chapter. Both pages are from the Graphic Maps Web site. Notice how each has the same white background, the same distinctive and simple logo, and similar heading styles. Using such elements consistently from page to page creates an identity that gives your business credibility and helps viewers find what they're looking for.

Figure 2-3: Through careful planning and design, the Graphic Maps site maintains a consistent look and feel, or graphic identity, on each page.

Step 7: Set Up a System for Processing Sales

Many businesses go online and then are surprised by their own success. They don't have systems in place for finalizing sales, shipping out purchased goods in a timely manner, and tracking finances as well as inventory.

An excellent way to plan for success is to set up ways to track your business finances and to create a secure purchasing environment for your online customers. That way, you can build on your success rather than be surprised by it.

Providing a means for secure transactions

Getting paid is the key to survival as well as success. When your business exists only online, the payment process isn't always straightforward. Make your Web site a safe place for customers to pay you. Provide different payment options and build a level of trust any way you can.

Some Web surfers are still squeamish about submitting credit card numbers online. And beginning businesspeople are understandably intimidated by the requirements of processing credit card transactions. In the early stages, you can simply create a form that customers have to print out and mail to you along with a check. (The Graphic Maps site is successful without having an online credit card system; clients phone in their orders.)

When you can accept credit cards, make your customers feel at ease by explaining what measures you're taking to ensure that their information is secure. Such measures include signing up for an account with a Web host that provides a *secure server,* a computer that uses software to encrypt data and uses digital documents, or *certificates,* to ensure its identity. (See Chapters 6 and 7 for more on Internet security and secure shopping systems.)

Becoming a credit card merchant

Electronic commerce, or *e-commerce,* brings to mind visions of online forms and credit card data that's transmitted over the Internet. Do you have to provide such service in order to run a successful online business? Not necessarily. Being a credit card merchant makes life easier for your customers, to be sure, but it also adds complications and extra costs to your operation.

The traditional way to become a credit card merchant is to apply to a bank. Small and home-based businesses can have difficulty getting their applications approved. Alternatively, you can sign up with a company that provides electronic shopping cart services and credit card payments online to small businesses. See Chapter 7 for suggestions. These days, you can also accept credit card payments through the popular electronic payment service PayPal; your customers have to have an account with PayPal and have their purchase price debited from their credit card accounts, but the service is popular enough that a substantial number of your online shoppers are probably members already.

If you do get the go-ahead from a bank to become a credit card merchant, you have to pay it a *discount rate,* which is a fee (typically, 2 to 3 percent of each transaction). You sometimes have to pay a monthly premium charge of $10 to $25 as well. Besides that, you may need special software or hardware to accept credit card payments.

To maximize your sales by reaching users who either don't have credit cards or don't want to use them on the Internet, provide low-tech alternatives (such as toll-free phone numbers and fax numbers) so that people can provide you with information, using more familiar technologies.

After much searching, Lucky Boyd signed with a company called Goemerchant (www.goemerchant.com), which provides him with the payment systems that many online shoppers recognize when they want to make a purchase. First, Goemerchant has a *shopping cart* — a set of pages that acts as an electronic holding area for items before they are purchased. Next, it has a secure way for people to make electronic purchases by providing online forms where people can safely enter credit card and other personal information. The note stating that the payment area is protected by Secure Sockets Layer (SSL) encryption tells people that, even if a criminal intercepts their credit card data, he can't read it.

Safeguarding your customers' personal information is important, but you also need to safeguard your business. Many online businesses get burned by bad guys who submit fraudulent credit card information. If you don't verify the information and submit it to your financial institution for processing, you're liable for the cost. Strongly consider signing up with a service that handles credit card verification for you in order to cut down on lost revenue.

Keeping your books straight

In the simplest sense, "keeping your books" means recording all financial activities that pertain to your business, including any expenses you incur, all the income you receive, as well as your equipment and tax deductions. The financial side of running a business also entails creating reports, such as profit and loss statements, that banks require if you apply for a loan. Such reports not only help meet financial institutions' needs, but also provide you with essential information about how your business is doing at any time.

You can record all this information the old-fashioned way, by writing it down in ledgers and journals, or you can use accounting software. (See Chapter 17 for some suggestions of easy-to-use accounting packages that are great for financial novices.) Because you're making a commitment to use computers on a regular basis by starting an online business, it's only natural for you to use computers to keep your books, too. Accounting software can help you keep track of expenses and provide information that may save you some headaches at tax time.

After you save your financial data on your hard drive, make backups so that you don't lose information you need to do business. See Chapter 6 for ways to back up and protect your files.

Step 8: Provide Personal Service

The Internet, which runs on wires, cables, and computer chips, may not seem like a place for the personal touch. But technology didn't actually create the Internet and all of its content; *people* did that. In fact, the Internet is a great place to provide your clients and customers with outstanding, personal customer service.

In many cases, customer service on the Internet is a matter of being available and responding quickly to all inquiries. You check your e-mail regularly; you make sure that you respond within a day; you cheerfully solve problems and hand out refunds if needed. By helping your customers, you help yourself, too. You build loyalty as well as credibility among your clientele. For many small businesses, the key to competing effectively with larger competitors is by providing superior customer service. See Chapter 8 for more ideas on how you can do this.

Selling by sharing your expertise

Your knowledge and experience are among your most valuable commodities. So you may be surprised when I suggest that you give them away for free. Why? It's a "try before you buy" concept. Helping people for free builds your credibility and makes them more likely to pay for your services down the road.

When your business is online, you can easily communicate what you know about your field and make your knowledge readily available. One way is to set up a Web page that presents the basics about your company and your field of interest in the form of Frequently Asked Questions (FAQs). Another technique is to become a virtual publisher/editor and create your own news-letter in which you write about what's new with your company and about topics related to your work. See Chapter 8 for more on communicating your expertise through FAQs, newsletters, and advanced e-mail techniques.

My brother was skeptical when I recommended that he include a page full of technical information explaining exactly what equipment he uses and describ-ing the steps involved in audio restoration. He didn't think anyone would be interested; he also didn't want to give away his "trade secrets." *Au contraire, mon frère!* People who surf the Internet gobble up all the technical details they can find. The more you wow them with the names and model numbers of your expensive equipment, not to mention the work you go through to restore their old records, the more they'll trust you. And trust gets people to place an order with you.

Making your site a go-to resource

Many *ontrepreneurs* (online entrepreneurs) succeed by making their Web sites not only a place for sales and promotion but also an indispensable resource, full of useful hyperlinks and other information, that customers want to visit again and again. For example, the Graphic Maps Web site, which I profile earlier in this chapter, acts as a resource for anyone who has a ques-tion about geography. To promote the site, John Moen gives away free maps for nonprofit organizations, operates a daily geography contest with a $100 prize to the first person with the correct answer (as shown in Figure 2-4), and answers e-mail promptly. "I feel strongly that the secret on the Web is to provide a solution to a problem and, for the most part, to do it for free," he suggests.

The MyTexasMusic site (www.mytexasmusic.com) uses the concept of membership to strengthen connections with customers. The main purpose of the site is to make money by selling the works of Texas musicians as well as tickets to concerts. But in order to make money, give people a reason to visit your site on a regular basis. When people are *members* rather than *shoppers,* they feel connected and privileged.

"Memberships work for us in two ways," comments Boyd. "Every vendor who consigns to us is a member. Customers can also be members. Membership invokes the idea of ownership, and everyone likes to feel as though they are a part owner of the process."

The site encourages music lovers and musicians to become members: They provide information about who they are and where they live, and they create their own username and password so that they can access special content and perform special functions on the site, such as selling their own CDs or posting song clips online. For an online business, knowing the names and addresses of people who visit and who don't necessarily make purchases is a gold mine of information. The business can use the contact information to send members special offers and news releases; the more frequently contact is maintained, the more likely those casual shoppers will eventually turn into paying customers.

The concept of membership also builds a feeling of community among customers. By turning the e-commerce site into a meeting place for members who love Texas musicians, those members make new friends and have a reason to visit the site on a regular basis. Community building is one way in which commerce on the Web differs from traditional brick-and-mortar selling, and it's something you should consider, too.

Another way to encourage customers to congregate at your site on a regular basis is to create a discussion area. In Chapter 8, I show you how to provide a discussion page right on your own Web site.

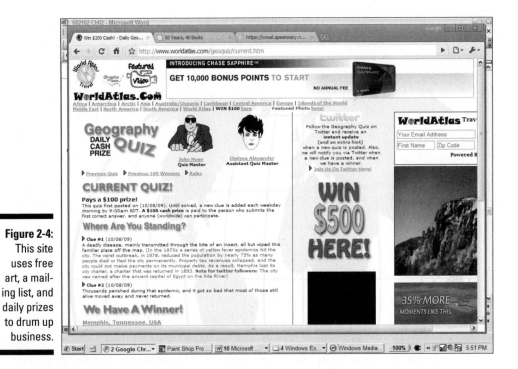

Figure 2-4:
This site uses free art, a mailing list, and daily prizes to drum up business.

Becoming a super e-mailer

E-mail is, in my humble opinion, the single most important marketing tool that you can use to boost your online business. Becoming an expert e-mail user increases your contacts and provides you with new sources of support, too.

The two best and easiest e-mail strategies are the following:

- ✔ Check your e-mail as often as possible.
- ✔ Respond to e-mail inquiries immediately.

Additionally, you can e-mail inquiries about comarketing opportunities to other Web sites similar to your own. Ask other online business owners if they will provide links to your site in exchange for you providing links to theirs. And always include a signature file with your message that includes the name of your business and a link to your business site. See Chapter 8 for more information on using e-mail effectively to build and maintain relations with your online customers.

I'm encouraging you to use e-mail primarily for one-to-one communication. The Internet excels at bringing individuals together. Mailing lists and newsletters can use e-mail effectively for marketing, too. However, I'm *not* encouraging you to send out mass quantities of unsolicited commercial e-mail, a practice that turns off almost all consumers and that can get you in trouble with the law, too. Spam artists have been convicted, and the sentences are getting more severe. In April 2005, a man was sentenced to nine years for masking his identity while bombarding Internet users with millions of unsolicited e-mail messages (`www.pcworld.com/news/article/0,aid,118493,00.asp`). In August of that year, a former America Online employee was sentenced to a year and three months for stealing 92 million screen names and e-mail addresses and sending them to spammers (`www.cbsnews.com/stories/2005/08/17/tech/main783512.shtml`).

Step 9: Alert the Media and Everyone Else

In order to be successful, small businesses need to get the word out to the people who are likely to purchase what they have to offer. If this group turns out to be only a narrow market, so much the better; the Internet is great for connecting to niche markets that share a common interest. (See Chapter 10 for more on locating your most likely customers on the Internet and figuring out how best to communicate with them.)

The Internet provides many unique and effective ways for small businesses to advertise, including search services, e-mail, newsgroups, electronic mailing lists, and more. It's encouraging to note, though, that you don't always have to depend on high-tech solutions to get publicity. "We still do not spend money on print advertising — and have more business than we can handle from word-of-mouth," says Jinele Boyd of MyTexasMusic.com.

Listing your site with Internet search services

How, exactly, do you get listed on the search engines such as Yahoo! and Lycos? Frankly, it's getting more difficult. Many of the big search services charge for listings (Yahoo!'s fees for commercial listings in its directory are particularly steep). But some let you contribute a listing for free, though there's no guarantee if or when you'll see your site included in their databases.

You can increase the chances that search services list your site by including special keywords and site descriptions in the titles, body text, and HTML commands for your Web pages. You place some of these keywords after a special HTML command (the `<meta>` tag), making them invisible to the casual viewer of your site. Turn to Chapter 11 for details.

John Moen and Lucky Boyd have both created multiple Web sites for different purposes. One purpose is to reach different markets. Another is to improve rankings on search engines, such as Google, by linking one site to several other sites, the site is considered more popular, and its ranking rises. See Chapter 11 for more on this and other tips on getting listed by Internet search engines.

Reaching the entire Internet

Your Web site may be the cornerstone of your business, but if nobody knows it's out there, it can't help you generate sales. Perhaps the most familiar form of online advertising are *banner ads,* those little electronic billboards that seem to show up on every popular Web page that you visit.

But banner advertising can be expensive and may not be the best way for a small business to advertise online. In fact, the most effective marketing for some businesses hasn't been traditional banner advertising or newspaper/ magazine placements. Rather, the e-marketers who run those businesses target electronic bulletin boards and mailing lists where people already discuss the products being sold. You can post notices on the bulletin boards where your potential customers congregate, notifying them that your services are now available. (Make sure that the board in question permits such solicitation before you do so, or you'll chase away the very customers you want.)

This sort of direct, one-to-one marketing may seem tedious, but it's often the best way to develop a business on the Internet. Reach out to your potential customers and strike up an individual, personal relationship with each one.

Chapter 10 contains everything you need to know about advertising with mailing lists, newsgroups, and even traditional banner ads.

Step 10: Review, Revise, and Improve

For any long-term endeavor, you need to establish standards by which you can judge its success or failure. You must decide for yourself what you consider success to be. After a period of time, take stock of where your business is and then take steps to do even better.

Taking stock

After 12 months online, Lucky Boyd took stock. His site was online, but he wasn't getting many page views. He redid the site, increased the number of giveaways, and traffic rose. Now, he makes music downloads available on his site; he also redid all his Web pages with the Hypertext Preprocessor (PHP) programming language. He has also expanded to include a business presence on the popular social networking sites MySpace, Facebook, and Twitter.

HTML is a markup language: It identifies parts of a Web page that need formatted as headings, text, images, and so on. It can be used to include scripts, such as those written in the JavaScript language. But by creating his pages from scratch with PHP, Lucky Boyd can make his site more dynamic and easier to update. He can rotate random images, process forms, and compile statistics that track his visitors by using PHP scripts, for instance. He can design Web pages in a modular way so that they can be redesigned and revised more quickly than with HTML, too.

When all is said and done, your business may do so well that you can reinvest in it by buying new equipment or increasing your services. You may even be in a position to give something back to nonprofits and those in need. The young founders of The Chocolate Farm set up a scholarship fund designed to bring young people from other countries to the United States to help them find out about free enterprise. Perhaps you'll have enough money left over to reward yourself, too — as if being able to tell everyone "I own my own online business" isn't reward enough!

Money is only one form of success. Plenty of entrepreneurs are online for reasons other than making money. That said, it *is* important from time to time to evaluate how well you're doing financially. Accounting software, such as the programs that I describe in Chapter 17, makes it easy to check your revenues on a daily or weekly basis. The key is to establish the goals you want to reach and develop measurements so that you know when and if you reach those goals.

Updating your data

Getting your business online now and then updating your site regularly is better than waiting to unveil the perfect Web site all at one time. In fact, seeing your site improve and grow is one of the best things about going online. Over time, you can create contests, strike up cooperative relationships with other businesses, and add more background information about your products and services.

Consider The Chocolate Farm, a business that was owned and operated for ten years by Evan and Elise MacMillan of Denver, Colorado. The business was started when Elise was just 10 years old and Evan was 13. They began by selling chocolates with a farm theme, such as candy cows; later, they focused more on creating custom chocolates — sweets made to order for businesses, many of which bore the company's logo. Evan and his sister eventually oversaw the work of 50 full- and part-time employees.

Today, Evan reports that he and his sister decided to wrap up their involvement with the Chocolate Farm. It was sold to another chocolate company. "We considered the exit a success," says Evan. He recalls how much the project brought to their lives: an appearance on "Oprah" and coverage in the *Wall Street Journal*. He adds: "And yes, it did help us with college expenses." Elise is a student at Stanford University, studying computer music and art. Evan graduated in the spring of 2009 and began work on his fifth startup company (he cofounded and operated a couple of energy software companies while still a college student). "Though we are out of the business, we still love chocolate, and Elise and I make things together on weekends."

Businesses on the Web need to evaluate and revise their practices on a regular basis. Lucky Boyd studies reports of where visitors come from before they reach his site, and what pages they visit on the site, so that he can attract new customers. Online business is a process of trial and error. Some promotions work better than others. The point is that it needs to be an ongoing process and a long-term commitment. Taking a chance and profiting from your mistakes is better than not trying in the first place.

Chapter 3

Choosing and Equipping Your New E-Business

In This Chapter

▶ Drawing up a plan for your own successful online business

▶ Understanding your options: Sales, services, auctions, hike!

▶ Making your cybershop stand out from the crowd

▶ Obtaining or upgrading your computer and other hardware

▶ Assembling a business software suite

Starting your own online business is like rehabbing an old house — something I'm constantly doing. Both projects involve a series of recognizable phases:

✔ **The idea phase:** You tell people about your great idea. They hear the enthusiasm in your voice, nod their heads, and say something like, "Good luck." They've seen you in this condition before and know how it usually turns out.

✔ **The decision phase:** Undaunted, you begin honing your plan. You read books (like this one), ask questions, and shop around until you find just the right tools and materials. Of course, when the project is staring you down in your own workshop, you may start to panic, asking yourself whether you're really up for the task. Don't worry: you are!

✔ **The assembly phase:** Still determined to proceed, you forge ahead. You plug in your tools and go to work. Drills spin, sparks fly, and metal moves.

✔ **The test-drive phase:** One fine day, out of the dust and fumes, your masterpiece emerges. You invite everyone over to enjoy the fruits of your labor. All of those who were skeptical before are now full of admiration. You get enjoyment from your project for years to come.

If rehabbing a house doesn't work for you, think about restoring an antique auto, planning an anniversary party, or devising a mountain-climbing excursion in Tibet. The point is that starting an online business is a project like any other — one that you can understand and accomplish in stages. Right now, you're at the first stage of launching your new cyberbusiness. Your creativity is working overtime. You have some rough sketches that only a mother could love.

This chapter helps you get from idea to reality. Your first step is to imagine how you want your business to look and feel. Then you can begin to develop and implement strategies for achieving your dream. You have a big advantage over those who started new businesses a few years ago: You have plenty of models to show you what works and what doesn't.

While you travel along the path from idea to reality, you must also consider properly equipping your online business — just like you would have to equip a traditional, brick-and-mortar business. One of the many exciting aspects of launching a business online, however, is the absence of much *overhead* (that is, operating expenses). Many non-cyberspace businesses must take out loans to pay rent, remodel their storefronts, and purchase store fixtures. In contrast, the primary overhead for an online business is computer hardware and software. Although it's great if you can afford top-of-the-line equipment, you'll be happy to know that the latest bells and whistles aren't absolutely necessary in order to get a business site online and maintain it effectively. But in order to streamline the technical aspects of connecting to the online world and creating a business presence, some investment may be a wise and profitable idea.

Don't rush into signing a contract to get your online business hosted. I've encountered experienced businesspeople who prepaid for a year's worth of Web hosting with nothing else yet in place. Be sure that you know your options and have a business strategy, no matter how simple, before you sign anything. Web sites are important, but they're not all there is to creating a presence and branding yourself, as you discover throughout this book.

Mapping Out Your Online Business

How do you get to square one? Start by imagining the kind of business that is your ultimate goal. This is the time to indulge in some brainstorming. Envisioning your business is a creative way of asking the all-important questions: Why do I want to go into business online? What are my goals? Table 3-1 illustrates some possible goals and suggests how to achieve them. By envisioning the final result you want to achieve, you can determine your online business goals.

Table 3-1	Online Business Models	
Goal	*Type of Web Site*	*What to Do*
Make big bucks	Sales	Sell items/gain paying advertisers.
Gain credibility and attention	Marketing	Start a blog; start Twittering; put your résumé and samples of your work online.
Promote yourself	Personal	Promote yourself in discussion groups or on your Web site so that people will hire you or want to use your goods or services.
Turn an interest into a source of income	Hobby/special interest	Invite like-minded people to share your passion, participate in your site, and generate traffic so that you can gain advertisers.

Looking around

You don't have to reinvent the wheel. Your ultimate destination can be the best source of information on how to get there. Sometimes, spending just half an hour surfing the Internet can stimulate your own mental network. Find sites with qualities you want to emulate. Throughout this book, I suggest business sites you can visit to find good models to follow.

Don't feel obligated to keep moving in the same direction all the time, either. One of the many advantages of starting an online business is the ability to change direction with relative ease.

Because you're not unlike your target audience, your likes and dislikes have value. Keep a low-tech pencil and pad of paper handy each time you surf for ideas. Make a list as you go of what you find appealing and jot down notes on logos, designs, and text. That way, you'll have raw data to draw upon when you begin to refine what you want to do.

Making your mark

The Web and other parts of the online world have undergone a population explosion that still shows no signs of slowing. According to Internet Systems Consortium's Domain Survey (www.isc.org), in July 2009, 625.2 million computers that hosted Web sites were connected to the Internet, compared with 439.3 million in 2006, 353.3 million in 2005, and 285 million in 2004. Twenty percent of those computers host Web addresses that end with the commercial (.com) designation.

As an *ontrepreneur* (online entrepreneur), your goal is to stand out from the crowd — or to "position yourself in the marketplace," as business consultants like to say. Consider the following tried-and-true suggestions if you want your Web site to be a go-to place:

✔ **Pursue something you know well.** Experience adds value to the information that you provide. In the online world, expertise sells.

✔ **Make a statement.** On your Web site, include a mission statement that clearly identifies what you do, the customers you hope to reach, and how you're different from your competitors. On your blog, give your opinions. On discussion groups, share your knowledge.

✔ **Give something away for free.** Giveaways and promotions are surefire ways to gain attention and develop a loyal customer base. In fact, entire Web sites are devoted to providing free stuff online; see iWon (www. iwon.com) or WebStakes (www.webstakes.com). You don't have to give away an actual product; it can be words of wisdom based on your training and experience.

✔ **Find your niche.** Web space is a great place to pursue niche marketing. In fact, it often seems that the quirkier the item, the better it sells. Some of the most successful sellers I know deal in things like flavored coffee, toy train accessories, fountain pens, women's purses, and the like. Don't be afraid to target a narrow audience and direct all your sales efforts to a small group of devoted followers.

✔ **Do something you love.** The more you love your business, the more time and effort you're apt to put into it and, therefore, the more likely it is to be successful. Such businesses take advantage of the Internet's worldwide reach, which makes it easy for people with the same interests to gather at the same virtual location.

Scan through the list of *Inc.* magazine's (www.inc.com) Top 500 privately held companies, and you find many examples of businesses that follow all the aforementioned strategies:

✔ The number 4 company for 2009, Perfect Fitness (www.perfect online.com/), has a niche selling fitness equipment online.

✔ The 26-year-old CEO of the number 2 company for 2004, uSight (www. usight.com), almost closed his company in its second year before finding his niche: a do-it-yourself Web site application called uBuilder.

✔ Go Daddy (www.godaddy.com) switched from Web-building software to domain-name registration and became number 8 in 2004.

✔ High Point Solutions (www.highpt.com), the top-ranked company in *Inc.* magazine's 500 List for 2001, was started by two brothers who skipped college and began the business in their home in Sparta, New Jersey. The company focuses on a niche: helping a small but very satisfied group of corporate customers iron out the logistical details of buying network hardware. They find good prices on new and used equipment and deliver products fast.

Evaluating commercial Web sites

How is your business the same as others? How is it different than others? Your customers will be asking these questions, so you may as well start out by asking them also. Commercial Web sites — those whose Internet addresses end with .com or .biz — are the fastest-growing segment of the Internet . This is the area you're entering, too. The trick is to be comfortable with the size and level of complexity of a business that's right for you. In general, your options are

- **A big commercial Web site:** The Web means big business, and plenty of big companies create Web sites with the primary goal of supplementing a product or business that's already well known and well established. Just a few examples are the Ragu Web site (www.ragu.com), the Pepsi World Web site (www.pepsiworld.com), and the Toyota Web site (www.toyota.com). True, corporations with thousands of dollars to throw into Web design created these commercial Web sites, but you can still look at them to get ideas for your own site.

- **A mid-size site:** Many a small business of ten to twelve employees makes good use of the Web to provide customer service, disseminate information, and post a sales catalog. You may find some features that mid-size companies use, such as a Frequently Asked Questions (FAQ) page or a sales catalog, useful to you. Look at the Golfballs.com site (www.golfballs.com) for good ideas.

- **A site that's just right:** You don't need prior business experience to guarantee success on the Web. A business can also start out as a single person, couple, or family. In fact, the rest of this book is devoted to helping you produce a very fine, homegrown entrepreneurial business. This chapter gets you off to a good start by examining the different kinds of businesses you can launch online and some business goals you can set for yourself.

Flavors of Online Businesses You Can Taste Test

If you're easily overstimulated, you may feel that you need blinders when you comb the Internet for ideas to give your online business a definite shape and form. Use the following brief descriptions of online businesses to create categories of interest and then zero in on the ones that will be most useful to you.

Selling consumer products

Leading Internet research firm Forrester Research (www.internet retailer.com/dailyNews.asp?id=30341) predicts that, despite slow-downs in the economy, total e-commerce sales in the United States will continue to grow to $156.1 billion in 2009, an increase of 10 percent over 2008's 141.3 billion in revenues. The online marketplace is a great venue if you have products to sell (such as auto parts, antiques, jewelry, or food). The Web has always attracted those looking for unique items or something customized just for them. Consider taking your wares online if any of the following applies to you:

- ✔ Your products are high in quality.

- ✔ You create your own products; for example, you design dishes, make fudge, or sell gift baskets of wine.

- ✔ You specialize in some aspects of your product that larger businesses can't achieve. Perhaps you sell regional foods, such as Chicago deep-dish pizza or live lobsters from Maine.

I have always admired the customization tools available on the Timbuk2 site (www.timbuk2.com), which manufactures bicycle messenger bags and sells them directly to the public. Other sites don't sell consumer goods directly, but they support consumer goods. For instance, ice cream may not be good for my waistline, but I often go to the Web site of Ben and Jerry's (www.benjerry.com) just to drool. These guys are entrepreneurs just like you, and I like their Web site as well as their products. The Web site focuses on the unique flavors and the high quality of their ice cream, as well as their personalities and business standards.

So c'mon in; the water's fine. The key is to find your niche, as many small-but-successful businesses have done. Use your Web space to declare your love for your products (and, by implication, why your customers will love them, too).

Hanging out your professional services

Either through a Web site or through listings in indexes and directories, offer-ing your professional services online can expand your client base dramati-cally. A Web presence also gives existing clients a new way to contact you: through e-mail. Here are just a few examples of professionals who are offering their services online:

- ✔ **Attorneys:** Immigration attorney Kevin L. Dixler is based in Chicago. Through his Web site (www.dixler.com), he can reach individuals around the world who want to come to the United States.

- ✔ **Psychotherapists:** Sarah Calothis uses a simple, nicely designed Web site (www.sarahcalothis.co.uk) to pursue a profession you might not think you could do online: psychotherapy. Her site is upfront about her work and the advantages of online counseling.

- ✔ **Physicians:** Dr. Rob Lamberts, a physician in Augusta, Georgia, maintains a blog called "Musings of a Distractible Mind" (http://distractible.org) that gives opinions and tips. He is also known as "The House Call Doctor" on the Quick and Dirty Tips Web site (quickanddirtytips.com).

- ✔ **Consultants:** Experts who keep their knowledge up-to-date and are willing to give advice to those with similar interests and needs are always in demand. Consultants in a specialized area often find a great demand for their services on the Internet. The Yahoo! Consulting page is crowded with fields in which online consultants are available: dir.yahoo.com/business_and_economy/business_to_business/consulting.

We're busy people who don't always have the time to pore over the fine print. Short and snappy nuggets of information can draw customers to your site and make them feel as though they're getting "something for free." One way you can put forth this professional expertise is by starting your own online newsletter. You get to be editor, writer, and mailing-list manager. Plus, you get to talk as much as you want, network with tons of people who are interested enough in what you have to say to subscribe to your publication, and put your name and your business before lots of people. Judy Vorfeld (whom I profile in Chapter 5) puts out a regular newsletter called Communication Expressway that supplements her online business site (www.ossweb.com).

Selling your expertise

The original purpose of the Internet was to share knowledge via computers, and information is the commodity that has fueled cyberspace's rapid growth. As the Internet and commercial online networks continue to expand, information remains key.

Finding valuable information and gathering a particular kind of resource for one location online can be a business in itself. People love to get knowledge they trust from the comfort of their own homes. For example, students and parents are eager to pay someone to help them sort through the procedures involved and the data required to apply for college. (See the intriguing Counselor-O-Matic Web site, www.princetonreview.com/college/research/advsearch/match.asp, run by the Princeton Review and *Seventeen* magazine, for example.)

Other online businesses provide gathering points or indexes to more specific areas. Here are just a few examples:

✔ **Search engines:** Some businesses succeed by connecting cybersurfers with companies, organizations, and individuals that specialize in a given area. Yahoo! (`www.yahoo.com`) is the most obvious example. Originally started by two college students, Yahoo! has practically become an Internet legend by gathering information in one index so that people can easily find things online.

✔ **Links pages:** On her Grandma Jam's Sweepstakes/Contest Guide (`www.grandmajam.com`), Janet Marchbanks-Aulenta gathers links to current contests along with short descriptions of each one. Janet says her site receives as many as 22,000 visits per month and generates income through advertising and affiliate links to other contest Web sites. She says she loves running her own business despite the hard work involved with keeping it updated. "The key to succeeding at this type of site is to build up a regular base of users that return each day to find new contests — the daily upkeep is very important," she says.

✔ **Personal recommendations:** The personal touch sells. Just look at sites like Lifehacker (`www.lifehacker.com`) and About.com (`www.about.com`). The latter is a guide to the online world that provides Web surfers with a central location where they can locate virtually anything. It works because real people do the choosing and provide evaluations (albeit brief) of the sites they list.

Resource sites, such as these, can transform information into money in a number of ways. In some cases, individuals pay to become members. Sometimes, businesses pay to be listed on a site; other times, a site attracts so many visitors on a regular basis that other companies pay to post advertising on the site. Big successes — such as About.com — carry a healthy share of ads and strike lucrative partnerships with big companies, as well.

Opportunities with technology or computer resources

What could be more natural than using the Web to sell what you need to get and stay online? The online world itself, by the very fact that it exists, has spawned all kinds of business opportunities for entrepreneurs:

✔ **Computer Services:** *U.S. News and WorldReport* listed computer services as one of the best small businesses to start, and mentioned Arlington Virginia Computer Repair (`arlingtonvacomputerrepair.com`) as an example. Owner Alex Chamandy fills a niche by dealing with customers face to face, and by locating his company in the basement of his residence, he saves on overhead and other costs. He is thus able to offer lower rates than repair services of the "big box" computer stores.

✔ **Internet service providers:** These businesses give you a high-speed connection to the Internet. Many ISPs, such as Comcast or AT&T, are big concerns. But smaller companies are succeeding as well — such as, YourNET Connection (`www.ync.net`), which is based in Schaumburg, Illinois, offers free online Web training for its customers.

✔ **Software:** Matt Wright is well known on the Web for providing free computer scripts that add important functionality to Web sites, such as processing information that visitors submit via online forms. Matt's Script Archive site (`www.scriptarchive.com`) now includes an advertisement for a book on scripting that he coauthored, as well as a Web postcard system for sale and an invitation to businesses to take out advertisements on his site.

Being a starving artist without the starving

Being creative no longer means you have to live out of your flower-covered van, driving from art fairs to craft shows. If you're simply looking for exposure and feedback on your creations, you can put samples of your work online. Consider the following suggestions for virtual creative venues (and revenues):

✔ **Host art galleries.** Thanks to online galleries, artists whose sales were previously limited to one region can get inquiries from all over the world. Art Gaga (formerly known as Art Xpo) (`www.artgaga.com`) reports thousands of dollars in sales through its Web site and aggressive marketing efforts. The personal Web site created by artist Marques Vickers (`www.marquesv.com`) has received worldwide attention; see Figure 3-1.

✔ **Publish your writing.** Blogs (Weblogs, or online diaries) are all the rage these days. The most successful, such as the one run by Andrew Sullivan (`www.andrewsullivan.com`) as part of the *Atlantic* magazine, are generating ad revenue. To find out how to create one, check out Blogger (`www.blogger.com`).

✔ **Get your art printed.** Two young men named Jake and Jacob met through a design forum and dropped out of college to start an online T-shirt business. Today, their Threadless T-Shirts (`www.threadless.com`) Web site rakes in millions.

✔ **Sell your music.** Singer-songwriter Michael McDermott sells his own CDs, videos, and posters through his online store (`www.michael-mcdermott.com`).

You can, of course, also sell all that junk that's been accumulating in your basement, as well as your relatives' and family members' junk, on eBay; see Chapter 13 for more information on this and other exciting marketplaces.

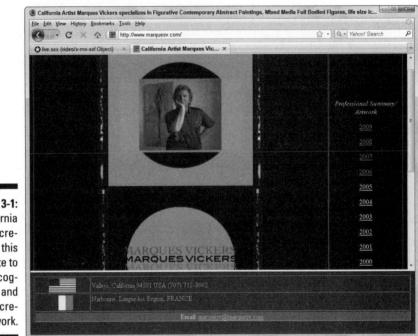

Figure 3-1:
A California
artist cre-
ated this
Web site to
gain recog-
nition and
sell his cre-
ative work.

Easyware (Not Hardware) for Your Business

Becoming an information provider on the Internet places an additional burden on your computer and peripheral equipment. When you're "in it for the money," you may very well start to go online every day, and perhaps hours at a time, especially if you buy and sell on eBay. The better your computer setup, the more e-mail messages you can download, the more catalog items you can store, and so on. In this section, I introduce you to many upgrades you may need to make to your existing hardware configuration.

Some general principles apply when assembling equipment (discussed in this section) and programs (discussed in a subsequent section, "Software Solutions for Online Business") for an online endeavor:

✔ **Look on the Internet for what you need.** You can find just about everything you want to get you started.

✔ **Be sure to pry before you buy!** Don't pull out that credit card until you get the facts on what warranty and technical support your hardware or software vendor provides. Make sure that your vendor provides phone support 24 hours a day, 7 days a week. Also ask how long the typical turnaround time is in case your equipment needs to be serviced.

If you purchase lots of new hardware and software, remember to update your insurance by sending your insurer a list of your new equipment. Also consider purchasing insurance specifically for your computer-related items from a company such as Safeware (www.safeware.com).

The right computer for your online business

You very well may already have an existing computer setup that's adequate to get your business online and start the ball rolling. After all, personal computers are becoming more powerful and at the same time generally less expensive; your personal computer may be more than adequate for your business. Or you may be starting from scratch and looking to purchase a new computer. In either case, it pays to know what all the technical terms and specifications mean. Here are some general terms you need to understand:

- ✔ **Gigahertz (GHz) and megahertz (MHz):** This unit of measure indicates how quickly a computer's processor can perform functions. The central processing unit (CPU) of a computer is where the computing work gets done. In general, the higher the processor's internal clock rate, the faster the computer.

- ✔ **Random access memory (RAM):** This is the memory that your computer uses to temporarily store information needed to operate programs. RAM is usually expressed in millions of bytes, or megabytes (MB). The more RAM you have, the more programs you can run simultaneously.

- ✔ **Synchronous dynamic RAM (SDRAM):** Many ultrafast computers use some form of SDRAM synchronized with a particular clock rate of a CPU so that a processor can perform more instructions in a given time.

- ✔ **Double data rate SDRAM (DDR SDRAM):** This is a type of SDRAM that can dramatically improve the clock rate of a CPU.

- ✔ **Auxiliary storage:** This term refers to physical data-storage space on a hard drive, tape, CD-RW, DVD, or other device.

- ✔ **Portable storage:** SD, XD, CF, and other memory cards can store data in cellphones, cameras, and other portable devices. And don't forget those little USB "flash drives" (also called "thumb drives") that can help you back up your data in a — well, in a flash.

- ✔ **Virtual memory:** This is a type of memory on your hard drive that your computer can "borrow" to serve as extra RAM.

- ✔ **Network interface card (NIC):** You need this hardware add-on if you have a cable or DSL modem or if you expect to connect your computer to others on a network. Having a NIC usually provides you with Ethernet data transfer to the other computers. (*Ethernet* is a network technology that permits you to send and receive data at very fast speeds.)

✔ **Wireless network card:** The laptop or desktop computer you purchase almost certainly has a wireless network card installed so that you can connect to your wireless modem if you have one. If your home or office has a wireless network and you need to connect by using a desktop computer with no built-in wireless capability, however, you need to purchase a card as an add-on. You can find one at your local computer store for $20 to $30.

The Internet is teeming with places where you can find good deals on hardware. A great place to start is the CNET Shopper.com Web site (`shopper.cnet.com`). Also visit the auction site uBid.com (`www.ubid.com`).

Processor speed

Computer processors are getting faster all the time. Don't be overly impressed by a computer's clock speed (measured in megahertz or even gigahertz). By the time you get your computer home, another, faster chip will already have hit the streets. Just make sure that you have enough memory to run the types of applications shown in Table 3-2. (Note that these are only estimates, based on the Windows versions of these products that were available at the time of this writing.)

Table 3-2	Memory Requirements	
Type of Application	*Example*	*Amount of RAM Recommended*
Web browser	Internet Explorer	64 or 128MB
Web page editor	Dreamweaver	256MB
Word processor	Microsoft Word	256MB (as part of Office 2007)
Graphics program	Paint Shop Pro	256MB
Professional drawing/ editing software	Adobe Photoshop CS4	512MB (1GB recommended)
Accounting software	Microsoft Excel	8MB (if you are already running an Office application)
Animation/Presentation	Adobe Flash Professional	256MB

The RAM recommended for the sample applications in Table 3-2 adds up to more than 1GB. If you plan to work, be sure to get at least 2GB of RAM — more if you can swing it. Memory is cheap nowadays, so get all the RAM you can afford.

Hard drive storage

RAM is only one type of memory your computer uses; the other kind, the memory in the hard drive, stores information, such as text files, audio files, programs, and the many essential files that your computer's operating system needs. Most new computers on the market come with hard drives that store many gigabytes of data. Any hard drive with a few gigabytes of storage space should be adequate for your business needs if you don't do a lot of graphics work. But most new computers come with hard drives that are 300 to 500GB or larger in size.

CD-RW/DVD±RW drive

Although a DVD and/or CD recordable drive may not be the most important part of your computer for business use, it can perform essential installation, storage, and data communications functions, such as installing software and saving and sharing data. Most machines are now being made available with a *digital versatile disc* (DVD) drive. You can fit 4.7GB or more of data on a DVD±RW, compared with the 700MB or so that a conventional CD-RW can handle. You can also add on a Blu-Ray drive if you want to create high-definition video; drives are currently available for $100 to $150.

Be sure to protect your equipment against electrical problems that can result in loss of data or substantial repair bills. At the very least, make sure that your home office has grounded three-prong outlets and a *surge suppressor*. A common variety is a five- or six-outlet strip that has a protection device built in. Also consider the option of an uninterruptible power supply (UPS), which keeps devices from shutting off immediately in the event of blackouts. Eaton Corporation presents a questionnaire on its Web site that leads you through the process of selecting just the right UPS device that's available for your device and your needs. Try it out at `http.powerquality.eaton.com/ UPS/selector/SolutionOverview.asp`.

Monitor

In terms of your online business, the quality or thinness of your monitor doesn't affect the quality of your Web site directly. Even if you have a poor-quality monitor, you can create a Web site that looks great to those who visit you. The problem is that you won't know how good your site really looks to customers who have high-quality monitors.

Flat-panel LCD (liquid crystal display) monitors are pretty much the norm at this point, and they've become far more affordable than they used to be, too. The quality of a monitor depends on several factors:

✔ **Resolution:** The resolution of a computer monitor refers to the number of pixels it can display horizontally and vertically. A resolution of 640 x 480 means that the monitor can display 640 pixels across the screen and 480 pixels down the screen. Higher resolutions, such as 800 x 600 or 1,024 x 768, make images look sharper but require more RAM in your computer. Anything less than 640 x 480 is unusable these days.

✔ **Size:** Monitor size is measured diagonally, as with TVs. Sizes, such as 21 inches, 24 inches, and up to 28 inches, are available. (Look for a 21-inch LCD monitor, which can display most Web pages fully and is now available for less than $150.)

✔ **Refresh rate:** This is the number of times per second that a video card redraws an image on-screen (at least 60 Hz to 120 Hz [hertz] is preferable).

Keep in mind that lots of Web pages seem to have been designed with 21-inch or 24-inch monitors in mind. The problem isn't just that some users (especially those with laptops) have 15-inch monitors but also that you can never control how wide the viewer's browser window will be. The problem is illustrated in the page from the Web Style Guide, one of the classic references of Web site design (www.webstyleguide.com/).

Computer monitors display graphic information that consists of little units — *pixels.* Each pixel appears on-screen as a small dot — so small that it's hard to perceive with the naked eye unless you magnify an image to look at details closely. Together, the patterns of pixels create different intensities of light in an image as well as ranges of color. A pixel can contain one or more bytes of binary information. The more pixels per inch (ppi), the higher a monitor's potential resolution. The higher the resolution, the closer the image appears to a continuous-tone image such as a photo. When you see a monitor's resolution described as 1,280 x 1,024, for example, that refers to the number of pixels that the monitor can display. *Dot pitch* refers to the distance between any two of the three pixels (one red, one green, and one blue) that a monitor uses to display color. The lower the dot pitch, the better the image resolution that you obtain. A dot pitch of 0.27 mm is a good measurement for a 17-inch monitor.

Fax equipment

A fax machine is an essential part of many home offices. If you don't have the funds available for a standalone machine, you can install software that helps your computer send and receive faxes. You have three options:

✔ You can install a fax modem, a hardware device that usually works with fax software. The fax modem can be an internal or external device.

✔ You can use your regular modem but install software that enables your computer to exchange faxes with another computer or fax machine.

✔ You can sign up for a service that receives your faxes and sends them to your computer in the body of an e-mail message.

If you plan to fax and access the Internet from your home office, get a second phone line or a direct connection, such as a DSL or cable modem. The last thing a potential customer wants to hear is a busy signal.

Image capture devices

When you're ready to move beyond the basic hardware and on to frill, think about obtaining a tool for capturing photographic images. (By *capturing*, I mean *digitizing* an image or, in other words, saving it in computerized, digital format.) Photos are often essential elements of business Web pages: They attract a customer's attention, they illustrate items for sale, and they can provide before-and-after samples of your work. If you're an artist or designer, having photographic representations of your work is vital.

Including a clear, sharp image on your Web site greatly increases your chances of selling your product or service. You have two choices for digitizing: a scanner or digital camera. To decide which is best for you, read on.

Digital camera

Not so long ago, digital cameras cost thousands of dollars. These days, you can find a very serviceable camera made by a reputable manufacturer, such as Nikon, Fuji, Canon, Olympus, or Kodak, for around $100 or less. The small investment in this particular tool can pay off for you big time in the long run. With the addition of a color printer, you can even print your own photos. But before you invest in a color printer, try the photo kiosk at your local drug store. You can usually scan or print there and only pay a few cents for a print. If you print photographs only occasionally, this may be a more economical option than buying your own printer.

Don't hesitate to fork over the extra dough to get a camera that gives you good resolution. Cutting corners doesn't pay when you end up with images that look fuzzy, but you can find many low-cost devices with good features. For example, the Canon PowerShot A490, which costs about $100, has a resolution of 10 megapixels — fine enough to print on a color printer and enlarge to a size such as 5 x 7 inches — and a zoom feature. *Megapixels* are calculated by multiplying the number of pixels in an image — for instance, when actually multiplied, $1,984 \times 1,488 = 2,952,192$ pixels or 2.9 megapixels. The higher the resolution, the fewer photos your camera can store at any one time because each image file requires more memory.

Having super-high resolution images isn't critical for Web images because they display on computer monitors (which have limited resolution). Before you can display an image on a Web browser, you have to compress it by putting it in GIF or JPEG format. (See Chapter 5 for more scintillating technical details on GIF and JPEG.) Also, smaller and simpler images (as opposed to large, high-resolution graphics) generally appear more quickly on the viewer's screen. If you make your customers wait too long (more than just ten seconds or so) for an image to appear on-screen, they're highly likely to go to someone else's online store.

When shopping for a digital camera, look for the following features:

✔ The ability to download images to your computer via a FireWire or USB connection

✔ Bundled image-processing software

✔ The ability to download image files directly to a memory card that you can easily transport to a computer's memory card reader

✔ A macro function that enables you to capture clear close-up images

✔ An included LCD screen that lets you see your images immediately

Digital photography is a fascinating and technical process, and you'll do well to read more about it in other books, such as *Digital Photography All-in-One Desk Reference For Dummies*, 4th Edition, by David Busch, or *Digital Photography For Dummies,* 6th Edition, by Julie Adair King and Serge Timacheff (both by Wiley).

Scanners

Scanning is the process of turning the colors and shapes contained in a photographic print or slide into digital information (that is, bytes of data) that a computer can understand. You place the image in a position where the scanner's camera can pass over it, and the scanner turns the image into a computer document that consists of tiny bits of information — *pixels.* The type that I find easiest to use is a flatbed scanner. You place the photo or other image on a flat glass bed, just like what you find on a photocopier. An optical device moves under the glass and scans the photo.

The best news about scanners is that they've been around for a while, which, in the world of computing, means that prices are going down at the same time that quality is on the rise. Many good scanners are built in to printers, so you can buy both in one device. The bargain models are well under $100, and I've even seen a couple standalone photo scanners for as low as $59.95 new.

A type of scanner that has lots of benefits for small or home-based businesses is a multifunction device. You can find these units, along with conventional printers and scanners, everywhere: at computer outlets, office-supply shops, big-box stores such as Target and Costco, and online through TigerDirect.com and many other vendors. I use a multifunction device in my home office that sends and receives faxes, scans images, acts as a laser printer, and makes copies — plus it includes a telephone and answering machine. Now, if it could just make a good cup of espresso. . . .

A low-budget alternative

These days, you really need a digital camera, and if you're on a tight budget, you can buy a slightly used model on eBay or elsewhere. But if you truly want to get a computerized version of a photo on your Web without investing in any of the hardware that I mention in this chapter, not to worry. Just call your local photo shop or copy center. Many FedEx Office outlets (formerly known as Kinko's), for example, provide computer services that include scanning photos. If you do your photo processing through Kodak, you can have the images placed online or on a CD. If you're a member of America Online, you can get your photos online through its "You've Got Pictures" service and delivered to a location that you set up with AOL. Or stop by just about any chain drugstore, Target, Kmart, or the like, which have scanning and photomaking self-serve kiosks.

Wherever you go, be sure to have the image saved in GIF or JPEG format so that it's in a usable format for display on the Web. You can save the image in the size that you want, too, so that you don't have to resize it later in a graphics program.

Getting Online: Connection Options

After you purchase the computer hardware that you need, telephone bills are likely to be the biggest monthly expense you'll encounter in connection with your online business. At least they are for me: I pay for local service, long-distance service, cellphone service, plus DSL service over my phone lines. It pays to choose your *telco* (telephone company) connection wisely.

A second phone line

Having a second line is pretty much a given if you plan to do business online regularly. A cellphone works fine for business purposes if you don't want to pay your telephone company's fees for the extra land line. Having a separate phone line dedicated to your business also makes your operation look more legitimate in case you're applying for a business checking account or merchant account from a financial institution.

Ask your telco about a *call pack* so that you can call one number a lot for the same rate: 100 calls per month for a flat $10 fee, for example. Or check out Skype (www.skype.com). For just pennies a minute, you can call anywhere in the world, including phone calls from your computer to cellphones or land lines.

Cable modem

Cable modem connections offer a really attractive way to get a high-speed connection to cyberspace. So go ahead and ask your local cable TV providers whether they provide this service. But other options, such as AT&T (www. att.com) and EarthLink (www.earthlink.net/access/cable.faces) provide high-speed Internet access through affiliations with cable TV providers in many parts of the country. In my neighborhood in Chicago, a company called RCN Chicago (www.rcn.com/about-rcn) offers Internet access via cable modem for $24.99 to $59.99 plus a $5 fee for the cable modem device itself. AT&T (www.att.com), however, offers several high-speed Internet packages ranging from $19.95 to $24.95 per month.

The advantages of having a cable modem connection are many: It's a direct connection, it frees up a phone line, and it's super fast. Cable modems have the capacity to deliver 4 or 5MB of data per second. But some providers don't tell you what kind of connection you're getting: You might pay for the speed of the connection instead. Currently AT&T provides a connection of up to 6.0 Mbps for $24.95 per month, which is a good deal.

In reality, of course, the speed is going to be less than this because you're sharing access with other users. Plus, you have to purchase or lease the cable modem itself, pay an installation fee, and purchase an Ethernet card (if your computer doesn't already have one installed). But a cable modem is going to be far faster than a dialup connection.

You can find out which cable modem and DSL providers cover your area by using the Service Availability tool provided by Cable-Modem.net (www.cable-modem.net/cable_service/service_availability.html).

DSL

If your telephone company offers its customers Digital Subscriber Line (DSL) connections, you may be able to get a connection that approaches the speed of cable. With DSL, you can use your existing, conventional phone lines rather than have to install a new line to your house. That's because DSLs "borrow" the part of your phone line that your voice doesn't use, the part that transmits signals of 3,000 Hz (hertz) or higher. DSLs can *upload* (send) data to another location on the Internet at up to 6.0 Mbps (megabits per second) and *download* (receive) data at up to 2.560 Mbps. (Your may get half that speed, though, depending on your location.)

DSL comes in different varieties. Asymmetrical Digital Subscriber Line (ADSL) transmits information at different speeds, depending on whether you're sending or receiving data. Symmetrical Digital Subscriber Line (SDSL) transmits information at the same speed in both directions. As DSL gets more popular, it becomes more widely available and the pricing drops. While I'm writing this, EarthLink DSL is available for just $12.95 per month with free DSL modem and installation. Your local phone provider might offer DSL, too. In the Chicago area, AT&T has a DSL option for just $19 per month plus free installation and a free DSL modem.

Smart phone

One of the most convenient ways to get online, when I'm on the road, is through my Palm Pro cellphone, which has Web access. After I obtained unlimited access through my provider, I never looked back. I'm on the phone all the time, checking my Gmail, my Webmail, and even posting on Twitter and my blog occasionally.

For an online businessperson, a cellphone is a necessity rather than a luxury. A smart phone will enable you to respond quickly to queries from customers who visit your Web site and ask questions about your products and services.

Software Solutions for Online Business

One of the great things about starting an Internet business is that you get to use Internet software. As you probably know, the programs you use online are inexpensive (sometimes free), easy to use and install, and continually being updated.

Although you probably already have a basic selection of software to help you find information and communicate with others in cyberspace, the following sections describe some programs you may not have as yet that may come in handy when you create your online business.

Don't forget to update your homeowner's or renter's insurance by sending your insurer a list of new software (and hardware) or even by purchasing insurance specifically for your computer-related items from a company such as Safeware (www.safeware.com). With homeowner's or renter's insurance, some accidents are not covered, and you don't always get replacement coverage for items such as computers. Check with your insurance provider to be sure.

Anyone who uses firewall or antivirus software will tell you how essential these pieces of software are for home or business use. Find out more about such software in Chapter 6. See Chapter 17 for suggestions about accounting software — other important software you need.

Web browser

A *Web browser* is software that serves as a visual interface to the images, colors, links, and other content contained on the Web. The most popular such programs are Microsoft Internet Explorer, Firefox, Safari, and Google Chrome.

Your Web browser is your primary tool for conducting business online, just as it is for everyday personal use. When it comes to running a virtual store or consulting business, though, you have to run your software through a few more paces than usual. You need your browser to

- ✔ Preview the Web pages you create
- ✔ Display animations, play sounds and movie clips, and other goodies you plan to add online
- ✔ Support some level of Internet security, such as Secure Sockets Layer (SSL), if you plan to conduct secure transactions on your site

In addition to having an up-to-date browser with the latest features, install-ing more than one kind of browser on your computer is a good idea. For example, if you use Microsoft Internet Explorer because that's what came with your operating system, be sure to download the latest copy of Firefox and Safari, as well. That way, you can test your site to make sure that it looks good to most of your visitors.

Web page editor

HyperText Markup Language (HTML) is a set of instructions used to format text, images, and other Web page elements so that Web browsers can cor-rectly display them. But you don't have to master HTML to create your own Web pages. Plenty of programs — *Web page editors* — are available to help you format text, add images, make hyperlinks, and do all the fun assembly steps necessary to make your Web site a winner. Among the most popular are Adobe Dreamweaver, Adobe GoLive, and Microsoft Expression Web.

Sometimes, programs that you use for one purpose can also help you create Web documents: Software you use to create blogs, such as WordPress, can help you format other types of Web content. Microsoft Word enables you to save text documents as HTML Web pages, and Microsoft Office enables you to export files in Web page format automatically.

Taking e-mail a step higher

You're probably very familiar with sending and receiving e-mail messages. But when you start an online business, make sure that e-mail software has some advanced features:

- ✔ **Autoresponders:** Some programs automatically respond to e-mail requests with a form letter or document of your choice.

- ✔ **Mailing lists:** With a well-organized address book (a feature that comes with some e-mail programs), you can collect the e-mail addresses of visitors or subscribers and send them a regular update of your business activities or, better yet, an e-mail newsletter.

- ✔ **Quoting:** Almost all e-mail programs let you quote from a message to which you're replying so that you can respond easily to a series of questions.

- ✔ **Attaching:** Attaching a file to an e-mail message is a quick and convenient way to transmit information from one person to another.

- ✔ **Signature files:** Make sure that your e-mail software automatically includes a simple electronic signature at the end. Use this space to list your company name, your title, and your Web site URL.

Both Outlook, the e-mail component of Microsoft Internet Explorer, and Thunderbird (which is associated with the Web browser Firefox) include most or all of these features. Because these functions are all essential aspects of providing good customer service, I discuss them in more detail in Chapter 8.

Discussion group software

When your business site is up and running, consider taking it a step farther by creating your own discussion area right on your Web site. This sort of discussion area isn't a newsgroup as such; it doesn't exist in Usenet, and you don't need newsgroup software to read and post messages. Rather, it's a Web-based discussion area where your visitors can compare notes and share their passion for the products you sell or the area of service you provide.

If you set up a page on Facebook (`www.facebook.com`), you can invite your customers to say they "like" you, and you get a discussion area included with your page as well as an area where you can post information about your business or photos of your products.

FTP software

FTP (File Transfer Protocol) is one of those acronyms you see time and time again when you move around the Internet. You may even have an FTP program that your ISP gave you when you obtained your Internet account. But chances, are you don't use it that often.

In case you haven't used FTP yet, start dusting it off. When you create your own Web pages, a simple, no-nonsense FTP program is the easiest way to transfer the files for them from your computer at home to your Web host. If you need to correct and update your Web pages quickly (and you will), you'll benefit by having your FTP software ready and set up with your Web site address, username, and password so that you can transfer files right away.

To work on this book, I used the free FTP program FileZilla (www.filezilla.org), which I find to be convenient and easy to use. And did I mention that it's free?

Image editors

You need a graphics-editing program either to create original artwork for your Web pages or to crop and adjust your scanned images and digital photographs. In the case of adjusting or cropping photographic image files, the software you need almost always comes bundled with the scanner or digital camera, so you don't need to buy separate software for that.

In the case of graphic images, the first question to ask is, "Am I really qualified to draw and make my own graphics?" If you feel like taking the plunge, three programs I recommend are Adobe Photoshop Elements (www.adobe.com), LView Pro by Leonardo Haddad Loureiro (www.lview.com), and Paint Shop Pro by Corel (www.corel.com). You can download all these programs from the Web to use on a trial basis. After the trial period is over, you have to pay a small fee to the developer in order to register and keep the program. Photoshop Elements costs $99; LView Pro version 2006 costs $29.95; Paint Shop Pro costs $69.95 to download for Version Photo X2.

The ability to download and use free (and almost free) software from shareware archives and many other sites is one of the nicest things about the Internet. Keep the system working by remembering to pay the shareware fees to the nice folks who make their software available to individuals like you and me.

Instant messaging

You may think that MSN Messenger, AOL Instant Messenger, ICQ, and PalTalk are just for social "chatting" online, but instant messaging has its business applications, too. Here are a few suggestions:

- ✔ If individuals you work with all the time are hard to reach, you can use a messaging program to tell you whether those people are logged on to their computers. You can contact them the moment they sit down to work (provided that they don't mind your greeting them so quickly, of course).
- ✔ You can cut down on long-distance phone charges by exchanging instant messages with far-flung colleagues.
- ✔ With a microphone, sound card, and speakers, you can carry on voice conversations through your messaging software.

MSN Messenger enables users to do file transfers without having to use FTP software or attaching files to e-mail messages.

Internet phone software

Skype (pronounced *skipe*; rhymes with *snipe*) is the best known of a group of software programs that provide you with Internet phone service. Skype allows you to talk to other computer users over the Internet, provided that you have a microphone connected to your computer and a headset if your built-in speakers aren't loud enough. (Mine aren't.) Skype gives you a highly cost-effective alternative to long-distance or international phone calls. Skype really works best if both parties have a high-speed Internet connection. When they do, Skype is convenient and a lot of fun. When one Skype member calls another, the connection is free. In addition, you can

- ✔ Type messages to one individual, either in a real-time "chat"-like session, or by typing a message that the individual will read when he or she is back online
- ✔ Put the Skype logo on your Web site to help market your business by letting people know that you'll speak to them personally, for free

Giving your customers the chance to "meet" you in person, at least virtually, will help build their trust. The program is free; find out more at www. skype.com.

Backup software

Losing copies of your personal documents is one thing, but losing files related to your business can hit you hard in the pocketbook. That makes it even more important to make backups of your online business computer files. Iomega Prestige or eGodrives (www.iomega.com) come with software that lets you automatically make backups of your files. If you don't own one of these programs, I recommend that you get really familiar with the backup program included with Windows XP or look into Backup Exec by Symantec Corporation (www.symantec.com/business/products/family. jsp?familyid=backupexec). Or just buy a USB flash drive that holds 2GB or more of information and use that to back up your files.

Instead of (or along with) purchasing a disk drive to back your files up, you can store your files in an online "cloud." Cloud computing is all the rage these days. A "cloud" is a huge storage space on a server provided by an online provider. Perhaps the best-known example is Google. Google not only gives people access to many gigabytes' worth of e-mail storage space through its Gmail service but also gives Gmail users free access to a service called Google Docs (docs.google.com). Google Docs lets you work on Google's servers, doing word processing and spreadsheet computing while storing your files online so that you can access them from anywhere you have an Internet connection. Some service providers provide space in the "cloud" (that is, on their servers) specifically for storage and backup. These include Microsoft's SkyDrive (skydrive.live.com/), which gives you 25GB of free storage space, and Box (box.net), which has a free option with 1GB of space or 10GB for $9.95 per month.

Chapter 4

Selecting Your E-Commerce Host and Design Tools

*Y*ou *can* sell items online without having a Web site. But do you really want to? Doing real online business without some sort of online "home base" is time consuming and inefficient. The vast majority of online commercial concerns use their Web sites as the primary way to attract customers, convey their message, and make sales. Ambitious capitalists use online auction sites such as eBay (www.ebay.com) to make money, but the auctioneers who depend on eBay for regular income often have their own Web pages, too — plus storefronts on other hosting sites, where they can gather all the profit without having to pay fees to the auction marketplace.

The success of a commercial Web site depends in large measure on two important factors: where it's hosted and how it's designed. These factors affect how easily you can create and update your Web pages; what special features, such as multimedia or interactive forms, you can have on your site; and even how your site looks. Some hosting services provide Web page creation tools that are easy to use but limit the level of sophistication you can apply to the page's design. Other services leave the creation and design up to you. In this chapter, I provide an overview of your Web hosting options as well as different design approaches that you can implement.

Plenty of Web hosting services and CDs claim that they can have your Web site up and running online "in a matter of minutes" by using a "seamless" process. The actual construction may indeed be quick and smooth — as long as you do all your preparation work beforehand. This preparation work includes identifying your goals for going online, deciding what market you want to reach, deciding what products you want to sell, writing descriptions and capturing images of those products, and so on. Before you jump over to Yahoo!

Small Business or Microsoft Small Business Center and start assembling your site, be sure that you do all the groundwork that I discuss in Chapter 2, such as identifying your audience and setting up your hardware.

Getting the Most from Your Web Host

An Internet connection and a Web browser are all you need if you're primarily interested in surfing through cyberspace, consuming information, and shopping for online goodies. But when you're starting an online business, you're no longer just a consumer; you're becoming a provider of information and consumable goods. Along with a way to connect to the Internet, you need to find a hosting service that will make your online business available to your prospective customers.

A *Web hosting service* is the online world's equivalent of a landlord. Just as the owner of a building gives you office space or room for a storefront where you can hang your shingle, a hosting service provides you with space online where you can set up shop. A Web hosting service may or may not advertise itself as such. On Zazzle (www.zazzle.com), for example, you can set up a storefront for free, customize it to your liking, and take advantage of a store-builder utility. Essentially, you're setting up your own Web site with Zazzle as the host.

You can operate an online business without a Web site if you sell regularly on eBay, Zazzle, or another marketplace. On eBay, you can create an About Me page or an eBay store; eBay itself is your host in both cases. (You pay a monthly fee to eBay in order to host your store. See Chapter 13 for more information.)

A Web host provides space on special computers — *Web servers* — that are connected to the Internet all the time. Web servers are equipped with software that makes your Web pages visible to people who connect to them by using a Web browser. The process of using a Web hosting service for your online business works roughly like this:

1. **Decide where you want your site to appear on the Internet.**

   Do you want it to be part of a virtual shopping mall that includes many other businesses? Or do you want a standalone site that has its own Web address and doesn't appear to be affiliated with any other organization?

2. **Sign up with the host.**

   Sometimes you pay a fee. In some cases, no fee is required. In all cases, you're assigned space on a server. Your Web site gets an address, or *URL,* that people can enter in their browsers to view your pages.

3. **Create your Web pages.**

   Usually, you use a Web page editor to do this step, though many hosts will help you by providing you with a "store builder" or other utility.

4. **Transfer your Web page files (HTML documents, images, and so on) from your computer to the host's Web server.**

   You generally need special File Transfer Protocol (FTP) software to do the transferring. But many Web hosts can help you through the process by providing their own user-friendly software. (The most popular Web editors, such as Dreamweaver, let you do this, too.)

5. **Access your own site with your Web browser and check the contents to make sure that all the images appear correctly and that any hyper-text links you created go to the intended destinations.**

   At this point, you're open for business — visitors can view your Web pages by entering your Web address in their Web browser's Go To or Address box.

6. **Market and promote your site to attract potential clients or customers, as described in Chapter 10.**

Choose your Web host carefully, because the host affects which software you need to use to create your Web pages and get them online. The Web host also affects the way your site looks, and it may determine the complexity of your Web address. (See the "What's in a name?" sidebar, later in this chapter, for details.)

If you have a direct connection to the Internet, such as through DSL or cable, and are competent with computers (or know someone who is), you can host your own site. However, turning your own computer into a Web server is more complicated than signing up with a hosting service. (Your ISP may not allow you to set up your own server anyway; check your user agreement first.) You need to install server software and set up a domain name for your computer. You also have to purchase a static IP address for your machine. (An *IP address* is a number that identifies every computer that's connected to the Internet; it consists of four sets of numerals separated by dots, such as 206.207.99.1. A *static IP address* is one that doesn't change from session to session.) If you're just starting a simple home-based or part-time business, hosting your own Web site is probably more trouble than you care to handle, but you should be aware that it's an option. If you're interested in becoming a Webmaster, check out Speakeasy (`www.speakeasy.net`). This ISP encourages users to set up their own Web servers and even offers eight static IP addresses with a DSL line for $59.95 per month.

One of the best shortcuts to success is to find a good Web servicing host or ISP and then depend on that company's software tools and service reps when you need help building your Web site, processing forms, running scripts, and performing similar tasks.

Before you sign up with a host, check out its customer service options. Specifically, find out when the service staff is available by telephone. Also ask whether telephone support costs extra.

A Web host called pair Networks (www.pair.com) offers a pretty typical selection of hosting options and has been praised by some technical writers I know. It also provides the following kinds of e-commerce services that go above and beyond the basic hosting arrangements, which range from $5.95 to $49.95 per month: a secure server, a shopping card, credit card authorization, and a dedicated server.

Instead of getting locked into a long-term contract with a Web host, go month to month or sign a one-year contract. Even if you're initially happy with your host, you want a chance to back out if the company takes a turn for the worse or your needs change.

Domain-name registration

Some ISPs also function as domain-name registrars by enabling anyone to purchase the rights to use a domain name for one or more years. Having your own domain name lets you associate the name with your site rather than have to point the name at the server that holds your site.

By *pointing* your domain name at your server, you purchase the rights to a domain name from a registrar. You then need to associate the name with your Web site so that when people connect to your site, they won't have to enter a long URL such as username.home.earthlink.com. Instead, they'll enter www.mybusiness.com. To do this, you tell the registrar that your domain name should be assigned to the IP address of your server. Your ISP or Web host tells you the IP address to give to the registrar.

New domains have been made available that can provide you an alternative in case your ideal name on the dot-com (.com) domain is unavailable. Even if you do get a dot-com name (.com is still the most recognizable and desirable domain-name extension), you may want to buy the same name with .biz, .info, or .tv at the end so that someone else doesn't grab it.

Marketing utilities

Some people are great at promotion and marketing. Others excel at detail work. If you're not among the lucky people who can do both kinds of business tasks well, find a hosting service that helps you get noticed.

Some hosts, such as Microsoft Small Business Center (`www.microsoft.com/smallbusiness/bc/default.mspx`), give you access to a variety of marketing services if you sign with it as your host. Not all the services are free, of course.

Catalog creators

Some of the biggest Web hosts (such as Yahoo! Small Business Merchant Solutions) give you software that enables you to create an online sales catalog by using your Web browser. In other words, you don't have to purchase a Web design program, figure out how to use it, and create your pages from scratch.

On the downside, a Web-based catalog creation tool doesn't give you the ultimate control over how your pages look. You probably can't pull off fancy layout effects with tables or layers. (See Chapter 5 for more on using tables and layers to design your site's Web pages.) On the plus side, however, you can use one of these tools to get your pages online quickly all by yourself.

Database connectivity

If you plan to sell only a few items at a time, your e-commerce site can be a *static* site, which means that every time a customer makes a sale, you take the time to manually adjust inventory. A static site also requires you to update descriptions and revise shipping charges or other details by hand, one Web page at a time. In contrast, a *dynamic* e-commerce site presents catalog sales items on the fly (dynamically) by connecting to a database whenever a customer requests a Web page.

If you need to create a dynamic Web site, another factor in choosing a Web host is whether it supports the Web page and database software that you want to use. For Doug Laughter of The Silver Connection, LLC (whom I profile elsewhere in this chapter), the choice of host was essential. He wanted to develop his site himself by using technologies he was familiar with and regarded highly, such as Microsoft Active Server Pages (ASP) technology. If you use a database program, such as MySQL, you may want to sign up with a Web host that allows you to run SQL Server on one of its servers.

Finding a Web Server to Call Home

Hi! I'm your friendly World Wide Web real estate agent. Call me Virtual Larry. You say you're not sure exactly what kind of Web site is right for you, and you want to see all the options, from a tiny storefront in a strip mall to your own landscaped corporate park? Your wish is my command. Just hop into my 2010-model Internet Explorer, buckle your seat belt, and I'll show you around the many different business properties available in cyberspace.

Here's a road map of our tour:

- **Online Web-host-and-design-kit combos:** Microsoft Office Live, Google Space, Yahoo! Small Business Merchant Solutions, and Microsoft Small Business Center (formerly called bCentral), among other names.

- **Electronic merchant CD-ROMs:** ShopSite and WebSite Complete, to name two.

- **eBay:** A site that lets its users create their own About Me Web pages and their own stores.

- **Auxiliary companies:** These folks do something that doesn't seem directly related to e-commerce, but they let you build a store online, such as FedEx eCommerce Builder.

- **An online marketplace:** You can rent a space in these sites, where you can offer specialty items for sale, such as clothing, artwork, or antiques.

- **Your current Internet service provider (ISP):** Many ISPs are only too happy to host your e-commerce site — for a monthly fee in addition to your access fee.

- **Companies devoted to hosting Web sites full time:** These are businesses whose primary function is hosting e-commerce Web sites and providing their clients with associated software, such as Web page building tools, shopping carts, catalog builders, and the like.

The first four options combine Web hosting with Web page creation kits. Whether you buy these services or get to use them on the Web for free, you simply follow the manufacturer's instructions. Most of these hosting services enable you to create your Web pages by filling in forms; you never have to see a line of HTML code if you don't want to. Depending on which service you choose, you have varying degrees of control over how your site ultimately looks.

The last three options (online marketplaces, ISPs, and full-time Web hosts) tend to be do-it-yourself projects. You sign up with the host, you choose the software, and you create your own site. However, the distinction between this category and the others is blurry. As competition between Web hosts grows keener, more and more companies are providing ready-made solutions that streamline the process of Web site creation for their customers. For you, the end-user, this competition is a good thing: You have plenty of control over how your site comes into being and how it grows over time.

Web site homesteading for free

Free Web hosting is still possible for small businesses. If you're on a tight budget and looking for space on a Web server for free, turn first to your ISP, which probably gives you server space to set up a Web site. You can also check out one of a handful of sites that provide customers with hosting space for no money down and no monthly payments, either. Rather than money, you pay in terms of advertising: You may have to include some ads or other things on your site, but if you don't mind that, here are some good deals you can enjoy:

✔ **Microsoft Office Live** (officelive. microsoft.com): This service comes in three "levels" — Basics, Essentials, and Premium. Each one (including the free Basics service) includes user-friendly Web-based software for creating a Web site, e-mail, and a free domain name. You have to display the Office Live logo on your site, however. And you can access the service only with Internet Explorer. You get 500MB of free Web storage space.

✔ **Google Apps** (www.google.com/ enterprise/apps/index.html): As long as you have a domain name, you can use Google's services. These include Google's Gmail e-mail service and Google Page Creator for creating Web pages. You can access Google Apps with Internet Explorer, Firefox, and other browsers. You get 100MB of Web storage space, too.

✔ **Freeservers** (www.freeservers.com): In exchange for banner ads and pop-up ads, which you're required to display if you set up a Web site on one of its servers, this site gives you add-ons (such as guest books and hit counters) and an online Web page building tool for creating your site — not to mention 50MB of server space.

You can find more free Web hosting services on Yahoo! here:

```
dir.yahoo.com/Business_and_Economy/
        Business_to_Business/
        Communications_and_Networking/
        Internet_and_World_Wide_Web/
        Network_Service_Providers/
        Hosting/Website_Hosting/Free_
        Hosting/
```

Be sure that the site you choose lets you set up for-profit business sites for free.

If you simply need a basic Web site and don't want a lot of choices, go with one of the kits. Your site may look like everyone else's and seem a little generic, but setup is easy, and you can concentrate on marketing and running your business.

However, if you're the independent type who wants to control your site and have lots of room to grow, consider a do-it-yourself project. The sky's the limit as far as the degree of creativity you can exercise and the amount of sweat equity you can put in are concerned (as long as you don't make your site so large and complex that shoppers have a hard time finding anything, of course).

Using software to build your Web site

Virtually all the free Web hosting services mentioned in the "Web site home-steading for free" sidebar have caught on to the concept of making things easy and affordable for would-be *ontrepreneurs* (online entrepreneurs). These sites act as both a Web host and a Web page creation tool. You connect to the site, sign up for service, and fill out a series of forms. Submitting the completed forms activates a script on the host site that automatically generates your Web pages based on the data you entered.

Some Web site creation packages are available at the following sites:

- **CafePress** (www.cafepress.com): CafePress (www.cafepress.com) allows you to easily create and sell music CDs, photos, or artwork online for free. The hard part is deciding what you want to sell, how best to describe your sales items, and how to promote your site.

- **Freeservers** (www.freeservers.com): Freeservers, the free hosting site mentioned in the preceding section, makes a user-friendly Web site building tool available to all its customers, even those who use its free package.

- **Babylon Mall** (www.babylonmall.com): This site, which caters to vintage clothing sellers, charges $15 per month and gives members software that helps them design their storefronts.

Investigating electronic storefront software

All the options that this chapter provides for publishing your business site are ones that you access and use online. Yet another option for creating a business site and publishing it online is to purchase an application that carries you through the entire process of creating an electronic storefront. The advantage is control: You own and operate the software and are in charge of the entire process (at least until the files get to the remote Web servers). The speed with which you develop a site depends on how quickly you master the process, not on the speed of your Internet connection.

Similarly to hosting services such as Yahoo! Store and Tripod, electronic storefront software is designed to facilitate the process of creating Web pages and to shield you from having to master HTML. Most storefront software provides you with predesigned Web pages, called *templates,* which you customize for your particular business. Some types of storefront options provide you with shopping cart systems that enable customers to select items and tally the cost at checkout. They may also provide for some sort of electronic payment option, such as credit card purchases. Usually, you purchase the software and either download it online or obtain a CD, install the package as you do any other application, and follow a series of steps that mirror the primary aspects of an offline business:

✔ **The storefront:** The Web pages that you create. Some packages, such as WebSite Complete, include predesigned Web pages that you can copy and customize with your own content.

✔ **The inventory:** You can stock your virtual storefront shelves by presenting your wares in the form of an online catalog or product list.

✔ **The delivery truck:** Some storefront packages streamline the process of transferring your files from your computer to the server. Rather than use FTP software, you publish information simply by clicking a button in your Web editor or Web browser.

✔ **The checkout counter:** Most electronic storefront packages give you the option to accept orders by phone, fax, or online with a credit card.

Besides providing you with all the software that you need to create Web pages and get them online, electronic storefronts instruct you on how to market your site and present your goods and services in a positive way. In addition, some programs provide you with a backroom for your business, where you can record customer information, orders, and fulfillment.

The problem with many electronic storefront packages is that they're more expensive than the average software program — some cost $489 to $699 or more. They're not intended for individuals starting their own small businesses, but rather are for large corporations that want to branch out to the Web. However, a few packages (two of which I describe in the following sections) provide a Ford-type alternative to the Rolls-Royce storefronts.

CASE STUDY

Finding a host that makes your business dynamic

Whether you choose America Online or another ISP, which Web host you choose can have a big impact on how easy it is to get online and run your business successfully. Just ask Doug Laughter. He and his wife Kristy own The Silver Connection, LLC, which sells sterling silver jewelry imported from around the world. They began their endeavor when Kristy brought back some silver jewelry from Mexico. The Silver Connection went online in April 1998 at www. silverconnection.com and is hosted by CrystalTech Web Hosting, Inc. (www.crystaltech.com). As of 2010, CrystalTech was still their host: "[It is] a sound business that keeps getting better," says Doug.

Q. Why did you choose CrystalTech as your Web host?

A. Although many reliable companies today offer complete Web site hosting solutions, I settled on CrystalTech for a few reasons. It has a Windows-based environment that supports virtually every technology needed for your Web site development and needs. CrystalTech also offers a wide variety of hosting plans that are suitable for small personal Web sites and large business commercial sites at reasonable prices with options of shared hosting, dedicated hosting, and SharePoint hosting.

(continued)

(continued)

Q. What makes CrystalTech such a good Web host?

A. CrystalTech offers a robust Control Center that allows complete administrative control for the Web site and business. Clients are able to manage every aspect of their sites, which includes administrative tools, such as automatic database connections, complete customer information overview, custom site and file permissions, domain setting, mail, and much more. Some very nice resources also offer merchant applications and helpful information with legal forms to assist the client with Web site legalities.

Q. What kinds of customer service features do you use that other business owners should look for?

A. One feature that CrystalTech is very good with is keeping clients informed with informational items that include monthly newsletters and timely notifications of maintenance or system enhancement issues. CrystalTech also has a very knowledgeable and helpful technical support department, an in-depth knowledge base, and various community forums to interact with other clients.

Q. What kinds of questions should small business owners and managers ask when they're shopping for a hosting service? What kinds of features should they be looking for initially?

A. I would first suggest considering how you want to develop your Web site. Today's business site needs to be dynamic in nature, so the business needs to research and determine what Web server application it will use. A Web server application consists of the following:

- ✔ **Server-side technology:** Active Server Pages (ASP, ASP.NET), ColdFusion, Java Server Pages, PHP, XML

- ✔ **Database solution:** Microsoft SQL Server, MS Access, MySQL, Oracle

- ✔ **Server application:** IIS, Apache, iPlanet, Sun Java System Web Server

- ✔ **Operating Platform:** Windows, UNIX

So the decision about how the e-commerce Web site will be developed and in what technology is a very key decision to make from the onset. After this is decided, choose a Web host that supports your environment of choice.

Q. After the development platform is determined, what features should you look for?

A. Look for essentials that are wholesale elements to develop, maintain, and enhance the Web presence. These items are common with most hosting plans but always need attention paid to them. This cursory list includes Web disk space, bandwidth limitations, FTP and mail accounts, site statistics, backup plans, merchant applications with payment gateways, and other customary plan offers. Finally, make sure there's an application that can analyze traffic, such as WebTrends.

Take time to shop around and compare. Select a Web hostingcompany that you're comfortable with to avoid having to move shop too soon if something doesn't work out. After you select a hosting company, get down to the business of developing your presence on the Web and not having to spend time wondering about moving your Web site identity.

Laughter says that sales "did slide" in 2009 due to the economic slowdown. But he urges small business owners "not to give up too soon or too easily." Even though silver prices are on the rise, he plans to maintain fair prices for his silver and wait for business to come back.

"There are a lot of plateaus and times when the business flattens, but if you are able to keep your business online for a long time, it will pay off in the long run," he adds. "Also, be in contact with your local chamber [of commerce] and other local businesses. Have a good Web presence and have easy access to customers. Try not to extend your assets too far or too soon, and enjoy having your own business that you can slowly build."

ShopSite

ShopSite, by ShopSite, Inc., isn't software that you purchase and install on your computer. Rather, you find a Web hosting service, such as Verio (www.verio.com), that runs ShopSite on its servers. You then set up an account with the host and use the ShopSite software over the Internet, using your Web browser. With this kind of setup, which is a *hosted application,* you don't have to worry about having enough memory or hard drive space to run the program yourself. You also don't have to bother with updating or trouble-shooting the software; that, too, is the hosting service's responsibility.

To find a hosting service that runs ShopSite, go to the ShopSite Web site (www.shopsite.com) and scan a list of hosts. You pick a company and arrange for an account. Pricing varies, depending on the host and the version of the service that you want. ShopSite comes in three varieties:

- ✔ **Starter:** Lets you create a catalog of only 15 items for sale and five Web pages.
- ✔ **Manager:** Gives you an unlimited number of pages, plus templates, themes, a shopping cart, and real-time credit card processing.
- ✔ **Pro:** Adds the ability to track inventory as products are purchased.

I have seen ShopSite Lite advertised for free with some hosting packages, Manager for $29.95 per month, and Pro for $74.95 per month.

Miva Merchant

Miva Merchant, a competitor to ShopSite, handles all the basics required for an e-commerce storefront, including Web site templates, a product cata-log, electronic payments, inventory tracking, and shipping. It's available on Web hosts such as Hostasaurus.com. The package lets you go beyond the basics and set up an affiliate program or a mailing list. Find out more at mivacentral.com.

ecBuilder Pro

ecBuilder Pro, by Maximizer Software, Inc. (www.maximizer.com/webstore/?panel=3#crm-purchase), is software that you purchase and install on your computer. You either download the program from its own Web site for $379 or purchase it on a CD-ROM for $399. (That's for the most basic version; other versions are more expensive.) The software makes it easy for you not only to create basic Web pages but also to make a site searchable by keyword, set up password-protected pages, and set up a shop-ping cart.

ecBuilder Pro comes with 40 templates and interactive wizards for creating Web sites and works with Windows.

Easyhosting

If ecBuilder Pro seems expensive, you can sign up with a host that includes similar software among the services it gives you for a monthly fee. Easyhosting (`www.easyhosting.com`) includes Easy StoreMaker shopping cart/catalog builder software with its Intermediate and Advanced hosting packages, which range from $50.99 to $80.99 per month.

Moving into an online mall

In addition to Web site kits, ISPs, and businesses that specialize in Web hosting, online shopping malls provide another form of Web hosting. You set up your site, either on your own or by using special Web page authoring utilities that some malls provide. You pay a monthly fee, transfer your files to the mall's Web site, and your store appears online. The basic steps are the same with an online mall as with any of the other hosting businesses that I mention in this chapter.

What's the difference, then, between a shopping mall that does Web hosting, an ISP that does hosting, and a Web hosting service? Their names and the features they offer differ slightly, but the important thing to remember is that they all do essentially the same thing. After you open your virtual business on the Web (and as long as you get a custom URL that takes the form `www.mybusiness.com`), your customers can't always tell whether you're part of America Online, a mall, or a Web host such as EarthLink.

What *is* an online shopping mall, anyway? It's a collection of online businesses that are listed in a directory or index provided by a single organization. The directory may be a simple list of stores on a single Web page. For larger malls with a thousand stores or more, the online businesses are arranged by category and can be found in a searchable index.

In theory, an online shopping mall helps small businesses by giving them additional exposure. A customer who shops at one of the mall's stores might notice other businesses on the same site and visit it, too. Some malls function as Web hosts that enable their customers to transfer Web page files and present their stores online, using one of the mall's Web servers. Other malls let people list their business in the mall with a hyperlink, even if the store is actually hosted by another company.

Perhaps the only thing that really distinguishes online malls from other hosting services is presentation:

✔ Some malls, such as Access Market Square (`amsquare.com`), use the metaphor of a town's market square to organize their businesses. Stores are presented as being on particular parts of the square, but the metaphor is just that; other than the fact that many different owners operate the storefronts, the site is no different than a big marketplace such as Amazon.com.

✔ Another online mall to look into is AOL Shopping (`shopping.aol.com`), which gathers in one location a number of businesses both small and large. You add your products to the shopping area by sending a "feed." A feed is a version of your product catalog that has been converted to the programming language XML (eXtensible Markup Language). Most hosts provide utilities that convert your catalog to a feed so that you can list your products in such areas; make sure that your host does this, too. To find out how to add your products to AOL's shopping area, send an e-mail to `AddYourProducts@aol.com`.

Consider joining an online mall if you find one that offers an attractive hosting package, particularly if it has Web page forms that help you set up your site or create an online catalog quickly. But remember that to Web shoppers, it doesn't matter who your host is; what's more important is that you develop compelling content for your site to attract customers and encourage sales.

Amazon.com doesn't look like an online mall, but it has instituted some opportunities for entrepreneurs to sell items on its site. If you don't want to create an entire storefront, you also have the option of selling items individually on the Amazon.com site. You pay fees to list items for sale and for completed sales as well. Find out more by clicking the Selling on Amazon link at the left side of the Amazon.com home page (`www.amazon.com`).

Turning to your ISP for Web hosting

People sometimes talk about Internet service providers (ISPs) and Web hosts as two separate types of Internet businesses, but that's not necessarily the case. Providing users with access to the Internet and hosting Web sites are two different functions, to be sure, but the same organization may well perform them.

In fact, it's only natural to turn to your own ISP first to ask about its Web hosting policies for its customers. If you already go online with Comcast, trying out its Web hosting facilities makes sense. If you have an Internet access account with the popular ISP EarthLink (`www.earthlink.net`), by all means consider EarthLink as a Web host for your business site.

EarthLink has different Web hosting options depending on the kind of account you have. Like most ISPs, however, EarthLink provides Web space to its customers so that they can publish Web pages that are primarily personal in nature. Yes, you *can* publish a business Web site, and EarthLink won't complain or cancel your account. But EarthLink really prefers that business users spring for special business services that include oodles of Web space, support for forms and CGI scripts, and a "vanity" URL of the `www.company.com` variety.

EarthLink offers two separate types of Web hosting options. Its StarterSite packages range from $9.98 to $12.48 per month with no setup fee. Its EarthLink Store packages range from $14.98 to $49.98 per month with no setup fee, which provides individual users with the following Web hosting options:

- ✔ 5GB to 50GB of storage space

- ✔ 100 to 500 separate e-mail accounts for personal or family members' use

- ✔ Free CGI scripts that you can run to capture information submitted in a Web page form to either an e-mail message or a file that you can read

- ✔ Miva Merchant, the EarthLink Web page editing tool

- ✔ The ability to put 50 items for sale in a catalog (for the $14.98 per month option) to an unlimited number with the $49.98 option

What should you look for in an ISP Web hosting account, and what constitutes a good deal? For one thing, price: A rate of $14.98 per month for 5GB of Web site space is a pretty good deal. Look for a host that doesn't limit the number of Web pages that you can create. Also, find one that gives you at least one e-mail address with your account and that lets you add extra addresses for a nominal fee. Finally, look for a host that gives you the ability to include Web page forms on your site so that visitors can send you feedback.

What to expect from an ISP Web hosting service

The process of setting up a Web site varies from ISP to ISP. Here are some general features that you should look for, based on my experience with my own ISP:

- ✔ **Web page editor:** You don't necessarily need to choose a provider that gives you a free Web page editor. You can easily download and install the editor of your choice. I tend to use one of three programs, Netscape Composer, Expression Web Designer, or Dreamweaver, to create Web pages. (I describe these programs later in this chapter.)

- ✔ **Password and username:** When my Web pages are ready to go online, I get to use the same username and password to access my Web site space that I use when I connect to the Internet. Although you don't need to enter a password to view a Web site through a browser (well, at least at most sites), you do need a password to protect your site from being accessed through an FTP program. Otherwise, anyone can enter your Web space and tamper with your files.

✔ **FTP software:** When I signed up for a hosting account, I received a CD-ROM containing a basic set of software programs, including a Web browser and an FTP program. FTP is the simplest and easiest-to-use software to transfer files from one location to another on the Internet. When I access my Web site space from my Macintosh, I use an FTP program — Fetch. From my PC, I have used a program called WS-FTP. Cute FTP (www.cuteftp.com) is another program that many Web site owners use, which costs $39.99. (I like the free FileZilla even better, however; find it at www.filezilla.com). Most FTP programs are available for free on the Internet or can be purchased for a nominal fee.

✔ **URL:** When you set up a Web site by using your ISP, you're assigned a directory on a Web server. The convention for naming this directory is ~*username*. The ~*username* designation goes at the end of your URL for your Web site's home page. However, you can (and should) register a shorter URL with a domain-name registrar, such as Network Solutions. You can then "point" the domain name to your ISP's server so that it can serve as an "alias" URL for your site.

After you have your software tools together and have a user directory on your ISP's Web server, it's time to put your Web site together. Basically, when I want to create or revise content for my Web site, I open the page in my Web page editor, make the changes, save the changes, and then transfer the files to my ISP's directory with my FTP program. Finally, I review the changes in my browser.

What's the ISP difference?

What's the big difference between using a kit, such as Microsoft Office Live or Yahoo! Small Business, to create your site and using your own inexpensive or free software to create a site from scratch and post it on your ISP's server? It's the difference between putting together a model airplane from a kit and designing the airplane yourself. If you use a kit, you save time and trouble; your plane ends up looking pretty much like everyone else's, but you get the job done faster. If you design it yourself, you have absolute control. Your plane can look just the way you want. It takes longer to get to the end product, but you can be sure that you get what you want.

On the other hand, three differences lie between an ISP-hosted site and a site that resides with a company that does *only* Web hosting rather than provides Internet dialup access and other services:

✔ A business that does only Web hosting charges you for hosting services, whereas your ISP may not.

✔ A Web hosting service lets you have your own domain name (www.company.com) whereas an ISP or a service, such as Microsoft Office Live, may not. (Some ISPs require that you upgrade to a business hosting account in order to obtain the vanity address. See the "What's in a name?" sidebar for more about how Web hosting services offer an advantage in the domain-name game.)

✔ A Web hosting service often provides lots of frills, such as super-fast connections, one-button file transfers with your Web browser, and tons of site statistics, as well as automatic backups of your Web page files.

To find out more about using a real, full-time Web hosting service, see the section, "Going for the works with a Web hosting service," later in this chapter.

Where to find an ISP

What if you don't already have an Internet service provider, or you're not happy with the one you have? On today's Internet, you can't swing a mouse without hitting an ISP. How do you find the one that's right for you? In general, you want to look for the provider that offers you the least expensive service with the fastest connection and the best options available for your Web site.

Bigger doesn't necessarily mean cheaper or better; many regional or local ISPs provide good service at rates that are comparable to the giants such as Verio or EarthLink. When you're shopping around for an ISP, be sure to ask the following types of questions:

✔ What types of connections do you offer?

✔ How many dialup numbers do you have?

✔ What is your access range? (Do you provide only local coverage, or regional or international coverage as well?)

✔ What type of tech support do you offer? Do you accept phone calls or e-mail inquiries around the clock or only during certain hours? Are real human beings always available on call or are clients sent to a phone message system?

Some Web sites are well known for listing ISPs by state or by the services they offer. Here are a few starting points in your search for the ideal ISP:

✔ **The List:** This site lists about 8,000 ISPs. You can search the list by area code or by country code, or you can focus on the United States or Canada.

```
thelist.internet.com
```

✔ **Yahoo's List of Internet Access Providers:** This is a good source for directories of national and international ISPs.

```
dir.yahoo.com/Business_and_Economy/Business_to_
        Business/Communications_and_Networking/
        Internet_and_World_Wide_Web/Network_Service_
        Providers/Internet_Service_Providers__ISPs_/
```

What's in a name?

Most hosts assign you a URL that leads to your directory (or folder) on the Web server. For example, the typical personal account with an ISP includes space on a Web server where you can store your Web pages, and the address looks like this:

`http://homepage.speakeasy.net/~gholden`

This is a common form of URL that many Web hosts use. It means that my Web pages reside in a directory called ~gholden on a computer named `homepage`. The computer, in turn, resides in my provider's domain on the Internet: `speakeasy.net`.

However, for an extra fee, some Web hosts allow you to choose a shorter domain name, provided that the one you want to use isn't already taken by another site. For example, if I paid extra for a full-fledged business site, my provider would have let me have a catchier, more memorable address, like this:

`www.gregholden.com`

Going for the works with a Web hosting service

After you've had your site online for a while with a free Web host, such as Freeservers.com, you may well decide that you need more room, more services (such as inventory tracking or electronic payments), and a faster connection that can handle many visitors at one time. In that case, you want to locate your online business with a full-time Web hosting service.

As the preceding sections attest, many kinds of businesses now host Web sites. But in this case, I'm defining *Web hosting service* as a company whose primary mission is to provide space on Web servers for individual, nonprofit, and commercial Web sites.

What to look for in a Web host

Along with providing lots of space for your HTML, image, and other files (typically, you get anywhere from 1GB to 50GB of space), Web hosting services offer a variety of related services, including some or all of the following:

- **E-mail addresses:** You can likely get several e-mail addresses for your own or your family members' personal use. Besides that, many Web hosts give you special e-mail addresses called *auto-responders.* These are e-mail addresses, such as `info@yourcompany.com`, that you can set up to automatically return a text message or a file to anyone looking for information.

- **Domain names:** Virtually all the hosting options that I mention in this chapter give customers the option of obtaining a short domain name, such as `www.mycompany.com`. But some Web hosts simplify the process by providing domain-name registration in their flat monthly rates.

- ✔ **Web page software:** Some hosting services include Web page authoring/editing software, such as Adobe Dreamweaver. Some Web hosting services even offer Web page forms that you can fill out online in order to create your own online shopping catalog. All you have to provide is a scanned image of the item you want to sell, along with a price and a description. You submit the information to the Web host, which then adds the item to an online catalog that's part of your site.

- ✔ **Multimedia/CGI scripts:** One big thing that sets Web hosting services apart from other hosts is the ability to serve complex and memory-intensive content, such as RealAudio sound files or RealVideo video clips. They also let you process Web page forms that you include on your site by executing computer programs called *CGI scripts.* These programs receive the data that someone sends you (such as a customer service request or an order form) and present the data in readable form, such as a text file, e-mail message, or an entry in a database. See Chapter 6 for more about how to set up and use forms and other interactive Web site features.

- ✔ **Shopping cart software:** If part of your reason for going online is to sell specific items, look for a Web host that can streamline the process for you. Most organizations provide you with Web page forms that you can fill out to create sale items and offer them in an online shopping cart, for example.

- ✔ **Automatic data backups:** Some hosting services automatically back up your Web site data to protect you against data loss — an especially useful feature because disaster recovery is important. The automatic nature of the backups frees you from the worry and trouble of doing it manually.

- ✔ **Site statistics:** Virtually all Web hosting services also provide you with site statistics that give you an idea (perhaps not a precisely accurate count, but a good estimate) of how many visitors you have received. Even better is access to software reports that analyze and graphically report where your visitors are from, how they found you, which pages on your site are the most frequently viewed, and so on.

- ✔ **Shopping and electronic commerce features:** If you plan to give your customers the ability to order and purchase your goods or services online by using their credit cards, be sure to look for a Web host that provides you with secure commerce options. A *secure server* is a computer that can encrypt sensitive data (such as credit card numbers) that the customer sends to your site. For a more detailed discussion of secure electronic commerce, see Chapter 6.

Having so many hosting options available is the proverbial blessing and curse. It's good that you have so many possibilities and that the competition is so fierce because that can keep prices down. On the other hand, deciding which host is best for you can be difficult. In addition to asking about the preceding list of features, To help narrow the field, here are a few more questions to ask prospective Web hosts about their services:

✔ **Do you limit file transfers?** Many services charge a monthly rate for a specific amount of electronic data that is transferred to and from your site. Each time a visitor views a page, that user is actually downloading a few kilobytes of data in order to view it. If your Web pages contain, say, 1MB of text and images and you get 1,000 visitors per month, your site accounts for 1GB of data transfer per month. If your host allocates you less than 1GB per month, it will probably charge you extra for the amount you go over the limit.

✔ **What kind of connection do you have?** Your site's Web page content appears more quickly in Web browser windows if your server has a super-fast T1 or T3 connection. Ask your ISP what kind of connection *it* has to the Internet. If you have a DSL line, speeds differ depending on the ISP: You might get a fast connection (1.5Mbps) or a more common, slower one (684Kbps). Make sure that you're getting the fastest connection you can afford.

✔ **Will you promote my site?** Some hosting services (particularly online shopping malls) help publicize your site by listing you with Internet search indexes and search services so that visitors are more likely to find you.

Besides these, the other obvious questions that you would ask of any contractor apply to Web hosting services as well. These include questions such as "How long have you been in business?" and "Can you suggest customers who will give me a reference?"

The fact that I include a screen shot of a particular Web hosting service's site in this book doesn't mean that I'm endorsing or recommending that particular organization. Shop around carefully and find the one that's best for you. Check out the hosts with the best rates and most reliable service. Visit some other sites that they host, and e-mail the owners of those sites for their opinion of their hosting service.

Competition is tough among hosting services, which means that prices are going down. But it also means that hosting services may seem to promise the moon in order to get your business. Be sure to read the fine print and talk to the host before you sign a contract, and always get statements about technical support and backups in writing.

What's it gonna cost?

Because of the ongoing competition in the industry, prices for Web hosting services vary widely. If you look in the classified sections in the back of magazines that cover the Web or the whole Internet, you'll see ads for hosting services costing from $9.95 to $24.95 per month. Chances are, these prices are for a basic level of service: Web space, e-mail addresses, domain name, and software. This may be all you need.

The second level of service provides CGI script processing, the ability to serve audio and video files on your site, regular backups, and extensive site statistics, as well as consultants who can help you design and configure your site. This more sophisticated range of features typically runs from $20 per month up to $75 or more per month. At Verio, for instance, you can conduct secure electronic commerce on your site as part of hosting packages that begin at $28.95 per month.

Fun with Tools: Choosing a Web Page Editor

A woodworker has his or her favorite hammer and saw. A cook has an array of utensils and pots and pans. Likewise, a Web site creator has software programs that facilitate the presentation of words, colors, images, and multimedia in Web browsers.

A little HTML is a good thing — but just a little. Knowing HTML comes in handy when you need to add elements that Web page editors don't handle. Some programs, for example, don't provide you with easy buttons or menu options for adding `<meta>` tags, which enable you to add keywords or descriptions to a site so that search engines can find them and describe your site correctly.

If you really want to get into HTML or to find out more about creating Web pages, read *HTML, XHTML & CSS For Dummies*, 6th Edition, by Ed Tittel and Jeff Noble, or *Creating Web Pages For Dummies*, 9th Edition, by Bud Smith (both by Wiley).

It pays to spend time choosing a Web page editor that has the right qualities. What qualities should you look for in a Web page tool and how do you know which tool is right for you? To help narrow the field, I've divided this class of software into different levels of sophistication. Pick the type of program that best fits your technical skill.

For the novice: Use your existing programs

A growing number of word processing, graphics, and business programs are adding HTML to their list of capabilities. You may already have one of these programs at your disposal. By using a program with which you're already comfortable, you can avoid having to install a Web page editor.

Here are some programs that enable you to generate one type of content and then give you the option of outputting that content in HTML, which means that your words or figures can appear on a Web page:

✔ **Microsoft Word:** The most recent versions of the venerable word processing standby work pretty much seamlessly with Web page content. Although most professional Web designers would say it generates messy code, it does get the job done for beginners. You can open Web pages from within Word and save Word files in Web page format.

✔ **Adobe PageMaker/Quark Xpress:** The most recent versions of these two popular page layout programs let you save the contents of a document as HTML. Only the words and images are transferred to the Web, however; any special typefaces become generic Web standard headings.

✔ **Microsoft Office 2010:** Word, Excel, and PowerPoint all give users the option of exporting content to Web pages.

✔ **WordPerfect and Presentations:** These two component programs within Corel's suite of tools let you save files as an HTML page or a PDF file that you can present on the Web. If you chose to present one slide per Web page, the program adds clickable arrows to each slide in your presentation so that viewers can skip from one slide to another.

Although these solutions are convenient, they probably won't completely eliminate the need to use a Web page editor. Odds are, you'll still need to make corrections and do special formatting after you convert your text to HTML.

For intermediate needs: User-friendly Web editors

If you're an experienced Web surfer and eager to try a simple Web editor, make it a program that lets you focus on your site's HTML and textual content, provides you with plenty of functionality, and is still easy to use. Here are some user-friendly programs that are inexpensive (or, better yet, free) but allow you to create a functional Web site.

The following programs don't include some of the bells and whistles you need to create complex, interactive forms, format a page by using frames, or access a database of information from one of your Web pages. These goodies are served up by Web page editors that have a higher level of functionality, which I describe in the upcoming section for advanced commerce sites.

BBEdit

If you work on a Macintosh and you're primarily concerned with textual content, BBEdit is one of the best choices you can make for a Web page tool. It lives up to its motto: "It doesn't suck." BBEdit is tailored to use the Mac's highly visual interface, and version 9.2 runs on the Mac OS 10.4 or later. You can use Macintosh drag and drop to add an image file to a Web page in progress by dragging the image's icon into the main BBEdit window, for example. Find out more about BBEdit at the Bare Bones Software, Inc. Web site (www.barebones.com/products/bbedit/index.html).

Editors that'll flip your whizzy-wig

Web browsers are multilingual; they understand exotic-sounding languages, such as FTP, HTTP, and GIF, among others. But English is one language browsers don't speak. Browsers don't understand instructions, such as "Put that image there" or "Make that text italic." HyperText Markup Language, or HTML, is a translator, if you will, between human languages and Web languages.

If the thought of HTML strikes fear into your heart, relax. Thanks to modern Web page creation tools, you don't have to master HTML in order to create Web pages. Although knowing a little HTML does come in handy at times, you can depend on these special user-friendly tools to do almost all your English-to-HTML translations for you.

The secret of these Web page creation tools is their WYSIWYG (pronounced whizzy-wig) display. WYSIWYG stands for "What You See Is What You Get." A WYSIWYG editor lets you see on-screen how your page will look when it's on the Web, rather than force you to type (or even see) HTML commands like this:

```
<H1> This is a Level 1
    Heading </H1>
<IMG SRC = "lucy.gif"> <BR>
<P>This is an image of
    Lucy.</P>
```

A WYSIWYG editor, such as CoffeeCup HTML Editor for Windows (www.coffeecup.com), shows you how the page appears even as you assemble it. Besides that, it lets you format text and add images by means of familiar software shortcuts such as menus and buttons.

Other good choices of Web editors for the Macintosh are Taco HTML Edit by Taco Software (www.tacosw.com) or PageSpinner by Optima System (www.optima-system.com).

Macromedia HomeSite

HomeSite was an affordable tool for Web site designers who feel at ease working with HTML code. However, HomeSite is no longer being released or supported by its owner, Adobe Systems. If you can find a copy, though, try it. HomeSite also provides you with step-by-step utilities — *wizards* — to quickly create pages, tables, frames, and JavaScript elements.

CoffeeCup HTML Editor

CoffeeCup HTML Editor, by CoffeeCup Software (www.coffeecup.com), is a popular Windows Web site editor that contains a lot of features for a small price ($49). You can begin typing and formatting text by using the CoffeeCup HTML Editor menu options. You can add an image by clicking the Insert Image toolbar button, or use the Forms toolbar to create the text boxes and radio buttons that make up an interactive Web page form. You can even add JavaScript effects and choose from a selection of clip art images that come with the software.

CoffeeCup HTML Editor doesn't let you explore database connectivity, add Web components, or other bonuses that come with a program like Dreamweaver. But it does have everything you need to create a basic Web page.

Nvu

When I read reviews of Web page software, I don't often see Nvu included in the list. But to me, it's an ideal program for an entrepreneur on a budget. Why? Let me spell it out for you: F-R-E-E.

Nvu is the successor to Mozilla Composer, a Web page editing and authoring tool that came with the full version of the Mozilla browser suite. Although Mozilla is no longer supporting Composer, you can download Nvu for free at http://net2.com/nvu/. The software was developed by using Composer's original source code. With Nvu, you can create sophisticated layout elements, such as tables (which I discuss further in Chapter 5), with an easy-to-use graphical interface. After you edit a page, you can preview it in Firefox with the click of a button. In my opinion, it's worth going through a few extra steps to try this program.

For advanced commerce sites: Programs that do it all

If you plan to do a great deal of business online or even to add the title of Web designer to your list of talents (as some of the entrepreneurs profiled in this book have done), it makes sense to spend some money upfront and use a Web page tool that can do everything you want — today and for years to come.

The advanced programs that I describe here go beyond the simple designation of Web page editors. They not only let you edit Web pages but also help you add interactivity to your site, link dynamically updated databases to your site, and keep track of how your site is organized and updated. Some programs can even transfer your Web documents to your Web host with a single menu option. This way, you get to concentrate on the fun part of running an online business — meeting people, taking orders, processing payments, and the like.

Dreamweaver

What's that you say? You can never hear enough bells and whistles? The cutting edge is where you love to walk? Then Dreamweaver, a Web authoring tool by Adobe (www.adobe.com), is for you. Dreamweaver is a feature-rich, professional piece of software.

Dreamweaver's strengths aren't so much in the basic features, such as making selected text bold, italic, or a different size; rather, Dreamweaver excels in producing Dynamic HTML (which makes Web pages more interactive through scripts) and HTML style sheets. Dreamweaver has ample FTP (File Transfer Protocol) settings, and it gives you the option of seeing the HTML codes you're working with in one window and the formatting of your Web page in a second, WYSIWYG window. The latest version is a complex and powerful piece of software. A recent version of Dreamweaver MX is shown in Figure 4-1.

Dreamweaver lets you create Active Server pages and connect to the ColdFusion database, and it contains lots of templates and wizards. Dreamweaver is available for both Windows and Macintosh computers; find out more at the Adobe Web site (www.adobe.com/products/dreamweaver/).

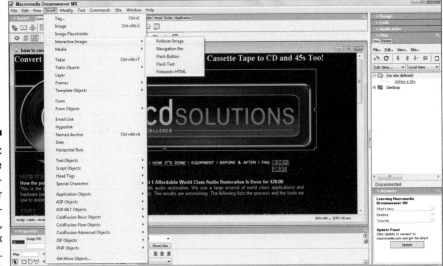

Figure 4-1:
Adobe
Dream-
weaver
is a full-
featured,
complex
program.

Microsoft Expression Web

Expression Web is a user-friendly yet powerful editor that has strong support for Cascading Style Sheets (CSS), a technology that allows you to format multiple Web pages consistently by using standard commands that all Web browsers can interpret. The program also lets you develop Web sites with ASP.NET and XML markup. Expression Web includes Dynamic Web Templates — sets of Web pages that have master areas that appear on each Web page. If you make a change to the master area, the change is carried out through the whole site. Find out more at www.microsoft.com/expression/products/Web_Overview.aspx. A related program from Microsoft, Silverlight, works in tandem with Expression Web and lets you create sites by using Extensible Application Markup Language (XAML); find it at www.silverlight.net/.

Check out *Silverlight 4 For Dummies*, by Mahesh Krishnan and Philip Beadle (Wiley), to find out all about Silverlight.

Part II
Establishing and Organizing Your Online Business

The 5th Wave   By Rich Tennant

"The top line represents our revenue, the middle line is our inventory, and the bottom line shows the rate of my hair loss over the same period."

In this part . . .

Just as business owners in the real world have to rent or buy a facility and fix it up to conduct their businesses, so, too, do you have to develop an online storefront to conduct your online business. In this part, I explain how to put a virtual roof over your store and light a cyberfire to welcome your customers. In other words, this part focuses on the nuts and bolts of your Web site itself. You'll be happy to discover that getting a Web storefront online is easier than ever, thanks to some new and inexpensive services designed especially for novices.

The World Wide Web is the most exciting and popular place to open an online store. Merely creating a set of Web pages isn't enough to succeed online, though. Your site needs to be compelling — even irresistible. You also need to streamline purchases and payments.

This part shows you how to organize your site and fill it with useful content that attracts customers in the first place and encourages them to stay and browse. I also show you how to get your pages up and running quickly, to equip your site (and yourself) to handle many different kinds of electronic purchases, and to provide a high level of customer service. Finally, you explore new sourcing options around the world.

Chapter 5

Organizing Your Business Presence and Attracting Customers

*I*n the previous edition of this book, the title of this chapter began with "Organizing Your Business Site . . ." This time around, I changed the word "site" to "presence." It's a subtle but significant difference. A Web site is still a "home base" for an online business. But even more important is a business *presence*. A presence can include a blog, ads on Craigslist, or storefronts on a variety of marketplaces. Wherever you do business, the same basic principles work on the Web just as well as they do in the brick-and-mortar world: Attracting customers is important, but real success comes from establishing relationships with customers who come to trust you and rely on you for providing excellent products and services.

Achieving these goals on the Web requires some special strategies, however. First and foremost, you want to be found. Update your content frequently, and market yourself by using multiple points of entry. That way, you'll reach Web surfers who are increasingly mobile and increasingly accustomed to sophisticated content.

This chapter examines some of the best ways for standing out from the crowd and attracting customers even as cyberspace becomes increasingly crowded and competitive. The chapter title might make it sound as though organizing a site and making it attractive are two mutually exclusive activities, but they go together: Creating an organized Web site and a supplementary presence is sure to attract not only first-time but return customers. In this chapter, you explore ways to achieve these goals, including making your site easy to navigate; creating compelling content; optimizing your images so that they appear quickly; and building interactivity into your site so that customers want to return to you on a regular basis.

Feng Shui Your Web Site

Feng Shui is the art of arranging objects in an environment to achieve (among other things), success in your career, wealth, and happiness. If that's true, try practicing some Feng Shui with your online business environment — that is, your Web site.

Although you may be tempted to jump right into the creation of a cool Web site, take a moment to plan. Whether you're setting off on a road trip across the nation or building a new addition for your house, you'll progress more smoothly by drawing a map of where you want to go. Dig down into your miscellaneous drawer until you find pencil and paper and then make a list of the elements you want to have on your site.

Look over the items on your list and break them into two or three main categories. These main categories will branch off your _home page,_ which functions as the grand entrance for your online business site. You can then draw a map of your site that assumes the shape of a triangle, as shown in Figure 5-1.

Figure 5-1:
A home page is the point from which your site branches into more specific levels of information.

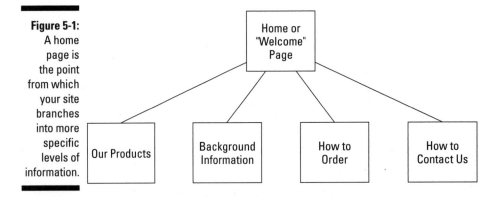

Note: The page heading "Background Information" is a placeholder for detailed information about some aspect of your online business. For my brother's audio restoration business, I suggested that he include a page of technical information listing the equipment he uses and describing the steps he takes to process audio. You can write about your experience with what you buy and sell. You can also include your love for your products, or anything else that personalizes your site and builds trust.

The preceding example results in a very simple Web site — but there's nothing wrong with starting out simple. When my brother was creating his first Web site, just getting started was intimidating, and this simple model worked well for him. Many other businesses start with a three-layered organization for their Web sites. This arrangement divides the site into two sections: one about the company and one about the products or services for sale (see Figure 5-2).

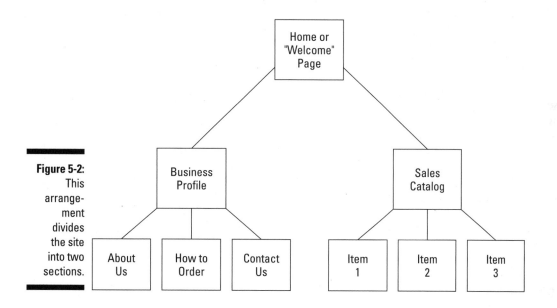

Figure 5-2: This arrangement divides the site into two sections.

Think of your home page as the lobby of a museum, where you get the help of the friendly person at the information desk, who hands you a list of the special exhibits you can visit that day and shows you a map so that you can begin to figure out how you're going to get from here to there. Remember to include the following items on your home page:

- ✔ The name of the store or business.

- ✔ Your logo, if you have one.

- ✔ Links to the main areas of your site or, if your site isn't overly extensive, to every page.

- ✔ Contact information, such as your e-mail address, phone/fax numbers, and (optionally) your business address so that people know where to find you in the Land Beyond Cyberspace.

✔ A privacy policy. If you collect personal information from California residents, or if you accept some charge cards on your site, you are required to have one. (Find out more at `blog.redclayinteractive.com/privacy-policy-required/`). To find out about standard guidelines for creating one, go to the W3 Consortium's P3P (The Platform for Privacy Preferences) Web page, at `www.w3.org/P3P/`. You can use the OCED Privacy Policy Generator (`www.oecd.org/document/39/0,2340,en_2649_34255_28863271_1_1_1_1,00.html`) to help you write one.

Some Web design programs, such as Microsoft's Expression Web, give you the ability to create your own visual site map. You can create new pages and see how they link to one another in Hyperlinks view.

Devising a structure for your Web site is only one way to organize it — the outer or top-down organizational method, you might say. Organization also comes from the inside — from the content you create. The words, images, and interactive features that help your site get organized are discussed in the sections that follow.

Making them fall in love at first site

First impressions are critical on the Web, where shoppers have the ability to jump from site to site with a click of their mouse. A few extra seconds of downtime waiting for complex images or mini-computer programs — *Java applets* — to download can cause your prospective buyer to lose patience and you to lose a sale.

How do you make visitors to your welcome page feel as though they're being greeted with open arms? Here are some suggestions:

✔ **Remember, less is more:** Don't overload any one page with more than three or four images. Keep all images 20K or less in size. You do this by saving images with a resolution of 72 dpi (dots per inch), as described in "A picture is worth a thousand words," later in this chapter.

✔ **Find a fast host:** Some Web servers have super-fast connections to the Internet and others use slower lines. Test your site; if your pages take 10 or 20 seconds or more to appear, ask your host company why and find out whether it can move you to a faster machine. These days, cable connections of 1MB to 2MB are easy to find and affordable as well.

✔ **Offer a bargain:** Nothing attracts attention as much as a contest, a giveaway, or a special sales promotion. If you have anything that you can give away, either through a contest or a deep discount, do it.

✔ **Provide instant gratification:** Make sure that your most important information appears at or near the top of your page. Visitors to the Web don't like having to scroll through several screens' worth of material to get to the information they want.

Creating Content That Attracts Customers

What sells on the Web? Look no farther than the search engine you probably use on a regular basis: Google. Google proves that information sells online. Making information easy to find and organizing much of the Web's content in one place has helped make this one of the most successful businesses of recent years. When it comes to a business Web site, you need to present the *right* content in the *right* way to make prospective clients and customers want to explore your site the first time and then come back for more later on. What, you ask, is the "right" content? It's content that

- ✔ Helps people absorb information fast

- ✔ Makes it easy for visitors to find out who you are and what you have to offer

- ✔ Is friendly and informal in tone, concise in length, and clear in its organization

- ✔ Helps develop the all-important one-to-one relationship with customers and clients by inviting dialogue and interaction, both with you and with others who share the same interests

The place to begin is by identifying your target audience. Envision the customers you want to attract and make your site appear to speak directly to them, person to person. Ask around and try to determine what people want from your Web site. Speak informally and directly to them by using "you" rather than "we" or "us," and make sure that your site has plenty of action points — links to click, forms to fill out, or product descriptions to view. Also, follow the general principles outlined in the sections that follow.

Consider doing what professional marketing consultants do and write detailed descriptions of the individuals you're trying to reach. Make your customer profiles complete with fictitious names, ages, job descriptions, type of car they drive, and so on. The more detailed you get, the better you can tailor your content to those people.

The KISS principle: Keep it simple, sir (or sister)

Studies of how information on a Web page is absorbed indicate that people don't really read the contents from top to bottom (or left to right, or frame to frame) in a linear way. In fact, most Web surfers don't *read* in the traditional sense at all. Instead, they browse so quickly that you'd think they have an itchy mouse finger. They "flip through pages" by clicking link after link. More and more Internet users go online with palm devices, pocket PCs, Web-enabled cellphones, and even Internet-ready automobiles. Because your prospective customers don't necessarily have tons of computing power or hours' worth of time to explore your site, the best rule is to *keep it simple.*

Blogs and Twitter posts are simple and easy to read. They are also ideally suited for harried customers. You can use both to market your products or services. See Chapter 15 for more on these new social networking/marketing strategies.

People who are looking for things on the Web are often in a state of hurried distraction. Think about a TV watcher browsing during a commercial or a parent stealing a few moments on the computer while the baby naps. Imagine this person surfing with one hand on a mouse and the other dipping chips into salsa. This person isn't in the mood to listen while you unfold your fondest hopes and dreams for success, starting with playing grocery store cashier as a toddler. Attract your potential customer immediately by answering these questions:

- ✔ Who are you, anyway?
- ✔ All right, so what is your main message or mission?
- ✔ Well then, what do you have here for me?
- ✔ Why should I choose your site to investigate rather than all the others that seem to be about the same?

When it comes to Web pages, it pays to put the most important components first: who you are, what you do, how you stand out from any competing sites, and contact information.

Keep in mind that people who come to a Web site give that site less than a minute (in fact, I've heard only 20 seconds) to hold their attention.

If you have a long list of items to sell, you probably can't fit everything you have to offer right on the first page of your site. Even if you could, you wouldn't want to: It's better to prioritize the contents of your site so that the "breaking stories" or the best contents appear at the top, and the rest of what's in your catalog is arranged in order of importance.

Think long and hard before you use features that may scare people away rather than wow them. I'm talking about a splash page that contains only a logo or short greeting and then reloads automatically and takes the visitor to the main body of a site. I also don't recommend loading your home page with Flash animations or Java applets that take your prospective customers' browsers precious seconds to load.

Striking the right tone with your text

Business writing on the Web differs from the dry, linear report writing one is often called upon to compose in the corporate world. So this is your chance to express the real you: Talk about your fashion sense or your collection of salt and pepper shakers. Your business also has a personality, and the more striking you make its description on your Web page, the better. Use the tone of your text to define what makes your business unique and what distinguishes it from your competition.

Satisfied customers are another source of endorsements. Approach your customers and ask whether they're willing to provide a quote about how you helped them. If you don't yet have satisfied customers, ask one or two people to try your products or services for free and then, if they're happy with your wares, ask permission to use their comments on your site. Your goal is to get a pithy, positive quote that you can put on your home page or on a page specifically devoted to quotes from your clients.

Making your site easy to navigate

Imagine Web surfers arriving at your Web site with only a fraction of their attention engaged. Making the links easy to read and in obvious locations makes your site easier to navigate. Having a row of clickable buttons at the top of your home page, each of which points the visitor to an important area of your site, is always a good idea. Such navigational pointers give visitors an idea of what your site contains in a single glance and immediately encourage viewers to click into a primary subsection of your site and explore farther. By placing an interactive table of contents right upfront, you direct surfers right to the material they're looking for.

The links to the most important areas of a site can go at or near the top of the page on either the left or right side. The Dummies.com home page, shown in Figure 5-3, has a few links as part of the top banner, but also sports links down *both* the center and right sides.

Navigation can help with marketing: If you want to be ranked highly by search engines (and who doesn't?), you have another good reason to place your site's main topics near the top of the page in a series of links. Some search services index the first 50 or so words on a Web page. Therefore, if you can get lots of important keywords included in that index, the chances are better that your site will be ranked highly in a list of links returned by the service in response to a search. See Chapter 11 for more on embedding keywords.

Figure 5-3:
Putting at
least one
or two links
near the
top of your
home page
is a good
idea.

Open the Web page you want to edit and follow these steps to create links to
local files on your Web site by using Dreamweaver, the powerful and popular
Web site creation software by Adobe Systems Inc., (www.adobe.com):

1. **Select the text or image on your Web page that you want to serve as
   the jumping-off point for the link.**

2. **Choose Insert⇨Link or press Ctrl+L.**

   The Properties dialog box appears, as shown in Figure 5-4.

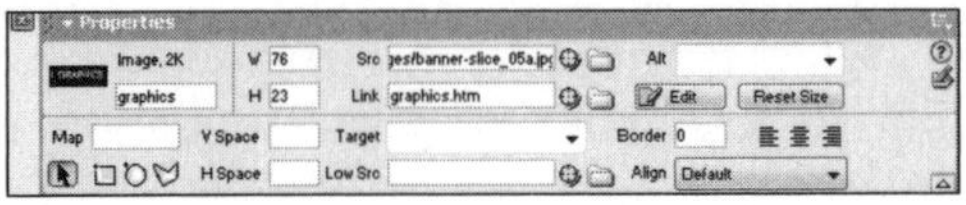

Figure 5-4:
Enter the
name of the
file you want
to link to.

3. **In the box in the Link section, enter the name of the file you want to
   link to if you know the filename.**

   If the page you want to link to is in the same directory as the page that
   contains the jumping-off point, you need to enter only the name of the
   Web page. If the page is in another directory, you need to enter a path
   relative to the Web page that contains the link.

4. Click OK.

You return to the main Dreamweaver screen. If you made a textual link, the selected text is underlined and in a different color. If you made an image link, a box appears around the image.

Presenting the reader with links upfront doesn't just help your search engine rankings but also indicates that your site is content rich and worthy of exploration.

Pointing the way with headings

One hard-to-miss Web page element that's designed to grab the attention of your readers' eyes is a heading. Every Web page needs to contain headings that direct the reader's attention to the most important contents. This book provides a good example. The chapter title (I hope) piques your interest first. Then the section headings and subheadings direct you to more details on the topics you want to read about.

Most graphics designers label their headings with the letters of the alphabet: A, B, C, and so on. In a similar fashion, most Web page editing tools designate top-level headings with the style Heading 1. Beneath this, you place one or more Heading 2 headings. Beneath each of those, you may have Heading 3 and, beneath those, Heading 4. (Headings 5 and 6 are too small to be useful, in my opinion.) The arrangement may look like this (I've indented the following headings for clarity; you don't have to indent them on your page):

```
Miss Cookie's Delectable Cooking School (Heading 1)
    Kitchen Equipment You Can't Live Without (Heading 2)
    The Story of a Calorie Counter Gone Wrong (Heading 2)
    Programs of Culinary Study (Heading 2)
        Registration (Heading 3)
        Course Schedule (Heading 3)
            New Course on Whipped Cream Just Added!
            (Heading 4)
```

You can energize virtually any heading by telling your audience something specific about your business. Rather than "Ida's Antiques Mall," for example, say something like "Ida's Antiques Mall: The Perfect Destination for the Collector and the Crafter." Instead of simply writing a heading like "Stan Thompson, Pet Grooming," say something specific, such as "Stan Thompson: We Groom Your Pet at Our Place or Yours."

Building an online presence takes time

Judy Vorfeld, who goes by the *nom de Net* Webgrammar, knows all about finding different ways to attract regular clientele. She also knows how important it is to have good content in a business Web site. She started the online version of her business Office Support Services (www.ossweb.com) from her home in Arizona in early 1998. She now has a second business site (www.editingandwritingservices.com) and a third (www.webgrammar.com), which serves as a resource for students, educators, writers, and Web developers.

I've been following Judy for several years now, and I noticed that she's followed a popular business trend: She started her own blog. Her home page, which is also her blog page, displays photos of flowers, wildlife, and other scenes from her personal life. She knows that on the Web, getting personal lets you strike up a relationship with potential clients and builds interest as well as trust. "It's difficult to separate who I am from what I do, and almost everything I do in terms of work is based on some kind of presentation or communication," she comments. "Thus, the photos."

Q. What would you describe as the primary goal of your online business?

A. To help small businesses achieve excellent presentation and communication by copyediting their print documents, books, and Web sites.

Q. How many hours a week do you work on your business sites?

A. Three to six hours, which includes my syndicated writing tips, surveys, and newsletter, *Communication Expressway* (www.ossweb.com/ezine-archive-index.html).

Q. How do you promote your site?

A. I participate in newsgroups, write articles for Internet publications, add my URLs to good search engines and directories, moderate discussion lists and forums for others, offer free articles and tips on my sites, and network locally and on the Web.

Q. Has your online business been profitable financially?

A. Yes, although slowly. I rarely raise my rates because my skills seem best suited to the small business community, and I want to offer fees these people can afford.

Q. Who creates your business's Web pages?

A. Basic design is done by a Web designer, and I take over from there. I want the ability to make extensive and frequent changes in text and design. I do hire someone to format my e-zine pages, graphics, and programming.

Q. What advice would you give to someone starting an online business?

A. I have a bunch of suggestions to give, based on my own experience:

✔ **Network.** Network with small business people who have complementary businesses and with those who have similar businesses. Also, network by joining professional associations participating in the activities. Volunteer time and expertise. Link to these organizations from your site.

✔ **Join newsgroups and forums.** Study netiquette first. Lurk until you can adequately answer a question or make a comment. Also, keep on the lookout for someone with whom you can build a relationship, someone who might mentor you and be willing to occasionally scrutinize your site, news release, and so on. This person must be brutally honest, but perhaps you can informally offer one of your own services in return.

✔ **Learn Web development and the culture.** Get a Twitter account (`www.twitter.com`). Subscribe to some blogs at Blogger (`www.blogger.com`). Learn the lingo. Even if you don't do the actual design, you have to make decisions on all the offers you receive regarding how to make money via affiliate programs, link exchanges, hosts, Web design software, and so on. Keeping active online and making those judgments yourself is vital unless you thoroughly trust your Webmaster. Find online discussion lists that handle all areas of Web development and keep informed.

✔ **Include a Web page that shows your business biography or profile.** Mention any volunteer work you do, groups to which you belong, and anything else you do in and for the community. You need to paint as clear a picture as possible in just a few words. Avoid showcasing your talents and hobbies on a business site unless they're directly related to your business.

✔ **In *everything* you write, speak to your visitors.** Use the word "you" as much as possible. Avoid the words "I," "we," and "us." You, as a businessperson, are there to connect with your visitors. You can't give them eye contact, but you can let them know that they matter, that they're (in a sense) the reason for your being there.

✔ **Become known as a specialist in a given field.** Be someone who can always answer a question or go out and find the answer. Your aim is to get as many potential clients or customers to your site as possible, not to get millions of visitors. Forget numbers and concentrate on creating a site that grabs the attention of your target market.

✔ **Get help.** If you can't express yourself well with words (or graphics, or both), and know little about layout, formatting, and so on, hire someone to help you. You'll save yourself a lot of grief if you get a capable, trustworthy editor or designer.

She concludes, "Don't start such a business unless you are passionate about it and willing to give it some time and an initial investment. But when you do start, resources are everywhere — many of them free — to help people build their businesses successfully."

Becoming an expert list maker

Lists are simple and effective ways to break up text and make your Web content easier to digest. They're easy to create and easy for your customer to view and absorb. For example, suppose that you import your own decorations and you want to offer certain varieties at a discount during various seasons. Rather than bury the items you're offering within an easily overlooked paragraph, why not divide your list into subgroups so that visitors find what they want without being distracted by holidays they don't even celebrate?

Lists are easy to implement. If you're using Microsoft Expression Web, open your Web page and follow these steps:

1. **Type a heading for your list and then select the entire heading.**

   For example, you might type and then select the words **This Month's Specials**.

2. **Choose a heading style from the Style drop-down list.**

   Your text is formatted as a heading.

3. **Click anywhere in Expression Web's Design View (the main editing window) to deselect the heading you just formatted.**

4. **Press Enter to move to a new line.**

5. **Type the first item of your list, press Enter, and then type the second item on the next line.**

6. **Repeat Step 5 until you enter all the items of your list.**

7. **Select all the items of your list (but not the heading).**

8. **Choose Format⇨Bullets and Numbering.**

   The List Properties dialog box appears.

9. **Choose one of the four bullet styles and click OK.**

   A bullet appears next to each list item, and the items appear closer together on-screen so that they look more like a list. That's all there is to it! Figure 5-5 shows the result.

Most Web editors let you vary the appearance of the bullet. For example, you can make the bullet a hollow circle rather than a solid black dot, or you can choose a rectangle rather than a circle.

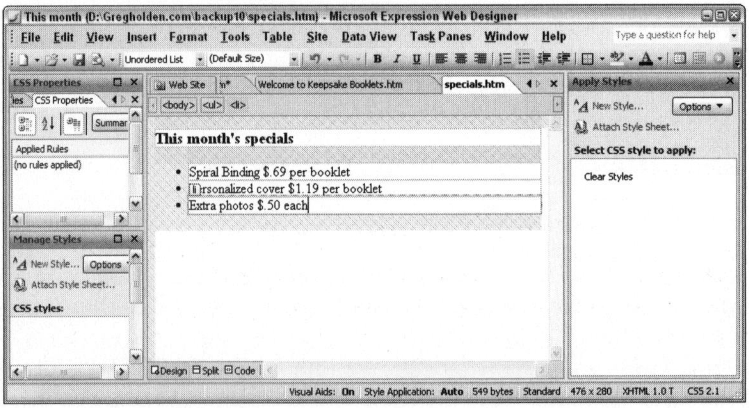

Figure 5-5:
A bulleted list is an easy way to direct customers' attention to special promotions or sale items.

Your Web page title: The ultimate heading

When you're dreaming up clever headings for your Web pages, don't overlook the "heading" that appears in the narrow title bar at the very top of your visitor's Web browser window: the *title* of your Web page.

The two HTML tags `<title>` and `</title>` enclose the text that appears within the browser title bar. But you don't have to mess with these nasty HTML codes: All Web page creation programs give you an easy way to enter or edit a title for a Web page. Make the title as catchy and specific as possible, but make sure that the title is no longer than 64 characters. An effective title refers to your goods or services while grabbing the viewer's attention. If your business is Myrna's Cheesecakes, for example, you might make your title "Smile and Say Cheese! With Myrna's Cakes" (40 characters).

Leading your readers on with links

I mean for you to interpret the preceding heading literally, not figuratively. In other words, I'm not suggesting that you make promises on which you can't deliver. Rather, I mean that you should do anything you can to lead your visitors to your site and then get them to stay long enough to explore individual pages. You can accomplish this goal with a single hyperlinked word that leads to another page on your site:

More . . .

I see this word all the time on Web pages that present a lot of content. At the bottom of a list of their products and services, businesses place that word in bold type: **More . . .** I'm always interested in finding out what more they could possibly have to offer me.

Magazines use the same approach. On their covers you find "refer" phrases that refer you to the kinds of stories that you find inside. You can do the same kind of thing on your Web pages. For example, which of the following links is more likely to get a response?

Next

Next: Paragon's Success Stories

Whenever possible, tell your visitors what they can expect to encounter as a benefit when they click a link. Give them a tease — and then a big payoff for responding.

Enhancing your text with well-placed images

You can add two kinds of images to a Web page: an *inline image,* which appears in the body of your page along with your text, or an *external image,* which is a separate file that visitors access by clicking a link. The link may take the form of highlighted text or a small version of the image — a *thumbnail.*

The basic HTML tag that inserts an image in your document takes the following form:

```
<img src="URL">
```

This tag tells your browser to display an image (`<img>`) here. `"URL"` gives the location of the image file that serves as the source (`src`) for this image. Whenever possible, also include `width` and `height` attributes (as follows) because they help speed up graphics display for many browsers:

```
<img height=51 width=48 SRC="target.gif">
```

Most Web page editors add the `width` and `height` attributes automatically when you insert an image. Typically, here's how you add an image:

1. **Click the location in the Web page where you want the image to appear.**

2. **Click an Image toolbar button or choose Insert⇨Image to display an image selection dialog box.**

3. **Enter the name of the image you want to add and click OK.**

   The image is added to your Web page.

A well-placed image points the way to text that you want people to read immediately. Think about where your own eyes go when you first connect to a Web page. Most likely, you first look at any images on the page; then you look at the headings; finally, you settle on text to read. If you can place an image next to a heading, you virtually ensure that viewers read the heading.

Making your site searchable

A search box is one of the best kinds of content you can put on your Web site's opening page. A *search box* is a simple text-entry field that lets a visitor enter a word or phrase. By clicking a button labeled Go or Search, the search term or terms are sent to the site, where a script checks an index of the site's contents for any files that contain the terms. The script then lists documents that contain the search terms in the visitor's browser window.

Search boxes are commonly found on commercial Web sites. You usually see them at the top of the home page, right near the links to the major sections of the site. The Dummies.com Technology page, shown in Figure 5-6, includes a search box in the upper-right corner of the page.

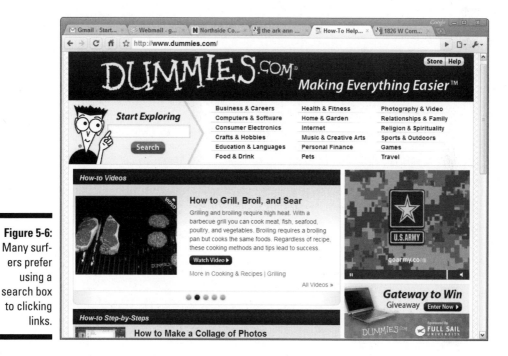

Figure 5-6: Many surfers prefer using a search box to clicking links.

Search boxes let visitors instantly scan the site's entire contents for a word or phrase. They put visitors in control right away and get them to interact with your site. They're popular for some very good reasons.

Yes, I recommend some sort of search utility for e-commerce sites. However, adding a search box to your site doesn't make much sense if you have only five to ten pages of content. If your site has a sales catalog driven by a database, your customers can use the database search tool instead.

The problem is that search boxes usually require someone with knowledge of computer programming to create or implement a program called a CGI script to do the searching. Someone also has to compile an index of the documents on the Web site so that the script can search the documents. An application such as ColdFusion works well, but it's not a program for beginners.

Make a map of your Web site

Maps are especially important when navigating the information superhighway. When it comes to your e-commerce Web site, a site map can help you make your site easier to navigate. A *site map* is a graphical representation of your Web site — a diagram that graphically depicts all the pages in the site and how they connect to one another. When you create pages and link them to one another, a site map is created. The following figure shows the site map on the left side of the window and a list of files on the right.

Keep in mind that you don't have to invest in a fancy (and expensive) software program to create a site map. You can also create one the old-fashioned way, with a pencil and paper.

Or you can draw boxes and arrows with a computer graphics program you're familiar with. The point is that your site map can be a useful design tool for organizing the documents within your site.

If your sales are sluggish, make sure that your customers can actually find what they're looking for. Take a typical product in your sales catalog and then visit your own site to see how many clicks you need to make to find it. Then see how many clicks it takes to complete its purchase. Eliminating any unnecessary navigational layers (such as category opening pages) makes your site easier to use.

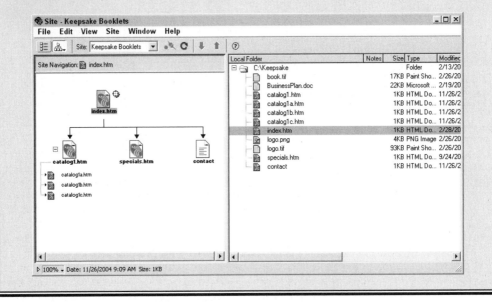

You can get around having to write CGI scripts to add search capabilities to your site, however. Choose one of these options:

- ✔ **Let your Web host do the work.** Some hosting services do the indexing and creation of the search utility as part of their services.

- ✔ **Use a free site search service.** The server that does the indexing of your Web pages and holds the index doesn't need to be the server that hosts your site. A number of services make your site searchable for free. In exchange, you display advertisements or logos in the search results you return to your visitors.

✔ **Pay for a search service.** If you don't want to display ads on your search results pages, pay a monthly fee to have a company index your pages and let users conduct searches. FreeFind (www.freefind.com) has some economy packages, a free version that forces you to view ads, and a professional version that costs $5 per month for a site of 250 pages or fewer and $9 per month for a site of 500 pages or fewer. SiteMiner (siteminer.mycomputer.com) charges $19.95 per month for up to 1,500 pages but lets you customize your search box and reindex your site whenever you add new content.

You say you're up to making your site searchable, and you shudder at the prospect of either writing your own computer script or finding and editing someone else's script to index your site's contents and actually do the searching? Then head over to AtomZ (www.atomz.com) and check out the hosted application Site Search. Other organizations that offer similar services include FreeFind (www.freefind.com), PicoSearch (www.picosearch.com), and Webinator (www.thunderstone.com/texis/site/pages/webinator.html).

Nip and Tuck: Establishing a Visual Identity

The prospect of designing a Web site may be intimidating if you haven't tried it before. But just remember that designing a site really boils down to a simple principle: *effective visual communication that conveys a particular message.* The first step in creating graphics is not to open a painting program and start drawing, but rather to plan your page's message. Next, determine the audience you want to reach with that message and think about how your graphics can best communicate what you want to say. Some ways to do this are as follows:

✔ **Gather ideas from Web sites that use graphics well.** Award-winning sites and sites created by designers who are using graphics in new or unusual ways can help you. To find some award winners, check out The Webby Awards (www.webbyawards.com) and The International Web Page Awards (www.webpageawards.com).

✔ **Use graphics consistently from page to page.** You can create an identity and convey a consistent message.

✔ **Know your audience.** Create graphics that meet visitors' needs and expectations. If you're selling fashions to teenagers, go for neon colors and out-there graphics. If you're selling financial planning to senior citizens, choose a distinguished and sophisticated typeface.

How do you become acquainted with your customers when it is likely that you'll never actually meet them face to face? Find newsgroups and mailing lists in which potential visitors to your site are discussing subjects related to what you plan to publish on the Web. Read the posted messages to get a sense of the concerns and vocabulary of your intended audience.

Choosing wallpaper that won't make you a wallflower

The technical term for the wallpaper behind the contents of a Web page is its *background*. Most Web browsers display the background of a page as light gray or white unless you specify something different. In this case, leaving well enough alone isn't good enough. If you choose the wrong background color (one that makes your text hard to read and your images look as though they've been smeared with mud), viewers are likely to get the impression that the page is poorly designed or that the author of the page hasn't put a great deal of thought into the project.

Most Web page creation programs offer a simple way to specify a color or an image file to serve as the background of a Web page. For example, in Expression Web, you use the Document Colors and Background options in the Page Properties dialog box to set your Web page wallpaper.

Color your Web site effective

You can use background and other colors to elicit a particular mood or emotion and to convey your organization's identity on the Web. The right choice of color can create impressions ranging from elegant to funky.

The basic colors chosen by the United Parcel Service Web site (www.ups.com) convey to customers that it is a staid and reliable company, and the U.S. Postal Service (www.usps.gov) sticks to the patriotic choice of red, white, and blue. In contrast, the designers of the HotHotHot hot sauce site (www.hothothot.com) combine fiery colors to convey a spice that sizzles.

When selecting colors for your own Web pages, consider the demographics of your target audience. Do some research on what emotions or impressions are conveyed by different colors and which colors best match the mission or identity of your business. Refer to resources, such as the online essay by Web Resources (www.webdesignoutsource.net/articles/web-design-color-theory/the-psychology-of-color-in-web-design), which examines the subject of how color choices make Web surfers react differently.

Even if you have the taste of a professional designer, you need to be aware of what happens to color on the Web. The best color choices for Web backgrounds are ones that don't shift dramatically from browser to browser or platform to platform. The best palette for use on the Web is a set of 216 colors that is common to all browsers. These are called *browser-safe colors* because they appear pretty much the same from browser to browser and on different monitors. The palette itself appears on Victor Engel's Web site (`the-light.com/netcol.html`).

Keep in mind that the colors you use must have contrast so that they don't blend into one another. For example, you don't want to put purple type on a brown or blue background, or yellow type on a white background. Remember to use light type against a dark background; likewise, use dark type against a light background. That way, all your page's contents show up.

Tiling images in the background

You can use an image rather than a solid color to serve as the background of a page. You specify an image in the HTML code of your Web page (or in your Web page editor), and browsers automatically *tile* the image, reproducing it repeatedly to fill the current width and height of the browser window.

This isn't the time to be totally wild and crazy. Background images work only when they're subtle and don't interfere with the page contents. Choose an image that doesn't have any obvious lines that create a distracting pattern when tiled. The effect you're trying to create should literally resemble wallpaper. Visit the Maine Solar House home page (`www.solarhouse.com`) for a rare example of a background image that is faint enough to not interfere with foreground images and that adds something to the page's design.

Using Web typefaces like a pro

If you create a Web page and don't specify that the text be displayed in a particular font, the browser that displays the page uses its default font — which is usually Times or Helvetica (although individual users can customize their browsers by picking a different default font).

However, you don't have to limit yourself to the same old, same old. As a Web page designer, you can exercise a degree of control over the appearance of your Web page by specifying that the body type and headings be displayed in a particular nonstandard font. A few of the choices available to you have names such as Arial, Courier, Century Schoolbook, and so on. But just because you fall in love with a particular typeface doesn't mean your audience will be able to admire it in all its beauty. The problem is that you don't have ultimate control over whether a given browser can display the specified typeface because you don't know for sure whether the individual user's system has access to your preferred typefaces. If the particular font you specified is not available, the browser falls back on its default font (which, again, is probably Helvetica or Times).

That's why you're better off picking a generic typeface that is built into virtually every computer's operating system. This convention ensures that your Web pages look more or less the same no matter what Web browser or what type of computer displays them.

Where, exactly, do you specify type fonts, colors, and sizes for the text? Again, special HTML tags tell Web browsers what fonts to display, but you don't need to mess with these tags yourself if you're using a Web page creation tool. The specific steps you take depend on what Web design tool you're using. In Dreamweaver, you have the option of specifying a group of preferred typefaces rather than a single font in the Properties inspector (see Figure 5-7). If the viewer doesn't have one font in the group, another font displays. Check the Help files with your own program to find out exactly how to format text and what typeface options you have.

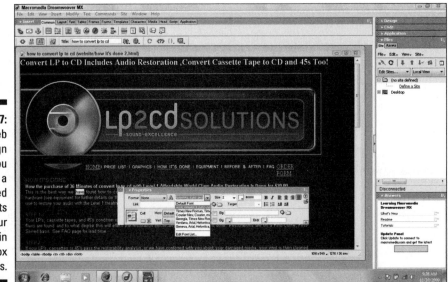

Figure 5-7: Most Web page design tools let you specify a preferred font or fonts for your Web page in a dialog box like this.

Not all typefaces are equal in the eye of the user. Serif typefaces, such as Times Roman, are considered to be more readable (for printed materials, at least) than sans-serif fonts, such as Helvetica. However, an article on the Web Marketing Today Web site (www.wilsonweb.com/wmt6/html-email-fonts.htm) found that by a whopping 2 to 1 margin, the sans-serif font Arial is considered more readable on a Web page than Times Roman.

If you want to make sure that a heading or block of type appears in a specific typeface (especially a nonstandard one that isn't displayed as body text by Web browsers), scan it or create the heading in an image-editing program and insert it into the page as a graphic image. But make sure that it doesn't clash with the generic typefaces that appear on the rest of your page.

Clip art is free and fun

Not everyone has the time or resources to scan photos or create their own original graphics. But that doesn't mean you can't add graphic interest to your Web page. Many Web page designers use clip-art bullets, diamonds, or other small images next to list items or major Web page headings to which they want to call special attention. Clip art can also provide a background pattern for a Web page or highlight sales headings, such as Free!, New!, or Special!

When I first started in the print publications business, I bought catalogs of illustrations, literally clipped out the art, and pasted it down. It's still called clip art, but now the process is different. In keeping with the spirit of exchange that has been a part of the Internet since its inception, some talented and generous artists have created icons, buttons, and other illustrations in electronic form and offered them free for downloading.

Here are some suggestions for sources of clip art on the Web:

- clipart.com (`www.clipart.com`)
- Clip Art Universe (`clipartuniverse.com`)
- The Yahoo! page full of links to clip-art resources (`dir.yahoo.com/Computers_and_Internet/Graphics/Clip_Art`)

If you use Microsoft Office, you have access to plenty of clip-art images that come with the software. In Word, choose Insert➪Picture➪Clip Art to open the Insert Clip Art dialog box. If these built-in images aren't sufficient, you can connect to the Microsoft Clip Gallery Live Web site by clicking the Clips Online toolbar button in the Insert Clip Art dialog box. Web page editors — such as CoffeeCup HTML Editor — come with their own clip-art libraries, too.

Be sure to read the copyright fine print *before* you copy graphics. All artists own the copyright to their work. It's up to them to determine whether or how they want to give someone else the right to copy their work. Sometimes, the authors require you to pay a small fee if you want to copy their work, or they may restrict use of their work to nonprofit organizations.

A picture is worth a thousand words

Some customers know exactly what they want from the get-go and don't need any help from you. But most customers love to shop around or could use some encouragement to move from one item or catalog page to another. This is where images can play an important role.

Even if you use only some basic clip art, such as placing spheres or arrows next to sale items, your customer is likely to thank you by buying more. A much better approach, though, is to scan or take digital images of your sale items and provide compact, clear images of them on your site. Here's a quick step-by-step guide to get you started:

1. **Choose the right image to scan.**

   The original quality of an image is just as important as how you scan or retouch it. Images that are murky or fuzzy in print are even worse when viewed on a computer screen.

2. **Preview the image.**

   Most digital cameras let you preview images so that you can decide whether to keep or delete individual pictures before downloading to your computer. If you're working with a scanner, scanning programs let you make a quick *preview scan* of an image so that you can get an idea of what it looks like before you do the actual scan. When you press the Preview button, the optical device in the scanner captures the image. A preview image appears on-screen, surrounded by a *marquee box* (a rectangle made up of dashes), as shown in Figure 5-8.

Figure 5-8:
The marquee box lets you crop a preview image to make it smaller and reduce the file size.

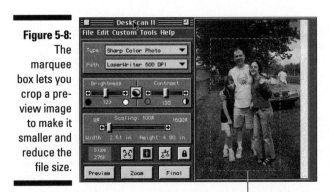

Marquee box

3. **Crop the image.**

   Cropping means that you resize the box around the image to select the portion of the image that you want to keep and leave out the parts of the image that aren't essential. Cropping an image is a good idea because it highlights the most important contents and reduces the file size. Reducing the file size of an image should always be one of your most important goals — the smaller the image, the quicker it appears in someone's browser window.

Almost all scanning and graphics programs offer separate options for cropping an image and reducing the image size. By cropping the image, you eliminate parts of the image you don't want, and this *does* reduce the image size. But it doesn't reduce the size of the objects within the image. Resizing the overall image size is a separate step, which enables you to change the dimensions of the entire image without eliminating any contents.

4. **Select an input mode.**

   Tell the scanner or graphics program how you want it to save the visual data — as color, line art (used for drawings), or grayscale (used for black-and-white photos).

5. **Set the resolution.**

   Digital images are made up of little bits (dots) of computerized information called *pixels.* The more pixels per inch, the higher the level of detail. When you scan an image, you can tell the scanner to make the dots smaller (creating a smoother image) or larger (resulting in a more jagged image). This adjustment is called *setting the resolution* of the image. (When you take a digital photo, the resolution of the image depends on your camera's settings.)

   When you're scanning for the Web, your images appear primarily on computer screens. Because many computer monitors can display resolutions only up to 72 dpi, 72 dpi — a relatively rough resolution — is an adequate resolution for a Web image. Using this coarse resolution has the advantage of keeping the image's file size small. Remember, the smaller the file size, the more quickly an image appears when your customers load your page in their Web browsers. (Alternatively, many designers scan at a fine resolution such as 300 dpi and reduce the file size in a graphics program.)

6. **Adjust contrast and brightness.**

   Virtually all scanning programs and graphics-editing programs provide brightness and contrast controls that you can adjust with your mouse to improve the image. If you're happy with the image as is, leave the brightness and contrast set where they are. (You can also leave the image as is and adjust brightness and contrast later in a separate graphics program, such as Paint Shop Photo Pro, which you can try by downloading it from the Corel Web site, `www.corel.com`.)

7. **Reduce the image size.**

   The old phrase "good things come in small packages" is never more true than when you're improving your digital image. If you're scanning an image that is 8" x 10" and you're sure that it needs to be about 4" x 5" when it appears on your Web page, scan it at 50 percent of the original size. This step reduces the file size right away and makes the file easier to transport, whether it's from your camera to your computer or your computer to your hosting service. Even more important, it appears more quickly in someone's Web browser.

8. **Scan away!**

Your scanner makes a beautiful whirring sound as it turns those colors into pixels. Because you're scanning only at 72 dpi, the process shouldn't take too long.

9. **Save the file.**

Now you can save your image to disk. Most programs let you do this by choosing File⇨Save. In the dialog box that appears, enter a name for your file and select a file format. (Because you're working with images to be published on the Web, remember to save either in GIF or JPEG format.)

Be sure to add the correct filename extension. Web browsers recognize only image files with the extensions .gif, .png, .jpg, or .jpeg. If you name your image product and save it in GIF format, call it product.gif. If you save it in JPEG format and you're using a PC, call it product.jpg. On a Macintosh, call it product.jpeg.

For more details on scanning images, check out Epson's beginners' instructions at ftp.epson.com/htmldocs/pr126_/pr126_rf/scani_1.htm.

GIF, JPEG, and PNG

Web site technology and HTML may have changed dramatically over the past several years, but for the most part, there are only three types of images as far as Web pages are concerned: GIF, PNG, and JPEG. These formats use methods that compress computer image files so that the visual information contained within them can be transmitted easily over computer networks. PNG, a third format designed several years ago as a successor to GIF, has never gained wide acceptance and still isn't as widely used as GIF although it's far superior in terms of compression and image quality.

GIF (pronounced either *jiff* or *giff*) stands for Graphics Interchange Format. GIF is best suited to text, line art, or images with well-defined edges. Special types of GIF allow images with transparent backgrounds to be *interlaced* (broken into layers that appear gradually over slow connections) and animated. JPEG (pronounced *jay-peg*) stands for Joint Photographic Experts Group, the name of the group that originated the format. JPEG is preferred for large photos and continuous tones of grayscale or color that need greater compression.

If you have a choice, I suggest that you try PNG (Portable Network Graphics). Its images are ideal for the Web. The quality is so good that I've even blown up images, printed them on a color inkjet printer, and put them on the wall of my office. All the major browsers support PNG, so you'll have no problem getting your visitors to enjoy them.

Creating a logo

An effective logo establishes your online business's graphic identity in no uncertain terms. A logo can be as simple as a rendering of the company name that imparts an official typeface or color. Whatever text it includes, a *logo* is a small, self-contained graphic object that conveys the group's identity and purpose. Figure 5-9 shows an example of a logo.

Figure 5-9: A good logo effectively combines color, type, and graphics to convey an organization's identity or mission.

A logo doesn't have to be a fabulously complex drawing with drop-shadows and gradations of color. A simple, type-only logo can be as good as gold. Pick a typeface you want, choose your graphic's outline version, and fill the letters with color.

Inviting Comments from Customers

Quick, inexpensive, and *personal:* These are three of the most important advantages that the Web has over traditional printed catalogs. The first two are obvious pluses. You don't have to wait for your online catalog to get printed and distributed. On the Web, your contents are published and available to your customers right away. Putting a catalog on the Web eliminates (or, if publishing a catalog on the Web allows you to reduce your print run, dramatically reduces) the cost of printing, which can result in big savings for you.

But the fact that online catalogs can be more personal than the printed variety is perhaps the biggest advantage of all. The personal touch comes from the Web's potential for *interactivity*. Getting your customers to click links makes them actively involved with your catalog.

Getting positive e-mail feedback

Playing hide and seek is fun when you're amusing your baby niece, but it's not a good way to build a solid base of customers. In fact, providing a way for your customers to interact with you so that they can reach you quickly may be the most important part of your Web site.

Add a simple *mailto* link like this:

> Questions? Comments? Send e-mail to: info@mycompany.com

A mailto link gets its name from the HTML command that programmers use to create it. When visitors click the e-mail address, their e-mail program opens a new e-mail message window with your e-mail address already entered. That way, they have only to enter a subject line, type the message, and click Send to send you their thoughts.

Most Web page creation programs make it easy to create a mailto link. For example, if you use Dreamweaver, follow these steps:

1. **Launch and open the Web page to which you want to add your e-mail link.**

2. **Position your mouse arrow and click the spot on the page where you want the address to appear.**

   The convention is to put your e-mail address at or near the bottom of a Web page. A vertical blinking cursor appears at the location where you want to insert the address.

3. **Choose Insert➪Email Link.**

   The Insert Email Link dialog box appears.

4. **In the Text box, type the text that you want to appear on your Web page.**

   You don't have to type your e-mail address; you can also type **Webmaster**, **Customer Service**, or your own name.

5. **In the E-Mail box, type your e-mail address.**

6. **Click OK.**

The Insert Email Link dialog box closes, and you return to the Dreamweaver Document window, where your e-mail link appears in blue and is underlined to signify that it is a clickable link.

Other editors work similarly but don't give you a menu command called Email Link. For example, in World Wide Web Weaver, a shareware program for the Macintosh OS, you choose Tags⇨Mail. A dialog box called Mail Editor appears. Enter your e-mail address and the text you want to appear as the highlighted link; then click OK to add the mailto link to your page.

The drawback to publishing your e-mail address directly on your Web page is that you're certain to get unsolicited e-mail messages (commonly called *spam*) sent to that address. Hiding your e-mail address behind generic link text (such as Webmaster) may help reduce your chances of attracting spam.

Web page forms that aren't off-putting

You don't have to do much Web surfing before you become intimately acquainted with how Web page forms work, at least from the standpoint of someone who has to fill them out to sign up for Web hosting or to download software.

When it comes to creating your own Web site, however, you become conscious of how useful forms are as a means of gathering essential marketing information about your customers. They give your visitors a place to sound off, ask questions, and generally get involved with your online business.

Be clear and use common sense when creating your order form. Here are some general guidelines on how to organize your form and what you need to include:

- ✔ **Make it easy on the customer.** Whenever possible, add pull-down menus with preentered options to your *form fields* (text boxes that visitors use to enter information). That way, users don't have to wonder about things such as whether you want them to spell out a state or use the two-letter abbreviation.

- ✔ **Validate the information.** You can use a programming language — for example, JavaScript — to ensure that users enter information correctly, that all fields are completely filled out, and so on. You may have to hire someone to add the appropriate code to the order form, but the expense is worth it to save you from having to call customers to verify or correct information that they missed or submitted incorrectly.

> ✔ **Provide a help number.** Give people a number to call if they have questions or want to check on an order.
>
> ✔ **Return an acknowledgment.** Let customers know that you have received their order and will be shipping the merchandise immediately or contacting them if more information is needed.

As usual, good Web page authoring and editing programs make it a snap to create the text boxes, check boxes, buttons, and other parts of a form that the user fills out. The other part of a form, the computer script that receives the data and processes it so that you can read and use the information, is not as simple. See Chapter 8 for details.

Not so long ago, you had to write or edit a scary CGI script to set up forms processing on your Web site. These days, the process of creating a working Web page form is accessible to nonprogrammers like the rest of us. Web businesses such as Response-O-Matic (www.response-o-matic.com) and FormMail.To (www.formmail.to) lead you through the process of setting up a form and providing you with the CGI script that receives the data and forwards it to you.

Blogs that promote discussion

Most blogs give readers the chance to comment on individual comments the author has made. On my own blog, for instance, which was created with Blogger, I make comments, and readers can immediately respond. This is a standard feature to give readers the opportunity to comment on what you've written.

On blogs that attract a wide following, such as Talking Points Memo (www.talkingpointsmemo.com) or the Julie/Julia Project, the blog that inspired the movie *Julie and Julia* (blogs.salon.com/0001399), comments by the respective authors generate long discussions by a community of devoted readers. Find out more about blogs in Chapter 1.

Providing a guestbook

If you don't have a blog, a guestbook on your Web site can add a whole other dimension to your business by making your customers feel that they're part of a thriving community. When you provide a guestbook on one of your business's Web pages, your clients and other visitors can check out who else has been there and what others think about the site, and then add their own comments as well.

If you set out to create your own Web page guestbook from scratch, you'd have to create a form, write a script (fairly complicated code that tells a computer what to do), test the code, and so on. Thankfully, an easier way to add a guestbook is available: You simply register with a special Web business that provides free guestbooks to users. One such organization, Lycos, offers a guestbook service through its Html Gear site.

If you register with Html Gear's service, you can have your own guestbook right away with no fuss. (Actually, Html Gear's guestbook program resides on one of its Web servers; you just add the text-entry portion to your own page.) Here's how to do it:

1. **Connect to the Internet, start up your Web browser, and go to** `htmlgear.lycos.com/specs/guest.html`.

2. **Scroll down the page and click the Get This Gear! link.**

   You go to the Network Membership page.

3. **Click the Sign Me Up! button and follow the instructions on subsequent pages to register for the guestbook and other software on the Html Gear site.**

   The program asks you to provide your own personal information, choose a name and password for your guestbook, enter the URL of the Web page on which you want the guestbook to appear, and provide keywords that describe your page.

   After you register, a page titled Gear Manager appears.

4. **Click Add Gear and then Get Gear next to Guest Gear.**

   After a few seconds, the Create Guest Gear page appears. This page contains a form that you need to fill out to create the guestbook *text-entry fields* (the text boxes and other items that visitors use to submit information to you) to your Web page.

5. **Fill out the Create Guest Gear form.**

   This form lets you name your guestbook and customize how you want visitors to interact with you. For instance, you can configure the guestbook to send you an e-mail notification whenever someone posts a message.

6. **When you're done filling out the form, click Save & Create.**

   The Get Code page appears. A box contains the code you need to copy and add to the HTML for your Web page.

7. **Select the code.**

   Position your mouse arrow at the beginning of the code (just before the first line, which looks like this: `<!-- \/ GuestGEAR Code by http://htmlgear.com \/ ->`), press and hold down your mouse button, and scroll across the code to the last line, which reads: `<!-- /\ End GuestGEAR Code /\ -->`.

   The code is highlighted to show that it has been selected.

8. **Choose Edit⇨Copy to copy the selected code to your computer's Clipboard.**

9. **Launch your Web editor, if it isn't running already, and open the Web page you want to edit in your Web editor window.**

   If you're working in a program (such as Dreamweaver or HotDog Pro) that shows the HTML for a Web page while you edit it, you can move on to Step 10. If, on the other hand, your editor hides the HTML from you, you have to use your editor's menu options to view the HTML source for your page. The exact menu command varies from program to program. Usually, though, the option is contained on the View menu. In Expression Web, for example, you click the Code tab at the bottom of the window. The HTML code for the Web page you want to edit then appears.

10. **Click the spot on the page where you want to paste the HTML code for the guestbook.**

    How do you know where this spot is? Well, you have to add the code in the BODY section of a Web page. This is the part of the page that is contained between two HTML tags, `<BODY>` and `</BODY>`. You can't go wrong with pasting the code just before the `</BODY>` tag — or just before your return e-mail address or any other material you want to keep at the bottom of the page. The following example indicates the proper placement for the guestbook code:

```
<HTML>
<HEAD>
<TITLE>Sign My Guestbook</TITLE>
</HEAD>
<BODY>
The body of your Web page goes here; this is the part
        that appears on the Web.
Paste your guestbook code here!
</BODY>
</HTML>
```

11. **Choose Edit⇨Paste.**

    The guestbook code is added to your page.

12. **Close your Web editor's HTML window.**

Exactly how you do this depends on the program. If you have a separate HTML window open, click the close box (X) in the upper-right corner of the HTML window — if you're working in a Windows environment. (If you're working on a Mac, close the window by clicking the close box in the upper-left corner of the window that displays the HTML.)

The HTML code disappears, and you return to your Web editor's main window.

13. **Choose File⇨Save to save your changes.**

14. **Preview your work in your Web browser window.**

The steps involved in previewing also vary from editor to editor. Some editors have a Preview toolbar button that you click to view your page in a Web browser. Otherwise, launch your Web browser to preview your page as follows:

- If you use Google's Chrome browser, press Ctrl+O. When the Open dialog box appears, click the name of the file you just saved in the Open Page dialog box, and then click Open to open the page.

- If you use Internet Explorer, press Ctrl+O. When the Open dialog box appears, click Browse. Click the name of the file you just saved in the Windows Internet Explorer dialog box, and then click Open to open the page.

The page opens in your Web browser, with a new Guestbook button added to it, as shown in Figure 5-10.

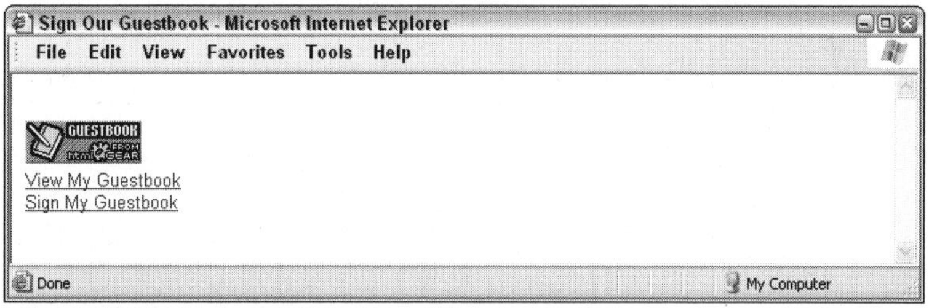

Figure 5-10:
Add a guestbook link to your Web page.

Now when visitors to your Web page click the Sign My Guestbook link, they go to a page that has a form they can fill out. Clicking the View My Guestbook link enables visitors to view the messages that other visitors have entered into your guestbook.

The problem with adding a link to a service that resides on another Web site is that it makes your Web pages load more slowly. First, your visitor's browser loads the text on your page. Then it loads the images from top to bottom.

Besides this, it has to make a link to the Html Gear site in order to load the guestbook. If you decide to add a guestbook, images, or other elements that reside on another Web site, be sure to test your page and make sure that you're satisfied with how long the contents take to appear. (If it takes more than 10 seconds — 20, absolute max — you're liable to lose visitors.) Also make sure to use the "Moderation" feature that enables you to screen postings to your guestbook. That way, you can delete obscene, unfair, or libelous postings before they go online.

Chit-chat that counts

After visitors start coming to your site, the next step is to retain those visitors. A good way to do this is to build a sense of community by posting a bulletin-board-type discussion area.

A discussion area takes the form of back-and-forth messages on topics of mutual interest. Each person can read previously posted messages and either respond or start a new topic of discussion. For an example of a discussion area that's tied to an online business, visit the AuctionBytes (`www.auction bytes.com`) discussion areas (called Forums on this site), one of which is shown in Figure 5-11. AuctionBytes is a highly regarded site that provides information about the online auction industry. Its discussion boards give readers a place to bring up questions and issues in a forum that's independent from those provided by auction sites like eBay.

The talk doesn't have to be about your own particular niche in your business field. In fact, the discussion will be more lively if your visitors can discuss concerns about your area of business in general, whether it's flower arranging, boat sales, tax preparation, clock repair, computers, or whatever.

How, exactly, do you start a discussion area? The basic first step is to install a special computer script on the computer that hosts your Web site. (Discussing this prospect with your Web hosting service beforehand is essential.) When visitors come to your site, their Web browsers access the script, enabling them to enter comments and read other messages.

Here are some specific ways to prepare a discussion area for your site:

- ✔ Copy a bulletin board or discussion-group script from either of these sites:
  - Extropia.com (`www.extropia.com/applications.html`)
  - Matt's Script Archive (`www.worldwidemart.com/scripts`)
- ✔ Start your own forum on a service such as HyperNews, by Daniel LaLiberte, or install the HyperNews program yourself:
  - `www.hypernews.org/HyperNews/get/hypernews.html`

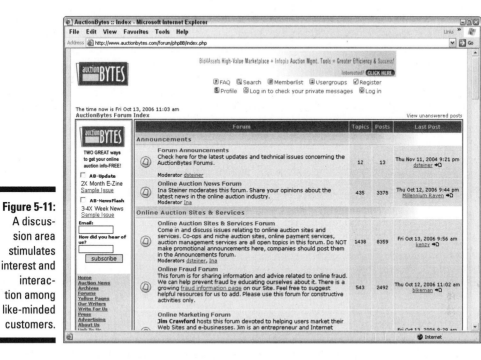

Figure 5-11:
A discussion area stimulates interest and interaction among like-minded customers.

Moving from Web Site to Web Presence

After you have established a visual identity through colors, images, and a logo, you can "brand" yourself by "popping up" in as many Web venues as possible. Make no mistake about it: Tending to your own image and building a name for yourself takes time and effort. It might take one, two, or more hours every day. After you start blogging and building an audience, you need to keep at it every few days, if not *every* day. Otherwise, those fickle Web visitors you worked so hard to cultivate will flit away to someone else's Web site or blog or Facebook page.

How do you "pop up" in places where people will find you? You'll find suggestions throughout this book. Here are a few ideas:

✔ Start a blog and use it to comment on your area of interest. (See Chapter 12.)

✔ Twitter as much as possible; short "tweets" can advertise new products or sales you have running (again, see Chapter 12.)

✔ Get on Facebook and start cultivating a circle of friends. Use Facebook to point them to your Web site — and your blog, your tweets, and so on. (You guessed it — see Chapter 12.)

✔ Open a storefront on eBay or a free site such as eCrater (`www.ecrater.com`). See Chapter 13 for more about storefronts.

✔ List your products on Google Base, a free listing service mentioned in Chapter 14.

The art of having a Web presence is using all these sites to point to one another so that no matter where you are, shoppers will be directed to your products or services or will at least be prompted to find out more about you.

Extreme Web Pages: Advanced Layouts

Usually, people who place frames and tables on a Web site have some experience creating Web sites. However, taking on the challenge of using these items might be right up the alley of an adventurous type (you) who wants to start an online business.

Setting the tables for your customers

Tables are to designers what statistics are to sports fans. They provide another means to present information in a graphically interesting way. Tables were originally intended to present "tabular" data in columns and rows, much as a spreadsheet does. But by using advanced HTML techniques, you can make tables a much more integrated and subtle part of your Web page.

Because you can easily create a basic table by using Web page editors, such as HotDog, Composer, and Expression Web, starting with one of these tools makes sense. Some adjustments with HTML are probably unavoidable, however, especially if you want to use tables to create blank columns on a Web page (as I explain later in this section). Here is a quick rundown of the main HTML tags used for tables:

✔ `<table> </table>` encloses the entire table. The `border` attribute sets the width of the line around the cells.

✔ `<tr> </tr>` encloses a table row, a horizontal set of cells.

✔ `<td> </td>` defines the contents of an individual cell. The `height` and `width` attributes control the size of each cell. For example, the following code tells a browser that the table cell is 120 pixels wide:

```
<td width=120> Contents of cell </td>
```

A quick HTML primer

Thanks to Web page creation tools, you don't have to master HyperText Markup Language (HTML) to create your own Web pages, although some knowledge of HTML is helpful when it comes to editing pages and understanding how they're put together.

HTML is a markup language, not a computer programming language. You use it in much the same way that old-fashioned editors marked up copy before they gave it to typesetters. A markup language allows you to identify major sections of a document, such as body text, headings, title, and so on. A software program (in the case of HTML, a Web browser) is programmed to recognize the markup language and to display the formatting elements that you have marked.

Markup tags are the basic building blocks of HTML as well as eXtensible Markup Language (XML). Tags enable you to structure the appearance of your document so that when it is transferred from one computer to another, it looks the way you described it. HTML tags appear within caret-shaped brackets. Most HTML commands require a *start tag* at the beginning

of the section and an *end tag* (which usually begins with a backslash) at the end.

For example, if you place the HTML tags <b> and </b> around the phrase "This text will be bold," the words appear in bold type on any browser that displays them, no matter whether it's running on a Windows-based PC, a UNIX workstation, a Macintosh, a palm device that's Web enabled, or any other computer.

Many HTML commands are accompanied by *attributes,* which provide a browser with more specific instructions on what action the tag is to perform. In the following line of HTML, src is an attribute that works with the <img> tag to identify a file to display:

    <img src="house.jpg">

Each attribute is separated from an HTML command by a single blank space. The equal sign (=) is an operator that introduces the value on which the attribute and command functions. Usually, the value is a filename or a directory path leading to a specific file that is to be displayed on a Web page. The straight (as opposed to curly) quotation marks around the value are essential for the HTML command to work.

Cells in a table can contain images as well as text. Also, individual cells can have different colors from the cells around them. You can add a background color to a table cell by adding the bgcolor attribute to the <td> table cell tag.

The clever designer can use tables in a hidden way to arrange an entire page, or a large portion of a page, by doing two things:

> ✔ **Set the table border to 0.** Doing so makes the table outline invisible, so the viewer sees only the contents of each cell, not the lines bordering the cell.

> ✔ **Fill some table cells with blank space.** They act as empty columns that add more white space to a page.

An example of the first approach, that of making the table borders invisible, appears in Figure 5-12: David Nishimura's Vintage Pens Web site (www.vintagepens.com) where he sells vintage writing instruments. This page is divided into table columns and cells, which give the designer a high level of control over the layout.

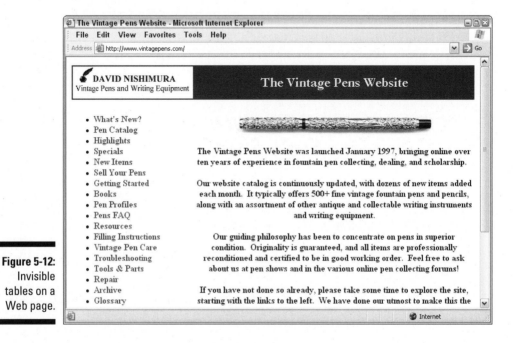

Figure 5-12:
Invisible
tables on a
Web page.

Breaking the grid with layers

Tables and another set of virtually obsolete layout tools called frames bring organization and interactivity to Web pages, but they confine your content to rows and columns. If you feel confined by the old up-down, left-right routine, explore layers for arranging your Web page content.

Layers, like table cells and frames, act as containers for text and images on a Web page. Layers are unique because they can be moved around freely on the page — they can overlap one another and they can "bleed" right to the page margin.

Layers carry some big downsides: You can't create them with just any Web editor. Microsoft Expression Web is the Web editor I recommend because it lets you create layers by using Cascading Style Sheets (CSS) commands so that they display accurately by almost all browsers. See the product's Web site (`http://www.microsoft.com/expression/products/Web_Overview.aspx`) to find out more about current availability and pricing.

With either Dreamweaver or Expression Web, you can draw a layer directly on the Web page you're creating. You add text or images to the layer and then resize or relocate it on the page by clicking and dragging it freely. The result is some innovative page designs that don't conform to the usual grid.

Achieving consistency with Cascading Style Sheets

Cascading Style Sheets (CSS) are the tools of choice among designers who want to observe standards that have been established on the Internet and who want to make sure that their Web pages appear the same from browser to browser and from one computer to another. If you have a choice as to how you want to lay out a page, and you want to precisely position items while at the same time creating layouts that are easily updatable, I urge you to look into CSS.

CSS is a subject for a book all by itself, so I don't get into the subject in any great detail here. Suffice it to say that if you want to create full-featured, cutting-edge Web layouts, you need to use CSS. The major Web design programs — Dreamweaver and Expression Web — all support CSS designs. Rather than master CSS from scratch, choose one of these applications and let it do the work for you.

Standards such as CSS and XML are important because they enable you to reach the widest set of viewers possible. A *style sheet* is a document that contains the formatting for a Web page. By separating the formatting from the content, you quickly apply the same formatting to multiple Web pages. You can also update the design of an entire Web site easily: Rather than change a heading from Arial to Verdana 20 separate times on 20 Web pages, for example, you have to change it only once, and all the pages that have the style sheet *attached* to it have their headings updated all at one time.

When in doubt, hire a pro

Part of the fun of running your own business is doing things yourself. Most of the entrepreneurs I interviewed in the course of writing this book do their own Web page design work. They discovered how to create Web sites by reading books or taking classes on the subject. But in many cases, the initial cost of hiring someone to help you design your online business can be a good investment in the long run. Keep in mind that after you pay someone to help you develop a look, you can probably implement it in the future more easily yourself. For example:

✔ If you need business cards, stationery, brochures, or other printed material in addition to a Web site, hiring someone to develop a consistent look for everything at the beginning is worth the money.

✔ You can pay a designer to get you started with a logo, color selections, and page layouts. Then you can save money by adding text yourself.

✔ If, like me, you're artistically impaired, consider the benefits of having your logo or other artwork drawn by a real artist.

Most professional designers charge $40–$60 per hour for their work. You can expect a designer to spend five or six hours to create a logo or template. But if your company uses that initial design for the foreseeable future, you're not really paying that much per year.

Chapter 6

Making Shopping Easy on Your E-Commerce Site

*W*alk into any Wal-Mart or other megastore and you're likely to feel overwhelmed with the sheer size of the place. Not to worry: Wal-Mart makes life (and spending money) easier for their shoppers by having an employee greet you at the door, ready to give directions, and by carefully arranging merchandise in aisles where management thinks you'll find them easily. Online businesses work much the same; in fact, shoppers want to move even more quickly and easily through an online store than a brick-and-mortar one. Your job is to make your sales items easy to find and purchase, and to make customers feel secure so that you're paid promptly and reliably. You also need to protect yourself financially and guard your business data. In this chapter, I discuss some technologies and strategies that can keep your data secure and make your customers feel at ease, too.

Fostering a good atmosphere for e-commerce is also a matter of presenting your merchandise clearly and making it easy for customers to choose and purchase it. Making changes to your Web site is relatively easy. You can remake your store's *front door* (your home page) in a matter of minutes. You can revamp your sales catalog in less than an hour. Making regular improvements and updates to your online store doesn't just mean changing the colors or the layout, which is the part of your operation that customers notice, on your Web site. It also means improving back-office functions that customers don't see, such as inventory management, invoices, labels, packing, and shipping. When you test, check, and revise your Web site based on its current performance, you can boost your revenue and increase sales as well as make your Web site more usable.

Here's a short list of what you need to do to be a successful e-commerce businessperson: Set up the right atmosphere for making purchases, provide options for payment, and keep sensitive information private. Oh, and don't forget that your main goal is to get goods to the customer safely and on time. In this chapter, I describe ways in which you can implement these essential online business strategies to ensure a positive shopping experience for your customers.

Giving Online Shoppers What They Need

You've heard it before, but I can't emphasize enough the importance of understanding the needs of online shoppers and doing your best to meet those needs. That's the best way to end up with a healthy balance in your bank account.

Showing what you've got

Customers may end up buying an item in a brick-and-mortar store, but chances are good that they saw it online first. Shoppers now routinely assume that legitimate stores have a Web site and an online sales catalog that is likely to include even more items, accompanied by detailed descriptions, than a shopper would find by going to the store in person.

"It's not enough to just say we have this or that product line for sale. Until we actually add an individual item to our online store, with pictures and prices, we won't sell it," says Ernie Preston, who helped create an 84,000-item online catalog for a brick-and-mortar tool company that I profile later in this chapter. "As soon as you put it in your online catalog, you'll get a call about it. Shopping on the Web is the convenience factor that people want."

Don't be coy about your prices

Because most customers are comparison shopping, it's wise to put the cost, measurements, and other important features right next to each item to promote speed and convenience.

Microsoft Office 2010 gives you access to clip art images that help highlight sales items. Figure 6-1 shows an example of how you can edit an HTML Web page file with Word by inserting an image from the Clip Art task pane. (You can find more clip art images at the Microsoft Office Clip Art and Media Center, office.microsoft.com/clipart/default.aspx.)

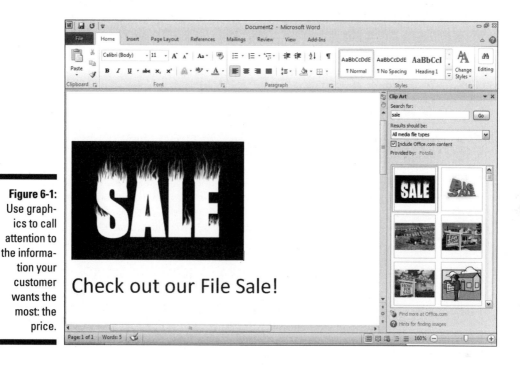

Figure 6-1:
Use graphics to call attention to the information your customer wants the most: the price.

Earning trust to gain a sale

Although e-commerce is more and more common, many customers who are relatively new still need to have their fears addressed. They want to be sure that providing their names, phone numbers, and credit card information won't lead to identity theft. Shoppers who are old pros at shopping online want to avoid being flooded with unwanted e-mails. In regard to the sale at hand, many fear that merchandise will be paid for but not received.

State your policies clearly and often, providing assurance that you don't give out personal data without consent. If you plan to accept credit card orders, get an account with a Web host that provides a *secure server,* which is software that encrypts data exchanged with a browser. Be sure to include comments from satisfied customers. If you run an eBay Store or a store on another marketplace such as Bonanzle (www.bonanzle.com), your feedback rating provides assurance.

If you're a member in good standing with the Better Business Bureau (www.bbb.org), you may be eligible to join the BBBOnLine program (www.bbbonline.org) to build credibility and confidence among your clients. Businesses that participate in the BBBOnLine program show their commitment to their customers by displaying a BBBOnLine Reliability Seal or Privacy Seal on their Web sites.

Giving the essentials

Remember that one of the big advantages of operating a business online is space. Not only do you have plenty of room in which to provide full descriptions of your sale items but you also have no reason to skimp on the details that you provide about your business and services. Here are some suggestions of how to provide information that your customer may want:

- ✔ If you sell clothing, include a page with size and measurement charts.
- ✔ If you sell food, provide weights, ingredients, and nutritional information.
- ✔ If you sell programming, Web design, or traditional graphic design, provide samples of your work, links to Web pages you've created, and testimonials from satisfied clients.
- ✔ If you're a musician, publish a link to at least one short sound file of your work.

Don't be reluctant to tell people how your products and services are better than others. Visit the Lands' End online catalog (www.landsend.com) for good examples of how this well-established marketer describes the quality of its wares.

Managing Goods and Services

Shoppers on the Web are continually in search of The New: the next new product, the latest price reduction or rebate, the latest comment in a blog, or today's headlines. As a provider of content, whether it's in the form of words, images, or products for sale, your job is to manage that content to keep it fresh and available. You also need to replenish stock when it's purchased, handle returns, and deal with shipping options, as I describe in the sections that follow.

Handling returns

Your returns policy depends on the venue where you make your sales. If you sell primarily on eBay or another marketplace, you should accept returns, if only because many of the most experienced and successful sellers do, too. That doesn't mean you need to accept every single item that is returned. Most businesses place restrictions on when they'll receive a return and send a refund. The items must be returned within 14 days, for instance; the packages must be unopened; the merchandise must not be damaged.

Adding shipping rates

As part of creating a usable e-commerce catalog, provide customers with shipping costs for your merchandise. Shipping rates can be difficult to calculate. They depend on your own geographic location as well as the location to which you're planning to ship. If you're a small-scale operation and you process each transaction manually, you may want to ship everything a standard way (UPS ground, FedEx Home Delivery, or USPS Parcel Post). Then you can keep a copy of your shipper's charges with you and calculate each package's shipping cost individually.

You can also save time by using the quick shipping calculator provided by iShip (`www.iship.com`). Just go to the site's home page, enter the origin and destination ZIP Codes, and click Go. You get a set of shipping rates from DHL, UPS, and USPS so that you can pick the most cost-effective option. If you want some help with shipping, you can set up your site with the help of a transaction hosting service, such as ChannelAdvisor (`www.channeladvisor.com`). This company has an agreement with the USPS so that it automatically calculates shipping charges and includes those charges in the invoices it sends to your customers.

If you sell the same type of item all the time, such as a particular type of clothing, you can provide flat-rate shipping by using a method such as the U.S. Postal Service's Priority Mail option. You can even add a few dollars to the purchase price to cover the standard shipping charge to most locations in the U.S. and offer free shipping to your domestic customers.

Maintaining inventory

Shoppers on the Web want things to happen instantly. If they discover that you're out of stock for an item they want, they're likely to switch to another online business rather than wait for you to restock that item. With that in mind, obey the basic principle of planning to be successful: Rather than order the bare minimum of this or that item, make sure that you have enough to spare. Too much inventory initially is better than running out at some point.

Rely on software or management services to help you keep track of what you have. If you feel at ease working with databases, record your initial inventory in an Access or SQL database. A database forces you to record each sale manually so that you know how many items are left. You could connect your sales catalog to your database by using a program such as ColdFusion from Adobe (www.adobe.com/products/coldfusion). Such a program can update the database on the fly when sales are made. But you may need to hire someone with Web programming experience to set up the system for you and make sure that it actually works.

If you sign up with an online store solution, such as Yahoo! Small Business or a sales management provider such as Marketworks Solutions from ChannelAdvisor (www.channeladvisor.com/mw/), inventory is tracked automatically for you. Whether you do the work yourself or hire an outside service, you have to be able to answer basic questions such as

- **When should you reorder?** Establish *reorder points* — points at which you automatically reorder supplies (when you get down to two or three items left, for instance).

- **How many do you have in stock right now?** Make sure that you have enough merchandise on hand, not only for everyday demand but also in case a product gets hot or the holiday season brings about a dramatic increase in orders.

An e-commerce hosting service can also help you with questions that go beyond the basics, such as the past purchasing history of customers. Knowing what customers have purchased in the past gives you the ability to suggest *up-sells* — additional items the person might want. But in the early stages, making sure that you have a cushion of additional inventory for the time when your site becomes a big success is your primary responsibility.

Keeping Your Web Site in Top Shape

The job of your hosting service or ISP is, of course, to monitor traffic and make sure that your Web site is up and running. But unless you keep an eye on your site and its availability to your customers, you may not be aware of technical problems that can scare potential business away. If your site is offline periodically or your server crashes or works slowly, it doesn't just waste your customers' time — it can cut directly into your sales.

If your site doesn't work well, a potential customer can find another site whose pages load more quickly just a few mouse clicks away. Outages can be costly, too. The Business Insider reported that an outage that hit the popular online payment service PayPal in summer 2009 cost businesses between $7 and $32 million. The site was offline for about 4 and a half hours. Sears' Web site suffered intermittent service disruptions on an especially bad day — "Black Friday," the day after Thanksgiving, 2008 — a day when competing retailers' Web sites were receiving millions of visits.

Using software to keep score

Although they take some effort to install, a number of programs are available for between $30 and $200 that continually keep an eye on your Web site and notify you of any problems. WebCheck is a utility that automatically checks your site and alerts you if it goes down or a page is accidentally renamed or deleted. You configure WebCheck to check your site's URLs; you can have the program load the URLs once a minute or even once every second (faster checking may slow down your site's performance, however). You can be notified by e-mail, fax, pop-up browser window, or taskbar icon. You can download WebCheck from the IT Utils Web site (www.itutils.com).

Some companies offer such monitoring as a service. You use the company's software, which resides on its computers, not yours. For example, @Watch (www.atwatch.com) provides an online service that checks your site's images and links periodically to see if everything is working correctly. The company offers several levels of service. The @Watch Advanced version costs $12.99 per month and checks your site once every 30 minutes. For $33.99 per month, the program will check your site every five minutes.

When your service goes out to lunch

Ideally, your Web host provides a page on its Web site that keeps track of its network status and records any recent problems. Receiving *one* site monitoring notification (from a program you install yourself or one that you "rent" as a service from an ASP — see the next section, "Outsourcing your business needs") probably isn't cause for concern. However, when you receive a *series* of notifications, call your Web hosting service and tell technical support exactly what the problems are/were.

If the problem with your site is a slow response to requests from Web browsers rather than a complete outage, the problem may be that your server is slow because you're sharing it with other Web sites. Consider moving from shared hosting to a different option. In *co-location,* you purchase the server on which your files reside, but the machine is located at your Web host's facility rather than at your own location. Your site is the only one on your machine. You also get the reliability of the host's technical support and high-speed Internet connection.

If you really need bandwidth, consider a *dedicated server.* In this case, you rent space on a machine that is dedicated to serving your site. This arrangement is far more expensive than sharing a Web server, and you should choose it only if the number of visits to your site at any one time becomes too great for a shared server to handle. You'll know that a shared server is becoming overtaxed if your site is slow to load.

Outsourcing your business needs

One of the most effective ways to save time and money doing business online is to let someone else install and maintain the computer software that you use. *Outsourcing* is a term whose use is increasingly common, but in terms of e-commerce, it refers to the practice of using a service to perform various tasks for you, such as Web hosting, form creation, or financial record keeping, rather than installing software and running it on your own computer. Outsourcing simply refers to the practice of having an outside company provide services for your business.

One of the companies that provides Web-based services on an outsourced basis is an *application service provider* (ASP). An ASP is a company that makes business or other applications available on the Web. For instance, when you fill out a form and create a Web page on CafePress.com (which I describe in Chapter 12), you're using CafePress.com as an ASP. Rather than create your Web page on your own computer, you use an application on the CafePress.com site and store your Web page information there.

How an ASP can help your company

You have to pay a monthly fee to use an ASP's services. You may incur installation fees, and you may have to sign a one- or two-year contract. In return, ASPs provide benefits to your company that include the following:

- ✔ **Payroll and administration:** AquaPrix, Inc. (`www.aquaprix.com`), a small Hayward, California, water systems distribution company, outsources some of its payroll functions to a company — QuikPay — for about $100 per month.

- ✔ **Tech support:** ComponentControl (`www.componentcontrol.com`) licenses software that enables aerospace companies to locate and trade aviation parts. Rather than travel all over the country to solve every problem that users encounter with its software, ComponentControl's tech support staff uses Desktop Streaming, an online application that enables them to "see" the problem a customer is encountering. ComponentControl can also show customers how to use the software from its own offices, which saves on travel costs and reduces the time to solve problems by 30 percent.

✔ **Online form creation:** FormSite.com (`www.formsite.com`) is a leader in creating a variety of forms that can help online shoppers provide essential functions, such as subscribing to newsletters or other publications, asking for information about your goods and services, or providing you with shipping or billing information. The sample pizza order form, shown in Figure 6-2, is an example of the type of form that this particular ASP can help you create.

✔ **Marketing and survey data gathering online:** LeadMaster (`www.leadmaster.com`) calls itself a "Web-based data mining tool." You store your customer information with LeadMaster, and LeadMaster provides you with an online database that you can access any time with your Web browser. LeadMaster enables you to develop mailing lists based on your customer database. You can use LeadMaster's online tools to do sales forecasting and develop surveys that give you a better idea of what your customers need and want.

Although ASPs can help you in many ways, they require research, interviewing, contract review, and an ongoing commitment on your part. I illustrate the potential pluses and minuses of outsourcing in Table 6-1.

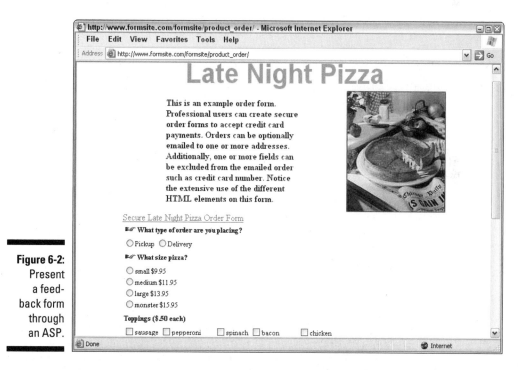

Figure 6-2:
Present a feedback form through an ASP.

Table 6-1	Outsourcing Benefits and Risks
Pros	**Cons**
Better customer service: By outsourcing scheduling or other functions, businesses give customers increased options for interacting with them online. Customers don't have to call or e-mail the company; in the case of online scheduling, customers can schedule or cancel appointments by accessing the company's online calendar.	**A contract is required:** When ASPs first began to appear in the late 1990s, they spoke in terms of "renting" software. These days, ASPs usually allow customers to try their services for a while, but then offer long-term contracts. The terms of these contracts can range from one to three years. Don't get yourself locked in to a long-term arrangement that prevents you from trying cheaper or better alternatives down the road.
Greater Web site functionality: ASPs enable your site to provide better service to your customers and allow you to get more work done.	**ASPs face stiff competition:** Many ASPs have failed in recent years. Make sure that the companies you sign agreements with will be around for a while by talking to current customers and reviewing résumés of senior staff and key employees. Scan the Web for any press releases or articles that serve as warning signs about the ASP's financial health.
Expanded scope: You don't have to become proficient in subjects that aren't part of your core business or expertise.	**Security risks:** The moment you hand over your business data to another online firm or give outside companies access to your internal network, you risk theft of data or virus infections from hackers. Make sure that the ASPs you work with use encryption and other Internet security measures.

In many cases, ASPs can provide a software solution and customize it to your needs. Outsourcing not only improves your company's bottom line but also helps you convey your message to potential customers that you might never reach otherwise.

Doing your homework before you sign up

After you try the software or other service that you want to lease, you usually need to sign a contract. This is the time to read the fine print. Contracts can last for 12 to 50 months; make sure that you don't get locked in to one that's longer than you need. You have a better chance of getting the service you want if you do the following:

✔ **Understand pricing schemes:** Some ASPs charge on a "per-employee" basis, whereas others charge "per-seat" fees based on each registered user. Still others charge "per-CPU," which means you're charged for each machine that runs the hosted application.

✔ **Pin down startup fees:** Virtually all ASPs charge a startup fee, or a service implementation fee, when you sign the contract. Make sure that the fee covers installation and any customization that you'll need.

✔ **Don't accept just any SLA:** Obtaining a *service level agreement* (SLA), a document that spells out what services you expect an ASP (or other vendor) to provide, is essential. But don't hesitate to add, delete, and change sections so that your needs are met.

Paula M. Hunter, vice-president of sales and marketing for cMeRun Corp (an ASP) and the president of the ASP Industry Consortium, says, "The SLA and/or hosting contract should outline additional monthly fees for data backup and recovery (often, these items are included). It's also important to review the contract regarding help desk support and any fees, which would be associated with placing support calls to the ASP."

✔ **Avoid "gotcha" fees:** Pricing arrangements are hardly standard with regard to ASPs. Some of the big hidden costs involve personalizing or customizing the service to adapt to legacy systems. You should ask these questions to avoid unpleasant surprises: Is there an additional cost for customizing or personalizing the application? Does it cost extra to back up my company's data and recover it if one of my computers goes down? Is help desk support included in my monthly fee, or will you charge me every time I call with a question or problem?

✔ **Make sure that your information is secure:** Some huge security risks are associated with transmitting your information across the wide-open spaces of the Internet. Make sure that your ASP takes adequate security measures to protect your data by asking informed questions, such as: Is my data protected by SSL encryption? Do you run a virtual private network? How often do you back up your customers' data?

If the answer to any of these questions seems inadequate, move on to the next ASP.

Keeping Your Business Safe

Working at home or even in a small office carries its own set of safety concerns for small business owners. Chances are, you don't have an IT professional at hand to make sure that your files and your network are safe from intrusion. Some safe computing practices, such as using password protection, making backups, and installing antivirus software, can go a long way toward keeping your data secure, even if you never have to get into more technical subjects such as public-key encryption.

Separating the personal and the professional

Many entrepreneurs who run businesses from their homes face a simple logistical problem: Their work takes over their home. Boxes, computers, phones, and other gadgets create disruptions that can drive everyone crazy. Following are some simple steps that can help you set more clearly defined boundaries between work and domestic life.

When the computer is a group sport

A lot to can be said for having at least two separate computers — one for personal use and one for business use. The idea is that you set up your system so that you have to log on to your business computer with a user-name and password. (For suggestions on how to devise a good password that's difficult to crack, see the section, "Picking passwords that are hard to guess," later in this chapter.)

If you have only one computer, passwords can still provide a measure of protection from other users in your house. Windows gives you the ability to set up different user profiles, each associated with its own password. User profiles and passwords don't necessarily protect your business files, but they convey to your family members that they should use their own software, stick to their own directories, and not try to explore your company data.

 Folder Guard, a program by WinAbility Software3 Corporation (www. winability.com/folderguard), enables you to hide or password-protect files or folders on your computer. The software works with all current versions of Windows. You can choose from the Standard version, which is intended for home users, or the Professional version, which is designed for business customers. A 30-day trial version is available for download from the WinAbility Web site; if you want to keep the Standard version of Folder Guard, you have to pay $29.95 (or $59.95 for the Professional version).

One phone may not be enough

Having a devoted phone line not only makes your business seem more serious but also separates your business calls from your personal calls. If you need a phone line to connect to the Internet, you then have a choice of which line to use for your modem.

The next step is to set up your business phone with its own answering machine or voice mail. You can then install privacy features, such as caller ID, on your business line as needed.

One place that provides tips and news on telephone service, not only for small businesses but also for personal use, is the Telecommunications Research & Action Center. Visit the group's Web site (www.trac.org) and read how to make smart decisions on telephone service for your home and business.

Heading off disasters

An old joke about the telegram from a mother reads, "Worry. Details to follow." When you're lying awake at night, you can be anxious about all sorts of grim disasters: flood, fire, theft, computer virus, you name it. Prevention is always better than a cure, so this chapter covers steps you can take to prevent problems. Should a problem arise, however, you do have some ways to recover more easily if you're prepared.

Insurance . . . the least you can do

I can think of ways to spend money that are a whole lot more fun than paying insurance premiums. Yet there I am every month, writing checks to protect myself in case something goes wrong with my house, car, body, and so on. And yes, there's another item to add to the list: protecting my business investment by obtaining insurance that specifically covers me against hardware damage, theft, and loss of data. You can also go a step further and obtain a policy that covers the cost of data entry or equipment rental that would be necessary to recover your business information. Here are some specific strategies:

- Make a list of all your hardware and software and how much each item cost, and store a copy of it in a place such as a fireproof safe or safe-deposit box.

- Take photos of your computer setup in case you need to make an insurance claim. Put the photos in the same safe place as your list of hardware and software.

- Save your electronic files on CD or DVD and put the disc in a safe storage location, such as a safe-deposit box.

Investigate the many options available to you for insuring your computer hardware and software. Your current homeowner's or renter's insurance may offer coverage, but make sure that the dollar amount is sufficient for replacement. You may also want to look into the computer hardware and software coverage provided by Safeware, The Insurance Agency, Inc. (www.safeware.com).

Think ahead to the unthinkable

The Gartner Group estimates that two out of five businesses that experience a major disaster will go out of business within five years. I would guess that the three that are able to get back up on their feet and running quickly are those that already had recovery plans in place. Even if your company is small, be prepared for trouble such as floods, hurricanes, or tornadoes. A recovery effort might include the following strategies:

- ✔ **Backup power systems:** What will you do if the power goes out and you can't access the Web? You need a backup power device — an electrical device that provides you with power in case your home or office electricity goes out. You can buy a backup power system for less than $50 at office supply stores or from Amazon.com.

- ✔ **Data storage:** This is probably the most practical and essential disaster recovery step for small or home-based businesses. Back up your files on a computer that's not located in the place where you physically work. At the very least, upload your files periodically to the Web space that your hosting service gives you. Also consider storing your files with an online storage service.

- ✔ **Telecommunications:** Having some alternative method of communication available in case your phone system goes down ensures that you're always in touch. The obvious choice is a cellphone. Also, set up a voice mailbox so that customers and vendors can leave messages for you even if you can't answer the phone.

Creating a plan is a waste of time if you don't regularly set aside time to keep it up-to-date. Back up your data on a regular basis, purchase additional equipment if you need it, and make arrangements to use other computers and offices if you need to — in other words, *implement* your plan. You owe it not only to yourself but also to your customers to be prepared in case of disaster.

Antivirus protection without a needle

As an online businessperson, you download files, receive discs from customers and vendors, and exchange e-mail with all sorts of people you've never met before. Surf safely by installing antivirus programs, such as

- ✔ **Norton Internet Security by Symantec Corporation** (`www.symantec.com/product`): This application, which includes an antivirus program as well as a firewall and lists for $69.99, automates many security functions and is especially good for beginners. A standalone version, Norton Anti-Virus, is available for $49.99, but I highly recommend the more full-featured package, which includes a firewall that blocks many other dangerous types of intrusions, such as Trojan horses.

- ✔ **AVG AntiVirus** (`www.avg.com`): Many users who find Norton Internet Security too intrusive (it leaves lots of files on your computer and consumes a great deal of memory) turn to this product, which comes in a free version as well as a fuller-featured version for $49.99.

- ✔ **Avira AntiVir Personal Edition Classic by H+BEDV** (`www.free-av.com`): Another popular free program.

✔ **VirusScan by McAfee (**www.mcafee.com/us**):** This is the leading competitor to Norton Anti-Virus, which comes bundled with Norton Internet Security. VirusScan is included in McAfee Internet Security, which includes a firewall and costs $44.99.

I love gadgets, and few things get me more excited than handheld devices, laptops, and other portable computing devices. But those devices, too, need protection from harmful software. You can install protection software designed especially for mobile devices, such as VirusScan Mobile by McAfee (http://us.mcafee.com/root/product.asp?productid=mobile_info).

Protecting your equipment from viruses is another area that demands your attention on a regular basis. Viruses change all the time, and new ones appear regularly. The antivirus program you install one day may not be able to handle the viruses that appear just a few weeks or months later. You may want to pick an antivirus program that doesn't charge excessive amounts for regular updates (for instance, charging you for a new version every year). Also check the ICSA's Product Testing Reports (go to www.icsalabs.com).

A visible sign that you're trustworthy

Same as with the office assistant whose work is visible only when he or she is not doing a good job, your site may be squeaky clean, but your customers won't know that unless you display a "seal of approval" from a reputable online organization. The two best-known seals (which are actually images you add to your Web pages to show visitors you're reputable) are TRUSTe and BBBOnline.

The nonprofit organization TRUSTe was created to boost the degree of trust that Web surfers have in the Internet. It does this through a third-party oversight "seal" program. If you demonstrate to TRUSTe that you're making efforts to keep your visitors' personal data secure, and if you pledge not to share your customers' data and to publish a privacy statement on your site, TRUSTe issues you a seal of approval that you can place on your site's home page. The TRUSTe seal is intended to function as the online equivalent of the Good Housekeeping seal of approval on a product.

By itself, the seal doesn't keep hackers from breaking into your site and stealing your data. That's still up to you. Earning the seal and displaying it on your site just gives visitors a reason to feel better about using your services. The TRUSTe site provides you with a wizard that leads you through the process of generating a privacy statement for your site. The statement tells visitors how you protect their information. Find out more by visiting the TRUSTe home page (www.truste.org) and clicking the For Businesses link.

BBBOnline, the Web-based arm of the Better Business Bureau, has a similar program for commercial Web sites. The BBBOnline Reliability Seal Program has several eligibility requirements, including a physical location in the U.S. or Canada, a business record for at least a year, a satisfactory complaint-handling record, membership in the Better Business Bureau, and a commitment to resolve disputes and respond promptly to consumer complaints. Find out more at www.bbbonline.org.

Installing firewalls and other safeguards

You probably know how important a firewall for your personal files and hardware. Firewalls filter out unwanted intrusions, such as executable programs that hackers seek to plant on your file system so that they can use your computer for their own purposes. When you're starting an online business, the objectives of a firewall become different: You're protecting not just your own information but also that of your customers. In other words, you're quite possibly relying on the firewall to protect your source of income as well as the data on your computers.

A *firewall* is an application or hardware device that monitors the data flowing into or out of a computer network and that filters the data based on criteria that the owner sets up. Acting like a security guard at the entrance to a building, a firewall scans the packets of digital information that traverse the Internet, making sure that the data is headed for the right destination and that it doesn't match known characteristics of viruses or attacks. Authorized traffic is allowed into your network. Attack attempts or viruses are either deleted automatically or cause an alert message to appear, to which you must respond with a decision to block or allow the incoming or outgoing packets.

Keeping out Trojan horses and other unwanted visitors

A *Trojan horse* is a program that enters your computer surreptitiously and then attempts to do something without your knowledge. Some folks say that such programs enter your system through a "backdoor" because you don't immediately know that they've entered your system. Trojan horses may come in the form of an e-mail attachment with the filename extension .exe (which stands for *executable*). For instance, I recently received an e-mail that purported to be from Microsoft Corporation and claimed to contain a security update. The attachment looked innocent enough, but had I saved the attachment to my computer, it would have used my computer as a staging area for distributing itself to many other e-mail addresses.

I didn't run into trouble, however. My firewall program recognized the attachment and alerted me to the danger. I highly recommend that anyone who, like me, has a cable modem, DSL, or other direct connection to the Internet install a firewall right away. You can try out the shareware program ZoneAlarm by Zone Labs, Inc. (www.zonealarm.com), that provides you with basic firewall protection, although more full-featured programs such as Norton Internet Security (www.symantec.com/product) are probably more effective.

Low- and high-tech locks

If you play the word game with a Web surfer or Web site and say "security," you're likely to get a response such as "encryption." But security doesn't need to start with software. The fact is, all the firewalls and passwords in the world won't help you if someone breaks into your home office and trashes it or makes off with the computer that contains all your files.

Besides insuring your computer equipment and taking photos in case you need to get it replaced, you can also invest in locks for your home office and your machines. They might not keep someone from breaking into your house, but they'll at least make it more difficult for intruders to carry off your hardware.

Here are some suggestions for how to protect your hardware and the business data your computers contain:

✔ **Lock your office:** Everyone has locks on the outer doors of their house, but you can go a step further and install a deadbolt lock on your office door.

✔ **Lock your computers:** Innovative Security Products (www.wesecure.com) offers several varieties of computer locking systems. It also sells ultraviolet pens that you can use to mark your equipment with your name and the serial number of your computer in case the police recover it.

✔ **Mark your modem:** Unbeknownst to someone who's up to no good, an innovative theft recovery system called CompuTrace can be installed on your hard drive. Then if your computer is stolen, the software is activated. When the thief connects its internal modem to a phone line, the authorities are notified. The system works with other types of Internet connections as well, including DSL and cable modems. CompuTrace Plus (www.absolute.com) is offered by Absolute Software Corp. and costs home office users $49.95 for one year of monitoring.

✔ **Make backups:** Be sure to regularly back up your information on Zip drives, USB drives, CDs, or similar storage devices. Also consider signing up with a Web-based storage service where files can be transferred from your computer. That way, if your computers and your extra storage disks are lost for whatever reason, you have an online backup in a secure location. Look into the online backup options mentioned in Chapter 3 for some free or low-cost options.

Cleaning out spyware

Watch out for software that "spies" on your Web surfing and other activities and then reports these activities to advertisers, potentially invading your privacy. Ad-Aware isn't a firewall, exactly, but it's a useful program that detects and erases any advertising programs you may have downloaded from the Internet without knowing it. Such advertising programs might be running on your computer, consuming your processing resources and slowing down operations. Some spyware programs track your activities when you surf the Web; others simply report that they have been installed. Many users regard these spyware programs as invasions of privacy because they install themselves and do their reporting without your asking for it or even knowing they're active.

When I ran Ad-Aware the first time, it detected a whopping 57 programs I didn't know about that were running on my computer and that had installed themselves when I connected to various Web sites or downloaded software. As you can see in Figure 6-3, when I ran Ad-Aware while I was working on this chapter, sure enough, it found four suspicious software components running.

I highly recommend Ad-Aware; you can download a version at `www.lava softUSA.com` and try it for free. If you decide to keep it, you pay a $15 share-ware fee.

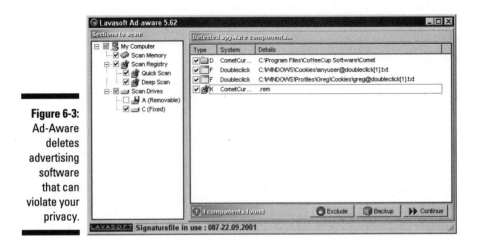

Figure 6-3:
Ad-Aware deletes advertising software that can violate your privacy.

Positioning the firewall

These days, most home networks are configured so that the computers on the network can share information as well as the same Internet connection. Whether you run a home-based business or a business in a discrete location, you almost certainly have a network of multiple computers. A network is far more vulnerable than a single computer connected to the Internet: A network has more entry points than a single computer, and more reliance is placed on each of the operators of those computers to observe good safety practices. And if one computer on the network is attacked, others have real potential to be attacked as well.

You probably are acquainted with software firewalls, such as Norton Personal Firewall or Zone Alarm. Software firewalls protect one computer at a time. In a typical business scenario, however, multiple computers share a single Internet connection through a router that functions as a gateway. Many network admin-istrators prefer a *hardware firewall* — a device that functions as a filter for traffic both entering and leaving it. A hardware firewall may also function as a router, but it can also be separate from the router. The device is positioned at the perimeter of the network, where it can protect all the company's comput-ers simultaneously. One example of this type of hardware is the WatchGuard Firebox X10e, by WatchGuard (`www.watchguard.com`). It costs about $480.

Companies that want to provide a Web site that the public can visit as well as secure e-mail and other communications services create a secure subnetwork of one or more specially hardened computers. (*Hardened* means they're secured because all unnecessary services have been removed from them.) This kind of network is called a *Demilitarized Zone* (DMZ).

Keeping your firewall up-to-date

Firewalls work by means of *attack signatures* (or *definitions*), which are sets of data that identify a connection attempt as a potential attack. Some attacks are easy to stop: They've been attempted for years, and the amateur hackers who attempt intrusions don't give much thought to them. The more danger-ous attacks are new ones. These have signatures that emerged after you installed your firewall.

You quickly get a dose of reality and find just how serious the problem is by visiting one of the Web sites that keeps track of the latest attacks, such as the Distributed Intrusion Detection System or DShield (www.dshield.org). On the day I visited, DShield reported that the "survival time" for an *unpatched computer* (a computer that has security software that isn't equipped with the latest updates called *patches*) after connecting it to the Internet was only 16 minutes. Therefore, such a computer only has 16 minutes before someone tries to attack it. If that doesn't scare you into updating your security soft-ware, I don't know what will.

Providing security with public keys

The conversations I overhear while I drive my teenage daughters and their friends to events leave no doubt in my mind that different segments of soci-ety use code words that only their members can understand. Even comput-ers use encoding and decoding to protect information they exchange on the Internet. The schemes used online are far more complex and subtle than the slang used by kids, however. This section describes the security method that is used most widely on the Internet, and the one you're likely to use yourself: Secure Sockets Layer (SSL) encryption.

The keys to public-key/private-key encryption

Terms such as *SSL* and *encryption* might make you want to reach for the remote. But don't be too quick to switch channels. SSL is making it safer to do business online and boosting the trust of potential customers. Anything that makes shoppers more likely to spend money online is something you need to know about.

The term *encryption* is the process of encoding data, especially sensitive data, such as credit card numbers. Information is encrypted by means of complex mathematical formulas — *algorithms*. Such a formula may trans-form a simple-looking bit of information into a huge block of seemingly incomprehensible numbers, letters, and characters. Only someone who has the right formula, called a *key* (which is a complex mass of encoded data), can decode the gobbledygook.

Here's a very simple example. Suppose that my credit card number is `12345`, and I encode it by using an encryption formula into something like the following: `1aFgHx203gX4gLu5cy`.

The algorithm that generated this encrypted information may say something like: "Take the first number, multiply it by some numeral, and then add some letters to it. Then take the second number, divide it by x, and add y characters to the result," and so on. (In reality, the formulas are far more complex than this, which is why you usually have to pay a license fee to use them. But this is the general idea.) Someone who has the same formula can run it in reverse, so to speak, to decrypt the encoded number and obtain the original number, `12345`.

In practice, the encoded numbers that are generated by encryption routines and transmitted over the Internet are very large. They vary in size depending on the relative strength (or *uncrackability*) of the security method used. Some methods generate keys that consist of 128 bits of data. A *data bit* is a single unit of digital information. These formulas are *128-bit keys*.

Encryption is the cornerstone of security on the Internet. The most widely used security schemes, such as the Secure Sockets Layer protocol (SSL), the Secure Electronic Transactions protocol (SET), and Pretty Good Privacy (PGP), all use some form of encryption.

With some security methods, the party that sends the data and the party that receives it both use the same key (a method known as *symmetrical encryption*). This approach isn't considered as secure as an asymmetrical encryption method, such as public-key encryption, however. In public-key encryption, the originating party obtains a license to use a security method. (In the following section, I show you just how to do this yourself.) As part of the license, you use the encryption algorithm to generate your own private key. You never share this key with anyone. However, you use the private key to create a separate public key. This public key goes out to visitors who connect to a secure area of your Web site. When they have your public key, users can encode sensitive information and send it back to you. Only you can decode the data — by using your secret, private key.

Getting a certificate without going to school

When purchasing an item via the Internet, however, how do people know that sellers are who they say they are when all the buyer has to go on is a URL or an e-mail address? The solution in the online world is to obtain a personal certificate that you can send to Web site visitors or append to your e-mail messages.

How certificates work

A *certificate,* which is also sometimes dubbed a Digital ID, is an electronic document issued by a certification authority (CA). The certificate contains the owner's personal information as well as a public key that can be exchanged with others online. The public key is generated by the owner's private key, which the owner obtains during the process of applying for the certificate.

In issuing the certificate, the CA takes responsibility for saying that the owner of the document is the same as the person actually identified on the certificate. Although the public key helps establish the owner's identity, certificates do require you to put a level of trust in the agency that issues it.

A certificate helps both you and your customers. A certificate assures your customers that you're the person you say you are, plus it protects your e-mail communications by enabling you to encrypt them.

Obtaining a certificate from VeriSign

Considering how important a role certificates play in online security, obtaining one is remarkably easy. You do so by applying and paying a licensing fee to a CA. One of the most popular CAs is VeriSign, Inc., which lets you apply for a certificate called a *Class 1 Digital ID.*

A Class 1 Digital ID is useful only for securing personal communications. As an e-commerce Web site owner, you may want a business-class certificate called a 128-bit SSL Global Server ID (`www.verisign.com/products/site`). This form of Digital ID works only if your e-commerce site is hosted on a server that runs *secure server software* — software that encrypts transactions — such as Apache Stronghold. Check with your Web host to see whether a secure server is available for your Web site.

A VeriSign personal certificate, which you can use to authenticate yourself in e-mail, news, and other interactions on the Internet, costs $19.95 per year, and you can try a free certificate for 60 days. Follow these steps to obtain your Digital ID:

1. **Go to the VeriSign, Inc., Digital IDs for Secure E-Mail page at**

   ```
   www.verisign.com/authentication/individual-
        authentication/digital-id/index.html
   ```

2. **Click the Buy Now button regardless of whether you're certain you want an ID or want the trial version.**

   The Digital ID Enrollment page appears.

   A page may appear (if you don't have JavaScript support) that asks you to identify the Web browser you use most often and that you want to associate with the Digital ID. Click the browser you want. An application form for a Digital ID appears.

3. **Complete the application form.**

   The application process is pretty simple. The form asks for your personal information and a challenge phrase that you can use in case anyone is trying to impersonate you. This also requires you to accept a license agreement. (You don't need to enter credit card information if you select the 60-day trial option.) Make sure that you select the box for adding a private key; you'll need it in Step 4.

4. **Click the Accept button at the bottom of the screen.**

   A dialog box appears asking you to confirm your e-mail address. After you confirm by clicking OK, a dialog box appears asking you to choose a password. When you enter a password and click OK, VeriSign uses your password to generate a private key for you. The private key is an essential ingredient in public-key/private-key technology.

5. **Click OK to have your browser generate your private key.**

   A page appears asking you to check your e-mail for further instructions. In a few minutes, you receive a message that contains a Digital ID PIN.

6. **In your e-mail program, open the new message from VeriSign Customer Support Department.**

7. **Use your mouse to highlight (or select) the PIN and then choose Edit⇨ Copy to copy the PIN.**

8. **Go to the URL for Digital ID Services that's included in the e-mail message and paste your PIN in the Enter the Digital ID Personal Identification Number (PIN) box.**

9. **Click Submit.**

   The certificate is generated, and the Digital IDF Installation and Registration Page appears.

10. **Click the Install button.**

    The ID from VeriSign downloads, and you can view it with your browser. Figure 6-4 shows my certificate for the Google Chrome browser. (Copying this ID, or anyone else's, is pointless because this is only your public key; the public key is always submitted with your private key, which is secret.)

After you have your Digital ID, what do you do with it? For one thing, you can use it to verify your identity to sites that accept certificate submissions. Some sites that require members to log in use secure servers that give you the option of submitting your certificate instead of entering the usual username and password to identify yourself. You can also attach your Digital ID to your e-mail messages to prove that your message is indeed coming from you. See your e-mail program's Help files for more specific instructions.

You can't encrypt or digitally sign messages on any computer other than the one to which your certificates are issued. If you're using a different computer than the one you used when you obtained your certificates, you must contact your certificate issuer and obtain a new certificate for the computer you're now using. Or, if your browser allows transfers, you can export your certificate to the new computer.

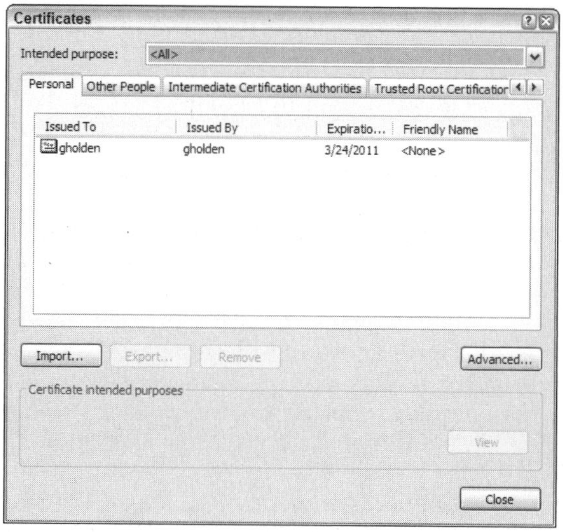

Figure 6-4:
A personal
certificate
assures
individuals
or Web sites
of your
identity.

Keeping other noses out of your business

Encryption isn't just for big businesses. Individuals who want to maintain their privacy, even while navigating the wilds of the Internet, can install special software or modify their existing e-mail programs to encode their online communications.

The CyberAngels Web site (www.cyberangels.org) presents some good tips and strategies for personal protection on the Internet.

Encryption software for the rest of us

PGP (Pretty Good Privacy), a popular encryption program, has been around for about as long as the Web itself. PGP lets you protect the privacy of your e-mail messages and file attachments by encrypting them so that only those with the proper authority can decipher the information. You can also digitally sign the messages and files you exchange, which assures the recipient that the messages come from you and the information hasn't been tampered with. You can even encrypt files on your own computer, too.

PGP (www.pgp.com) is a freely available personal encryption program. PGP is a *plug-in,* an application that works with another program to provide added functionality. You can integrate the program with popular e-mail programs such as Eudora and Microsoft Outlook.

To use either the free version of PGP or another, commercial version called PGP Personal Privacy, the first step is to obtain and install the program. After you install the program, you can use it to generate your own private-key/public-key pair. After you create a key pair, you can begin exchanging encrypted e-mail messages with other PGP users. To do so, you need to obtain a copy of their public keys, and they need a copy of your public key. Because public keys are just blocks of text, trading keys with someone is really quite easy. You can include your public key in an e-mail message, copy it to a file, or post it on a public-key server where anyone can get a copy at any time.

After you have a copy of someone's public key, you can add it to your *public keyring,* which is a file on your own computer. Then you can begin to exchange encrypted and signed messages with that individual. If you're using an e-mail application supported by the PGP plug-ins, you can encrypt and sign your messages by selecting the appropriate options from your application's toolbar. If your e-mail program doesn't have a plug-in, you can copy your e-mail message to your computer's Clipboard and encrypt it there by using PGP built-in functions. See the PGP User's Guide files for more specific instructions.

The commercial version of PGP's Encryption Platform runs on Windows 7, Vista, XP, Windows Server 2008, and the Mac OS 10.5 or later.

Encrypting e-mail messages

You can use your existing software to encrypt your mail messages rather than install a separate program such as PGP. In the following sections, I describe the steps involved in setting up the e-mail programs that come with the Big Two browser packages, Microsoft Internet Explorer and Firefox, to encrypt your messages.

If you use Outlook Express, you can use your Digital ID to do the following:

✔ **Send a digital signature:** You can digitally shrink-wrap your e-mail message by using your certificate in order to assure the recipient that the message is really from you.

✔ **Encrypt your message:** You can digitally encode a message to ensure that only the intended party can read it.

To better understand the technical details of how you can keep your e-mail communications secure, read the Digital ID User Guide, which you can access at

www.verisign.com/stellent/groups/public/documents/
guides/005326.pdf

After you have a digital ID, in order to actually make use of it, you need to follow these steps (which apply to Internet Explorer):

1. **After you obtain your own Digital ID, the first step is to associate it with your e-mail account. Choose Tools⇨Accounts.**

   The Internet Accounts dialog box appears.

2. **Click the Mail tab and then select your e-mail account and click Properties.**

   The Properties dialog box for your e-mail account appears.

3. **Click the Security tab to bring it to the front.**

4. **Click the Select button in the Signing Certificate section; then when the Select Default Account Digital ID dialog box appears, select your Digital ID.**

5. **Click OK to close the Select Default Account Digital ID dialog box; then click OK to close the Properties dialog box, and click Close to close the Internet Accounts dialog box.**

   You return to the main Outlook Express window.

6. **To send a digitally signed e-mail message to someone, click Create Message.**

   The New Message dialog box appears.

7. **Click either or both the security buttons at the extreme right of the toolbar, as shown in Figure 6-5.**

   The Sign button enables you to add your Digital ID. The Encrypt button lets you encrypt your message.

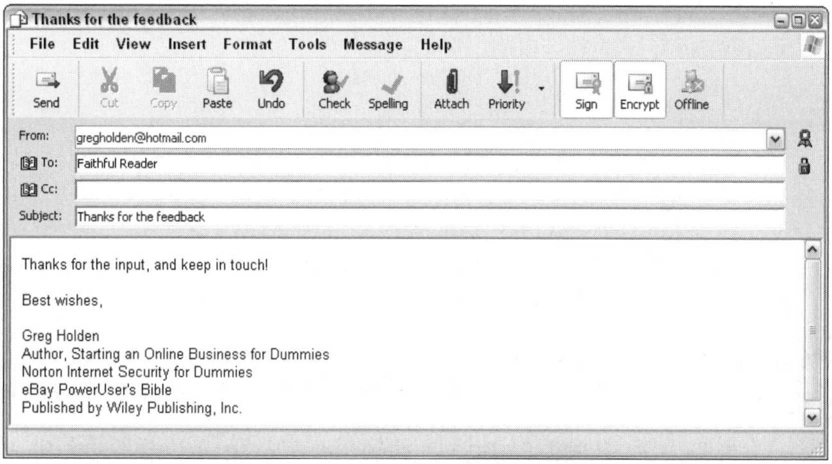

Figure 6-5: When you click the Sign and Encrypt buttons, your message goes out encrypted, with your certificate attached.

8. **Finish writing your message and then click the Send button.**

   Your encrypted or digitally signed message is sent on its way.

The preceding steps show you how to digitally sign or encrypt an individual message. You have to follow these steps every time you want to sign or encrypt a message. On the other hand, by selecting one or more of the options (Encrypt Contents and Attachments for all Outgoing Messages and Digitally Sign all Outgoing Messages) on the Security tab of the Options dialog box, you activate Outlook Express's built-in security features for *all* your outgoing messages. (You can still "turn off" the digital signature or encryption for an individual message by deselecting the Sign or Encrypt buttons in the toolbar of the New Message dialog box.)

If you use Mozilla Thunderbird, follow these steps (which apply to Thunderbird 3.0.4 or later) to encrypt your e-mail messages or include your certificate with them:

1. **With Thunderbird running, choose Tools⇨ Account Settings.**

   The Account Settings window appears.

2. **Click Security in the list of topics beneath your account name on the left side of the window.**

   The Security options appear on the right side of the window.

3. **In the Digital Signing section of the window, click Select.**

   The Select Certificate dialog box appears.

4. **Make sure the VeriSign, Inc. ID is displayed (choose this certificate from the drop-down list if it is not) and then click OK.**

   The Select Certificate dialog box closes. A dialog box appears asking whether you want to use the same certificate for reading and sending messages. Click OK to return to the Security settings.

5. **Select the Digitally Sign Messages (by default) check box and then click OK.**

   The Account Settings window closes, and you return to the main Messenger window.

6. **You can address and write your message and then click the Send button in the Message Composition toolbar.**

   Your encrypted or digitally signed message is sent on its way.

By checking one or more of the options in the Security dialog box, you activate Messenger's built-in security features for all your outgoing messages. In order to actually verify or undo those features (that is, if you want a message to be unencrypted or to be sent without a digital signature), you need to follow these additional steps:

1. **With any Messenger window open (Inbox, Message Center, or Message), click the Write toolbar button.**

   The Write window appears.

2. **In the Write window toolbar, click Security.**

   A drop-down list appears. A check mark appears next to the Encrypt This Message or Digitally Sign This Message options if you previously selected either option in the Security dialog box.

3. **If you want to undo either of these options, click the check box to deselect it.**

4. **You can now address and write your message and then click the Send button in the Write window` toolbar.**

   Your unencrypted or digitally unsigned message is sent on its way.

Picking passwords that are hard to guess

You put a lot of effort into picking the names of your kids and pets, and now you get to choose passwords. Whereas maybe you want others to think the names are cool, the point of creating a password is to make it difficult for thieves to figure out what it is. That is true whether you're protecting your own computer, downloading software, subscribing to an online publication, or applying for a certificate (as I explain earlier in this chapter).

One method for choosing a password is to take a familiar phrase and then use the first letter of each word to form the basis of a password. For example, the phrase "Every Good Boy Does Fine" would be EGBDF. Then mix uppercase and lowercase, add punctuation, and you wind up with eGb[d]f. If you *really* want to make a password that's hard to crack, add some numerals as well, such as the last two digits of the year you were born: eGb[d]f48.

Whatever you do, follow these tips for effective password etiquette:

- ✔ **Don't use passwords that are in a dictionary:** It takes time but not much effort for hackers to run a program that tries every word in an online dictionary as your password. So if it's in the dictionary, they'll eventually discover it.

- ✔ **Don't use the same password at more than one site:** Remembering more than one password is a pain, not to mention keeping track of which goes with what. Plus, you tend to accumulate lots of different passwords after you've been online for a while. But if you use the same password for each purpose and your password to one site on the Internet is compromised, all your password-protected accounts are in jeopardy.

- ✔ **Use at least six characters:** The more letters and numbers in your password, the more difficult you make the life of the code-crackers.

When it comes to passwords, duplication is not only boring but also dangerous. It's especially important not to reuse the password that you use to connect to your e-mail or your account with your Internet service provider as a password to an Internet site — or, worst of all, your online bank account. If a hacker discovers your password, that person can use it to read your e-mail or wreak havoc with your finances.

Chapter 7

Accepting Payments

Starting a new business and getting it online is exciting, but believe me, the real excitement occurs when you get paid for what you do. Nothing boosts your confidence and tells you that your hard work is paying off like receiving the proverbial check in the mail or having funds transferred to your business account.

The immediacy and interactivity of selling and promoting yourself online applies to receiving payments, too. You can get paid with just a few mouse clicks and some important data entered on your customer's keyboard. But completing an electronic commerce (*e-commerce* for short) transaction doesn't work the same way as in a traditional retail store. Online, customers can't personally hand you cash or a check. You, the seller, can't verify the user's identity by looking at a signature or photo ID.

In e-commerce, both buyers and sellers have the same concerns they've always had. Customers need a reliable way to pay you securely without worrying that their credit card information might be stolen. The seller needs to know that the customer isn't using a stolen credit card. Luckily, online payments are safer than ever, and more options exist than ever before.

To get paid promptly and reliably online, you have to go through some extra steps to make the customer feel secure — not to mention protecting yourself, too. Successful e-commerce is about setting up the right atmosphere for making purchases, providing options for payment, and keeping sensitive information private. It's also about making sure that the goods get to the customer safely and on time. In this chapter, I describe ways in which you can implement these essential online business strategies.

Sealing the Deal: The Options

As anyone who sells online knows, the point at which payment is transferred is one of the most eagerly awaited stages of the transaction. This is also one of the stages that's apt to produce the most anxiety. Customers and merchants who are used to dealing with one another face to face and to personally handing over identification and credit cards suddenly feel lost. On the Web, they can't see the person they're dealing with.

For customers, paying for something purchased over the Internet is still fraught with uncertainty even though security has improved dramatically. For merchants like you, it can still be nerve-racking; you want to make sure that checks don't bounce and purchases aren't being made with stolen credit cards.

In giving your customers the ability to provide payments online, your goal is to accomplish the following:

- ✔ **Give the customer options.** Online shoppers like to feel that they have some degree of control. Give them a choice of payment alternatives: phone, check, and credit cards are the main ones. Some also like a choice of online payment services; they want to see that you accept Google Checkout as well as PayPal, for instance.

- ✔ **Keep payment secure.** Pay an extra fee to your Web host to have your customers submit their credit card numbers or other personal information to a secure server — a server that uses Secure Sockets Layer (SSL) encryption to render it unreadable if stolen.

- ✔ **Make payment convenient.** Shoppers on the Web are in a hurry. Give them the Web page forms and the phone numbers they need so that they can complete a purchase in a matter of seconds.

Though the goals are the same, the options are different if you sell on eBay or on another Web site that functions as an e-commerce marketplace. If you sell on eBay, either through an auction or an eBay Store, you can take advantage of eBay's fraud protection measures: a feedback system that rewards honesty and penalizes dishonesty; fraud insurance; an investigations staff; and the threat of suspension. These safeguards mean that it's feasible to accept cash and personal checks or money orders from buyers. If you don't receive the cash, you don't ship. If you receive checks, you can wait until they clear before you ship.

On the Web, you don't have a feedback system or an investigations squad to ferret out dishonest buyers. You can accept checks or money orders, but credit cards are the safest and quickest option, and accordingly, they're what buyers expect. It's up to you to verify the buyer's identity as best you can to minimize fraud.

Enabling Credit Card Purchases

Having the ability to accept and process credit card transactions makes it especially easy for your customers to follow the impulse to buy something from you. You stand to generate a lot more sales than you would otherwise.

But although credit cards are easy for shoppers to use, they make *your* life as an online merchant more complicated. You have two options:

- ✔ **Let your customers pay with a credit card through an online payment service.** This requires them to sign up with the online payment service. But they gain protection from the payment service's security methods.

- ✔ **Sign up with your own merchant account.** This lets you shop around and choose the service with the lowest fees or the best service. But you have to jump through some hoops to get such an account.

I don't want to discourage you from becoming credit card ready by any means, but you need to be aware of the steps (and the expenses) involved, many of which may not occur to you when you're just starting out. For example, you may not be aware of one or more of the following:

- ✔ **Merchant accounts:** You have to apply and be approved for a special bank account called a *merchant account* for a bank to process the credit card orders that you receive. If you work through traditional banks, approval can take days or weeks. However, a number of online merchant account businesses are providing hot competition, which includes streamlining the application process.

- ✔ **Fees:** Fees can be high, but they vary widely, and it pays to shop around. Some banks charge a merchant application fee ($300–$800). On the other hand, some online companies, such as 1st American Card Service (`www.1stamericancardservice.com`), charge no application fee.

- ✔ **Discount rates:** All banks and merchant account companies (and even payment companies such as PayPal) charge a usage fee, deceptively called a *discount rate.* Typically, this fee ranges from 1 to 4 percent of each transaction. Plus, you may have to pay a monthly premium charge in the range of $30–$70 to the bank. Although 1st American Card Service saves you money with a free application, it charges Internet businesses a 2.19 percent fee that it calls a discount rate, plus 25 cents for each transaction, an $8 monthly statement fee, and a minimum charge of $15 per month.

- ✔ **American Express and Discover:** If you want to accept payments from American Express and Discover cardholders, you must make arrangements through the companies themselves. You can apply online to be an American Express card merchant by going to the American Express Merchant Homepage (`www.americanexpress.com/homepage/merchant.shtml`) and click an Accept the Card (or something similar)

link. At the Discover Card Network merchant site (www.discover
network.com), click the Get Started link and choose Merchants as
your business category, which leads you to the application for credit
card merchants.

✔ **Software and hardware:** Unless you depend on a payment service such as
PayPal, you need software or hardware to process transactions and transmit the data to the banking system. If you plan to accept credit card numbers online only and don't need a device to handle actual "card swipes"
from in-person customers, you can use your computer modem to transmit
the data. 1st American Card Service lets you use software dubbed Virtual
WebLink for processing transactions with your browser, but you have
to purchase the software for $39.95 and pay the usual discount rate and
fees. This particular package includes a Virtual WebTerminal that lets you
enter information manually and send it to the credit card network. Other
systems require you to get a hardware terminal or phone line, which you
can either purchase for $200 or more or lease for anywhere from $17 to
$26 per month, depending on the length of the lease.

As we move farther into the Web's second decade, the payment landscape
hasn't changed dramatically. But things have shifted a bit. The changes actually give buyers and sellers more options:

✔ **More and more people are paying bills online.** This change has been
taking place over several years and consumers are increasingly at ease
with the process.

✔ **PayPal is not the only game in town.** This payment service is owned by
eBay, but it can be used by anyone who wants to send or receive money
online. PayPal is used by millions of auction sellers every month, but
e-commerce storeowners can use it, too.

✔ **Google is gaining.** Google Payments charges fees that are no lower than
PayPal. Yet, shoppers and sellers alike flock to it. It provides an alternative to PayPal, which isn't popular with many buyers and sellers.

✔ **Overseas consumers are making use of new and innovative payment
systems.** At some point, if you accept payments from overseas, you might
be asked to accept Western Union money transfers or other payment
schemes. It's the wave of the future as e-commerce becomes globalized.

The steps in the upcoming section, in which I explain how to create your own
merchant account, are useful if you run a brick-and-mortar business that is
tied to your online store. But if you don't want to go through the trouble,
you might consider a payment service such as PayPal, Google Payments, or
PayByCash.

You also need to watch for credit card fraud — criminals using stolen numbers to make purchases. You, the merchant, end up being liable for most of the fictitious transactions. Cardholders are responsible for only $50 of fraudulent purchases. To combat this crime, before completing any transaction, verify that the shipping address supplied by the purchaser is the same (or at least in the same vicinity) as the billing address. If you're in doubt, you can phone the purchaser for verification — it's a courtesy to the customer as well as a means of protection for you. (See the upcoming section "Verifying credit card data.") You can do this check yourself or pay a service to do it for you.

Setting up a merchant account

The good news is that getting merchant status is becoming easier all the time for e-commerce enterprises because banks have accepted the notion that businesses don't have to have a physical storefront to be successful. Getting a merchant account approved, however, still takes a long time, and some hefty fees are involved as well. Banks look more favorably on companies that have been in business for several years and have a proven track record.

Traditional banks are reliable and experienced, and most are likely to be around for a while. The new Web-based companies that specialize in giving online businesses merchant account status welcome new businesses and give you wider options and cost savings, but they're new; their services may not be as reliable, and their future is less certain.

You can find a long list of institutions that provide merchant accounts for online businesses at one of the Yahoo! index pages:

```
dir.yahoo.com/Business_and_Economy/Business_to_Business/Financial_Services/
                Transaction_Clearing/Credit_Card_Merchant_Services
```

The list is so long that knowing which company to choose is difficult. I recommend visiting Wells Fargo Bank (`www.wellsfargo.com`), which has been operating online for several years and is well established. The Wells Fargo Web site provides you with a good overview of what's required to obtain a merchant account.

MyTexasMusic.com, the family-run business I profile in Chapter 2, uses a Web-based merchant account company called GoEmerchant.com (`www.goemerchant.com`) to set up and process its credit card transactions. This company offers a shopping cart and credit card and debit card processing to businesses that accept payments online. MyTexasMusic.com chose to use GoEmerchant after an extensive search because it found that the company would help provide reliable processing, while also protecting the business from customers who purchased items fraudulently.

One advantage of using one of the payment options set up by PayPal Merchant Services (merchant.paypal.com) is that the system (which originated with the well-known companies CyberCash and VeriSign) was well known and well regarded before PayPal acquired it. I describe the widely used electronic payment company in the section "Choosing an Online Payment System," later in this chapter.

In general, your chances of obtaining merchant status are enhanced if you apply to a bank that welcomes Internet businesses, and if you can provide good business records proving that you're a viable, moneymaking concern.

Be sure to ask about the discount rate that the bank charges for Internet-based transactions before you apply. Compare the rate for online transactions to the rate for conventional "card-swipe" purchases. Most banks and credit card processing companies charge 1 to 2 extra percentage points for online sales.

Do you use an accounting program, such as QuickBooks or MYOB Accounting? The manufacturers of these programs enable their users to become credit card merchants through their Web sites.

Finding a secure server

A *secure server* is a server that uses some form of encryption, such as SSL (which I describe in Chapter 6), to protect data that you receive over the Internet. Customers know that they've entered a secure area when the security key or lock icon at the bottom of the browser window looks locked.

If you plan to receive credit card payments, you definitely want to find a Web hosting service that can protect the area of your online business that serves as the online store. In literal terms, you need secure server software protecting the directory on your site that is to receive customer-sent forms. Some hosts charge a higher monthly fee for using a secure server; with others, the secure server is part of a basic business Web site account. Ask your host (or hosts you're considering) whether any extra charges apply.

Verifying credit card data

Unfortunately, the world is full of bad people who try to use credit card numbers that don't belong to them. The anonymity of the Web and the ability to shop anywhere in the world, combined with the ability to place orders immediately, can facilitate fraudulent orders, just as it can benefit legitimate orders.

Protecting yourself against credit card fraud is essential. Always check the billing address against the shipping address. If the two addresses are thousands of miles apart, contact the purchaser by phone to verify that the transaction is legit. Even if it is, the purchaser will appreciate your taking the time to verify the transaction.

You can use software to help check addresses. Here are three programs that perform this service:

- **ClearCommerce (**www.fisglobal.com/Products/Check/ E-Commerce/**):** This company sells both an automated payment system and payment authentication software that work with credit cards and banks.

- **PCCharge, VeriFone Payment Processing Software (**www.verifone. com/card-acceptance/pccharge.aspx**):** This software enables individuals who use the VeriFone payment service to accept payments online as well.

- **Payment Software for Windows (**www.firstdata.com/en_us/ products/merchants/support/payment-software-demo**):** Formerly known as IC*VERIFY,* this software verifies the address of the person making an online purchase as a defense against fraud.

Processing the orders

When someone submits credit card information to you, you need to transfer the information to the banking system. Whether you make this transfer yourself or hire another company to do it for you is up to you.

Do-it-yourself processing

To submit credit card information to your bank, you need point of sale (POS) hardware or software. The hardware, which you either purchase or lease from your bank, is a *terminal* — a gray box of the sort you see at many local retailers. The *software* is a program that contacts the bank through a modem.

The terminal or software is programmed to authorize the sale and transmit the data to the bank. The bank then credits your business or personal checking account. The bank also deducts the discount rate from your account weekly, monthly, or with each transaction.

If you have a small-scale Web site — perhaps with only one item for sale — you can use an online payment gateway, which enables you to add a Pay Button to a catalog page that securely processes a customer's payment information. When you receive the information, you can manually submit it for payment by using a program such as First Data Global Gateway Virtual

Terminal. The transaction is then processed on one of First Data's secure servers. Both you and your customer receive e-mail notifications that the transaction has been completed. You can find out more on the Cardservice International Web site at www.aboutcsi.com/secure-transaction-processing.html.

Automatic processing

You can hire a company to automatically process credit card orders for you. These companies compare the shipping and billing addresses to help make sure that the purchaser is the person who actually owns the card and not someone trying to use a stolen credit card number. If everything checks out, they transmit the data directly to the bank.

You can look into the different options provided by VeriFone, Inc. (www.verifone.com), or AssureBuy (www.otginc.com) for such services.

 Automatic credit card processing works so fast that your customer's credit card can be charged immediately, whether or not you have an item in stock. If a client receives a bill and is still waiting for an item that is on back order, the person can get very unhappy. For this reason, some business owners choose not to use this type of service.

Choosing an Online Payment System

A number of organizations have devised ways to make e-commerce secure and convenient for shoppers and merchants alike. These alternatives fall into one of three general categories:

- ✔ Organizations that help you complete credit card purchases (for example, VeriSign Payment Services).

- ✔ Escrow services that hold your money for you in an account until shipment is received and then pay you, providing security for both you and your customers.

- ✔ Organizations that provide alternatives to transmitting sensitive information from one computer to another. A number of attempts to create "virtual money" have failed. However, companies such as PayPal let customers make payments by directly debiting their checking accounts.

To use one of these systems, you or your Web host has to set up special software on the computer that actually stores your Web site files. This computer is where the transactions take place. The following sections provide general instructions on how to get started with setting up each of the most popular electronic payment systems.

To work smoothly, some electronic payment systems require you to set up programming languages such as Perl, C/C++, or Visual Basic on your site. You also have to work with techy documents called *configuration files.* This is definitely an area in which paying a consultant to get your business set up saves time and headaches. It also gets your new transaction feature online more efficiently than if you tackle it yourself. PayPal, for instance, provides support in setting up systems for its merchants; you can find an affiliate to help you or call the company directly. Visit the PayPal Merchant Services page (www. paypal.com/merchants) for links and phone numbers.

Shopping cart software

When you go to the supermarket or another retail outlet, you pick goodies off the shelves and put them in a shopping cart. When you go to the cash register to pay for what you've selected, you empty the cart and present your goods to the cashier.

Shopping cart software performs the same functions on an e-commerce site. Such software sets up a system that allows online shoppers to select items displayed for sale. The selections are held in a virtual shopping cart that "remembers" what the shopper has selected before checking out.

Shopping cart programs are pretty technical for nonprogrammers to set up, but if you're ambitious and want to try it, you can download and install a free program — PerlShop (www.waveridersystems.com/perlshop4/). Signing up with a Web host that provides you with shopping cart software as part of its services, however, is far easier than tackling this task yourself.

A shopping cart is often described as an essential part of many e-commerce Web sites, and Web hosts usually boast about including a cart along with their other businesses services. You don't *have* to use a shopping cart on your site, though. Some shoppers are put off by them; they're just as likely to abandon a purchase than follow through by submitting payment. Plenty of other e-businesses have users phone or fax in an order or fill out an online form instead.

PayPal Merchant Services

A good deal of this chapter is devoted to PayPal and its solutions for online buyers and sellers. The fact is that PayPal is becoming a bigger player in the field of e-commerce. When it purchased the security company VeriSign's payment services, it became even bigger. That's not necessarily a bad thing: The more users you have who take advantage of the same services, the more routine payments will become, and the more customers will trust the whole payment process.

Reach for your wallet!

One of the terms commonly thrown around in the jargon of e-commerce is wallet. A *wallet* is software that, like a real wallet that you keep in your purse or pocket, stores available cash and other records. You reach into the cyberwallet and withdraw virtual cash rather than submit a credit card number.

Wallets looked promising a few years ago, but they never really took off — at least not in the United States. The idea is that a cybershopper who uses wallet software, such as Windows Live ID (www.passport.com), can pay for items online in a matter of seconds, without having to transfer credit card data. What's more, some wallets can even "remember" previous purchases you have made and suggest further purchases. Such systems are popular in many countries, and don't be surprised if someone asks whether you accept the Paynova digital wallet system (www.paynova.com/merchant) or the Easecard Chinese wallet (www.easecard.com/index.jsp). You can accept payments from such services indirectly by signing up for PayByCash (www.paybycash.com).

The problem with wallets is that American shoppers just aren't comfortable with them. Credit cards are quick and convenient, and they've proven to be secure enough for most consumers. Consumers who are committed to using Microsoft's services can use Windows Live ID, which offers a "single sign-in" to register or make purchases on sites that support this technology. It also enables consumers to create a wallet that stores their billing and shipping information. (Credit card numbers are stored in an offline database when users sign up for a Windows Live ID.) Customers can then make purchases at participating sites with the proverbial single mouse click. In order for your online business Web site to support Windows Live ID, you need to download and install the Windows Live ID Software Development Kit (SDK) on the server that runs your Web site. You may need some help in deploying this platform. A list of consultants, as well as a link to the SDK, are included on the Windows Live ID SDK page (msdn.microsoft.com/en-us/library/bb404787.aspx).

PayPal's Merchant Services page (https://merchant.paypal.com) includes services such as Payflow, which lets your company accept payments online, and Website Payments, which facilitates payment with either credit cards or a PayPal account. Options include

- ✔ **E-mail Payments:** Your customers pay through e-mail communications; you don't even need to have a Web site.

- ✔ **Website Payments Standard:** Your customers choose an item to buy and are sent to PayPal's site, where they can pay with a credit card or their PayPal account, if they have one.

- ✔ **Website Payments Pro:** Your customers choose an item to buy from a shopping cart you have on your site. They pay with a credit card on the site (PayPal processes the payment in the background) or to PayPal if they prefer to use their PayPal account.

Trying one of the Payflow Payment Gateway options is free for 30 days to see how it works with your own business, but both options require that you have a merchant account. (If you don't have one, VeriSign suggests several financial institutions to which you can apply.) The Payflow services do carry some charges and require you to do some work, however:

- ✔ **Payflow Link:** The smallest and simplest of the VeriSign payment options, Payflow Link, is intended for small businesses that process 500 transactions or fewer each month. You add a payment link to your online business site and you don't have to do programming or other site development to get the payment system to work. You pay a $179 setup fee and a $19.95 monthly fee.

- ✔ **Payflow Pro:** With this service, you can process up to 1,000 transactions per month, and any additional transactions cost 10 cents each. To use this option, you begin by installing the Payflow software on the server that runs your Web site. The customer then makes a purchase on your site, and the Payflow software sends the information to VeriSign, which processes the transaction. Payflow Pro carries a $249 setup fee and costs $59.95 per month.

You can sign up for a trial of either Payflow Link or Payflow Pro on the Payflow Payment Gateway page (`www.paypal.com/cgi-bin/ webscr?cmd=_payflow-gateway-overview-outside`).

PayPal's personal payment services

PayPal was one of the first online businesses to hit on the clever idea of giving business owners a way to accept credit and debit card payments from customers without having to apply for a merchant account, download software, apply for online payment processing, or some combination of these steps.

PayPal's person-to-person payment services are ideal for transactions on eBay and other sites. In this sense, PayPal is essentially an *escrow service:* It functions as a sort of financial middleman, debiting buyers' accounts and crediting the accounts of sellers — and, along the way, exacting a fee for its services, which it charges to the merchant receiving the payment. The accounts involved can be credit card accounts, checking accounts, or accounts held at PayPal into which members directly deposit funds. In other words, the person making the payment sets up an account with PayPal by identifying which account (credit card or checking, for example) a payment is to be taken from. The merchant also has a PayPal account and has identified which checking or credit card account is to receive payments. PayPal handles the virtual "card swipe" and verification of customer information; the customer can pay with a credit card without the merchant's having to set up a merchant account.

PayPal is best known as a way to pay for items purchased on eBay. eBay, in fact, owns PayPal. But the service is regularly used to process payments both on and off the auction site. If you want to sell items (including through your Web site), you sign up for a PayPal Business or Premier account. You get a PayPal button that you add to your auction listing or sales Web page. (If you sell on eBay, this button is provided automatically.) The customer clicks the button to transfer the payment from his or her PayPal account to yours, and you're charged a transaction fee.

Setting up a PayPal account is free. Here's how you can set up a PayPal Business account:

1. **Go to the PayPal home page (**www.paypal.com**) and click the Sign Up Now button.**

   The PayPal Account Sign Up page appears.

2. **Choose your country of residence and your language, and click the Get Started button beneath Business.**

   The Select Payment Solution page appears.

3. **For this example, choose Website Payments Standard and click Continue.**

   The Sign up for a Business Account – Getting Started page appears.

4. **Click Go under the heading Sign Up for a Business Account.**

   The Business Account Sign Up page appears.

5. **Follow the instructions on the registration form page and set up your account with PayPal.**

   After you fill out the registration forms, you receive an e-mail message with a link that takes you to the PayPal Web site to confirm your e-mail address.

6. **Click the link contained in the e-mail message.**

   You go to the PayPal — Password page.

7. **Enter your password (the one you created during the registration process) in the Password box and then click the Confirm button.**

   You go to the PayPal — My Account page.

8. **Click the Merchant Tools tab at the top of the My Account page.**

9. **Click Buy Now under the Buttons link.**

   If you want to create a shopping cart, click the Shopping Cart link.

10. **Provide some information about the item you're selling:**

    - Enter a brief description of your sales item in the Item Name/Service box.

    - Enter an item number in the Item ID/Number Box.

    - Enter the price in the Price of Item/Service box.

    - Choose a button that shoppers can click to make the purchase. (You can choose either the PayPal logo button or a button that you've already created.)

11. **When you're done, click the Create Button Now button.**

    You go to the PayPal — Web Accept page, as shown in Figure 7-1.

12. **Copy the code in the For Websites box and paste it onto the Web page that holds your sales item.**

    That's all there is to it. When you receive a payment through eBay, you receive an e-mail notification to that effect. An example of an e-mail I received is shown in Figure 7-2. When someone sends you money directly through PayPal, you see that, too. You can then verify the payment by logging in to your account on the PayPal Web site.

You should realize that accepting money on PayPal is *not* free. Buyers don't pay to use PayPal, but sellers do. I have a Premier account, and every time I receive money from an eBay transaction, PayPal takes its fees off the top. For a purchase of about $23, PayPal takes about $1 in fees, for instance. On the plus side, PayPal does make a debit card available that you can use to make your own consumer purchases with the money in your account.

Figure 7-1:
Copy this code to your sales catalog Web page to enable other PayPal users to transfer purchase money to your account.

Figure 7-2:
When you
receive
payment
through
eBay or
directly
from an
individual,
you receive
a message
like this.

```
┌─────────────────────────────────────────────────────────────────────────────────┐
│ ✉ Colin has just sent you $10.00 USD with PayPal - Inbox for greg@gregholden.com - Netscape 7.0        ─□X │
│  File  Edit  View  Go  Message  Tools  Window  Help                                          │
│    ✉    🖊    ✉    ✉    ✉    ✉    📁    📄    🗑    🖨    ⊗       Ⓝ │
│      Get MsgsCompose   Reply  Reply All Forward  File   Next   Delete  Print  Stop              │
│  ▷  Subject: Colin has just sent you $10.00 USD with PayPal      From: gwd@pacbell.net   6/6/2005 1:09 PM │
│  Dear greg@gregholden.com,                                                        │
│                                                                                  │
│  You've got cash!                                                                │
│                                                                                  │
│  Colin just sent you money with PayPal.                                          │
│                                                                                  │
│  ---------------------------------                                               │
│  Payment Details                                                                 │
│  ---------------------------------                                               │
│                                                                                  │
│  Amount:  $10.00 USD                                                             │
│  Note:  thanks for your time                                                     │
│                                                                                  │
│  Simply click https://www.paypal.com/us/links/uni and complete PayPal's easy registration form to claim your money. │
│                                                                                  │
│  PayPal lets users send money to anyone with an email address. Use PayPal.com to settle restaurant tabs with colleagues, │
│  pay friends for movie tickets, or buy a baseball card at an online auction. You can also send personalized money │
│  requests to your friends for a group event or party.                            │
│                                                                                  │
│  For more information about PayPal, go to:                                       │
│                                                                                  │
│  http://www.paypal.com/us/                                                       │
│                                                                                  │
│  Welcome to PayPal!                                                              │
│  The PayPal Team                                                                 │
│  🌐 ✉ ☑ 📄  Document: Done                                                       │
└─────────────────────────────────────────────────────────────────────────────────┘
```

The nice thing about using PayPal is that the system enables you to accept payments through your Web site without having to obtain a merchant account. It does put a burden on your customers to become PayPal users, but chances are, those who buy or sell on eBay already have an account. The thing to remember is that both you and your customers place a high level of trust in PayPal to handle your money. If fraud is a problem, PayPal investigates it — or is supposed to, anyway. Some former PayPal users detest PayPal because of what they describe as a lack of responsiveness, and they describe their unhappiness in great detail on sites such as `www.paypalsucks.com`. Be aware of such complaints to have the full picture about PayPal and anticipate problems before they arise.

Google Checkout

Google seems to have a finger in just about every pie when it comes to e-commerce. Payments are no exception. Google Checkout (`checkout.google.com`) is a convenient and safe way to pay online. The process of signing up for Google Checkout is relatively easy because you probably already have a Google password to check your Gmail or perform other services with Google. If you don't, just go to the Google Checkout home page and click Sign Up Now to obtain one.

Google Checkout was originally seen as a quick payment system for Google itself. If you saw something on a Google search results page and wanted to buy it, you could do so immediately through Google Checkout. But the service also functions as a full-fledged payment system much like PayPal:

You sign up for Google Checkout and add "buy" buttons to your sale pages. Buyers can then click these buttons and pay you through Google Checkout. The service registers buyers and their credit card accounts, as well as sellers and their own account information. Google Checkout receives payments, passes them on to sellers, and, for its efforts, subtracts a discount rate.

Currently, the rate stands at 2.9 percent plus a 30-cent fee for a purchase under $3,000. Rates are lower for purchases of higher amounts. This is virtually the same as PayPal's rate, at this writing.

One big difference between Google Checkout and PayPal is in the method of payment. Google Checkout accepts only credit card payments. Paypal, on the other hand, also allows withdrawals from bank accounts as well as "eChecks" (payments taken from a buyer's checking account and deposited in the seller's account after a suitable time for the "check" to clear).

Another difference between Google Checkout and PayPal is customer service. You can reach a PayPal service person on the phone, but you can't reach Google Checkout this way.

An article on CNET (news.cnet.com/8301-30684_3-10348805-265. html) reported on problems with recurring payments not being processed by Google Checkout for weeks at a time. Trying to reach a human being at Google to discuss the problems seems nearly impossible for the average merchant. (Writers like me can sometimes get a response from a PR person.)

On the plus side, Google Checkout is integrated with Google's popular AdWords system. If you have an active AdWords account, your discount rate is lowered.

An article on the AuctionBytes Web site (www.auctionbytes.com/cab/abn/y09/m11/i05/s01) indicates that there may be another advantage to accepting Google Payments on your Web site. If you receive payments and then get positive rankings from your customers, you'll get better search placement for your site on Google.

Micropayments

Micropayments are very small units of currency that are exchanged by merchants and customers. The amounts involved may range from one-tenth of one cent (that's $.001) to a few dollars. Such small payments enable sites to provide content for sale on a per-click basis. For users to read articles, listen to music files, or view video clips online, some sites require micropayments in a special form of electronic cash that goes by names such as *scrip* or *eCash*.

Micropayments seemed like a good idea in theory, but they've never caught on with most consumers. On the other hand, they've never totally disappeared, either. The business that proved conclusively that consumers are willing to pay small amounts of money to purchase creative content online is none other than the computer manufacturer Apple, which revolutionized e-commerce with its iPod music player and its iTunes Store. Every day, users pay $.99 to download a song and add it to their iPod selections. But they make such payments with their credit cards, using real dollars and cents.

In other words, iTunes payments aren't true micropayments. But it's just about the only system I know that deals in small payments for items purchased or downloaded online that's really successful. While I was preparing an earlier version of this book, I wrote about a system called BitPass that provided a true micropayment system for online merchants. But the company went out of business in 2007. Micropayments simply look as though they won't be a popular option for the majority of online shoppers.

Other payment options

A number of new online payment options have appeared that let people pay for merchandise without having to submit credit card numbers or mail checks. Here are some additional options to consider:

- **PayByCash** (www.paybycash.com): Lots of individuals — especially those who live outside the United States — don't have credit cards. Or those who do have a card use a system (for example, the Chinese debit card system) that doesn't link up with the credit card providers in the United States. PayByCash consolidates approximately 25 different payment systems used around the world, ranging from PayPal and Western Union to local systems such as eNets in China or Paymate in Australia. There's one big catch, however: PayByCash requires that merchants expect sales of at least $50,000 in U.S. dollars or your native currency.

- **ClearTran** (www.cleartran.com): This service enables shoppers to make purchases by sending online checks to merchants. The shopper notifies the seller about the purchase and then contacts a special secure Web site to authorize a debit from his or her checking account. The secure site then transmits the electronic check to the merchant, who can either print the check on paper or save the check in a special format that can be transmitted to banks for immediate deposit.

Which one of these options is right for you? That depends on what you want to sell online. If you're providing articles, reports, music, or other content that you want people to pay a nominal fee to access, consider a micropayment system (see the preceding section). If your customers tend to be sophisticated, technically savvy individuals who are likely to embrace online checks or billing systems, consider ClearTran. The important things are to provide customers with several options for submitting payment and to make the process as easy as possible for them.

Fulfilling Your Online Orders

Being on the Internet can help when it comes to the final step in the e-commerce dance: order fulfillment. *Fulfillment* refers to what happens after a sale is made. Typical fulfillment tasks include the following:

- ✔ Packing up the merchandise
- ✔ Shipping the merchandise
- ✔ Solving delivery problems or answering questions about orders that haven't reached their destinations
- ✔ Sending out bills
- ✔ Following up to see whether the customer is satisfied

Order fulfillment may seem like the least exciting part of running a business, online or otherwise. But from your customer's point of view, it's the most important business activity of all. The following sections suggest how you can use your presence online to help reduce any anxiety your customers may feel about receiving what they ordered.

The back-end (or, to use the Microsoft term, BackOffice) part of your online business is where order fulfillment comes in. If you have a database in which you record customer orders, link it to your Web site so that your customers can track orders. Dreamweaver or ColdFusion can help you set up a database. (Dreamweaver contains built-in commands that let you link to a ColdFusion database.)

Providing links to shipping services

One advantage of being online is that you can help customers track packages after shipment. The FedEx online order-tracking feature, shown in Figure 7-3, gets thousands of requests each day and is widely known as one of the most successful marketing tools on the Web. If you use FedEx, provide your customers with a link to its online tracking page.

Figure 7-3:
Provide
links to
online track-
ing services
so that your
customers
can check
delivery
status.

The other big shipping services have also created their own online tracking systems. You can link to these sites, too:

- ✔ United Parcel Service (`www.ups.com`).

- ✔ U.S. Postal Service Express Mail (`www.usps.gov`).

- ✔ DHL (`www.dhl-usa.com/home/home.asp`). Be aware that DHL no longer accepts deliveries to the U.S. but will ship to other countries.

Presenting shipping options clearly

In order fulfillment, as in receiving payment, it pays to present your clients with as many options as possible and to explain the options in detail. Because you're online, you can provide your customers with as much shipping information as they can stand. Web surfers are knowledge hounds — they can never get enough data, whether it's related to shipping or other parts of your business.

When it comes to shipping, be sure to describe the options, the cost of each, and how long each takes. Here are some more specific suggestions:

✔ **Compare shipping costs.** Make use of an online service, such as InterShipper (www.intershipper.com), which allows you to submit the origin, destination, weight, and dimensions of a package that you want to ship via a Web page form and then returns the cheapest shipping alternatives.

✔ **Make sure that you can track.** Pick a service that lets you track your package's shipping status.

✔ **Be able to confirm receipt.** If you use the U.S. Postal Service, ship the package "return receipt requested" because tracking isn't available — unless you use Priority Mail or Express Mail. You can confirm delivery with Priority Mail (domestic) and Parcel Post.

Many online stores present shipping alternatives in the form of a table or bulleted list of options. (*Tables,* as you probably know, are Web page design elements that let you arrange content in rows and columns, making them easier to read; refer to Chapter 4 for more on adding tables to your site.) You don't have to look very far to find an example; just visit the John Wiley & Sons Web site (www.wiley.com) and order a book from its online store. When you're ready to pay for your items and provide a shipping address, you see the bulleted list, as shown in Figure 7-4.

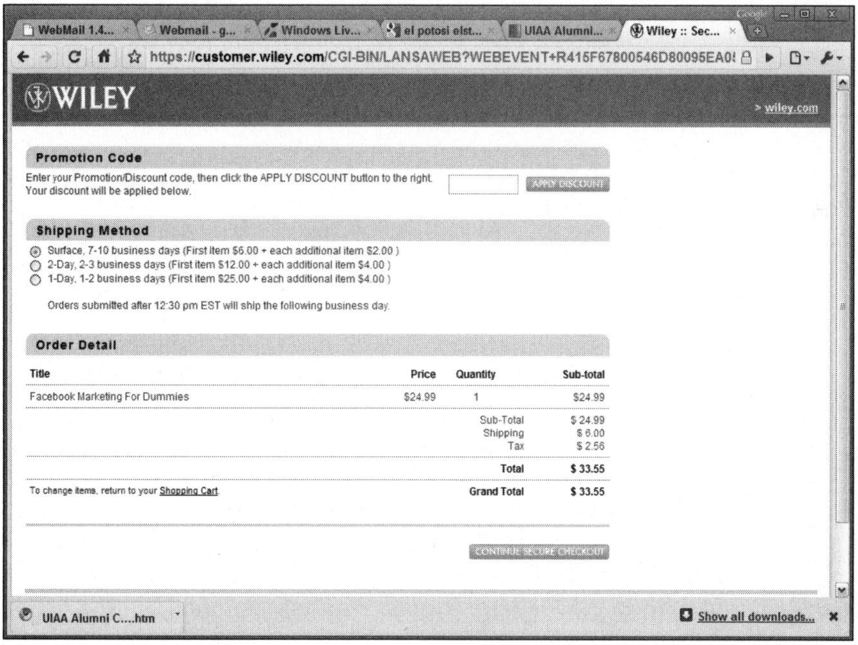

Figure 7-4:
Tables help shoppers calculate costs, keep track of purchases, and choose shipping options.

Joining the International Trade Brigade

International trade may seem like something that only multinational corporations practice. But the so-called little guys like you and me can be international traders, too. In fact, the term simply refers to a transaction between two or more individuals or companies in different countries. If you're a designer living in the United States and you create some stationery artwork and Web pages for someone in Germany, you're involved in international trade.

Keeping up with international trade issues

If you really want to be effective in marketing yourself overseas and become an international player in world trade, you need to follow the tried-and-true business strategies: networking, education, and research. Join groups that promote international trade, become familiar with trade laws and restrictions, and generally get a feel for the best marketing practices around the world.

Here are some suggestions for places you can start:

- ✔ **The Market Access Unit page of the Irish government's Department of Enterprise, Trade, and Employment Web site (**www.entemp.ie/trade/marketaccess**):** This page contains links to the European Union's Commercial Policy as well as requirements governing Export Licensing and Import Licensing.

- ✔ **Small Business Exporters Association (**www.sbea.org**):** A group of small- and mid-size business exporters devoted to networking, assistance, and advocacy.

- ✔ **globalEDGE (**globaledge.msu.edu/resourcedesk**):** This site is published by Michigan State University and includes hundreds of international trade links.

- ✔ **Newsletter Access (**www.newsletteraccess.com/subject/intertrade.html**):** This Web site has information on how to subscribe to hundreds of different newsletters that discuss international trade issues.

Researching specific trade laws

Rather than wait for overseas business to come to you, take a proactive approach. First, do some research into the appropriate trade laws that apply to countries with which you might do business. The Internet has an amazing amount of information pertaining to trade practices for individual countries.

You can seek out international business by using one or more message boards designed specifically for small business owners who want to participate in international trade. These message boards let users post *trade leads,* which are messages that announce international business opportunities.

For example, at the ECEurope.com B2B trade bulletin board (`www.eceurope. com`), you may find a message from a Finnish company selling surplus paint, a United States company that needs office equipment, or a British company offering X-ray equipment for export. Advertisements on this site typically include the URL for the business's Web site. The site charges a fee to post your own notices.

If you're in the business of creating computer software or hardware, you need to be aware of restrictions that the U.S. government imposes on the export of some computer-related products. In fact, you may incur a fine of more than $100,000 from the U.S. Treasury Department and the U.S. State Department for exporting just about anything high-tech to a Denied Person, Specially Designated National, or Restricted Country. The list of these people and countries changes frequently. Look for links to the current ones at `www.treas. gov/offices/enforcement/ofac/sdn/`.

The Buy & Sell Exchange site of the Federation of International Trade Associations (`www.worldbid.com`) lets you post your own trade leads or search for other leads by keyword. You can find the Trade Leads page of the extensive globalEDGE site (`http://globaledge.msu.edu/ resourcedesk/trade-leads/`), which includes links to sites that post trade leads in countries such as Egypt, India, and Taiwan.

Exploring free trade zones

A *free trade zone* (FTZ) is an officially designated business or industrial area within a country where foreign and domestic goods are considered to be "outside" the territory covered by customs. You don't have to pay customs duty, taxes, or tariffs on merchandise brought into, handled, or stored in an FTZ. You can find FTZs in many countries as well as in many U.S. states.

The purpose of FTZs is to reduce customs costs and make it easier for businesses to send goods into foreign countries. You can store your items in FTZs for a while, exhibit them, and, if necessary, change them to comply with the import requirements of the country in question, until the time comes when you want to import them into that country.

Shipping Overseas Goods

It never hurts to state the obvious, so here goes: Don't depend on ground mail (appropriately nicknamed *snail mail*) to communicate with overseas customers. Use e-mail and fax to get your message across — and, if you have to ship information or goods, use airmail express delivery. Surface mail can take weeks or even months to reach some regions of some countries — if it gets there at all.

Your customer may ask you to provide an estimate of your export costs by using a special set of abbreviations called incoterms. *Incoterms* (short for *international commercial trade terms*) are standardized acronyms originally established in 1936 by the International Chamber of Commerce. They establish an international language for describing business transactions to prevent misunderstandings between buyers and sellers from different countries. Incoterms thus provide a universal vocabulary that is recognized by all international financial institutions.

Incoterms are most likely to apply to you if you're shipping a large number of items to an overseas factory rather than, for example, a single painting to an individual's home. But just in case you hit the big time, you should be aware of common incoterms, such as

- ✔ **EXW (Ex Works):** This term means that the seller fulfills his or her obligation by making the goods available to the buyer at the seller's own premises (or *works*). The seller doesn't have to load the goods onto the buyer's vehicle unless otherwise agreed.

- ✔ **FOB (Free on Board):** This term refers to the cost of shipping overseas by ship — not something you're likely to do in this high-tech day and age. But if you sell a vintage automobile to a collector in France, who knows?

- ✔ **CFR (Cost and Freight):** This term refers to the costs and freight charges necessary to transport items to a specific overseas port. CFR describes only costs related to items that are shipped by sea and inland waterways and that go to an actual port. Another incoterm, CPT (Carriage Paid To) can refer to any type of transport, not just shipping, and refers to the cost for the transport (or *carriage*) of the goods to their destination.

You can find a detailed examination of incoterms at the International Chamber of Commerce Web site (`www.iccwbo.org/incoterms/id3045/index.html`).

If the item you're planning to ship overseas by mail is valued at more than $2,500, the United States requires you to fill out and use the Automated Export System (AES) and submit it to a U.S. customs agent. The AES collects

Electronic Export Information (EEI). To use the AES, you need to obtain either filer certification or, if you create computer programs, software certification. You have to file for certification and take a short test. Detailed instructions on how to use the AES are available on the U.S. Census Bureau's Web site (`www.census.gov/foreign-trade/aes/index.htmlf`). You can file your electronic export data with the AES through the U.S. Customs Service's Web site (`www.cbp.gov/xp/cgov/trade/automated/aes/`).

Some nations require a certificate of origin or a signed statement that attests to the origin of the exported item. You can usually obtain such certificates through a local chamber of commerce.

Some purchasers or countries may also ask for a certificate of inspection stating the specifications met by the goods shipped. Inspections are performed by independent testing organizations.

Wherever you ship your items, be sure to insure them for the full amount they are worth — and tell your customers about any additional insurance charges upfront. Finally, choose an insurance company that can respond quickly to claims made from your own country *and* from your customer's country.

Getting Paid in International Trade

Having an effective billing policy in place is especially important when your customers live thousands of miles away. The safest strategy is to request payment in U.S. dollars and to ask for cash in advance. This approach prevents any collection problems and gets you your money right away.

What happens if you want to receive payment in U.S. dollars from someone overseas but the purchaser is reluctant to send cash? You have a couple of options:

- ✔ You can ask the purchaser to send you a personal check — or, better yet, a cashier's check — but it's up to the buyer to convert the local currency to U.S. dollars.

- ✔ You can suggest that the buyer obtain an International Money Order from a U.S. bank that has a branch in his or her area, and specify that the money order be payable in U.S. dollars.

Suggest that your customers use an online currency conversion utility, such as the Bloomberg Online Currency Calculator (`www.bloomberg.com/invest/calculators/currency.html`), to do the calculation.

You can also use an online escrow service — such as Escrow.com (www.escrow.com) or Moneybookers.com (www.moneybookers.com) — to hold funds in escrow until you and your customer strike a deal. An *escrow service* holds the customer's funds in a trust account so that the seller can ship an item knowing that he or she will be paid. The escrow service transfers the funds from buyer to seller after the buyer has inspected the goods and approved them.

Escrow services usually accept credit card payments from overseas purchasers; this is one way to accept credit card payments even if you don't have a merchant account yourself. The credit card company handles conversion from the local currency into U.S. dollars.

If you're doing a lot of business overseas, consider getting export insurance to protect yourself against loss from damage or delay in transit. Policies are available from the Export-Import Bank of the United States (www.exim.gov) or from other private firms that offer export insurance.

Chapter 8

Providing Customer Service with a Virtual Smile

*N*o matter where you sell, you don't have to look far to figure out what separates the successful sellers from the struggling ones. Besides having a good idea and lots of chutzpah, the best sellers invariably provide the best customer service. They're the sellers who leave extras such as cards and gifts in packages; who make an effort to ship merchandise the same day it's purchased; who have a clear return policy and stick to it; and who answer questions promptly help to set off a positive feedback cycle: You provide good service and get good response from customers; you build more trust; you inspire more people to buy from you; and on and on. When I made an effort to include some "extras" with my packages and to ship quickly and carefully, I received my own glowing comments of appreciation, which proved highly satisfying.

Customer service is one area in which small, entrepreneurial businesses can outshine brick-and-mortar stores and even larger online competitors. Whether you're competing in the areas of e-trading, e-music, or e-tail sales of any sort doesn't matter. Tools such as e-mail, RSS feeds, and interactive forms, coupled with the fact that an online commerce site can provide information on a 24/7 basis, give you a powerful advantage when it comes to retaining customers and building loyalty. Make no mistake: Giving personal attention to customers who call you on the phone or demand instant shipment is hard work. But it pays off in the long run.

What constitutes good online customer service, particularly for a new business that has only one or two employees? For John Jacobs, CEO of ArtFire (`www.artfire.com`), it means forwarding e-mail inquiries from his Web site to his BlackBerry so that he can respond immediately.

Being responsive and available is only part of the picture, however. This chapter presents ways to succeed with the other essential components: providing information, communicating effectively, and enabling your clientele to talk back to you online.

Keeping Your Customers in the Loop

In a manner of speaking, satisfaction is all about expectations. If you give your customers what they're expecting or even a little bit more, they'll be happy. But how do you go about setting their level of expectation in the first place? Communication is the key. The more information you can provide upfront, the fewer phone queries or complaints you'll receive later. Printed pamphlets and brochures have traditionally described products and services at length. Online is now the way to go, though.

Say you're talking about a 1,000-word description of your new company and your products, services, or both. If that text were formatted to fit on a 4-x-9-inch foldout brochure, the contents would cover several panels and take at least a few hundred dollars to print.

On the other hand, if those same 1,000 words were arranged on a few Web pages and put online, they'd probably be no more than 5K–10K in size. The same applies if you distribute your content to a number of subscribers in an e-mail newsletter. In either case, you need pay only a little to publish the information.

Online publishing also has the advantage of easier updating. When you add new products or services, or even when you want a different approach, it takes only a little time and effort to change the contents or the look.

Providing FAQs

FAQs are as old as the Web. They're not high tech. They're not always elegant. But they can be found on nearly every organization's Web site. They have worked for an infinite number of online businesspeople, and they can work for you.

Even the format of FAQ pages is pretty similar from site to site, and this predictability is an asset. FAQ pages are generally presented in Q-and-A format, with topics appearing in the form of questions that have literally been asked by other customers or that have been made up to resemble real questions. Each question has a brief answer that provides essential information about the business.

Just because I'm continually touting communication doesn't mean I want you to bore your potential customers with endless words that don't apply to their interests. To keep your FAQ page from getting too long, I recommend that you list all the questions at the top of the page. This way, by clicking a hyperlinked item in the list, readers jump to the spot on the page where you present the question that relates to them and its answer in detail.

Just having a FAQ page isn't enough. Make sure that yours is easy to use and comprehensive. Take a look at one of the most famous of the genre, the venerable World Wide Web FAQ by Thomas Boutell (www.boutell.com/newfaq) to get some ideas. Be sure to check out the informative section "FAQs about the FAQ."

Sure, you could compose a FAQ page off the top of your head, but sometimes getting a different perspective helps. Invite visitors, customers, friends, and family to come up with questions about your business. You may want to include questions on some of the following topics:

- ✓ **Contact information:** If I need to reach you in a hurry by mail, fax, or phone, how do I do that? Are you available only at certain hours?

- ✓ **Instructions:** What if I need more detailed instructions on how to use your products or services? Where can I find them?

- ✓ **Service:** What do I do if the merchandise breaks or doesn't work for some reason? Do you have a return policy?

- ✓ **Sales tax:** Is sales tax added to the cost I see on-screen?

- ✓ **Returns or exchanges:** If I'm not satisfied, can I get my money back or get an exchange? Is there a time limit on this policy?

- ✓ **Shipping:** What are my shipping options?

You don't have to use the term *FAQ*, either. The retailer Lands' End, which does just about everything right in terms of e-commerce, does not use this term for its lists of questions and answers. Go to the Lands' End home page (www.landsend.com), click the Customer Service link, and then click Technical Information, Services & Policies, or any of the other sections to see how Lands' End presents the same type of material.

Nothing makes you look worse than an out-of-date FAQ page. Try to keep your page up-to-date as your business grows. Make sure that the questions match sales items and services that you actually provide.

Writing an online newsletter

You may define yourself as an online businessperson, not a newsletter editor. But sharing information with customers and potential customers through an e-mail newsletter is a great way to build credibility for yourself and your business.

For added customer service (not to mention a touch of self-promotion), consider producing a regular publication that you send out to a mailing list. Your mailing list would begin with customers and prospective customers who visit your Web site and indicate that they want to subscribe.

An e-mail newsletter doesn't happen by magic, but it can provide your business with long-term benefits that include

- ✔ **Customer tracking:** You can add subscribers' e-mail addresses to a mailing list that you can use for other marketing purposes, such as promoting special sales items for return customers.

- ✔ **Low bandwidth:** An e-mail newsletter doesn't require much memory. Such newsletters are great for businesspeople who get their e-mail on the road via laptops, palm devices, or appliances that are designed specifically for sending and receiving e-mail.

- ✔ **Timeliness:** You can get breaking news into your electronic newsletter much faster than you can put it in print.

The fun part is to name your newsletter and assemble content that you want to include. Then follow these steps to get your publication up and running:

1. **Create your newsletter by typing the contents in plain-text (ASCII) format.**

   Optionally, you can also provide an HTML-formatted version. You can then include headings and graphics, which show up in e-mail programs that support HTML e-mail messages.

   If you use a plain-text newsletter, format it by using capital letters; rules that consist of a row of equal signs, hyphens, or asterisks; or blank spaces to align elements.

2. **Save your file with the proper filename extension:** `.txt` **for the text version and** `.htm` **or** `.html` **if you send an HTML version.**

3. **Attach the file to an e-mail message by using your e-mail program's method of sending attachments — or paste it into the body of the message in case your recipients don't receive attachments.**

4. **Address your e-mail to the recipients.**

If you have lots of subscribers (many newsletters have hundreds or thousands), save their addresses in a mailing list. Use your e-mail program's address book function to do this.

5. **Send your newsletter.**

If you have a large number of subscribers, I recommend sending your publication late at night. I also recommend sending it in several stages — that is, to only so many subscribers simultaneously — rather than all at one time. Those are two good ways to help your words reach their destination quickly and reliably.

Managing a mailing list can be time consuming. You have to keep track of people who want to subscribe or unsubscribe, as well as those who ask for more information. You can save time and trouble by installing a management system such as FanBlast (`www.fanmass.com/`) or hiring a company such as Lyris SparkList (`www.sparklist.com`) to do the day-to-day list management for you.

Adobe's Portable Document Format (PDF) enables you to save a publication with the images, special typefaces, and other layout features intact. You can save your file as a PDF document and mail it. Recipients need the widely available program Adobe Reader to open it. You can create PDF files with the CutePDF (`www.cutepdf.com`) application.

Mixing bricks and clicks

If you operate a brick-and-mortar business as well as a Web-based business, you have additional opportunities to get feedback from your shoppers. Take advantage of the fact that you meet customers personally on a regular basis and ask them for opinions and suggestions that can help you operate a more effective Web site, too.

When your customers are in the checkout line (the real one with a cash register, not your online shopping cart), ask them to fill out a questionnaire about your Web site. Consider asking questions like the following:

✔ Have you visited this store's Web site? Are you familiar with it?

✔ Would you visit the Web site more often if you knew there was merchandise or content there that you couldn't find in our physical location?

✔ Can you suggest some types of merchandise, or special sales, you'd like to see on the Web site?

Including your Web site's URL on all the printed literature in your store is a good idea. The feedback system works both ways, of course: You can ask online customers for suggestions of how to run your brick-and-mortar store better and what types of merchandise they'd like to see on your real, as opposed to your "virtual," shelves.

Creating an RSS feed

E-mail newsletters and hyperlinks are becoming passé. These days, blogs and RSS feeds are the preferred options for getting the word out about just about anything. The phrase "send an RSS feed of your Web site or eBay listings" might sound really high-tech and complex. But it's Really Simple — Really Simple Syndication, or RSS, that is.

RSS is a way of converting the contents of a Web page to an eXtensible Markup Language (XML) file so that it can be read in a flash by anyone with an *RSS reader* software program. People subscribe to your RSS feed, and they receive it each time your site's contents are updated.

RSS is a marketing tool that is widely used in the world of blogs. Just as a blog publisher can, you can capture an RSS feed of your sales and offer it (you might say, *feed it*) to customers who want to subscribe to it. If you sell through an eBay Store (an option I describe in Chapter 13), it's easy to get started. Follow these steps:

1. **Subscribe to a feeder program, such as Feedburner (**www.feed burner.com**), or one of the readers I describe in Chapter 1.**

2. **Go to your eBay Store and click the Seller, Manage Store link near the bottom of the page.**

3. **Sign in with your User ID and password if needed.**

   The Manage My Store page appears.

4. **In the Marketing tools box on the left side of the window, click the RSS Feeds link.**

   The RSS Feeds options appear.

5. **Click the button next to Activate Your Fixed Price Listings via RSS.**

6. **Click Apply.**

7. **Go to your store's home page. Scroll to the bottom of the page, which has an orange button labeled RSS.**

8. **Click the RSS button on your page, copy the code presented, and paste it into your RSS feeder program.**

9. **Post the file and send it through the feeder program. (See eBay seller Doors2Stores's tutorial at** `www.doors2stores.com/resources2.html` **for more information.)**

If you don't sell through eBay, turning your catalog listings into an RSS feed isn't quite as simple. You need to come up with a standard description for your listings: a listing title, a description, and a hyperlink. You then format each item like this:

```
<item>
<title>Model 101 Widget</title>
<description>Check out the 101, the latest and greatest
          widget offering ever!</description>
<link>http://www.mywidgetcatalog.com/widget101.html</link>
</item>
```

You then go to a site, such as Feed Validator (`feedvalidator.org`), to make sure that your formatting is correct. Then subscribe to one of the RSS readers mentioned at `searchenginewatch.com/2175281` or in Chapter 1 of this book. Copy your feed to the reader and distribute it. More info about creating feeds is at `searchenginewatch.com/2175271`.

Helping Customers Reach You

I'm the type of person who has an unlisted home phone number. But being anonymous is not the way to go when you're running an online business. (I use a different number for business calls, by the way.) Of course, you don't have to promise to be available 24/7 to your customers in the flesh. But they need to believe that they can get attention no matter what time of day or night. When you're online, contact information can take several forms. Be sure to include

- ✔ Your snail-mail address
- ✔ Your e-mail address(es)
- ✔ Your phone and fax numbers as well as a toll-free number (if you have one)

My brother recently obtained a toll-free (800) number for his audio restoration business (`www.lp2cdsolutions.com`). He obtained the number for $30 and then had the number assigned to a land line (not a cellphone line). A service called Ureach (`www.ureach.com`) can forward a toll-free number to your cellphone. And businesses such as TollFreeNumber.org (`www.tollfreenumber.org`) will give you an 800 number that will ring on your cellphone. Of course, you also pay for the calls. Ask your local phone company for more information.

Most Web hosting services (such as the types of hosts that I describe in Chapter 4) give you more than one e-mail inbox as part of your account. So it may be helpful to set up more than one e-mail address. One address can be for people to communicate with you personally, and the other can be where people go for general information. You can also set up e-mail addresses that respond to messages by automatically sending a text file in response. (See the "Setting up autoresponders" section, later in this chapter.)

Even though you probably won't meet many of your customers in person, you need to provide them with a human connection. Keep your site as personal and friendly as possible. A contact page is a good place to provide some brief biographical information about the people visitors can contact, namely you and any employees or partners in your company.

Putting your contact information on a separate Web page makes your patrons have to wait a few seconds to access it. If your contact data is simple and your Web site consists of only a few pages, by all means put it right on your home page.

Going upscale with your e-mail

These days nearly everyone I know, including my parents, has an e-mail account. But when you're an online businessperson, you need to know more about the features of e-mail than just how to ask about the weather or exchange a recipe. The more you discover about the finer technical points of e-mail, the better you can meet the needs of your clients. The following sections suggest ways to go beyond simply sending and receiving e-mail messages so that you can use e-mail for business publishing and marketing.

Setting up autoresponders

An *autoresponder,* which also goes by the name *mailbot,* is software that you can set up to send automatic replies to requests for information about a product or service, or to respond to people subscribing to an e-mail publication or service.

You can provide automatic responses either through your own e-mail program or your Web host's e-mail service. If you use a Web host to provide automatic responses, you can usually purchase an extra e-mail address that can be configured to return a text file (such as a form letter) to the sender.

Look for a Web host that provides you with one or more autoresponders along with your account. Typically, your host assigns you an e-mail address that takes the form `info@mycompany.com`. In this case, someone at your hosting service configures the account so that when a visitor to your site sends a message to `info@yourcompany.com`, a file of your choice, such as a simple text document that contains background information about you and your services, automatically goes out to the sender as a reply. My own Web host and ISP, Speakeasy, lets me create and edit an autoresponse message for each of my e-mail accounts. First, I log on to my host's gateway, which is the service it provides customers for changing their e-mail settings. I click the Manage Email/Passwords link to go to the Autoreply Email Messaging page, as shown in Figure 8-1. I select the Enable Autoreply Message? box to turn on the feature and then click inside the Enter Autoreply Message Below box to set up my autoresponse text.

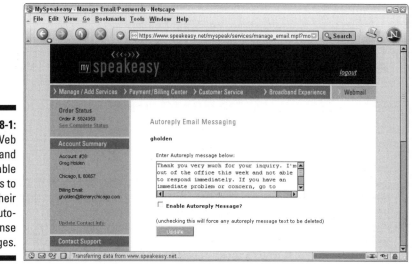

Figure 8-1:
Many Web hosts and ISPs enable users to create their own auto-response messages.

If the service that hosts your Web site doesn't provide free autoresponders, look into *SendFree,* an online service that provides you with autoresponder service for free but requires you to display ads along with your automatic response. (An ad-free version is available for $19.97 per month.) Read about it at `www.sendfree.com`.

Noting by quoting

Responding to a series of questions is easy when you use *quoting* — a feature that lets you copy portions of the message to which you're replying. Quoting, which is available in almost all e-mail programs, is particularly useful for responding to a mailing list or newsgroup message because it indicates the specific topic being discussed.

How do you tell the difference between the quoted material and the body of the new e-mail message? The common convention is to put a greater-than (>) character in the left margin, next to each line of the quoted material.

When you tell your e-mail software to quote the original message before you type your reply, it generally quotes the entire message. To save space, you can *snip* (delete) the part that isn't relevant. However, if you do so, it's polite to type the word <snip> to show that you've cut something out.

Attaching files

A quick and convenient way to transmit information from place to place is to attach a file to an e-mail message. In fact, attaching files is one of the most useful things you can do with e-mail. *Attaching,* sending a document or file along with an e-mail message, allows you to include material from any file to which you have access. Attached files appear as separate documents that recipients can download to their computers.

Many e-mail clients allow users to attach files with a simple button or other command. Compressing a lengthy series of attachments by using software, such as StuffIt or WinZip, conserves bandwidth. Using compression is also a necessity if you ever want to send more than one attached file to someone whose e-mail account (such as an AOL account) doesn't accept multiple attachments.

Protocols, such as MIME (Multipurpose Internet Mail Extensions), are sets of standards that allow you to attach graphics and other multimedia files to an e-mail message. Recipients must have an e-mail program that supports MIME (which includes almost all the newer e-mail programs) in order to download and read MIME files in the body of an e-mail message. In case your recipient has an e-mail client that doesn't support MIME attachments or you aren't sure whether it does, you must encode your attachment in a format such as BinHex (if you're sending files to a Macintosh) or UUCP (if you're sending files to a newsgroup).

Creating a signature file that sells

One of the easiest and most useful tools for marketing on the Internet is a signature file, or sig file. A *signature file* is a text blurb that your system appends automatically to the bottom of your e-mail messages and newsgroup postings. You want your signature file to tell the readers of your message something about you and your business. You can include information such as your company name and how to contact you.

Creating a signature file takes only a little more time than putting your John Hancock on the dotted line. First, to create the signature file itself, follow these steps:

1. **Open a text-editing program.**

   This example uses Notepad, which comes built in with Windows. If you're a Macintosh user, you can use SimpleText. With either program, a new, blank document opens on-screen.

2. **Press and hold down the hyphen (–) key or the equal sign (=) key to create a dividing line that separates your signature from the body of your message.**

   Depending on which symbol you use, a series of hyphens or equal signs forms a broken line. Don't make this line too long, or it runs onto another line, which doesn't look good; 30 to 40 characters is a safe measure.

3. **Type the information about yourself that you want to appear in the signature, pressing Enter after each line.**

   Include such information as your name, job title, company name, e-mail address, and Web site URL, if you have one. A three- or four-line signature is the typical length.

   If you're feeling ambitious at this point, you can press the spacebar to arrange your text in two columns. My agent (who's an online entrepreneur) does this with his own signature file, as shown in Figure 8-2.

   Always include the URL to your business Web site in your signature file and be sure to include it on its own line. Why? Most e-mail programs recognize the URL as a Web page by its prefix (`http://`). When your reader opens your message, the e-mail program displays the URL as a clickable hyperlink that, when clicked, opens your Web page in a Web browser window.

4. **Choose File⇨Save.**

   A dialog box appears, enabling you to name the file and save it in a folder on your hard drive.

5. **Enter a name for your file that ends in the filename extension** `.txt`.

   This extension identifies your file as a plain-text document.

6. **Click the Save button.**

   Your text file is saved on your computer's hard drive.

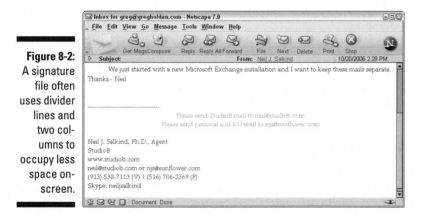

Figure 8-2:
A signature file often uses divider lines and two columns to occupy less space on-screen.

If you created a plain-text version of your electronic signature, the next step is to identify that file to the computer programs that you use to send and receive e-mail and newsgroup messages. Doing so enables the programs to make the signature file appear automatically at the bottom of your messages. The procedure for attaching a signature file varies from program to program; the following steps show you how to do this by using Microsoft Outlook Express 6:

1. **Start Outlook Express and choose Tools⇨Options.**

   The Options dialog box opens.

2. **Click the Signatures tab.**

3. **Click New.**

   The options in the Signatures and Edit Signature sections of the Signatures tab are highlighted.

4. **Click the File button at the bottom of the tab and then click Browse.**

   The Open dialog box appears. This is a standard Windows navigation dialog box that lets you select folders and files on your computer.

5. **Locate the signature file that you created in the preceding set of steps by selecting a drive or folder from the Look In drop-down list. When you locate the file, click the filename and then click the Open button.**

   The Signature File dialog box closes, and you return to the Options dialog box. The path leading to the selected file is listed in the box next to File.

6. **Click the Add Signatures to All Outgoing Messages check box and then click OK.**

   The Options dialog box closes, and you return to Outlook Express. Your signature file is added automatically to your messages.

To test your new signature file, choose File⇨New⇨Mail Message from the Outlook Express menu bar. A new message composition window opens. Your signature file appears in the body of the message composition window. You can compose a message by clicking before the signature and typing.

Signature files, autoresponders, and other techy gimmicks are fine, but the key to making them work is checking your e-mail and phone messages every single day. That includes weekends! If you can't do the job yourself, assign an employee to do it. That's the single most important customer service tip I can convey to you: Check your messages as frequently as possible, and respond to inquiries as quickly as you can.

Creating forms that aren't formidable

In the old days, people who heard "here's a form to fill out" usually started to groan. Who likes to stare at a form to apply for a job or for financial aid, or, even worse, to figure out how much you owe in taxes? But as an online businessperson, forms can be your best friends because they give customers a means to provide you with feedback as well as essential marketing information. With forms, you can find out where customers live, how old they are, and so on. Customers can also use forms to sound off and ask questions.

Forms can be really handy from the perspective of the customer as well. The speed of the Internet enables them to dash off information right away. They can then pretty much immediately receive a response from you that's tailored to their needs and interests.

The two components of Web page forms

Forms consist of two parts, only one of which is visible on a Web page:

- ✔ The *visible* part includes the text-entry fields, buttons, and check boxes that an author creates with HTML commands.

- ✔ The *invisible* part of the form is a computer script that resides on the server that receives the page.

The aforementioned script, which is typically written in a language such as Perl, AppleScript, or C++, processes the form data that a reader submits to a server and presents that data in a format that the owner or operator of the Web site can read and use.

How the data gets to you

What exactly happens when customers connect to a page on your site that contains a form? First, they fill out the text-entry fields, radio buttons, and other areas you have set up. When they finish, they click a button, often marked Submit, to transmit (or *post*) the data from the remote computer to your Web site.

A computer script called a Common Gateway Interface (CGI) program receives the data submitted to your site and processes it so that you can read it. The CGI may cause the data to be e-mailed to you, or it may present the data in a text file in an easy-to-read format.

Optionally, you can also create a CGI program that prompts your server to send users to a Web page that acknowledges that you received the information and thanks them for their feedback. This is a nice touch that your customers are sure to appreciate.

Writing the scripts that process form data is definitely in the province of Webmasters or computer programmers and is far beyond the scope of this book. But you don't have to hire someone to write the scripts: You can use a Web page program (such as Microsoft Expression WebDreamweaver) that not only helps you create a form but also provides you with scripts that process the data for you.

Some clever businesspeople have created some really useful Web content by providing a way for nonprogrammers, such as you and me, to create forms online. Appropriately enough, you connect to the server's Web site and fill out a form provided by the service to create your form. The form has a built-in CGI that processes the data and e-mails it to you. The Links page on this book's Web site includes some free form creation and processing services.

Using Expression Web to create a form

You can use Microsoft Expression Web to create the data-entry parts of forms, such as text boxes and check boxes. You can then link your form to a behind-the-scenes script that processes form data such as the popular FormMail program provided free online by Matt Wright in Matt's Script Archive (www.scriptarchive.com/formmail.html). Creating your own form gives you more control over how it looks and a greater degree of independence than if you use a ready-made forms service.

You might not have to look far to find FormMail. It's popular enough that many Web hosts provide it on their Web servers. I found it already up and running on mine. All I had to do was "point" the form to the script to process the data and send it to myself in an e-mail message.

The first step in setting up a Web page form is determining what information you want to receive from someone who fills out the form. Your Web page creation tool then gives you options to ask for the information you want. Start Expression Web and open the Toolbox by choosing Toolbox from the Task Panes menu. When the Toolbox opens, click the plus sign (+) next to Form Controls. Drag the form object into the page at the spot where you want the form to appear. The Toolbox also gives you a selection of the most commonly used options, including

- ✔ **Text Box:** Creates a single-line box in which someone can type text
- ✔ **Text Area:** Creates a scrolling text box
- ✔ **File Upload:** Lets the user send you a text file
- ✔ **Check Box:** Creates a check box
- ✔ **Input (Radio):** Creates an option button, sometimes called a radio button
- ✔ **Drop-Down Box:** Lets you create a drop-down list
- ✔ **Picture:** Lets you add a graphic image to a form

Figure 8-3 shows the most common form fields as they appear in a Web page form that you're creating.

When you add the Form control to a page you're designing, Expression Web inserts a dashed, marquee-style box in your document to signify that you're working on Web page form fields rather than normal Web page text.

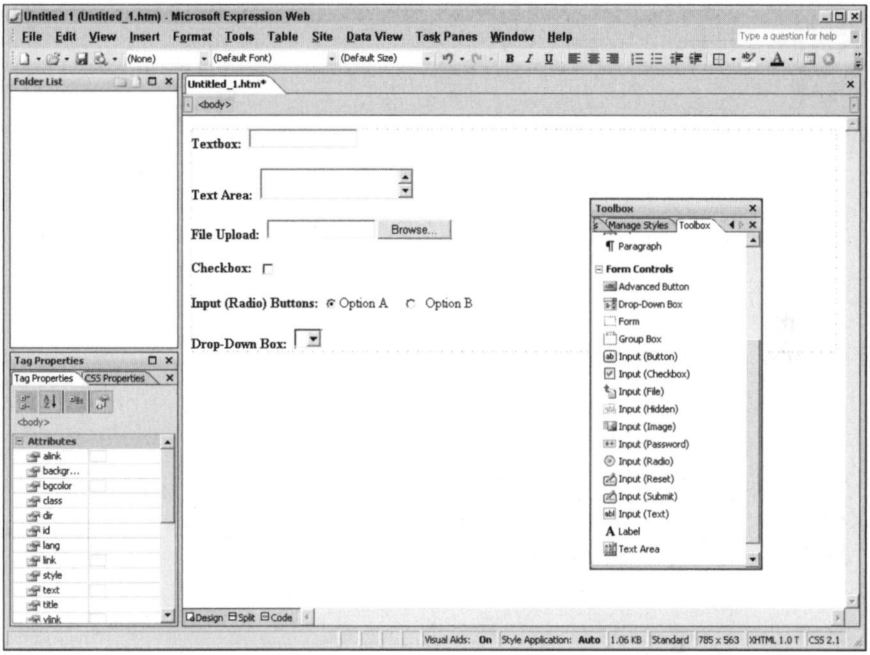

Figure 8-3:
Expression Web provides you with a Toolbox for quickly creating form elements.

Making Customers Feel That They Belong

In the old days, people went to the market often, sometimes on a daily basis. The shopkeeper was likely to have set aside items for their consideration based on individual tastes and needs. More likely than not, the business transaction followed a discussion of families, politics, and neighborhood gossip.

Good customer service can make your customers feel like members of a community that frequent a Mom-and-Pop store on the corner of their block — the community of satisfied individuals who regularly use your goods and services. In the following sections, I describe some ways to make your customers feel like members of a group, club, or other organization and who return to your site on a regular basis to interact with a community of individuals with similar interests.

CASE STUDY

Adding the personal touch that means so much

Sarah-Lou Morris started her business out of an apartment in London, England, in 1997. She developed an herbal insect repellent — Alfresco — while working in a botanical and herbal research center. Since then, sales have grown quickly — often doubling each year. One key to Morris's quick success is her personal approach to serving her customers, who include movie stars on location and other prominent entertainers such as Sir Paul McCartney.

Morris describes her Web site and operation (www.alfresco.uk.com), shown in the accompanying figure, as "an extremely lively business . . . an ever-growing, 24/7-demanding teenager that could easily drain my resources if I didn't keep a *very* tight shop." Over the years, she stuck to basic business practices and focused on cultivating the customer base she had already developed through selling her product by word of mouth. (The trendy term for this type of publicity is *viral marketing;* see Chapter 10 for more on this topic.) She started a fan club for Alfresco, and she has personally visited some of her best customers. Today, she is expanding her marketing to include social networks and is creating a new product line to reach younger customers.

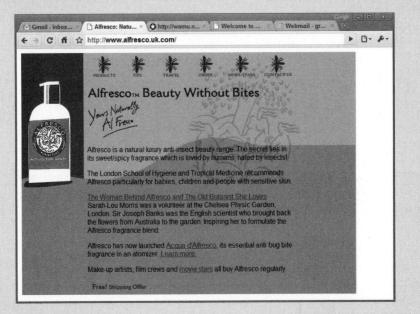

Q. How have you been able to keep a steady flow of business amid the ups and downs of the world economy?

A. We have built a bigger and bigger customer base by constantly giving good service to customers. We send out special editions for frequent buyers, have a fan club, and encourage customers to make recommendations. We listen to our customers — why wouldn't we? Our site could be more automated, making it easier for us to run, but we'd lose the personal touch. It's still rewarding, and I think profitable in the long term, to take a phone call or e-mail from some VIP in Rome or a badly bitten Chinese customer wanting quickly to buy what a friend just bought. The effort is still geared toward turning the products into a worldwide addiction-by-Internet.

I'm launching a new kids' product, Alfrescokids, that will bring in a new customer age range including young mums and dads, and young families. I decided to turn the concept of "insect repellant" on its head and make the theme for the site "attracting and preserving bugs" as they are part of our food chain. I have gathered good insect-related content and am hoping both children and adults will always think of our site as fun and contemporary.

Q. What are the one or two most important things people should keep in mind if they're starting an online business these days?

A. It isn't necessary to spend fortunes setting it up. Find a host that has been in business a number of years. (There *are* experts now.) A clean database that really works for you is vital because your customers are the most precious things a business can have. Keep in touch with them. Treat them with care and respect.

Q. What new approaches are you using to reach your customers?

A. Attracting the interest of search engines is a priority. We have spent enormous time researching our competition as well as the keywords people search for. And we are making sure we are sincere in our ethics. It's important to write intelligently about your products and services in a truthful and interesting way. Search engine robots wander about sites sifting the "worthwhile" from the "not so." If you don't spend time working on getting across clearly and precisely what is being sold, Google Robots will put you at the bottom of the pile.

I realize that including blogs, Twitter posts, newsletters, *et al.* is going to mean our staff will be extra busy. I have a Web site that attracts worldwide attention and I am very pleased to put on a good show. Most important is our customers' recommendations and word of mouth. Our Fan Club now enables lots of banter and travel tips, with offers and goodies from all kinds of areas. I hope to grow as a service similar to the travel clinic with advice and help incorporating travel companies participating by offering our customers good deals on holidays.

Q. What's the single best improvement you've made to your site to attract more customers or retain the ones you've had?

A. Putting on a special code that only special customers or fan club members can access for discounts and so on. For example, Royal Bank of Scotland employees have a special code dedicated to them.

Q. Is this a good time to start an online business?

A. It's a great time to start an e-commerce biz for a number of reasons, not the least being that the technical support is now well and truly in place. Let's just say more people know what they're doing than in earlier years. Secondly, most new customers aren't as concerned about credit card security, as there really has been hardly any fraud.

Q. What advice would you give to someone thinking of starting a new business on the Web?

A. Your customer is King, Queen, Prince, and Princess. Whatever you would like yourself is what you should aim to offer. "Do as you would like to be done by" should be your motto. Expose yourself any which way and as often as is acceptable to as many well-targeted customers as possible. Most of all, keep a positive attitude. Sir Paul McCartney once said to me when I felt depressed and almost ready to give up, "Always have faith." I'm glad I listened to him!

Putting the "person" into personal service

How often does an employee personally greet you when you walk through the door of a store? On the Web as well as in real life, people like a prompt and personal response. Your challenge is to provide live customer support on your Web site.

Some Web sites do provide live support so that people can e-mail a question to someone in real time (or close to real time) by using Internet technologies, such as chat and message boards. The online auction giant eBay has a New Users Board, for example, where beginners can post questions for eBay support staff, who post answers in response.

An even more immediate sort of customer support is provided by *chat* in which individuals type messages to one another over the Internet in real time. One way to add chat to your site is to start a Yahoo! Group, which I describe in the "Starting a Yahoo! Group" section, later in this chapter.

LivePerson (`www.liveperson.com`) provides a simpler alternative that allows small businesses to provide chat-based support. LivePerson is software that enables you to see who is connected to your site at any time and instantly lets you chat with them, just as if you're greeting them at the front door of a brick-and-mortar store.

LivePerson works like this: You install the LivePerson Pro software on your own computer (not the server that runs your site). With LivePerson, you or your assistants can lead the customer through the process of making a purchase. For instance, you might help show customers what individual sale items look like by sending them an image file to view with their Web browsers. You can try LivePerson Pro for free for 30 days and then pay $99.99 per month thereafter.

Not letting an ocean be a business barrier

You're probably familiar with terms such as "global village" and "international marketplace." But how do you extend your reach into the huge overseas markets? Making sure that products are easily and objectively described with words as well as clear images and diagrams, where necessary, is important. You can effectively overcome language and cultural barriers in other ways, some of which are common sense while others are less obvious.

Keep in mind the fact that shoppers in many developing nations still prefer to shop with their five senses. So that foreign customers never have a question on how to proceed, providing them with explicit descriptions of the shopping process is essential. Make information on ordering, payment, execution, and support available at every step.

Customer support in Asia is, in many ways, a different creature than in the West. Although personalization still remains critical, language and translation give an e-commerce site a different feel. A Western site that might work well by looking clean and well organized might have to be replaced with the more chaotic blitz of characters and options that's often found more compelling by Eastern markets. In Asia, Web sites tend to place more emphasis on color and interactivity. Many e-commerce destinations choose to dump all possible options on the front page instead of presenting them in an orderly, sequential flow.

Enhancing your site with a discussion area

Can we talk? Even my pet birds like to communicate by words as well as squawks. A small business can turn its individual customers into a cohesive group by starting its own discussion group on the Internet. Discussion groups work particularly well if you're promoting a particular type of product or if you and your customers are involved in a provocative or even controversial area of interest.

The three kinds of discussion groups are

- **A local group:** Some universities create discussion areas exclusively for their students. Other large companies set aside groups that are restricted to their employees. Outsiders can't gain access because the groups aren't on the Internet but rather are on a local server within the organization.

- **A Usenet newsgroup:** Individuals are allowed to create an Internet-wide discussion group in the `alt` or `biz` categories of Usenet without having to go through the time-consuming application and approval process needed to create other newsgroups. Although Usenet was originally one of the most popular parts of the Internet, my sense is that Web-based groups such as Google Groups (`groups.google.com`) are more frequently used these days.

- **A Web-based discussion group:** You can start a Yahoo! Group, which I describe in the upcoming section named (surprise!) "Starting a Yahoo! Group."

Of these three alternatives, the first isn't appropriate for your business purposes. So what follows focuses on the last two types of groups.

In addition to newsgroups, many large corporations host interactive chats moderated by experts on subjects related to their areas of business. Small businesses can also hold chats, most easily by setting up a chat room on a site that hosts chat-based discussions. However, the most common way these days to build goodwill and establish new connections with customers and interested parties is an interactive Web-based diary — a *blog* (short for Web log). Find out more about blogs in Chapter 1.

Starting an alt discussion group

Usenet is a system of communication on the Internet that enables individual computer users to participate in group discussions about topics of mutual interest. Internet newsgroups have what's referred to as a hierarchical structure. Most groups belong to one of seven main categories: comp, misc, news, rec, sci, soc, and talk. The category name appears at the beginning of the group's name, such as rec.food.drink.coffee. In this section, I discuss the alt category, which is just about as popular as the seven other categories and enables individuals to establish their own newsgroups.

In my opinion, the biz discussion groups aren't taken seriously because they're widely populated by unscrupulous people promoting get-rich-quick schemes and egomaniacs who love the sound of their own voices. The alt groups, although they can certainly address some wild and crazy topics, are at least as well known and often address serious topics. Plus, the process of setting up an alt group is well documented.

The prefix alt didn't originally stand for *alternative,* although it has come to mean that. The term was an abbreviation for Anarchists, Lunatics, and Terrorists, which wasn't so politically incorrect back when newsgroups were young. Now, alt is a catchall category in which anyone can start a group, if others show interest in the creator's proposal.

The first step to creating your own alt discussion group is to point your Web browser to Google Groups (groups.google.com) or launch your browser's newsgroup software. To start the Outlook Express newsgroup software, click the plus sign next to the name of the newsgroup software in the program's Folders pane (this assumes that you already configured Outlook Express to connect to your ISP's newsgroup server) and access the alt.config.newgroups group. This area contains general instructions on starting your own Usenet newsgroup. Also look in news.answers for the How to Start a New Usenet Newsgroup message.

To find out how to start a group in the alt category, go to Google (www.google.com), click Groups, and search for the How to Start an Alt Newsgroup message. Follow the instructions contained in this message to set up your own discussion group. Basically, the process involves the following steps:

1. **Write a brief proposal describing the purpose of the group you want to create and include an e-mail address for where people can respond with comments.**

   The proposal also contains the name of your group in the correct form (`alt.groupname.moreinfo.moreinfo`). Try to keep the group name short and professional if it is for business purposes.

2. **Submit the proposal to the newsgroup** `alt.config`.

3. **Gather feedback to your proposal through e-mail.**

4. **Send a special message, or a *control message*, to the news server that gives you access to Usenet.**

   The exact form of the message varies from server to server, so you need to consult with your ISP on how to compose the message correctly.

5. **Wait a while (a few days or weeks) as *news administrators* (the people who operate news servers at ISPs around the world) decide whether to adopt your request and add your group to their list of newsgroups.**

Before you try to start your own group, look through the Big 7 categories (`comp`, `misc`, `news`, `rec`, `sci`, `soc`, and `talk`) to make sure that someone else isn't already covering your topic.

Starting a Yahoo! Group

When the Internet was still fresh and new, Usenet was almost the only game in town. These days, the Web is pretty much (along with e-mail) the most popular way to communicate and share information. That's why starting a discussion group on the Web makes perfect sense. A Web-based discussion group is somewhat less intimidating than others because it doesn't require a participant to use newsgroup software.

Yahoo! Groups are absolutely free to set up. (To find out how, just go to the FAQ page, `help.yahoo.com/l/us/yahoo/groups/original/index.html` and click the How Do I Start a Group? link.) They enable users not only to exchange messages but also to communicate in real time by using chat. And as the list operator, you can send e-mail newsletters and other messages to your participants.

Simply operating an online store isn't enough. You need to present yourself as an authority in a particular area that is of interest. The discussion group needs to concern itself primarily with that topic and give participants a chance to exchange views and tips on the topic. If people have questions about your store, they can always e-mail you directly — they don't need a discussion group to do that.

Chapter 9

Sourcing Worldwide for Your Business

I occasionally get questions from budding entrepreneurs just like you who are wondering how to get started selling online. The question that comes up most often is simple: "What should I sell online?" A variation on this question that I hear almost as frequently goes like this: "What's the single best thing I can possibly sell online?" (Translation: "What can I sell on the Web that will make me the most money?")

Everyone who asks this question wants a simple answer, and so do you. But no single item sells better than anything else on the Web. Rather, people are hunting for thousands of things while they stare at their laptops and desktop computers. Your challenge is to find a connection between one of those things and you: You need to find something that's desirable that (1) you can find easily and inexpensively, (2) you're interested in, and (3) is easy to photograph, pack, and ship.

The list of desirable items changes all the time as new products catch the fancy of consumers. When it first came out, the Sony PlayStation 3 was a hot item, having come out in woefully limited quantities just before the holidays. More recently, the Amazon Kindle 2 was hard to find for a while, and sellers were marking it up on eBay. No matter what the hot item is, you want to find something that consumers want and that you can sell for a profit. Sites such as Alibaba make sourcing in China more feasible to small businesses and individual sellers, too. This chapter describes your options for finding such merchandise in a steady supply and presenting it in a way that will cause Web surfers to click your Buy button.

Knowing What Sells Well Online

My first job was as a clerk in my neighborhood pharmacy. Much of my time was spent on the look of the store and the merchandise within it, whether that involved cleaning, arranging items on shelves, creating signs, or rearranging window presentations. All traditional brick-and-mortar storeowners take care to show off their merchandise in a way that attracts attention. You should do the same, even though you're dealing in clicks rather than bricks. This isn't a complicated subject: The two sections that follow examine the basics of a good online sales presentation: choosing desirable merchandise and presenting it in its best light.

These are the kind of sales approaches that apply whether you're selling on a Web site, putting an ad on Craigslist, or setting up a storefront in a marketplace such as Artfire (`www.artfire.com`) or Etsy (`www.etsy.com`) — or all of these.

It's hard to predict what kinds of items can attract good profits. But if you can think of a hot product that's in short supply, you can realize such profits yourself. On a much smaller scale, I'm amazed to find merchandise that sold on eBay for far more than I paid for it. Here are a few examples:

- I found a pair of women's ballet-style slippers by the designer Taryn Rose secondhand for $2 and sold them for $132. (I don't have an image of this sale, but Figure 9-1 shows a pair of sandals by the same designer that I bought for $4 and sold for $51.)

- I sold a Cedar electronic device, a "de-clicker" for cleaning up audio files, for my brother for $1,500.

- My mother bought a set of antique wooden-shafted Spalding golf clubs for $10, and I sold them for more than $100.

Does a common thread run through these tales? Two threads, actually. You need to look for merchandise that's desirable, either new or in near new condition, and that is either difficult to find or sells for a high amount to begin with. The Cedar device normally sells for several thousand dollars; the ballet slippers sold at retail for $335; the golf clubs are hard to find because they're antique. Online shoppers, in fact, typically flock to two kinds of merchandise:

- Things that are rare and unusual

- Things that are very expensive when sold at retail

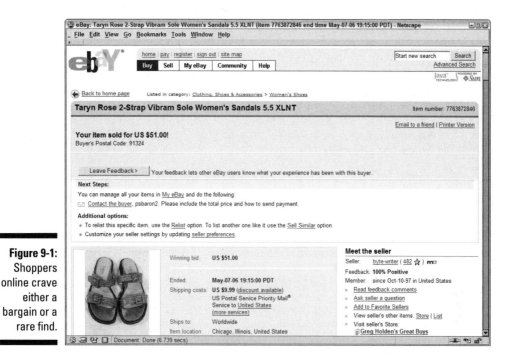

Figure 9-1:
Shoppers
online crave
either a
bargain or a
rare find.

They're looking on the Web either to find something they'd have trouble locating anywhere else or to find something at a much lower price than they'd pay anywhere else. Some enterprising sellers can deal in a variety of rare and desirable items. However, the majority of successful online entrepreneurs build their business by settling on a reliable source of desirable merchandise that they can buy in quantity from a wholesale supplier. They realize much slimmer profit margins than you might get from rare antiques. But they can sell a more-or-less predictable quantity of items each month, and what they don't get in profits, they make up for in the quantity and reliability of sales.

Finding Products Yourself

One of the many nice things about running an online business is the extent to which you can perform important functions no matter what your level of experience. This is both a blessing and a curse. Finding your own merchandise to sell is something you have to do on your own, for the most part — and yet, it's a subject that takes experienced retailers years to figure out. It can be a matter of trial and error, and it can be time consuming and difficult, too. But if you succeed with the central objective — finding a steady and reliable source for merchandise you can resell online at a profit — you've taken a huge step toward making your online business a success. I describe the most common options for do-it-yourself sourcing in the following sections.

Cleaning out your closets

Time and again, I interview successful online merchants (especially those who make a living selling on eBay) who began by selling what they found at hand. This kind of online commerce, in fact, is most practical when you're trying to sell on eBay: You start by cleaning your closets, attic, garage, and other storage areas. It's a sort of online garage sale: You get started and whet your appetite for future sales. Rummaging through your closets takes you only so far, though.

eBay isn't the only online marketplace for closet cleaners. If you find text-books, CDs, DVDs, or other common household items, you can add them to Amazon.com's marketplace. Your items appear alongside the same items offered for sale by "Earth's Biggest Bookstore." Selling in the marketplace is easier and quicker than on eBay; you don't even have to take photos. Find out more about Amazon.com in Chapter 12.

As a general rule, I tell budding sellers not to take a scattershot approach to sourcing and to avoid putting up anything and everything for sale. But in the beginning, when your primary goal is to clean out your house and make a few extra dollars, this approach has an advantage. When you're selling lots of different things, you might just discover one thing that interests you that you can sell in greater quantity. I know one eBay seller (a male, by the way) who sold a purse he found in his closet. It fetched a huge profit. He realized that certain brands of designer purses are eagerly sought on eBay. He has since gone on to become a leading seller of women's purses, an item he's never actually used.

Outsourcing your sourcing

Your closets are cleaned out; your attic is bare; you don't have a valuable antique to your name. How can you find merchandise to sell on the Web when you don't have anything of your own to start with? You sell other peoples' merchandise, that's how. In other words, you become a consignment seller — someone who puts items up for sale on behalf of the owner, who has given (or *consigned*) them to you to sell. This phenomenon is eBay-centric. In fact, finding eBay sellers who sell on behalf of friends, relatives, or total strangers is pretty common. I've never encountered a businessperson who sells on consignment through a Web site. The following sections, then, apply to eBay sellers, though they might be relevant to Web site or brick-and-mortar storeowners as well.

Somewhere in the world, a consignment seller probably sells through a conventional e-commerce Web site rather than an auction venue. But there are well-known consignment sellers who operate their own Web sites. The top dog among eBay trading assistants, Adam Hersh, has his own Web site (www.adamhershauctions.com), which includes a link to his eBay Store. As a consignment seller, you need to market and present yourself as effectively as people who are selling their own merchandise directly to customers.

Becoming a trading assistant

I'm using the term *trading assistant* loosely to refer to anyone who sells merchandise on eBay on behalf of the owners of the merchandise. The owner gets most of the profits; the seller earns a fee and does the work of photographing, listing, packing, and shipping the goods. Lots of eBay sellers peddle objects given to them by friends and family on an occasional basis. eBay uses the term *trading assistant* (TA) to designate someone approved by eBay to conduct consignment sales and who is listed in eBay's Trading Assistant directory (pages.ebay.com/tahub/index.html). In other words, you can become either an informal trading assistant or a formally designated one.

To become an informal trading assistant, you only have to find people who want to sell on eBay but who are unwilling to go through the work involved in conducting actual transactions. Chances are, they'll find you and you won't have to do much asking around. When word gets out that you're selling on eBay, you may well find that people come to you with boxes full of mementoes. You can also find clients by posting notices in your neighborhood stores or on your local version of Craigslist (www.craigslist.org), the popular classified ad service.

The advantage of taking on consignment sales is the ability to boost your feedback and your monthly gross sales figures in a relatively short amount of time. On eBay, a user's feedback rating is of great importance. *Feedback* is a numeric measurement of the comments left for you by people with whom you've done business. Someone who is satisfied with your performance as a buyer or seller can leave a positive feedback comment, which counts for 1 point. A negative comment counts for –1 point, and a neutral comment counts as 0 (zero). eBay sellers generally find that their sales go up if their feedback rating reaches into the hundreds, and if they can achieve PowerSeller status.

A *PowerSeller* has at least $1,000 in gross monthly sales or 100 sold items for three months in a row; at least 100 unique feedback results; a 98 percent positive feedback rating; and a good standing record as a seller. By turning around a substantial number of transactions for other people in a short amount of time and by shipping quickly, you can build both your feedback rating and your potential as a PowerSeller. You can make some extra money, to boot. (The merchandise is sold under your User ID, and buyers don't need to know that their objects belonged to someone other than you.) Another eBay designation, Top-Rated Seller, adds more requirements so that it is a little harder to maintain. Find out more about the criteria at pages.ebay.com/services/buyandsell/powerseller/criteria.html.

Just how much money can you make? The sky is the limit. Whether you're a formally designated TA or an informal consignment seller, you get to set your own payment terms. It's wise to look around the Trading Assistant directory to see what others are charging. The terms vary widely. Some TAs buy their customers' items outright and put them up for sale; others charge a flat fee of $10 per sale; most charge a fee for shipping and handling and a percentage of the sale price (perhaps 20–30 percent).

To find out more about the program, go to the Trading Assistants Program page (`pages.ebay.com/tahub/index.html`). You need to have a feedback score of more than 50, at least 97 percent positive feedback comments, and at least 4 items sold in the past 30 days to join the program. After you're a TA, you can create a profile about yourself and your area of interest, which is then included in a searchable database of such sellers.

Running a drop-off store

A few enterprising eBay sellers have taken consignment selling to a new level and opened brick-and-mortar outlets called *drop-off stores.* This is a big step that you should attempt only if you're an experienced PowerSeller and have a steady sales stream to cover the slowdowns and complications you'll inevitably encounter from opening a real physical store. On the other hand, with a physical location, you have lots of storage, a loading dock, and a location where wholesalers can ship to you. Depending on the location you choose, customers find you in the form of foot traffic. Choosing a good location (at an intersection, on a main street, or in a strip mall with plenty of parking) is only one consideration. Here are some others:

- ✔ You need lots of storage space to handle the increased sales volume you'll experience.

- ✔ You need to know how to say no to people whose merchandise just won't attract bids (or high enough bids; you might want to set a minimum of $50 per sale).

- ✔ You need a computer network for your employees, and possibly for customers who need to see the same search results you're conducting.

Some drop-off storeowners get a jump-start by signing up for a franchise with one of the big chains, such as iSOLD It (`877isoldit.com`). But drop-off stores are risky whether you open your own from scratch or join a franchise. I once interviewed a drop-off storeowner in northwest Illinois who grew tired of complaints, nonpaying bidders, and expenses associated with running a brick-and-mortar store. He bought a sign-making machine from a customer and decided to try his hand with that. The last I heard, he was enjoying making signs even more than he had liked selling on eBay.

CASE STUDY

Young trading assistant: No inventory, no worries

What do you when you're too young to have a storehouse of antiques and collectibles you can sell on eBay? You invite the owners of those valuable items to come to you, and you offer to sell them on eBay on their behalf. That's what Adam Hersh decided to do when he was a communications major at Northeastern University. "At the time, I had no idea what I was going to do with my life. Then I started taking night classes so I could be certified in e-commerce." He was still in college and didn't have venture capital funding or funds from previous occupations. "I said to myself, I can either buy or resell slowly or find another way to get inventory. I started as a trading assistant because it was a free way to have thousands of sales items at the same time."

In 2001, Hersh became an eBay trading assistant before there was a formal entity by that name. (eBay now has a program through which it certifies such sellers, as described earlier in this chapter.) Although he was a pioneer in the field, Hersh already had a history of entrepreneurship.

At age 12, he formed a corporation buying and selling baseball cards. He later did nightclub and concert promotions.

At this writing, Hersh is around 30 years old and is one of the highest profile and most successful sellers on eBay. Most trading assistants sell for individuals. Hersh has handled auction sales for some big-name entities, including MTV, Viacom, and the government of South Korea. He ran a charity auction for the New York Public Library. When he meets his clients in person, he often gets a strong reaction. "When I met with the South Korean government, they were satisfied with my presentation, but they flat out told me, 'I can't believe how young you are.'"

Hersh acknowledges that being a trading assistant can be more difficult and complex than selling for himself. "It is difficult, but it works well if you learn how to perfect it," he says. "If you perfect something that is difficult, you can be at the top."

Garage sales and flea markets

Garage sales and flea markets are the traditional ways to start selling, on eBay or Amazon.com, at least. You scrounge through your neighborhood garages sales, estate sales, house sales, rummage sales, and flea markets. You pick up some goodies at a bargain and put them up for sale. I know some PowerSellers who still get their merchandise this way. I'm thinking of a husband-and-wife team who sell on eBay under the User ID mrmodern. At this writing, their feedback rating is more than 9,000.

They don't waste their time with small-scale garage sales. Rather, they pick out big estate sales with care, and they show up before the sun rises so that they can be among the first in line. (Some sellers also pay students to wait in line for them until just before the sale opens.) Then they practically run through the sale, grabbing items that seem valuable, in a frenzy, trying to beat the competition. This is a perfectly viable way to run an eBay business — for some people, though not for me. If you're an incurable bargain hunter and you love the thrill of the hunt — and you have lots of time to spend — start looking in your local paper or online at sites like Craigslist for sales in your area.

Secondhand stores

Everyone has a thrift store, dollar store, or other secondhand shop in the immediate vicinity. These can be good sources of merchandise, provided that you can go there during the day when new stock is put out and competition is low. You have to be prepared to spend lots of time driving or walking from one venue to another, and you have to enjoy the hunt. Personally, I love the search and the thrill of discovering something that's like a hidden treasure. But I realize that for most sellers, finding a reliable wholesale supplier is a more practical option that carries lower stress with it as well.

Working with Wholesale Suppliers

Secondhand stores (such as those mentioned in the preceding section) are, in fact, wholesale suppliers. Getting to know the proprietors of your secondhand stores is a good idea; you can strike up relationships and let the owners know what you're looking for. If you're lucky, you might find that they put aside the items you want because they value your repeat business. These aren't the only kinds of wholesalers around, however. I give you some tips for finding and working with other sorts of suppliers in the following sections.

Finding wholesalers

If good wholesale suppliers were easy to find, everyone would use them. The fact is that finding good suppliers takes time and effort. One problem is that wholesalers don't advertise themselves in the places you're used to looking. Another is that they tend to want to deal with traditional, brick-and-mortar businesses. Some wholesalers look down on eBay or e-commerce sellers. They still don't understand that the Web is a legitimate marketplace.

What can you do to overcome these challenges? Other sellers have done the following:

✔ Rented a booth in an antiques mall and used that as a business address so that wholesalers could ship merchandise there.

✔ Listed themselves in the phone book for added credibility.

✔ Had a tax ID and a business license ready in case these items are requested.

To find wholesalers, look around. The Web is the logical place to start. The Chinese wholesale marketplace Alibaba (www.alibaba.com) is an increasingly popular venue for sellers seeking merchandise to sell. Another possibility is on eBay through the sales category Wholesale Lots.

But ask around, too. Often, wholesalers are found by word of mouth. Sometimes, you find products you like and that you're reasonably sure you can sell online. Going directly to the manufacturers is worth a try, but chances are, the manufacturer won't sell directly to you. I tried this once. I frequently sell a desirable line of high-end shoes for men that's manufactured in Wisconsin. When I called the company and talked to a sales rep, I was politely rebuffed. Producers are used to selling to wholesalers and not directly to eBay sellers. By selling to you at wholesale, they undercut their wholesalers as well as the retailers who sell their products to the public. You're much better off approaching the wholesalers.

Lots of online businesses advertise themselves as wholesale sellers. Many say they *drop-ship* their merchandise — in other words, they ship what's purchased directly from their wholesale facility so that they never actually have to handle it and may never see it.

Sound too good to be true? In many cases, it is, and you should always exercise a healthy dose of caution when you're looking for wholesale suppliers. The eBay sellers I've talked to who have faithful, reliable wholesalers guard the identities of those suppliers jealously. They usually find such suppliers only by word of mouth: Rather than answer an ad or visit a Web site, they ask someone who knows someone who . . . you get the idea.

If you aren't in the business of selling goods or services that you manufacture yourself, find a steady stream of merchandise that you can sell online. Your goal is to find a wholesaler who can supply you with good-quality items at rock-bottom prices. You can then mark up the prices and make a profit while keeping the prices low enough to make them attractive. Generally, the best wholesale items are small objects that can be packed and shipped inexpensively. On eBay, things like figurines, ornaments, stationery, and other small gift items are commonly sold by PowerSellers along with the occasional antiques and collectibles. Here are a few rules for finding items to resell:

✔ **Try them out yourself.** Purchase a few items yourself to start with or ask the wholesaler for samples. (Resist any attempts by the wholesaler to sell you, say, 10,000 items at a supposedly dirt-cheap price right off the bat.) Take a few of the items for a test-drive. It's easier to convince others to buy what you like yourself.

✔ **Try to sell many small, low-priced items rather than a few large ones.** Rather than computers or printers, consider selling computer memory chips or printer ink cartridges, for instance.

✔ **Ask for references.** Talk to businesspeople who have already worked with the supplier. Ask how reliable the supplier is and whether the prices are prone to fluctuate.

When looking for merchandise to sell, try to build on your own hobbies and interests. If you collect model cars, try to develop a sideline selling parts, paints, and components online. You'll find the process more enjoyable when you're dealing in products you love and know well.

You can find a page full of links to state Departments of Revenue, where you can apply for a state tax ID, at www.worldwidebrands.com/wwb/tax_popup.asp.

Approaching wholesalers

When you approach wholesalers, it helps to have a business address and a phone number dedicated to your business. Little things, such as an answering service or an assistant to answer your phone calls, can make a good impression on suppliers who aren't yet on board with the idea of individual entrepreneurs working at home and padding around their computer-laden offices in their bathrobe and slippers.

When you first talk to a wholesaler, don't immediately tell her that you're just creating your first Web site or that you're starting to sell on eBay and are hoping to build your feedback rating. Tell the sales rep your business name, your tax ID, and your address and then tell her what you're interested in doing. If the words "e-commerce" or "eBay" never come up in the conversation, so much the better. If they do, don't apologize for wanting to sell online, either: Be confident and straightforward. If the wholesaler is skeptical and doesn't want to sell to you, just move on to the next supply candidate.

Your first purchase from a wholesaler should be a small, trial run. Tell the wholesaler you want to buy a small quantity of what he offers to see what sells best. When you make a real purchase from a wholesaler, you'll have to buy a much larger quantity. You might have to take out a home equity loan or otherwise borrow to cover the initial cost if you don't have funds to begin with.

Giving your business a tax ID

Proper documentation is essential to ensure that wholesalers and other suppliers take your fledgling business seriously. The most important piece of documentation you can provide them is a tax ID. Another is a business license. In either case, you need to apply to the proper authorities to obtain the designation.

With respect to a business license, you may need to obtain that from your city, county, or state agency. A tax ID tells a tax agency that you collect sales tax. That tax agency might be your state tax department or the Internal Revenue Service (IRS). To get a tax ID (or Employer Identification Number, or

EIN), fill out a form designated for that purpose. To get one from the IRS, you can go to `www.irs.gov/businesses/small/article/0,,id=98350,00.html`. To get one from the state, contact your state's tax department.

You then need to turn over the sales tax you collect to your state. When the state sends you the forms needed for this purpose, your tax ID number (this might also be called your Business Tax ID or your Employer Identification Number, or EIN) is somewhere on the form. This is the number you can supply to wholesalers.

Turning to the Far East: Alibaba, Brokers, and More

China is known worldwide as a supplier of cheap consumer goods, and online sellers big and small are turning to China as an option for finding merchandise to resell at a profit. As you might expect, there are some potential pitfalls to keep in mind when you turn your attention to the Far East, and some special considerations that don't come into play when you are dealing with a wholesaler in the U.S. or in your own home country.

First, you have to keep in mind that a number of trade laws apply. You have to fill out forms to meet your import and export requirements. You have to pay duty and customs fees as well.

You can find out more about trade laws in Chapter 7.

But you need to keep some subtler issues in mind as well. First, you are hardly the first person to think about approaching the Chinese to buy wholesale. Many big-time sellers, including some of the biggest PowerSellers on eBay, have already been there. According to one of them, John Jacobs, a longtime seller on eBay and now CEO of Artfire (`www.artfire.com`), China tends to give preferential treatment to bigger sellers. "Typically, when you buy from China, you find that the profit margins are higher the more you buy," he says. In other words, the more you buy, the lower the price you're charged.

How do you compete with the big sellers? You have several options:

- ✔ **Make a personal appearance.** If you can go to China and meet factory owners yourself, the personal connection will help. That's what one eBay PowerSeller, Alan Warshauer, found out. He went to China and established connections that enabled him to sell charms on eBay.

- ✔ **Find a broker.** A broker functions as a middleman — someone who connects you with factories. Jacobs recommends this option. "Some brokers in China deal with as many as 200 different factories," he says. "They can offer you a wider selection than you would find on your own."

- ✔ **Go to trade shows.** You might meet Chinese manufacturers or brokers there. See "Working the Trade Shows," later in this chapter, for more details.

- ✔ **Search for a broker or supplier on Alibaba.** This site (www.alibaba.com) is explained further right after this list.

- ✔ **Look on eBay.** According to Jacobs, eBay is increasingly becoming a place where goods from China are sold at low prices — in some cases, low enough that you can resell the merchandise elsewhere.

Alibaba is a business-to-business marketplace: It brings together Chinese wholesale suppliers and overseas merchants. Go to the home page (www.alibaba.com) and you see listings for products that include health and beauty supplies, industrial materials, luggage, office supplies, printing and publishing, footwear and accessories, sports and entertainment, cellphones, jewelry, and toys. These are products made available by sellers in China to anyone who wants to meet their terms. You might be able to buy cellphone chargers, as long as you meet the minimum order quantity of 100 pieces. You don't always see the price on the site; you might have to contact the seller for that.

Alibaba is a convenient doorway into Chinese suppliers. It's more than 10 years old, having been founded by former English teacher Jack Ma in 1999. It has grown to be the second-largest Internet company in China. Alibaba is also moving into the U.S. market. As of this writing, it was planning to set up a marketplace that will directly compete with Amazon.com and Wal-Mart.

What are some potential pitfalls in working with suppliers on Alibaba? Testing the merchandise yourself isn't possible. Getting one or two sample items isn't always feasible, either — unless you use the company's new AliExpress site (http://wholesale.alibaba.com/), which is expressly designed for small wholesaler orders. Stories circulate about suppliers who aren't always trustworthy. Research sellers as much as you can, and try to deal with only those designated as Gold Sellers.

Working the Trade Shows

A *trade show* is a mass gathering where buyers and sellers meet in the hope of making business connections. For many entrepreneurs, trade shows are a mysterious thing — it seems that they're only for those "in the trade" and not amateurs like you. You need to get over this attitude and realize that you *are* the trade. In fact, you're on the cutting edge. By selling online, you have something to offer that wholesale suppliers are eager to know about. I highly recommend that after you settle on the kind of merchandise you want to sell, you find trade shows in that area so that you can go on the hunt for wholesale suppliers.

Don't travel all the way to a trade show without registering first and making sure that you're qualified to attend. Saying that you have a Web site or an eBay Store might not be enough. You might have to provide a tax ID number, a business phone number, or a business address to convince those in charge that you're a legitimate businessperson.

The problem is that trade shows aren't always easy to find. Very few are likely to advertise in the local media. Looking online is a better bet. Try the following possibilities:

✔ The Web site TSNN.com (`www.tsnn.com`), which calls itself "The Ultimate Trade Show Directory" and gathers information about upcoming trade shows

✔ Your local convention bureau, which probably has a list of upcoming events

✔ Trade journals in your chosen field

When you get to an event such as the L.A. Shoe Show, Coffee Fest Chicago, or the Jersey Shore Home Show, you can quickly get overwhelmed with the sheer size of the venue and the large number of people involved, especially if you've traveled a long way to attend. Make sure that you go with someone so that you can take a team approach and divide the searching. It's also a good idea for one person to "work the floor" while the other is stationed at a computer, either in a hotel room or at home. The person at the show can describe brand names and models, and the computer operator can look them up online to gauge the level of demand for such items.

Part III
Building Traffic through Social Networking and More

The 5th Wave   By Rich Tennant

"We have no problem funding your Web site, Frank. Of all the chicken farmers operating Web sites, yours has the most impressive cluck—through rates."

In this part . . .

If you've never run an online business before and you're starting out from scratch, it makes sense to advertise wisely. One option is to place expensive and old-fashioned banner ads. But you can also pay for keywords using Google AdWords. And you can take advantage of new approaches that help you reach customers directly — and sometimes without even spending a penny.

Chapter 10 gets you started with the basics of online advertising. Chapter 11 describes Search Engine Optimization (SEO), the practice of optimizing Web pages so that they are more easily found by search engines. In Chapter 12, I show you how to get up and running with Craigslist, Amazon.com, and CafePress.

Chapter 10

Advertising and Publicity:
The Basics

● ●

In This Chapter

▶ Branding your business for success

▶ Finding free advertising for businesses on a budget

▶ Making the most of mailing lists and word of mouth

▶ Maintaining an electronic address book

▶ Placing banner ads

▶ Broadening your customer base by shipping overseas

● ●

*E*very month — sometimes, every week, it seems — the Internet spawns a new superstar. As I write this, the star of the moment is a young man named Justin Bieber, who has become a household name from a new YouTube video, followed by an appearance on the television show "Saturday Night Live." A woman named Amber Lee Ellinger released a YouTube video called "Obama Girl" in 2007, before the presidential election of 2008. She went on to appear on "Saturday Night Live" as well, and her video has since been viewed an estimated 13 million times.

In these cases, word of mouth generated the attention — with a little help from the Web. As time goes on, such stories only become more common as more innovative online advertising venues become available and imaginative people find ways to get their work before the public. The Web can be a cost-effective way for a small business owner such as yourself to get a potential customer's attention. In fact, the most successful advertising strategies often involve one individual connecting with another. Targeted, personalized public-relations efforts work online because cyberspace is a personal place where intimate communication is possible. Blanketed advertising strategies of the sort you see in other media (most notably display ads, commercials, or billboards) are expensive and don't always work for online businesses. Why? They lack the personal edge you get with e-commerce. The Web is a one-to-one communications medium. Successful e-commerce sites thrive not just because you can find bargains there but also because they promote community through features such as newsletters and message boards.

Internet advertising is big business, and entrepreneurs like you can benefit from it as well. In this chapter, I describe cost-effective, do-it-yourself advertising techniques for the online entrepreneur who has a fledgling business on a tight budget. Usually, the more effort you put into attracting attention to your business, the more visits your site (or sites) receives.

If you don't toot your own horn, it may not get tooted at all.

Coming Up with a Marketing Strategy

Half the battle with running a successful online business is developing a plan for what you want to do. The next step is to get noticed. For many businesses, the plan frequently involves getting people to talk about you — to promote "viral marketing" in which consumers themselves sing your praises. The following sections describe two strategies for making your company name more visible to online customers and promoting word-of-mouth publicity.

A brand that speaks for you

In business-speak, *branding* has nothing to do with cattle roundups and everything to do with jacking up your profits. Branding is the process of raising awareness of a company's name and logo through advertising, public relations, or other means (for instance, getting people to say, "Did you hear about . . .?" and then mentioning you, your products, your Web site, and so on).

Despite recent economic crises, the Web is a great place for developing a business brand. A 2009 study by the Interactive Advertising Bureau (www. iab.net) reported that advertising revenue (the amount that businesses spend to advertise online) totaled more than $5.5 billion for the first half of that year — a modest decrease of 5 percent over the same period in the previous year. The report states that the Internet "continues to gain share of marketing trend" for advertisers, and that search revenue accounted for 47 percent of ad revenues in the second quarter of 2009, up from 44 percent in the second quarter of 2008. It was followed by more traditional options such as display advertising (35 percent), classified ads (10 percent) and lead generation (7 percent).

Online advertising works because you don't have to get potential shoppers to dress up, drive across town, and find a parking spot. Web users sit only a foot or two from the screen (or only inches away, if they're using a handheld device), which means your Web page can easily get a user's undivided attention — if your content is compelling enough, that is. Don't be shy about providing links to click, thumbnail images to view, and the like. (Just be sure to place these items where they work best; see Chapter 11 for more about that.) Previous studies have found that Web advertising that doesn't seem like advertising — that is, it's interactive and entertaining — is supported and liked by consumers. These studies also showed that brands advertised on the Web were seen as forward thinking.

But don't rely on your Web page alone to spread your name. Make use of the whole Internet — including e-mail, online communities, contests, and promotions. These days you have plenty of options to get the word out about your online business, such as the following:

- **Blogs:** These are online diaries that you can create to encourage connections with your customers and other interested individuals; you can use them to build visibility and generate advertising revenue.

- **Social networking:** A growing number of businesses are using popular places such as Facebook and MySpace to promote themselves and their products. In fact, BizFriendz (`www.bizfriendz.com`) is a social-networking site created especially for business owners.

- **Banner ads:** This type of ad is similar to the traditional print ads that you can place in a newspaper. See the "Waving a banner ad" section, later in this chapter, for more information.

- **Classifieds:** You can advertise your goods on a classified ad site such as Craigslist (`www.craigslist.org`).

- **Interstitials:** These pop-up ads appear in a separate window while a Web page is loading.

  Pop-ups are fairly common on the Web, but many users strongly dislike them and set their browsers to disallow them. Such ads also slow down the browsing/shopping process, which dampens the enthusiasm of impulse buyers. Before you use them, consider both the upside and downside, as described in the "Pop-up (and under, and over) ads" section, later in this chapter.

- **Keyword searches:** You can learn how search services work so that you can make your site appear more prominently in search results.

- **Newsletters:** You can generate goodwill and drive business to your Web site by distributing an e-mail newsletter.

- **Partnerships:** Find businesses whose goods and services complement yours and create links on each other's Web sites.

A Web site can also promote a brand that has already become well known through traditional sales and marketing strategies. The click-and-mortar version of Wal-Mart (`www.walmart.com`) works in conjunction with the giant retailer's many brick-and-mortar stores. The Web site provides a selection of styles and sizes that's generally wider than what customers can find in stores. The National Retail Federation's Stores magazine (`www.stores.org`) ranked Wal-Mart number 1 among all retail stores, with more than $13 million in revenue in 2008.

CASE STUDY

Painting a new business scenario

Marques Vickers has appeared in this book through several editions when he was primarily an artist based in California. His life has changed dramatically, and though he says he doesn't spend as much time online as he used to, he's an example of someone who has been able to change his life and circumstances profoundly, in part through the Web. "I can clearly say that Internet access enabled me to pursue my present course even if it meant shifting directions," he declares.

Through his self-named Web site (www.marquesv.com), he still markets his own painting, sculpture, and photography, as well as his books on marketing and buying fine art online. In 2009, he became an auction consultant, using eBay to market both paintings and collectible items; his new site is at www.artsinamerica.com. He first went online in November 1999, and his art-related sites have received anywhere from 25,000 to 40,000 visits per month.

Q. What have you done to market your work in a difficult economy?

A. Time is the lone commodity we often have control of, so I am focusing my selling activities on areas that are truly productive, and I pay greater attention to the response from advertising. Essentially, time management is my greatest form of cost control.

Q. What are the costs of running all your Web sites and doing the associated marketing?

A. Out-of-pocket expense is approximately $29 monthly for a Web site hosting and Internet access package. New domain name registrations and renewals probably add another $250 because I own more than 20 domain names.

Q. What would you describe as the primary goals of your online business?

A. My initial objective was to develop a personalized, round-the-clock global presence in order to recruit sales outlets, sell directly to the public, and create a reference point for people to access and view my work. I also have an intuitive sense that an online Web site presence will be a marketing necessity for any future visual artist and a lifelong exposure outlet. Having an online presence builds my credibility as a fine artist and positions me to take advantage of the evolution of the fine arts industry, too.

Q. Has your online business been profitable financially?

A. Absolutely — but make no mistake, achieving sales volume and revenue is a trial-and-error process and involves a significant time commitment. I'm still perfecting the business model, and it may require years to achieve the optimum marketing plan.

Q. How do you promote your site?

A. With the Internet, you are layering a collective web of multiple promotional sources. Experimentation is essential because recognition is not always immediate but may ultimately be forthcoming because postings in cyberspace are often stumbled across from unforeseen resources. I try multiple marketing outlets including paid ad positioning services, such as Overture and Google, bartered advertising space, and reciprocally traded links. Some have had moderate success, some unforeseen and remarkable exposure. Unlike traditional advertising media that have immediate response times, the Internet may lag in its response. It is a long-term commitment and one that cannot be developed by short-term tactics or media blitzes.

Q. Do you create your Web pages yourself or do you work with someone to do that?

A. I'm too particular about the quality of content to subcontract the work out. Besides, I know what I want to say, how I want to say it, and am capable of fashioning the design concepts I want to integrate. The rectangular limitations of HTML design make color a very important component, and the very minimal attention span of most Web viewers means that you'd better get to the point quickly and concisely. The more personalized, timely, and focused your content, the more reason an individual has to return to your Web site and ultimately understand your unique vision of what you're trying to create. A Web site is an unedited forum for telling your version of a story and a means for cultivating a direct support base.

Q. How are you using the Web these days?

A. A few years ago, I uprooted from Northern California with my wife, and we moved to the Languedoc region of southern France. I decided to focus my activities on areas more interesting to me and pursue a completely different direction. Much of the process is detailed in a column I write called "An American in the French Languedoc" (`http://www.the-languedoc-page.com/articles/languedoc-articles01g.htm`). I am still doing my artwork, but my primary "work" is buying and renovating houses (`www.UniqueSeek.com`). I've taken a decided step back from the pace of northern California. I still use the Internet for promoting the houses I renovate, however.

Q. What advice would you give to someone starting an online business?

A. Don't hesitate one minute longer than necessary. Read substantially and from a diverse selection of sources on the subject. Subscribe to e-zines on related subject matter and query the Webmasters of sites that impress you with their content. Go to informational seminars; ask questions. Distribute your message to multiple outlets, but focus your time and energy on what works best. Don't be afraid to experiment. Established sales outlets are usually best. The Internet is here to stay, and we have just scratched the surface in terms of potential.

You may not have thousands of dollars to spend on banner ads, but they aren't the most effective forms of online advertising anymore, anyway. It's just as effective to start with some simple, cost-effective techniques like this one: Make sure that your signature files, your domain name, and your e-mail address all refer to your company name as closely as possible. It may take a while for your business to develop name awareness among consumers, but these techniques give you a perfect way to start.

Being selective about your audience

Traditional broadcast advertising, such as commercials or radio spots, works kind of like standing on top of a tall building and screaming, "Hey, everyone, come to my store!" Such ads deliver short bits of information to huge numbers of people — everyone in the coverage areas who happens to be tuned in at a particular time. The Internet has its own form of broadcasting — getting your company mentioned or advertised on one of the sites that draws millions of visitors each day.

But where the Internet really excels is in one-to-one communication of the kind that TV and radio can't touch. I suggest that you try your own personalized forms of online advertising before you attempt to blanket cyberspace with banner ads. Often you can reach small, *targeted* groups of people — or even one prospect at a time — through free, do-it-yourself marketing strategies. These strategies include using the right keywords, sending newsletters, and taking part in mailing lists and newsgroups, all of which I discuss in the next section.

Publicity Strategies That Are Free

In the following sections, I describe some ways that you can publicize your online business yourself — for free. Prepare, however, to devote several hours a week to corresponding by e-mail and applying to have your business listed in search services, Internet indexes, or Web sites that have a customer base similar to yours.

The best way to generate first-time and return visits to your business site is to make yourself useful as well as ornamental. The longer people are inclined to stay on your Web site, the more likely they are to acquire your goods or services. (See Chapter 5 for some specific suggestions on generating compelling, useful content.)

A newsletter for next to nothing

It used to be said that the pen is mightier than the sword, but these days nothing beats a well-used mouse. No longer do you have to spend time and money to print a newsletter on actual paper and distribute it around the neighborhood. Now that you're online, you can say what you want — as often as you want — with your own publication. Online newsletters also help meet your clients' customer service needs, as I discuss in Chapter 8.

Many of the suggestions in this section apply to an even easier way of getting the word out: creating a blog. With a blog, you don't have to worry about design, distribution, and organization issues, either; you just have to focus on putting out content that your readers will actually find useful and that will encourage them to return on a regular basis.

Publish or perish

The work of producing an online newsletter is offset by the benefits you get in return. You may obtain hundreds — even thousands — of subscribers who find out about you and your online business.

To run your publishing venture smoothly, however, you have some areas to consider:

- ✔ **Topics:** If you run out of your own topics to write about, look to others for inspiration. Identify magazines in your field of business so that you can quote articles. Get on the mailing list for any press releases you can use.

- ✔ **Staff:** You don't have to do it all. Delegate the editing function to someone else, or line up colleagues to function as contributors.

- ✔ **Design:** You have two choices: Send a plain-text version that doesn't look pretty but that everyone can read easily, or send a formatted HTML version that looks like a Web page but is readable only by people who can receive formatted e-mail. Keep in mind, though, that many users are on corporate e-mail systems that either discourage or prohibit HTML-formatted e-mail. Others don't like HTML e-mail because it takes longer to download the graphics files.

- ✔ **Audience:** Identify your readers and make sure that your content is useful to them. (This last item certainly applies to business blogs: Keep the personal news about your trip to Ibiza or your new puppy for a personal blog; focus on your area of expertise and present news and tips for readers who will be interested in them.)

Newsletters work only if they appear on a regular basis *and* they consistently maintain a high level of quality. Whether yours comes out every week, every month, or just once a year, your subscribers expect you to re-create your publication with every new issue. Keep your newsletter simple and make sure that you have the resources to follow through.

Extra! Read all about it!

After you do your planning, the actual steps involved in creating your newsletter are pretty straightforward. Because you're just starting out, I suggest that you concentrate on producing only a plain-text version of your newsletter. Later on, you can think about doing an HTML version as well.

People like receiving inside tips and suggestions in plain text; they're happy that they don't have to wait for graphics files to download. On the other hand, a simple layout with colors and small photos can work well. Figure 10-1 shows an example: The Chicago publishing house that published my book *Literary Chicago* uses a two-column arrangement for its user-friendly newsletter. It's a standard layout provided by the e-mail marketing service Constant Contact (www.constantcontact.com).

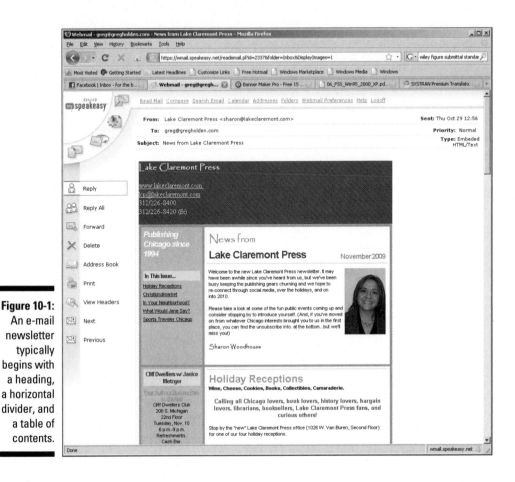

Figure 10-1:
An e-mail
newsletter
typically
begins with
a heading,
a horizontal
divider, and
a table of
contents.

Before you do anything, check with your ISP to make sure that you're permitted to have a mailing-list publication. Even if your newsletter consists of a simple announcement that you send out only once in a while (in contrast to a discussion list, which operates pretty much constantly), you'll be sending a *lot* more e-mail messages through your ISP's machines than you otherwise would.

Keep the size of your newsletters small; about 30K is the biggest e-mail file you can comfortably send. If you absolutely must have a larger newsletter, break it into two or three separate e-mail messages. Reducing the file size of your newsletter keeps your readers from getting irritated about how long your message takes to download or open. And keeping your customers happy should be one of your highest business priorities.

When you're all set with the prep work, follow these general steps for an overview of how to create and distribute your publication:

1. **Open a plain-text editor, such as Notepad (Windows) or SimpleText (Mac).**

2. **Start typing.**

   Just because your newsletter is in plain text doesn't mean that you can't spice it up. Consider the following low-tech suggestions for emphasizing text or separating one section from another:

   - *All caps:* Using ALL CAPITAL LETTERS is always useful for distinguishing the name of the newsletter or heads from subheads.

   - *Rules:* You can create your own homemade horizontal rules by typing a row of equal signs, hyphens, or asterisks to separate sections.

   - *Blank spaces:* Used carefully, that lowly spacebar on your keyboard can help you center plain text or divide it into columns.

   Be sure to proofread the whole newsletter before sending it. Better yet, enlist the help of an objective viewer to read over the text for you. Ask him or her to make suggestions on content, organization, and format, as well as to look for typos.

3. **Save your file.**

4. **Open your e-mail program's address book, select the mailing list of recipients, and compose a new message to them.**

5. **Attach your newsletter to the message, or paste it into the body of the message, and send it away.**

If you're sending many e-mail messages simultaneously, be sure to do your mailing at a time when Internet traffic isn't heavy. Many popular newsletters, such as *eWeek News,* go out on weekends, for example. Other e-commerce providers, such as 1shoppingcart.com (`www.1shoppingcart.com/news letter/Nov06/article5.html_`), say that Tuesday is the best day to mail.

Don't flood your Internet service provider's mail server with hundreds or thousands of messages at one time; you may crash the server. Break the list into smaller batches and send them at different times.

Be sure to mention your newsletter on your Web page and to provide an e-mail address where people can subscribe to it. In the beginning, you can ask people to send subscription requests to you. If your list swells to hundreds of members, consider automated mailing-list software or a mailing-list service to manage your list.

Managing your mailing list

When you make the decision to host and run your own mailing list, you assume the responsibility of processing requests to subscribe and unsubscribe from the list. This venture can start eating into the time that you need to spend on your other business activities. When mailing lists get to be too much to handle yourself, you have a couple of options to make life easier:

✔ **Purchase special mailing-list software.** This type of program automatically adds or subtracts individuals from a mailing list in response to special e-mail messages that they send to you. You can usually manage the mailing list from your home computer. If you're a Windows user, check out Mailing List Express by Mail-List-Software.com

(www.mail-list-software.com). Mac users can try ListSTAR by MCF Software (www.liststar.com).

✔ **Hire a company to run your mailing list for you.** Even though mailing-list software can help reduce the work involved in maintaining a list, you still have to install and use the software on a regular basis. So if you're really strapped for time, hiring a company to take care of your mailing list may be the way to go. Check out Constant Contact (www.constantcontact.com/index.jsp), StormPost (www.datranmedia.com/stormpost/), or Lyris ListHosting (www.lyris.com/solutions) for pricing information.

Participating in mailing lists and newsgroups

Many areas of the Internet can provide you with direct access to potential customers as well as a chance to interact with them. Two of the best places to market yourself directly to individuals are mailing lists and newsgroups. Mailing lists and newsgroups are highly targeted and offer unprecedented opportunities for niche marketing. Using them takes a little creativity and time on your part, but the returns can be significant.

Get started by developing a profile of your potential customer. Then join and participate in lists and newsgroups that may provide customers for your online business. For example, if you sell memorabilia of movie stars to fans online, you may want to join some newsgroups started by the fans themselves.

Where can you find these discussion forums? Topica (lists.topica.com) maintains a mailing-list directory that you can search by name or topic; it includes thousands of mailing lists. (Topica also helps you create your own e-mail newsletter, by the way.) Refdesk.com (www.refdesk.com) maintains links to Web sites, organized by category, that help you locate and participate in newsgroups, mailing lists, and Web forums.

A few newsgroups (in particular, the ones with `biz` at the beginning of their names) are especially intended to discuss small business issues and sales:

- ✔ `misc.entrepreneurs`
- ✔ `biz.marketplace.discussion`
- ✔ `biz.marketplace.international.discussion`
- ✔ `biz.marketplace.services.discussion`
- ✔ `alt.business.home`
- ✔ `alt.business.consulting`
- ✔ `aol.commerce.general`

The easiest way to access newsgroups is to use Google's Web-based directory (`groups.google.com`). You can also use the newsgroup software that comes built into Firefox or Microsoft Internet Explorer. Each browser or newsgroup program has its own set of steps for enabling you to access Usenet. Use your browser's online help system to find out how you can access newsgroups.

Mailing lists

A *mailing list* is a group of individuals who receive communications by e-mail. Two kinds of mailing lists are common online:

- ✔ **Discussion lists:** These are lists of people interested in a particular topic. People subscribe to the list and have messages on the topic delivered by e-mail. Each message sent to the list goes to everyone in the group. Each person can reply either to the original sender or to everyone in the group, too. The resulting series of messages on a topic is called a *thread*.

- ✔ **Announcement lists:** These lists provide only one-way communication. Recipients get a single message from the list administrator, such as an attached e-mail newsletter.

Discussion lists are often more specific in topic than newsgroups. These lists vary from very small lists to lists that include thousands of people. An example of a discussion list is ROOTS-L, which is a mailing list for individuals who are researching family history. People on this list exchange inquiries about ancestors that they're seeking and announce family tree information they've posted online.

By making contributions to a mailing list, you establish a presence, so when members are looking to purchase the kind of goods or services you offer, they're likely to come to you rather than to a stranger. By participating in the lists that are right for you, you also find out invaluable information about your customers' needs and desires. Use this information to fine-tune your business so that it better meets those needs and desires.

Marketing through lists and newsgroups requires a low-key approach. Participating by answering questions or contributing your opinion to ongoing discussion topics is far more effective than blatant self-promotion.

Always read the welcome message and list guidelines that you receive upon joining a mailing list. Figure out the rules before you post. Lurk in the background for a few weeks to get a feel for the topics and participants before you contribute. Let your four-to-six-line signature file establish your identity without selling your wares directly. Also, don't forget to spell check and proofread your messages before you send them.

Discussion groups

Discussion groups provide a different form of online group participation. On the Internet, you can find discussion groups in an extensive network called Usenet. America Online and CompuServe also have their own systems of discussion groups that are separate from Usenet. One of the easiest ways to access newsgroups, however, is with your Web browser. Just point it to Google Groups (`groups.google.com`). Many large corporations and other organizations maintain their own internal discussion groups as well. In any case, you can also access discussion groups with your Web browser's newsgroup or e-mail software. Microsoft Outlook Express can connect to newsgroup postings, for instance.

You can promote yourself and your business in discussion groups in the same way that you can make use of mailing lists: by participating in the group, providing helpful advice and comments, and answering questions. Don't forget that newsgroups are great for fun and recreation, too; they're a good way to solve problems, get support, and make new friends. For more information on newsgroups, see Chapter 3.

A contest in which everyone's a winner

In Chapter 2, I describe how cartographer John Moen uses contests and other promotions to attract attention to his online business. Remember that everyone loves to receive something for free. Holding a contest can attract visitors to your Web site, where they can find out about the rest of your offerings — the ones you offer for sale, that is.

You don't have to give away cars or trips around the world to get attention. SoftBear Shareware LLC — a company that offers Web hosting and manages several Web sites — gave away teddy bears and other simple items on its Web site (`www.799bear.com`). SoftBear's owner, John Raddatz, discontinued this particular contest, but he still provides free online games and a scholarship contest on other sites. When I asked John whether such contests had helped gain attention for his business, he responded as follows:

"Yes, yes, yes. Contests have increased traffic to my site. The response averages about 350 entries per month. I offer contests, free screensavers, and software, which still attract quite a few people from all over the world. My number-one contest draw is at Ice Puck University (www. ipucku.com), where I offer a free hockey diploma every month. My Johnny Puck Web site (www.johnnypuck.com) has spawned a local UHF TV show here in Muskegon, Michigan. You must offer something for free to draw people in to your site. Then you can draw their attention to your main offerings."

Cybersurfers regularly take advantage of freebies online, for example, by downloading shareware or freeware programs. They get free advice from newsgroups, and they find free companionship from chat rooms and online forums. Having already paid for network access and computer equipment, they actually *expect* to get something for free.

Your customers will keep coming back if you devise as many promotions, giveaways, or sales as possible. You can also get people to interact through online forums or other tools, as I describe in Chapter 5.

A 16-year-old cartoonist named Gabe Martin put his cartoons on his Web site, called The Borderline. Virtually nothing happened. But when his dad put up some money for a contest, young Gabe started getting hundreds of visits and inquiries. He went on to create 11 mirror sites (sites that provide duplicated information) around the world, develop a base of devoted fans, contribute to newspapers such as *The San Diego Union-Tribune,* and sell his own cartoon book. (You can read a brief bio at www.care2.com/ecards/bio/1022.)

Waving a banner ad

I'm not as big a fan of traditional banner ads as I am of the other strategies that I discuss in this chapter — especially where small entrepreneurial businesses are concerned. But banner ads have hardly gone away. You see them on the Microsoft Office Live hosting site and on popular sites such as YouTube (www.youtube.com) and MySpace (www.myspace.com). The latter venue reportedly attracts a billion page views per month, so it's a nearly irresistible place for advertisers. In general, though, banner ads are being used online less frequently than *targeted ads* — that is, ads that appear when specified keyword searches are conducted on sites such as Google (www.google.com) and Ask.com (www.ask.com).

Banner ads are like the traditional print ads you might take out in local newspapers. In some limited cases, banner ads are free, as long as you or a designer can create one. Otherwise, you have to pay to place them on someone else's Web page, the same way you pay to take out an ad in a newspaper or magazine.

Even these days, however, many commercial operations *do* use banner ads successfully on the Web. Banner ads can be effective promotional tools under certain circumstances:

- ✔ If you pay enough money to keep them visible in cyberspace for a long period of time
- ✔ If you pay the high rates charged by the most successful Web sites, which can steer you the most traffic

Banner ads differ from other Web-specific publicity tactics in one important respect: They publicize in a one-to-many rather than a one-to-one fashion. Banner ads broadcast the name of an organization indiscriminately, without requiring the viewer to click a link or in some respect choose to find out about the site.

Anteing up

You have to pay the piper to play the banner ad game. In general, Web sites have two methods of charging for banner ads:

- ✔ **CPM, or Cost Per Thousand:** This is a way of charging for advertising based on the number of people who visit the Web page on which your ad appears. The more visits the Web site gets, the higher the ad rates that site can charge. In this type of advertising, you have to pay depending on the number of times your ad is *viewed,* regardless of whether anyone clicks it to actually visit your site.
- ✔ **CTR, or Clickthrough Rate:** A *clickthrough* occurs when someone clicks a banner ad that links to your (the advertiser's) Web site. (Virtually all banner ads are linked this way.) In this case, you are billed after the ad has run for a while and the clicks have been tallied.

Say that 100,000 people visit the site on which your banner runs. If the site charges a flat $20 CPM rate, your banner ad costs $2,000 (100 × $20). If the same site charges a $1 per clickthrough rate, and 2 percent of the 100,000 visitors click through to your site (the approximate average for the industry), you pay the same: $2,000 (2,000 × $1).

Obviously, the more popular the site on which you advertise, the more your ad costs. Back in 1999, when Yahoo! was still publishing its advertising rates online, it charged a CPM rate of $20 to $50 for each 1,000 visits to the Yahoo! page on which the banner ad appears. If the page on which your banner runs received 500,000 visits, such ads could cost $10,000 to $25,000. Not all advertising sites are so expensive, of course.

These days, many advertisers are following Google's lead and charging for ads with a Cost Per Click (CPC) model, or some form of CPC. CPC is similar to CTR in that you, the advertiser, pay when someone clicks a link or graphic image that takes that person to your Web site. But the big difference is that in

Google's CPC model, *you* determine how much you pay for each click; in traditional CTR, the advertisers set the rates. In this system, the advertiser pays only when someone actually clicks an ad. In the case of Google's AdWords program (adwords.google.com), the amount paid per click is one that the advertiser decides by placing a bid on keywords used to display the ad. See Chapter 11 for more information on AdWords.

CPM rates are difficult to calculate because of the number of repeat visitors a site typically receives. For example, a Web page designer may visit the same site a hundred times in a day when testing scripts and creating content. If the site that hosts your ad charges a rate based on CPM, make sure that the site weeds out such repeat visits. You're better off advertising on sites that charge on not only a CPM but also a clickthrough basis — or, better yet, *only* on a clickthrough basis. The combination of CPM and CTR is harder for the hosting site to calculate but ultimately fairer for you, the advertiser.

Positioning banner ads can be a substantial investment, so be sure that your ad appears on a page whose visitors are likely to be interested in your company. If your company sells automotive parts, for example, get on one of the Yahoo! automotive index pages.

Profiting from someone else's banner ads

Banner ads may be out of favor, but they're not dead by any means. When used economically and targeted to the right audience, banner ads can help you achieve one of your goals: attracting visitors to your Web site. Attract enough visitors, and banner ads can help you achieve another, even more important goal: making money.

If you attract thousands or (if you're lucky) even millions of visitors to your site each month, you become an attractive commodity to advertisers looking to gain eyespace for their own banner advertisements. By having another business pay you to display their ads, you can generate extra revenue with very little effort.

Of course, the effort involved in soliciting advertisers, placing ads, keeping track of how many visitors to your site actually click ads, and getting paid *is* considerable — but you don't have to manage ads yourself.

For John Moen, owner of a pair of map-related Web sites (including Graphic Maps, which I profile in Chapter 2), the move from marketing his own Web site to becoming an advertiser came when his WorldAtlas.com (www.worldatlas.com) site began to attract 3 million hits per month. He turned to advertising giant DoubleClick (www.doubleclick.com) to serve the ads and handle the maintenance.

"We place [DoubleClick's] banner code on our pages, and [DoubleClick] pays us monthly for page impressions, direct clicks, page hits, and the like," says John. "[DoubleClick] also provides a daily report on site traffic. With [its] reports, I can tell which page gets the most hits and at what time of day. Banner advertising now pays very well."

Designing your ad

The standard "medium rectangle" and "large rectangle" banner ads are the traditional ones. Some standard square configurations or small buttonlike shapes are common, too. These days, ads appear on the side of a page (often, on the right, as on Facebook) and they are relatively small. The measurements for ads usually appear in pixels. An inch contains roughly 72 pixels, so a 110-x-80-pixel ad (the size seen on Facebook) is less than 2 inches wide and about 1 inch in height.

The rectangular ads appear most often at the top of a Web page, so they load first while other page contents have yet to appear; smaller ads may appear anywhere on a page. (Ensuring that your ad appears at the top of a Web page is always a good idea.)

Many banner ads combine photographic images, type, and color in a graphically sophisticated way. However, simple ads can be effective as well. You can create your ad yourself if you have some experience with a graphics program such as Paint Shop Pro. (You can download a trial copy of Paint Shop Pro at www.corel.com.)

Need some help in creating your own banner ad? If you have only a simple, text-only ad in mind and you don't have a lot of money to spend on design, try a create-your-own-banner-ad service or software program. I've had mixed results with the online banner-ad services such as The Banner Generator, provided for free by Prescient Code Solutions (www.coder.com/creations/banner). See Figure 10-2 for an ad that I created in just a couple of minutes by using a shareware program called Banner Maker Pro (www.bannermakerpro.com).

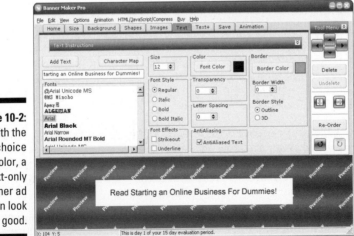

Figure 10-2: With the right choice of color, a text-only banner ad can look good.

Guerrilla Marketing and Advertising Strategies

I didn't make up the term *guerilla marketing*. As you may already know, the term appears in the titles of a series of popular books by Jay Conrad Levinson and Michael McLaughlin. It appears to be a buzzword that encompasses many (actually sensible) marketing techniques — from providing good customer service to knowing what your competition is doing. It also means going beyond the passive placement of ads on Web pages or other venues and taking a proactive, aggressive approach to getting your business name and brand in the marketplace. With competition growing all the time among online businesses, it pays to know all the options when dealing with online advertising — including the ones I describe in this section.

Pop-up (and under, and over) ads

The moment you connect to the CNN.com news site (www.cnn.com), a window pops up on your computer. In previous years, the window prompted you to choose the version of the news you want to see. When I checked recently, the window popped up and then under the CNN home page; it was an ad for the travel site Orbitz. Other sites typically urge you to sign up for news alerts or subscribe to a newsletter. Anything you can do to induce your visitors to identify themselves and provide contact information, from an e-mail address to a street address, is to your advantage.

Many Web surfers consider pop-up ads a bane, and some utilities — like the Google add-on browser toolbar and firewalls like Norton Internet Security, as well as browsers such as Internet Explorer and Firefox — can block them from appearing in the first place. But they can still get through to some individuals who don't have software configured to block them. And if your Web site becomes popular enough, you'll be approached by a company that wants to place its ad on your page, either as a banner ad that is part of the page or as a window that does one of several things:

- ✔ **Pops up:** This type of ad window is probably the most common one. It appears when a page is viewed and pops up atop the page you want to view. These ads work best when their content is related to the page you've opened: Subscribe to our newsletter, buy our book, attend our seminar, or other supplementary information.

- ✔ **Pops under:** When you open Web pages on many sites that display ads, a new window opens. But this window, which contains an ad unrelated to the Web page, opens underneath the primary window. Its content is visible only when the user specifically tries to close it, or closes or minimizes the other window(s) sitting on top of it.

✔ **Pops on top:** These ads, also called *interstitials,* totally replace the content you want to view. You are forced to look at them for a period of time and close them before you can view the page you wanted to see. I see these ads used on online magazines from time to time. When you click an article, a totally new window appears, with animated content, and it is big enough that it completely covers the article you want to read. You have to close the ad window in order to keep reading. You can read more about interstitials at

```
www.ecommerce-guide.com/news/news/article.
        php/6311_771181
```

John Moen told me that he has received criticism for pop-up and other ads on his clip-art site. But there's a trade-off here: The ad revenue makes it possible for him to keep creating the art and giving it away for free. In the end, whether consumers realize it or not, they benefit from the ads because they get free art. All they have to do is click the close box to delete the window that pops up.

Adding life to your ads

Ads on billboards, the sides of buildings, the sides of buses, the lights on top of cabs, and the pages of a newspaper and magazine have one thing in common: They basically sit there and don't do anything. They can have lights pointed at them, and magazine ads for perfumes can be scented — but that's about it.

On the Web, ads can get interactive in several different ways. The aim is to gain more attention from the jittery, hurried Web surfer who is, after all, looking for something else on the current Web page. You see several examples of interactive ads on the Graphic Maps clip-art pages (`worldatlas.com/clipart.htm`). On one particular visit to this page, I saw an ad for Walt Disney World that seemed to have snow falling, and another travel service ad presented a slide show. On YouTube (`www.youtube.com`), ads for popular movies immediately start playing video clips.

Creating ads that appear to move around is easy. You need software that's used to create animated GIF images, such as GIF Construction Set Professional, a Windows-only program available for $24.99 (`www.mindwork shop.com/alchemy/gifcon.html`), or the Macintosh application GIF.glf. giF, available for $28 (`www.peda.com/ggg`). When you create the initial ad image and save it in GIF format, you create a series of variations and string them together to create the animation. The animation software leads you through the process.

Minding Your Ps and Qs (Puns and Quips)

What is it that attracts shoppers to your business and encourages them to place orders from thousands of miles away? It's what you have to sell and how you present it. But how can customers understand what you're selling if they speak a different language? You must make your site accessible to *all* your potential customers.

Speaking their language

Put yourself in your customer's place. Suppose that you're from Spain. You speak a little English, but Spanish is your native tongue, and other Romance languages, such as French or Italian, are definitely easier for you to understand than English. You're surfing around an Internet shopping mall and you come across sentences such as

> Hey, ratchet-jaws. Shoot me some e-mail with your handle, and steer clear of Smokeys with ears.

> Whatever. All you home boys will be down with my superfly jive.

> Like, this cable modem is totally awesome to the max.

Get the picture? Your use of slang and local dialect may have customers from your own hometown or region in stitches, but it can leave many more people scratching their heads and clicking to the next site. The first rule in making your site accessible to a worldwide audience is to keep your language simple so that people from all walks of life — and various places on the planet — can understand you.

Using the right salutations

First impressions mean a lot. The way you address someone can mean the difference between getting off on the right foot and stumbling over your shoelaces. The following useful tidbits are from the International Addresses and Salutations Web page (`www.bspage.com/address.html`), which, in turn, borrowed them from Merriam Webster's *Guide to International Business Communication:*

   ✔ In Austria, address a man as *Herr* and a woman as *Frau;* don't use *Fräulein* for business correspondence.

   ✔ In southern Belgium, use *Monsieur* or *Madame* to address someone, but the language spoken in northern Belgium is Flemish, so be sure to use *De heer* (Mr.) when addressing a man, or *Mevrouw,* abbreviated to *Mevr.* (Mrs.) when addressing a woman.

   ✔ In India, use *Shri* (Mr.) or *Shrimati* (Mrs.). Don't use a given name unless you're a relative or close friend.

   ✔ In Japan, given names aren't used in business. Use the family name followed by the job title. Or, add *-san* to the family name (for example, Fujita-san), or the even more respectful *-sama* (Fujita-sama).

Adding multilingual content to your Web site is a nice touch, particularly if you deal on a regular basis with customers or clients from a particular area. Regional differences abound, so it's prudent to find a person familiar with the area you're trying to target and ask that person to read your text before you put it up on the Web. Let a friend — not the absence of orders for your goods — tell you that you've committed a cultural *faux pas.* That way, you can fix it before you put it out there.

Making your site multilingual

One of the best ways to expand your business to other countries is to provide alternative translations of your content. You can either hire someone to prepare the text in one or more selected languages or use a computer program to do the work for you. Then provide links to the Web pages that contain the translated text right on your site's home page, like this:

```
Read this page in:
French
Spanish
German
```

One translation utility that's particularly easy to use — and, by the way, free — is available from the search service Yahoo!. Just follow these steps to get your own instant translation:

   1. **Connect to the Internet, launch your Web browser, and go to** `babelfish.yahoo.com`.

      The Yahoo! Babel Fish Translation page appears.

   2. **If you have a specific bit of text that you want to translate, click in the Translate a Block of Text text box on this page and type the text or paste it from a word processing program. If you want the service to translate an entire Web page, enter the URL in the Translate a Web Page text box.**

Be sure to include the first part of the URL (for example, `http://www.mysite.com` rather than just `mysite.com`).

Obviously, the shorter and simpler the text, the better your results.

3. **Choose the translation path (that is, *from* what language you want to translate) by clicking the Select From and To Languages drop-down list.**

    At this writing, the service offers translation to or from Chinese, English, French, Korean, Spanish, German, Italian, Japanese, Dutch, Greek, Portuguese, and Russian.

4. **Click the Translate button.**

    Almost as fast as you can say "Welcome to the new Tower of Babel," a new Web page appears on-screen with the foreign-language version of your text. (If you selected a Web page to translate, the Web page appears in the new language. The title of the page, however, remains in the original language.)

A computer can never be as good as a human being when it comes to language translation. I once tried to translate my own Web page into French, showed it to a friend who is a native speaker, and watched her laugh at the results. If you try a computer translation, attempt only the simplest of sentences. And get someone who *really* understands the language to proofread the results.

Instead of creating a foreign-language version of your Web page, you can provide a link to the Yahoo! translation page on your own page. That way, your visitors can translate your text for themselves.

You can download the software behind the translation service, Systran Translator, from the Systran Software, Inc., Web site (`www.systransoft.com`). The program costs anywhere from $49 to $799 depending on the number of languages you need. It is available for Windows only, requiring at least 512MB of RAM and at least 500MB of hard drive space and 90MB of space per language pair during installation. If you need translation to or from Japanese, Chinese, or Korean (or from Russian to English), look into Systran Professional Premium, which costs $799. This program has the same software requirements as the Personal package, as well as a driver for displaying Asian fonts, which is essential for translation into Asian languages.

You don't have to translate your entire Web site. Just providing an alternative version of your home page may be sufficient. The important thing is to give visitors an overview of your business and a brief description of your products and services in a language they can understand easily. Always include a `mailto` link (see Chapter 5) so that people can send mail to you. However, if you aren't prepared to receive a response in Kanji or Swahili, request that your guests send their message in a language that you can read.

Marketing through global networking

Jeffrey Edelheit knows the potential for making connections around the world by taking advantage of the networking value of the World Wide Web. Edelheit, a business planning and development consultant based in Sebastopol, California, supports fledgling entrepreneurs' dreams of getting their businesses off the ground. You can find some of his advice for small business owners on the Bplans.com Web site, which is associated with the Business Plan Pro software product (http://help.bplans.com). He also helps established businesspeople extend their reach by looking at ways of gaining greater market exposure — including going online. In addition, Jeffrey works closely with management and staff to develop the internal systems necessary to build a strong operational base for the company.

Edelheit provides the following guidance:

- **Be deliberate in the creation of your Web site.** "I've worked with clients who are able to attract overseas customers and express themselves through creating their own Web sites," he says. A well-thought-out Web site can create a relationship between you and your customers; in other words, the stronger the relationship, the greater the opportunity for sales.

- **Know your market.** "The most important suggestion I can make," Jeffrey says, "is to know the overseas market that you want to reach and be aware of the issues associated with doing business there. I recommend getting contact information for an international trade group from the country's consulate."

- **Research shipping costs and regulations.** Shipping costs and restrictions are among the most common problems new businesspeople encounter when dealing with foreign customers, he says. "Check with the U.S. Customs Service and find out what the duty charges are before you ship overseas. Once, in the '80s, a company I was working with shipped an IBM computer to Sweden, but because there were still restrictions on exporting high-tech equipment, I nearly got arrested by U.S. Customs for not having received the required special clearance."

- **Avoid being ethnocentric.** "Also be aware of how consumers in other cultures regard your products," he suggests. Make sure that nothing about your products would be considered offensive or bad luck to someone from another part of the world.

- **Be visible:** Edelheit emphasizes that after you figure out the inside tricks to the search engines and cooperative links, you have an unlimited potential to reach people. He believes that one of the keys to a successful Web site is providing information that your targeted market would find useful — and then providing product offerings as an attractive supplement.

"Consumers, whether in this country or overseas, want to know who they are doing business with, and to develop a relationship with that person. A commercial Web site not only enables you to express yourself but also lets you create a 'value-added' experience for your customers," he concludes.

Although you probably don't have sufficient resources to pay for a slew of translation services, having someone translate your home page so that you can provide an alternative version may be worthwhile — especially if you sell products that are likely to be desirable to a particular market where a different language is the order of the day. Consider hiring a competent graduate student to do some translation for you. Plenty of translation services are available online. Yahoo! has an index of translation services at

```
dir.yahoo.com/Business_and_Economy/Business_to_Business/
            Translation_Services/Website_Translation
```

Using the right terms

Sometimes communicating effectively with someone from another country is a matter of knowing the terms used to describe important items in that language. The names of the documents you use to draw up an agreement or pay a bill are often very different in other countries than they are in your own. For example, if you're an American merchant and someone from Europe asks you to provide a *proforma invoice,* you may not know what the person wants. You're used to hearing the document in question called a *quote.*

When you and your European buyer have come to terms, a *Commercial Invoice* is an official form you may need to use for billing purposes. Many of these forms have to do with large-scale export/import trade, and you may never have to use them. But if you do undertake trade with people overseas, be aware that they may require you to use their own forms, not yours, to seal the deal. To avoid confusion later on, ask your overseas clients about any special requirements that pertain to business documents before you proceed too far with the transaction.

You'll find a sample plan for a Web-based business contributed by Edelheit and the founder of Business Plan Pro at www.gregholden.com/appendix.htm.

Chapter 11

Search Engine Optimization

· ·

In This Chapter

▶ Analyzing how search engines find your site — so that you can help them

▶ Focusing on ways to improve your coverage on Google

▶ Adding keywords and registering your site with search engines

▶ Making your Web site search-engine friendly

▶ Tracking referrals and visits to focus on the search services that count

· ·

*I*f you can get your business mentioned in just the right place, customers can find you more easily. Consider my local electronics repair shop. The store has been in business for more than three decades but never seemed to be busy. This time, however, the owner told me he was overwhelmed with hundreds of back orders and couldn't get to my job for several weeks. His store had just been featured on a local public television show, and now people were driving long distances to bring him retro audio equipment to fix.

On the Web, too, being found is the key to success. Search engines are the most important places to get yourself before the public. The key requirements for any business are to match your products or services with potential customers, to ensure that your company shows up in lots of search results, and to have your site near the top of the first page. *Search engine optimization* (SEO) is a set of practices designed to improve your site's placement in search results and is a cost-effective form of advertising that any Web site owner can tackle. SEO gives you a measure of control over the quality of your placement in search results, and this chapter describes strategies for improving it.

The Web analytics firm WebSideStory reported in 2006 on the two types of marketing on search engines: paying a per-click fee to place ads off to the side of search results pages or improving your site so that you get better placement in *organic* search results — results that are generated by individuals searching for Web content. The report (summarized at http://clickz. com/3623514) found that both methods had about the same results as far as converting Web shoppers (causing shoppers to click links and subsequently make a purchase). Paid search ads converted visitors 3.4 percent of the time, whereas all organic search listings converted visitors 3.13 percent of the time. More recent studies are finding that it pays to cultivate organic search results rather than spend money on ads. A study of prepaid wireless services by comScore Marketing found that between 2008 and 2009, traffic to these sites from organic searches increased at a higher rate than it did from paid search ads.

Understanding How Search Engines Find You

Have you ever wondered why some companies manage to find their way to the top page of search engine results — and occasionally pop up several times on the same page — while others get buried deep within pages and pages of Web site listings? In an ideal world, search engines would rank e-commerce sites by how well designed they are and how responsive their owners are. But with so many millions of Web sites crowding the Internet, the job of processing searches and indexing Web site URLs and content has to be automated. Because it's computerized, you can perform some magic with the way your Web pages are written that can help you improve your placement in a set of search results.

Your site doesn't necessarily need to appear right at the top of the first search results page. But you have to keep in mind that consumers on the Web are in a rush, and if you can get your site on the first page of search results — if not at the top of that page — you get more attention. The important thing is to ensure that your site appears before that of your competition. To begin, you need to think like a searcher, which is probably easy because you do plenty of Web-based searches yourself. How do you find the Web sites you want? Two things are of paramount importance: keywords and links.

Keywords are key

A *keyword* describes a subject that you enter in a search box to find information on a Web site or on the wider Internet. Suppose you're trying to find a source for an herbal sweetener called Stevia that low-carb dieters like. You'd naturally enter the term **Stevia** in the search box on your search service of choice, click a button — Search, Search Now, Go, or something similar — and then wait a few seconds for search results to gather.

When you send a keyword to a search service, you set a number of possible actions in motion. The keyword is processed by a script on a Web server operated by the search service. The script makes a request (which in computerspeak is a *query*) to a database file. The database contains contents culled from millions (even billions, depending on the service) of Web pages.

The database contents are gathered from two sources. In some cases, search services employ human editors who record selected contents of Web pages and write descriptions for those pages. But Web pages are so changeable that most of the work is actually done by computer programs that automatically scour the Web. These programs don't record every word on every Web page. Some take words from the headings; others index the first 50 or 100 words on a Web site. Accordingly, when I searched for Stevia on Google, the sites listed at the top of the first page of search results had two attributes:

✔ Some sites had the word Stevia in the URL, such as `www.stevia.net` or `www.stevia.com`.

✔ Other sites had the word Stevia mentioned several times at the top of the home page.

Observers agree that including the most relevant keywords in the titles and headings of the Web page is essential. In addition, pages that are updated with fresh content on a regular basis and are thus reindexed frequently get good search placement as well.

Wordtracker (`www.wordtracker.com`) does daily surveys of the keyword queries made to various search engines. It creates lists of the most popular search terms it finds. Those terms don't likely apply to your e-commerce site, of course. But if you want to maximize the number of visits to your site or just to make your site more prominent in a list of search results, you would do well to know what's trendy and write your text accordingly.

Adding your site's most important keyword to the URL is one solution to better search placement. But you can't always do this. When it comes to keywords, your job is to load your Web site with as many words as you can find that are relevant to what you sell. You can do this by

✔ Burying keywords in the `<meta>` tag in the HTML for your home page so that they won't be visible to your visitors but do appear to the spider programs that index Web pages (see the section "Adding keywords to your HTML," later in this chapter).

✔ Adding keywords to the headings and initial body text on your pages. Check out the section "Adding keywords to key pages," later in this chapter.

Adding keywords that are similar to your primary keywords will help with Microsoft's relatively new search engine Bing (`www.bing.com`). Bing categorizes its two types of search results: a set of primary results, and Web sites that are similar to the primary results. The latter results are presented in a column labeled Related Searches on the left side of a results page. By broadening the keywords you use on your pages, you increase your chances of turning up on Bing's "Related Searches" area on more people's search results.

Find out more in Microsoft's white paper "Bing for Webmasters" (`www.microsoft.com/downloads/details.aspx?FamilyID=b93cfee4-7dfb-40ae-a405-dfa269a33a18&displaylang=en`).

A keyword doesn't have to be a single word. You can use a phrase containing two or more words. Think beyond single words to consider phrases people might enter when they're trying to find products or services you're offering.

Links help searchers connect to you

Keywords aren't the only items that point search services to Web sites. Services such as Google keep track of the number of links that point to a site. The greater the number of links, the higher that site's ranking in a set of Google search listings. It's especially good if the URLs that form the links make use of your keywords. Suppose your ideal keywords are "Greg's Shoe Store." The ideal URL would be `www.gregsshoestore.com`, `www.gregsshoestore.biz`, and so on. You could create the following HTML link to your e-commerce Web site on a personal Web page, an eBay About Me page (see Chapter 13), or your profile on Amazon.com (see Chapter 12):

```
<a href="http://www.gregsshoestore.com"> Visit Greg's Shoe Store </a>
```

Such a link is doubly useful: A search service, such as Google, would find your desired keywords ("Greg's Shoe Store") in the visible, clickable link on your Web page as well as in the HTML for the link.

Don't forget the human touch

Search engines don't work solely by means of computer programs that automatically scour Web pages and by paid advertisements. Computer programs are perceived as the primary source, but the human factor still plays a role. Yahoo!, one of the oldest search engines around, originally compiled its directory of Web sites by means of real, live employees. These days, its Web directory (`dir.yahoo.com`) isn't as easy to find on Yahoo! as it once was. But editors still index sites and assign them to a New Additions category, which includes sites that are especially cool in someone's opinion.

There's almost no way to make sure that a human editor indexes your Web site. The only thing you can do is to make your site as unique and content rich as possible. That helps your business not only show up in directories and search results but also drum up more paying customers for you, too.

Having your site added to the Yahoo! Directory greatly increases your e-commerce site's visibility. But Yahoo! charges a $299 fee for businesses that want to be included. Focus on free directories, such as MSN and Google, and try to improve your visibility that way before you put down the big bucks.

Taking the initiative: P

You can't get much better placement than r
a set of search results, either at the top of th
side. It's even better if your site's name and U
only way to get such preferred treatment is to
a growing number of online businesses are do
list their sites in a prominent location. See the
ings can pay off," later in this chapter, for more

Knowing who supplies the search resu

Also important to remember about search engines is that they often gather
results from *other* search services. You may be surprised to find that if you
do a search of the Web on America Online (AOL), your search results are primarily gathered from Google. That's because AOL has a contract with Google
to supply such results. Not only that, but many search services are owned
by parent search services. Just what are the most popular search services
and where do they get their results? A rundown appears in Table 11-1. The
services are presented in rank order, beginning in the first row with Google,
which is number 1. Rankings of the top five were reported by comScore
Media Metrix in February 2010.

Table 11-1		**Internet Search Services**		
Parent Company	*Its Search Services*	*URLs*	*Source (Search Results)*	*Source (Paid Listings)*
Google	Google	www.google.com	Google	Google
Yahoo!	AltaVista, AllTheWeb, Overture	www.yahoo.com, www.altavista.com, www.overture.com	Yahoo!	Overture
Microsoft	Bing	www.bing.com	Microsoft	Microsoft adCenter
Ask Network	Ask Jeeves, Teoma	www.ask.com, www.teoma.com	Teoma	Google
AOL	AOL Search, Netscape Search	search.aol.com	Google	Google

The important thing to note is that many of the most popular search engines receive their listings not from their own database of Web sites but rather from other search services. If you pay for a listing with Google, in other words, your ad is likely to appear not only on Google but also on HotBot, Lycos, Teoma, AOL Search, and other places.

These are by no means the only search services around. Other search engines focus on Web sites and Internet resources in specific countries. You can find more of them by going to Search Engine Watch (`searchenginewatch.com`) and clicking the Search Engine Listings link.

Going Gaga over Google

When it comes to search engines, Google is at the top of the heap. In fact, Neilsen/NetRatings and comScore Networks both consistently reported that Google does more than 65 percent of all search referrals. The next highest competitor, Yahoo!, typically has 17–19 percent of the search market business.

Google is a runaway success thanks to its effectiveness. You're simply more likely to find something on Google, more quickly, than you are on its competitors. Any search engine placement strategy has to address Google first and foremost. But that doesn't mean you should ignore Google's competitors. Not long before this book was published, Microsoft came out with its own Internet search engine, Bing.

Googling yourself

To evaluate the quality of your search results placement on Google, start by taking stock of where you currently stand. That's easily done: Just go to Google's home page (`www.google.com`) and do a search for your own name or your business's name (a pastime that's also been called *egosurfing*). See where your Web site turns up in the results and also make note of which other sites mention yours.

Next, click Advanced Search or go directly to `www.google.com/advanced_search?hl=en`. Click the plus sign next to Date, Usage Rights, Numeric Range, and More to show more options on the Advanced search page. Under the heading Page-Specific Search, enter the URL for your e-commerce site in the Find Pages That Link to the Page text box and then click Search. The results that appear in a few seconds consist of Web sites that link to yours. The list suggests the kinds of sites you should approach to solicit links. It also suggests the kinds of informational Web sites you might create for the purpose of steering business to your Web site. (See the section "Maximizing links," later in this chapter, for a specific example.)

Playing Google's game to reach #1

A while back, some bloggers got together and decided to play a game called *Google bombing.* The game is simple: It consists of making links to a particular Web site in an attempt to get that site listed on Google. The more links the site has pointing to it, the higher that site will appear in a set of search results. Of course, the links that are made all have to be connected with a particular keyword or phrase.

The Google game applies to your e-commerce Web site, too. Suppose you sell yo-yos and your Web site URL is `www.yoyoplay.com`. (This is actually one of the sites run by Lars Hundley, the entrepreneur I profile in the sidebar "Paying for search listings can pay off," later in this chapter.) The game is to get as many other Web sites as possible to link to this URL. The terms that a visitor clicks to get to this URL can be anything: *Yo-Yos, Play Yo-Yos,* and so on. The more links you can make, the better your search results will be.

Getting started with Google AdWords

When most people think about search engine marketing, they immediately think about a single program: Google AdWords. AdWords revolutionized advertising on the Web and, not coincidentally, has made a fortune for Google as a company. What makes AdWords special is its do-it-yourself aspect, which puts a huge amount of control in the hands of individual businesspeople. You decide what programs to advertise; you specify how much you want to pay every time someone clicks one of your ads; you write the ads; you fine-tune your advertising programs to bid higher on those that are getting results and end the ones that aren't getting much attention.

 This section presents you with a brief introduction on how to get started with AdWords. It isn't meant to be the last word on the subject. Entire books could be written about AdWords, and they have been. Consult the latest edition of *Search Engine Optimization For Dummies,* by Peter Kent, or *Google AdWords For Dummies,* by Howie Jacobson (both published by Wiley).

Getting the big picture

What is AdWords? It's a service provided by Google that allows individuals and companies to take out ads that appear at the top or along the right side of a page of Google search results. Do a search on Google right now and you'll see what I mean: They're the ads enclosed in small boxes containing links to Web sites. Perhaps you have clicked those ads yourself, perhaps not. The fact is that hundreds of thousands — perhaps millions — of clicks are placed on those ads every single day. Every time someone clicks an ad, the person who placed the ad is charged a small fee by Google (that's why they're called cost-per-click, or CPC, ads).

If the "clicker" goes on to make a purchase on the Web site that is being advertised, or if he or she fills out a form or takes out a new membership, however, the person who took out the AdWords ad (for the purposes of this discussion, I'll call this person the affiliate) earns money in two possible ways. If your own Web site is being advertised, you make money from the purchase. If you advertise someone else's site and that site pays affiliates, you earn a referral fee. The exact fee varies from site to site.

One thing that makes AdWords effective is that the ads are targeted. The ads appear only on search results that are similar to the product or service being advertised. The connection between the advertiser and search results is made by keywords that the affiliate associates with the ad. If the affiliate is advertising a site that sells dog and cat supplies and specifies keywords such as dog food, cat collar, flea spray, and the like, the ad appears when a Web surfer searches for those terms. Another advantage is that you write the ad and you specify how much you'll pay for each click. You're in control.

You might think that specifying common keywords is a good thing because it causes your advertised site to appear in its AdWords ad more often: More people likely search for "dog" or "cat" than "dog food" or "dog hip dysplasia," for instance. But your goal is to target your search and find just the shoppers who are hunting for what the advertiser wants. If 100,000 people view your ad with the keyword "dog" and only two clicks are made, the ad is ineffective. If 100 people view the ad for "dog flea collars" but 30 clicks are made and they lead to 10 purchases, you have a far more effective ad.

Signing up for the service

Taking out an account with AdWords is the easy part. Before you start, you should decide what you want to advertise. For this example, I assume you're advertising your own Web site. You can also advertise for someone else, as long as you're willing to pay for the clicks.

You also need to obtain a Google account, with a username and password. You do this by going to Google's home page, clicking the Sign In link, and clicking the Create an Account Now link.

After you sign in, follow these steps:

1. **Go to the Google Advertising Programs page.**

   Click Advertising Programs at the bottom of the home page or go directly to www.google.com/ads.

2. **Click Sign Up Now to go to the Create Google Account page.**

3. **Fill out the first online form by clicking buttons that describe any existing Google accounts you might have. Follow the steps shown on the screens that follow to finish creating your account.**

After you have an account set up on AdWords, you can move to the next step: advertising your products.

Writing AdWords ads

When you have the URL of the Web page you want to link to, return to your AdWords window and click the Campaigns tab. Under the All online campaigns heading, click the New campaign button. When the Select campaign settings page shown in Figure 11-1 appears, follow these steps:

1. **Click the Campaign type button and, from the drop-down list that appears, choose the type of advertising campaign you want to create.**

   (If you're in doubt, choose Default.)

2. **In the Campaign Name box, enter the name of the business you are advertising.**

3. **Select a language and location if you want to target your ad to a particular group of Web surfers.**

4. **Fill out the rest of the form.**

   Pay special attention to Budget. This is the maximum amount you will be charged for your ads. It's important to limit your spending so that you don't use up your available funds if a campaign "takes off" with lots of clicks, but those clicks aren't necessarily going to lead to purchases. You might start with a limit of $99.

5. **Click Save and continue.**

   The Create ad group form appears; see Figure 11-2.

6. **In the Ad group name box, enter a name that describes your ad.**

   This is only for your convenience and can be as simple as Web Site Ad.

7. **Click the button next to the type of ad you want to create: text, image, a display ad (with text and images) or a Mobile ad (a short ad that will appear on cell phones).**

8. **Write an attention-grabbing, click-inducing, action-producing ad for this product.**

   You have only 35 characters per line to do so — and you'll see in a moment just how short a space that is.

9. **Write a heading (25 characters or less) in the Headline box.**

10. **Write lines 1 and 2 (each 35 characters or less).**

11. **In the box next to Display URL, type the URL that will appear in the body of the ad.**

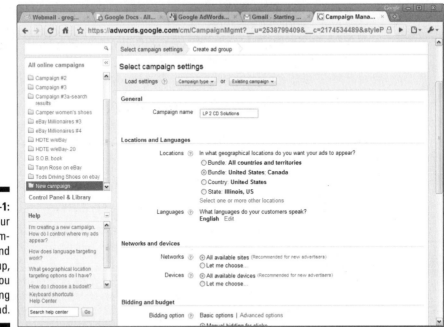

Figure 11-1: Name your ad campaign and ad group, even if you are creating only one ad.

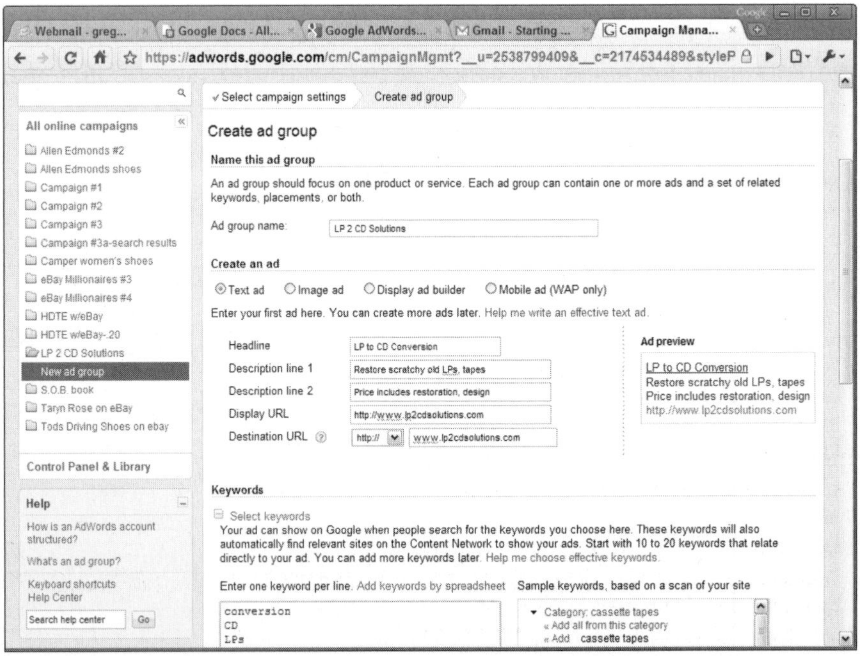

Figure 11-2: Create a short, pithy ad to induce clicks and purchases.

12. In the Destination URL box, type the same URL as the Display URL.

If you are advertising as an affiliate for a Web site such as Amazon. com, this box will contain a complex link that you need to obtain from Amazon.com. Here's an example of an ad I wrote:

```
LP to CD Conversion
Restore scratchy old LPs, tapes
Price includes restoration, design
www.lp2cdsolutions.com
```

13. In the Keywords section of the page (see Figure 11-3), choose keywords to accompany your ad.

You can use Google's suggestions, which are presented on this page. Or you can consult an online service such as Wordtracker (www. wordtracker.com), which suggests keywords for you.

14. In the Ad group default bids section, choose a default amount for each click.

This is the amount you commit to pay Google if someone clicks on your ad and goes to the destination URL. The higher the amount, the better your placement will be on a search results page. You might start with $.10 per click.

15. When you're done, click Save Ad Group.

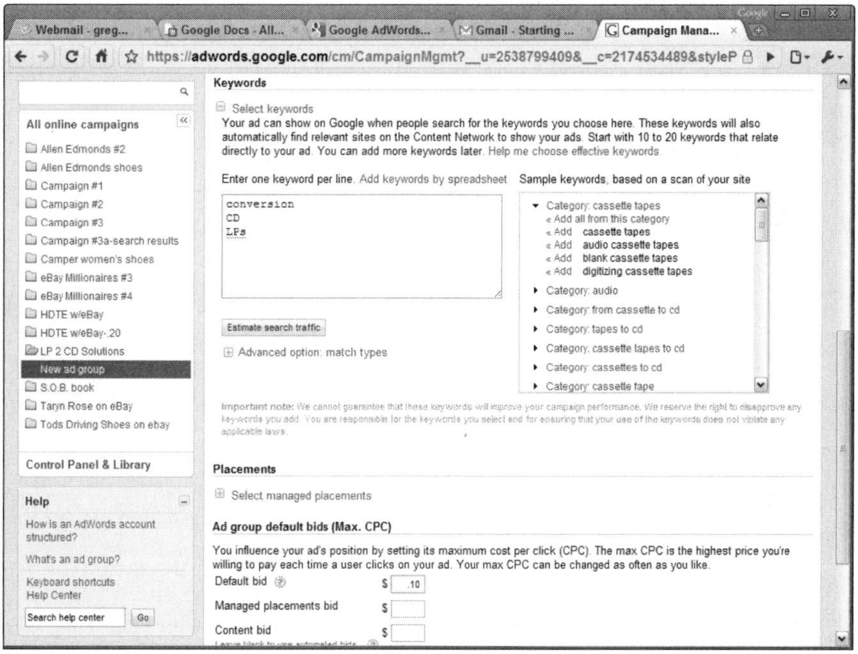

Figure 11-3:
Choose your keywords and set minimum bids.

Eventually, you launch your campaign, which goes online in a matter of minutes, if it meets Google's review standards. After your ad is online, you can create variations and see which ones get the best results. It can be quite an entertaining game to see which of your ads gets lots of page views and which attracts clicks. Figure 11-4 shows a group of ads I prepared as an affiliate for Amazon.com that are still awaiting approval from AdWords.

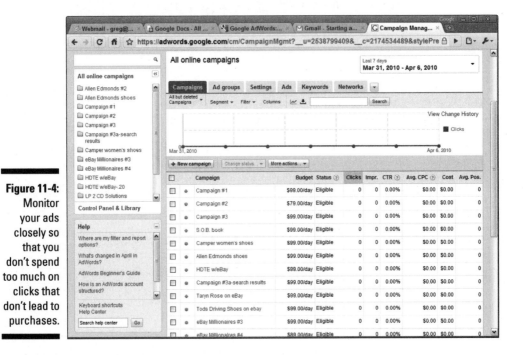

Figure 11-4: Monitor your ads closely so that you don't spend too much on clicks that don't lead to purchases.

Leaving a Trail of Crumbs

To improve your site's search placement, make it easy for searchers to find you. Leave a trail of digital crumbs, add keywords to the HTML for your Web pages, and make sure that your site is included in the most popular services' databases.

Keep in mind that most Web surfers don't enter single words in search boxes. They tend to enter phrases. Combinations of keywords are extra effective. If you sell tools, don't just enter *tools* as a keyword. Enter keywords, such as *tool box, power tool, tool caddy, pneumatic tool, electric tool,* and so on.

Adding keywords to your HTML

What keywords should you add to your site? Take an old-fashioned pencil and paper and write all the words you can think of that are related to your site, your products, your services, or you — whatever you want to promote, in other words. You may also enlist the help of a printed thesaurus or the one supplied online at Dictionary.com (www.dictionary.com). Look up one term associated with your goods or services and you're likely to find a number of similar terms.

Where to put the <meta> tag

Every Web page is enclosed by two specific tags: <html> and </html>. These tags define the page as being an HTML document. The <html> tag goes at the beginning of the document and </html> goes at the end.

Between the <html> and </html> tags reside two main subdivisions of a Web page:

- ✔ **The header section:** This section, enclosed by the <head> and </head> tags, is where the <meta> tags go.
- ✔ **The body section:** This section, enclosed by the <body> and </body> tags, is where the contents of the Web page — the part you actually see on-screen — go.

You don't have to include <meta> tags on every page on your site; in fact, your home page is the only page where doing so makes sense.

How to create a <meta> tag

The following steps show how to add your own <meta> tags from scratch to the source code of a Web page by using a popular Web site creation tool, Microsoft Expression Web. (Steps are similar for other Web editors, such as Adobe Dreamweaver.) To add <meta> tags to your site's home page by working directly with the underlying HTML code (which helps you master Web page structure), start Expression Web and follow these steps:

1. **Choose File⇨Open.**

   If you already have your Web site open, you can double-click the folder that holds your site in the Expression Web Folder List.

   Either way, the Open File dialog box appears.

2. **Find the Web page document to which you want to add <meta> tags.**
   Usually, this is your site's home page.

   - If the file resides on your computer's hard drive, locate the Webpage file in the standard Windows navigation dialog box and then click the Open button.

- If the file resides on the Web, enter the URL in the Location box of the Open File dialog box and then click OK.

The Web page opens in the Design view, the main editing area in the center of the Expression Web window. To add the `<meta>` tags, you must type them directly into the HTML source code for the page.

3. **Click the Code tab near the bottom of Design view.**

   Expression Web displays the HTML source code for your Web page.

4. **Scroll to the top of your page's HTML source code, between the** `<head>` **and** `</head>` **tags, and enter your keywords and description.**

   Use the following format:

   ```
   <meta name="description" content="Your short Web site
           description goes here.">
   <meta name="keywords" content="keyword1, keyword2,
           keyword3, and so on">
   ```

   The output appears in the View HTML window, as shown in Figure 11-5.

5. **Click the Design tab.**

   The Code view closes, and you return to the normal view of your Web page. Your additions aren't visible on the Web page because they're intended for search engines, not visitors to your site.

6. **You can now make more changes to your page, or you can save your Web page and then close Expression Web.**

Figure 11-5:
Insert your
`<meta>`
tags in
the HEAD
section of
your HTML
document.

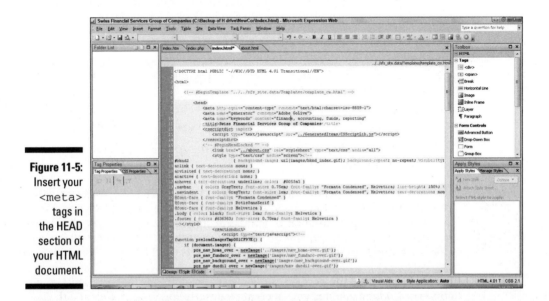

Most Web page editors also make this user friendly for you: You can type your information in specially designated boxes. Figure 11-6 shows Expression Web's commands; open the page you want to edit by choosing File➪Properties, and type the words in the Keywords box. You can also write your official description in the Description box.

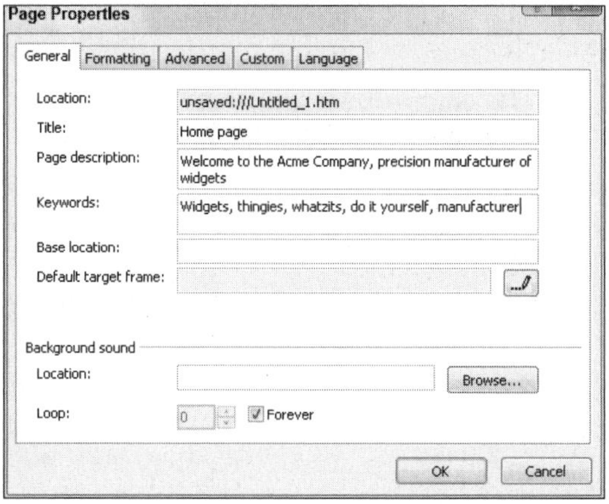

Figure 11-6: Some Web page editors make it easy to add keywords and descriptions for search services to find.

You can also spy on your competitors' Web sites to see if they added any keywords to their Web pages by following these steps:

1. **Go to your competitor's home page and choose View➪Source if you use Internet Explorer or choose View➪Page Source if you use Firefox.**

   A new window opens with the page source supplied.

2. **Scroll through the code, looking for the** `<meta>` **tags if they're present. (Press Ctrl+F, enter** META, **and click the Find button if you can't find them on your own.)**

   If the page's author used `<meta>` tags to enter keywords, you see them on-screen. They probably appear toward the top of the code.

3. **Note the keywords supplied and see whether you can apply any to your own Web site.**

Keywords, like Web page addresses, are frequently misspelled. Make sure that you type several variations on keywords that might be subject to typos: for instance, **Mississippi**, **Misissippi**, **Mississipi**, and so on. Don't worry about getting capitalization just right, however; most searchers simply enter all lowercase characters and don't bother with capital letters at all.

Besides keywords, the `<meta>` tag is also important for the `Description` command, which enables you to create a description of your Web site that search engines can index and use in search results. Some search services scan the description for keywords, too, so make sure that you create a description at the same time that you type your keywords in the `<meta>` tags.

Don't place too much importance on picking the ultimate, perfect keywords for use with your `<meta>` tags. They're not all that effective anymore — not with search placement on Google, for instance. Keeping your content updated and promoting links to other Web sites are just as effective.

. . . and don't forget about Bing

The bulk of this chapter discusses SEO techniques that work with most search sites, and especially with Google. Google, after all, is still the "big dog" among search engines. But the initial reviews of Bing are very positive, and when you're leaving a trail of crumbs for your prospective customers to find you, you should keep Microsoft's search service in mind, too.

A comparison published on the blog SEOWizz.net of how Google and Bing handle SEO finds that they both take titles, keywords, links, and other factors into account when ranking Web sites in a set of search results. But two factors are considered more important by Bing: the age of your Internet domain (the `.net` or `.com` part of your URL) and the number of sites that link to you and that have your keywords in their title. (Google, in contrast, gives higher rank to sites that have your keywords in the body of their Web pages.) So try to hold on to your domain, and cultivate links from sites that have titles with your favorite keywords in them. Find out more at `www.seowizz.net/2009/06/bing-seo-how-does-it-differ-to-google.html`.

Registering your site with Google

Google has a program — Googlebot — that automatically indexes Web pages all over the Internet. However, you don't have to wait for Googlebot to find your site: You can fill out a simple form that adds your URL to the sites indexed by this program. Go to `www.google.com/addurl.html`, enter your URL and a few comments about your site, and click the Add URL button. That's all there is to it. Expect to wait a few weeks for your site to appear among Google's search results if it doesn't already appear there.

Getting listed on Yahoo!

If you want to get the most bang for your advertising buck, get your site listed on the most popular locations in cyberspace. For several years now, the many sites owned by Yahoo! have ranked near the top most popular sites on the Internet in the Media Metrix Top 50 list of Web Properties published by comScore Media Metrix. Although many people think of Yahoo! primarily as a search engine, it's also a categorical index to Web sites. Getting listed on Yahoo! means being included on one of its index pages. An *index page* is a list of Web sites grouped together by category, much like a traditional yellow-pages phone book.

Aside from its steadily increasing size and popularity, one thing that sets Yahoo! apart is the way in which it evaluates sites for inclusion on its index pages. For the most part, real human beings do the Yahoo! indexing; they read your site description and your own suggested location and then deter-mine what category to list your site under. Usually, Yahoo! lists sites in only one or two categories, but if Yahoo! editors feel that a site deserves its own special category, they create one for it.

The Yahoo! editors don't even attempt to process all the thousands of site applications they receive each week. Reports continue to circulate on the Web as to how long it takes to get listed on Yahoo! and how difficult it is to get listed at all. The process can take weeks, months, or even years. That's why Yahoo! has instituted a Yahoo! Directory Submit listing system — your business site gets reviewed in exchange for a $299, nonrefundable annual fee, though you *still* aren't guaranteed that you'll get listed. Find out more at `https://ecom.yahoo.com/dir/sub/`.

Search Engine Watch (`searchenginewatch.com`) is a great place to go for tips on how search engines and indexes work and how to get listed on them.

Paying for Yahoo! Search Marketing

What *can* you do to get listed on Yahoo!? You can always sign up for Yahoo!'s paid search option (also called sponsored search), Yahoo! Search Marketing (`searchmarketing.yahoo.com`). Paid search won't get you listed in the Yahoo! Directory, but it does ensure with some measure of certainty that you'll at least appear in search results on the site.

What sets Yahoo! Search Marketing is that an editorial teams review your keywords and ads, much as they do the Web site listings at Yahoo!. Google AdWords listings are also reviewed thoroughly, but the results come back in a matter of seconds and appear to be automated. Yahoo! Search Marketing originally used Google's search technology but later developed its search marketing system. Yahoo! is a notable search engine because its search results mix together organic results (the results the search service retrieves as a result of a query) and paid listings, and the paid ads appear at the top, along the right, and at the bottom of a results page.

Listing in the Yahoo! index

If you want to show up in the Yahoo! Directory, consider following these three steps:

1. **Make your site interesting, quirky, or somehow attention grabbing.**

   You never know — you may just stand out from the sea of new Web sites and gain the attention of one of the Yahoo! editors.

2. **Go ahead and apply to Yahoo! through its Yahoo! Site Explorer service (**`siteexplorer.search.yahoo.com/submit`**).**

   The Site Explorer – Submit page appears.

   a. **Click Submit a Website or Webpage.**

      A text box appears.

   b. **Type the URL of the page you want to submit and then click Submit URL.**

      A page appears, prompting you to sign in to Yahoo with your username and password.

   c. **Sign in to Yahoo!.**

      After you sign in, a page appears, notifying you that your page will soon be indexed for inclusion in Yahoo!'s index.

3. **Try a local Yahoo! index.**

   Major areas around the country as well as in other parts of the world have their own Yahoo! indexes. Go to `http://yp.yahoo.com/yp/states.html` to browse by city. Find the local index closest to you and apply it, as I describe in the preceding step. Your chances are much better of getting listed locally than on the main Yahoo! site.

Improve your listing on Yahoo! by shelling out anywhere from $25–$300 or more per year to become a sponsored Web site. Your site is listed in the Sponsored Sites box at the top of a Yahoo! category. The exact cost depends on the popularity of the category. There is life beyond Yahoo!, too. Several Web-based services are trying to compete by providing their own way of organizing and evaluating Web sites. Try submitting a listing to Best of the Web (`http://botw.org`) or contact one of the guides employed by About.com (`www.about.com`).

Getting listed with other search services

Search services can steer lots of business to a commercial Web site, based on how often the site appears in the list of Web pages that the user sees and how high the site appears in the list. Your goal is to maximize your site's chances of being found by the search service. But Google is hard to crack, and Yahoo! charges for commercial sites that want to be listed. What about other search services?

Not so long ago, search services allowed you to list your site for free. After that, services adopted polices that guaranteed listings in their index only if you paid a subscription fee. These days, the preeminence of Google and Yahoo! has changed the playing field even further. Some services have consolidated; others "borrow" the search technology used by the competition. Only a few search services provide you with a Submit Your Site or an Add a URL link that enables you to include your site in their index.

Microsoft's Bing lets you submit your site by entering its URL at `www.bing.com/docs/submit.aspx`.

One of the few sites that allows individuals to submit personal or commercial Web sites for addition in its index is the Open Directory Project (`dmoz.org/add.html`). The advantage is that other well-known search services (AOL Search, Google, Netscape Search, and Yahoo! Search) use Open Directory data to update and augment their own databases. After you get your site in the Open Directory, anywhere from a few days to a few weeks later, you'll likely see it appear in other directories as well.

Follow these steps to submit your site to the Open Directory:

1. **Connect to the Internet, start your Web browser, and go to the Open Directory home page at** `dmoz.org`.

   The ODP – Open Directory Project home page appears.

2. **Enter the name of the site you want to add in the box at the top of the page and click Search.**

   A set of search results appears.

3. **Check to see whether your site is included already in the directory.**

   If it isn't, scan the search results for the category "tree" that appears at the end of each listing and find the category that fits your own site. A category tree looks like this:

   ```
   Regional: North America: United States: Business and
             Economy: Shopping: Sporting Goods
   ```

4. **Click the category tree.**

   The Category page on the Open Directory appears.

5. **Click the Suggest URL link near the top of the Category page.**

   The Submission form appears.

   Not all categories in the Open Directory include Suggest URL links. If you don't see one, that particular category doesn't allow submissions. But others will: Click a more specific subcategory to suggest your site.

6. **Type the URL as well as a brief but specific description for your site and then click Submit.**

   Your page is submitted to one of the Open Directory staff members, who reviews it to decide whether the site is suitable for inclusion in the directory. It may take several weeks for your site to be added.

CASE STUDY

Paying for search listings can pay off

Listing with search sites is growing more complex all the time. Many sites are owned by other sites. On top of that, you can list your products on shopping aggregation sites as well. You can make the consolidation of search sites work to your advantage by choosing a few services carefully: You can then find your business listed with many other sites.

Lars Hundley, who in 1998 started his first online store, Clean Air Gardening (shown in the following figure), has received lots of publicity thanks to energetic marketing and good use of search engine resources. He's also had great success with a site that's not often regarded as a search engine: YouTube. "I use Yahoo! Search Marketing (also known as Overture) and Google AdWords," Lars comments. "I also sometimes use shopping aggregation sites, like Yahoo! Shopping, Shopzilla, and Shopping.com." Sales were down in 2009, so he is closely watching AdWords spending to make sure that he is not paying too much for each sale his ads generate. Hundley hosts Clean Air Gardening and other e-commerce sites with Yahoo! Small Business. Other informational sites are hosted on his own Web server.

Hundley uses many of the search engine placement tools that I mention in this chapter. He says, "I also use tools, like Wordtracker and the Overture search term Suggestion tool, to make sure that I use important keywords in all my product descriptions. I always try to name and describe things in the words that people are searching for, and I think that really pays off over time."

Hundley points out that YouTube is the fifth most popular Web site around, according to Hitwise (www.hitwise.com/us/datacenter /main/dashboard-10133.html).

"YouTube has been a phenomenal success for us, and has been our most successful new marketing technique in the last two or three years," he comments. "We shoot short product videos for all of our major products, demonstrating the product in action. We use a $600 Canon HD camcorder, and edit on a Mac using iMovie or Final Cut Pro. Then we upload the movie to YouTube. We embed the YouTube video directly on our product page. So when someone is reading about the product, [he or she] can just click play on the video and watch it." An example appears in the following figure.

Hundley uses his previous journalism experience to write and distribute his own press releases and to pitch articles to magazines such as *U.S. News and World Report, The Wall Street Journal, This Old House,* and others. He also has an e-mail marketing campaign. "With Clean Air Gardening, I use Constant Contact to manage an e-mail newsletter that I send out every two weeks. I have approximately 25,000 subscribers. I use the newsletter to give gardening tips and promote my products at the same time — they are informational, but they also show how you can use Clean Air Gardening products for more successful gardening."

Hundley gives the following advice to budding entrepreneurs: "If you're thinking about starting your own Internet business, just do it! Start a small site and do it in your spare time to test the waters. I kept my day job for the first year when I started this business, until it started to take off and make money. Now, 11 years later, it is a multimillion-dollar-a-year company with 14 employees and a large, 14,000 square foot warehouse and office. You can do it, too, if you try!"

It's hard to argue with success: Hundley reports that Clean Air Gardening was named one of the 5,000 fastest-growing companies by *Inc.* magazine in 2008 and 2009.

Businesses on the Web can get obsessed with how high their sites appear on the list of search results pages. If a Web surfer enters the exact name of a site in the Google or Bing search text box, for example, some people just can't understand why that site doesn't come back at the top — or even on the first page — of the list of returned sites. Of the millions of sites listed in a search service's database, the chances are good that at least one has the same name as yours (or something close to it) or that a page contains a combination of the same words that make up your organization's name. It's important to be on the first page of search results, to be sure, but you'll get there by concentrating on creating a top-notch Web site and making sales.

Adding keywords to key pages

Earlier in this chapter, I show you how to add keywords to the HTML for your Web pages. Those keywords aren't ones that visitors normally see unless they view the source code for your Web page. You can add other keywords to parts of your Web page that are visible — that is, parts of the page that programs called *crawlers* or *spiders* scan and index, as follows:

- ✔ **The title:** Be sure to create a title for your page. The title appears in the title bar at the very top of the browser window. Many search engines index the contents of the title because it appears not only at the top of the browser window but also at the top of the HTML.

- ✔ **The headings:** Your Web page's headings should be specific about what you sell and what you do.

- ✔ **The first line of text:** Some search services index every word on every page, but others limit the amount of text they index. So the first lines might be indexed whereas others aren't. Get your message across quickly; pack your first sentences with nouns that list what you have for sale.

The best way to ensure that your site gets indexed is to pack it with useful content. I'm talking about textual content: Search programs can't view photos, animations, or sounds. Make sure that your pages contain a significant amount of text as well as these other types of content.

Web sites that specialize in SEO talk about *keyword density:* the number of keywords on your page, multiplied by the number of times each one is used. Keyword density is a way to gain a good search engine ranking. In other words, if you sell shoes and you use ten different terms once, you won't achieve as high a ranking as you would by using six or seven words twice, or a handful of well-chosen keywords several times each.

Don't make your pages hard to index

Sometimes, the key to making things work is simply being certain that you aren't putting roadblocks in the way of success. The way you format Web pages can prevent search services from recording your text and the keywords you want your customers to enter. Avoid these obvious hindrances:

- ✔ **Your text begins too far down the page.** If you load the top of your page with images that can't be indexed, your text is indexed that much slower, and your rankings suffer.

- ✔ **Your pages are loaded with Java applets, animations, and other objects that can't be indexed.** Content that slows down the automatic indexing programs reduces your rankings, too.

- ✔ **Your pages don't actually include the ideal keyword phrase you want your searchers to use.** If you have a business converting LP records to CDs, you want the phrase "LP to CD" or "convert LPs to CDs" somewhere on your home page and on other pages as well.

Every image on your Web page can and should be assigned a textual label (also known as *ALT text* because the `alt` element in HTML enables it to be used). The immediate purpose of the label is to tell visitors what the image depicts in case it can't be displayed in the browser window. (ALT text is actually required by the W3 Consortium [an international body that maintains standards of communication on the Web] to make sites more accessible — see `www.w3.org/TR/WAI-WEBCONTENT` for more information.) As a trick to produce more keyword density, you can assign keywords or keyword phrases to these names instead.

Maximizing links

Along with keywords, hyperlinks are what search engines use to index a site and include it in a database. By controlling two types of links, you can provide search services with that much more information about the contents of your site:

- ✔ The hyperlinks contained in the bodies of your Web pages
- ✔ The links that point to your site from other locations around the Web

The section "Links help searchers connect to you," earlier in this chapter, mentions the links in the bodies of your own Web pages. One of the most effective tricks for increasing the number of links that point to your online store is to create several different Web sites, each of which points to that store. That's just what Lars Hundley did with his main e-commerce site,

Clean Air Gardening (`www.cleanairgardening.com`). "Creating my own network of gardening sites that provide quality information helps me rise to the top of the search engines in many categories," says Lars. "People find the content sites sometimes and click through to Clean Air Gardening to buy related products."

It's true. Do an Advanced Search on Google for sites that link to `www.clean airgardening.com`. First, some sites are just a sampling that link to Clean Air Gardening and that aren't run by Lars:

- ✔ National Gardening Association (`garden.garden.org`)
- ✔ GardenTool Buyer's Resource (`www.gardentoolguide.com`)
- ✔ Master Composter (`www.mastercomposter.com`)
- ✔ Organic Gardening (`www.organicgardening.com`)

Farther down in the search results, you might also find these sites that *are* run by Lars:

- ✔ Gardening Guide (`www.gardenplantcare.com`)
- ✔ Organic Pest Control (`www.organicgardenpests.com`)
- ✔ Reel Mower Guide (`www.reelmowerguide.com`)
- ✔ Organic Garden Tips (`www.organicgardentips.com`)
- ✔ CompostGuide.com (`www.compostguide.com`)
- ✔ Rain Barrel Guide (`www.rainbarrelguide.com`)

For the sites that Lars doesn't run himself, he solicits links. "I also exchange links with other high-ranking related sites, both to improve my rankings and to provide quality links for my visitors. If you stick with quality links, you can never go wrong." For more about Lars and how he uses the Overture search network to help users find him on the Web, see the sidebar "Paying for search listings can pay off," earlier in this chapter.

Monitoring Traffic: The Science of Web Analytics

How do you improve the number of times your site is found by search engines? One way is to analyze the traffic that comes to your site, a practice often called *Web analytics.* When it comes to search engine placement, the type of research you need to perform is *log file analysis,* which can tell you exactly what keywords were used already to find your site. You can then combine those words into new keyword phrases and hope that doing so helps even more people find your site. You can get software that does the analysis for you or you can do it yourself. I briefly describe each way in this section.

Software to improve SEO

Some software options are specifically designed to help improve SEO. OptiLink (www.optilinksoftware.com/download.html) counts the number of keywords on a Web page. It analyzes the links that point at the page and helps you analyze what the best keywords are, where they need to be located, and what specific text can make the links rank higher in Google's search results.

Google Analytics (www.google.com/analytics) is one of the most useful tools you can have for studying who comes to your site and how they get there. Even better, it's free. Find out more in Chapter 14.

Do-it-yourself options

The other, more labor-intensive way to analyze what drives visitors to your Web site is by analyzing log files. A *log file* is an electronic document that a Web server compiles as a record of every visit made to a Web page, image, or other object on a site. Most Web hosting services let you look at the log file for your Web site. The log file gives you a rough idea of where your visitors are from and which resources on your Web site are the most visited. By focusing on particular types of log file data, you can evaluate how visitors find your site and which search services are doing the best job of directing visitors to you.

If you look at log file information in its raw-text form, you're probably mystified by page after page of numbers and techie gibberish. Log files typically record information such as the IP address and the domain name of the computer that accesses a Web page. They don't tell you the name and address of the person using the machine at the time. They give you an idea of where the computer is located geographically, based on the suffix at the end of a domain name (such as .de for Germany or .fr for France). You probably need to make use of a log file analyzer, such as WebTrends (www.webtrends.com), which presents the data in a format that is easy to interpret.

When you're viewing log files, one important thing to track is *referrer reporting,* which gives you the site the visitor was viewing just before coming to yours. This tells you what sites are directing visitors to yours. Make note of the search engines that appear most frequently; these are the ones you need to work on when it comes to improving your placement in sets of search results.

Chapter 12

Selling on Craigslist, Amazon.com, and CafePress

*W*hen it comes to making money online, the conventional notion is to think about creating a Web site or opening a storefront where you list many items for sale. You don't have to take such a structured approach, however. It's a lot of work to create a home page, set up a shopping cart, and establish a way to collect payments all by yourself. By listing individual items for sale on a well-established and well-known e-commerce venue, you can rack up sales without spending the big bucks on marketing and infrastructure. You can take advantage of the marketing tools the site gives you and the traffic the e-commerce venue already generates.

Even if you have a commercial site, you might still want to sell specialty items on venues that are set up to handle them — such as Craigslist for big items that are difficult to ship, Amazon.com for used books, and CafePress or other sites for artwork. In fact, the more places you "pop up" as a Web merchant, the better. Your stores can sell different products and link to one another, which boosts your business overall. This chapter examines some of the best-known alternatives for making money with hosting services.

Selling the Smart Way on Craigslist

Craigslist, the classified ad service started in the mid-1990s by Craig Newmark, has become an institution on the Web and beyond. It's so popular that it's cutting into the business of traditional print newspapers, which depend in part on their own classified ad postings for revenue. It's also popular enough that it's become a target for scam artists who try to trick sellers out of their money.

For entrepreneurs, Craigslist is a good way to sell merchandise locally. Sometimes, you just have big-ticket items that don't work well on eBay or another site because the cost of shipping is prohibitive. Craigslist is perfect for furniture, major appliances, motor vehicles, and other items that need to be picked up by the buyer. I recently sold a trailer for my father, and most of the experience went smoothly. It's important, though, to be aware of some of the quirks and unique features of selling on Craigslist so that you don't end up with a bad experience.

 eBay also has an extensive marketplace designated especially for motor vehicles and related items such as parts. eBay Motors (motors.ebay.com) includes extensive protections for both buyers and sellers. That makes it a good alternative to Craigslist, if you are looking to sell a car.

To illustrate the Craigslist sales system, I run through the process of listing items online, using two examples from my own experience. My father asked me to sell a trailer and a motorized chair lift. Some parts of the sales went well and some parts were alarming.

Gather details

On Craigslist, just as on eBay and other auction sites, the more details you have about an item, the better off you are. Details sell: sizes, colors, and serial numbers are all good to gather beforehand. Don't be surprised if you are asked about them. I did field some amazingly detailed questions. Get out a tape measure and measure your item. Get the exact model number and serial number. In your description, be sure to play up any desirable features.

Take photos

Next, take good, clear JPEG images of your item. If the item is especially large (such as a motor vehicle), be sure to photograph it from all sides. (Buyers want to make sure that you aren't concealing scratches or "dings" on a side you aren't showing.) Save the images in a graphics program, if necessary, so that each image is 72 dots per inch (dpi) in resolution. The ideal file size for an image is 50–100K.

List the item

Find the version of Craigslist that is closest to you geographically by search-ing the list on the site's home page (`www.craigslist.org`). Go to the local site and search for objects that are similar to yours. See where they are sold, and list your item in the same category. To list the trailer, I went to the North Chicagoland page, marked All for Sale (`chicago.craigslist.org/nch/sss`). I clicked the Post link in the upper-right corner. When a page full of more specific categories appeared, I clicked General for Sale. A list of items for sale appeared. Next, I clicked North Chicagoland and got a shorter list of items for sale located on the north side of Chicago and the surrounding suburbs, which is where the items were located. I typed the description shown in Figure 12-1.

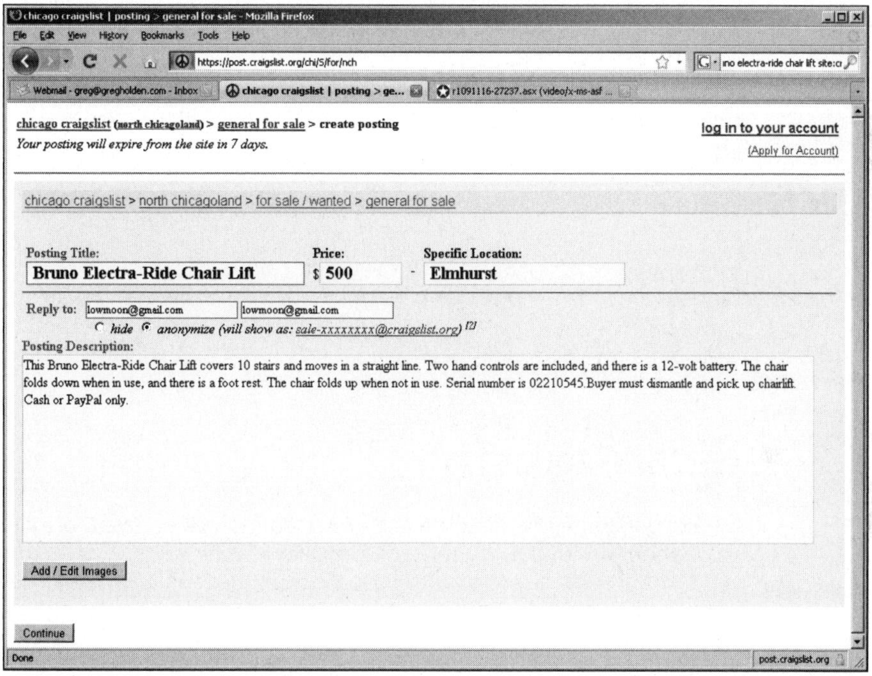

Figure 12-1:
Be specific with your Craigslist descrip-tion and be careful about what payment you accept.

As you can see, I added the sentence "Cash or PayPal only" at the end of the description. I did this for a reason. Craigslist, in its guidelines for sellers, warns against scams involving cashier's checks. Fraudulent buyers will buy items with forged cashier's checks. When the checks bounce, the seller has lost the merchandise and is out the value of the check as well.

Be wary of buyers who offer to have a shipper pick up the item and who say they'll pay with a cashier's check. Buyers should pick up in person and either pay cash or via PayPal. Be very wary of buyers who offer to pay more than you advertise and then ask you to reimburse the shipper for the difference. This is an age-old scam designed to take even more from you than the merchandise — you'll lose the money, too.

After you have written the description, click Add/Edit Images. Choose up to four images to include with the listing. (You can post no more than four.) Click Continue and preview your listing (see Figure 12-2). Read carefully for any mistakes. If you need to make revisions, click Edit. If everything seems OK, click Continue.

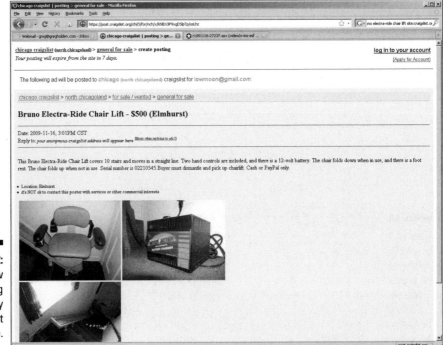

Figure 12-2:
Review your posting carefully before it goes online.

Click Continue, accept the terms of use, and read the e-mail that Craigslist sends to you. Click the link supplied in the e-mail, which takes you back to Craigslist to approve your listing. After you click the Publish button, your listing goes online. Be aware that the sale is online for only seven days. After that, it is removed, and you have to list it again. Keep the description and photos handy should you need to relist.

When you receive e-mail responses, be selective. Respond only to the e-mails that seem to be from people who are eager to pick your item up themselves and who will pay you either by cash or PayPal. I received plenty of responses from people who would not pick up in person but insisted on sending a "shipper." One e-mail read as follows (I am leaving misspellings intact):

```
Thanks for your prompt reply.Well,i must say you ve
got a nice item and as a matter of fact, In a trans-
action like this, i will appreciate it if we can put
trust first so that the transaction can go smoothly.I
would have love to come by with cash and pick it up but
at the moment am a kinda of too busy to come over,so
i think i can send you a cashier check via Fedex Or
UPS overnight and my shipping company could come pick
it up once payment is cleared.The Check will be excess
and all what you will need to do is to just send the
remaining balance to my Shipper for pick up after
deducting your money,if you are ok with this pls do get
back to me with your full name,address and phone number
so i can proceed with the payment and pls do keep this
item for me and inform other interested party that its
been sold..ok
```

Needless to say, I told the buyer that I was insisting on cash or PayPal and that the item be picked up in person. I never heard back from him. Craigslist can be a great place to sell, but remember that you're in charge. Don't be rushed by people who claim to be in a big hurry and who don't want to meet your terms. There will be others after them who will be more compliant.

Becoming an Amazon.com Seller

Over the years, Amazon.com has become known as "Earth's biggest book-seller." It has done so by selling books on the site all by itself. Having conquered the world of online bookselling, Amazon.com is attempting to give individual entrepreneurs different options for generating revenue. You'll find links leading to many of the options for selling with Amazon.com if you go to the home page (www.amazon.com) and click the Selling on Amazon link below the various department headings.

Amazon.com gives entrepreneurs a variety of ways to sell through its existing marketplace. If you have an item to sell, you can list it on Amazon.com. You also get to place your ad alongside the listing for the same book that's being sold brand new on the site.

Become an Amazon.com Associate

You're probably already familiar with the idea of an affiliate program. The Amazon.com Associates program works as you would expect: When you become an Amazon.com Associate, you place a link to Amazon.com on your Web site. When someone makes a purchase after following the link from your site, you earn a referral fee.

Becoming an affiliate

If you've written or created books, CDs, or other materials that are sold on Amazon.com, you can create links to those items on your own Web site and refer your visitors to the bookseller's site so that you can potentially earn the referral fee. I have a few books that are sold on Amazon.com, and I include images of several of these books on my own Web site (www.gregholden. com). I already had several of the ingredients for generating referral income: a Web site, books to sell, and a need for extra revenue. All that remained was to sign up with the Amazon.com Associates program and create specially-formatted links that I associate with each of the book images on my home page.

To get started with the program, just follow these steps:

1. **Go to the Amazon.com home page and click the Join Associates link at the bottom of the page.**

2. **Click the Join Now for FREE! button (on the right side).**

3. **Fill out the forms provided to become a member.**

   You have to tell Amazon.com all about your Web site and its content. When you're done, click Finish.

4. **Choose the type of content you want Amazon to add to your site. The first section is for the Associates program. Click Get Started Now under this section.**

   You have to set up a payment program by telling Amazon whether you want to receive a check or direct deposit into your bank account. I chose the direct deposit method, so I entered my bank account number and bank routing number.

5. **Click Get Started Now and then click Continue on subsequent pages to read about setting up links to Amazon.com products on your Web site.**

   You have to set up the Associates links according to Amazon.com's specifications so that it can track when the links are clicked and determine whether purchases are subsequently made.

6. **From the Associates Central welcome page, click the Links & Banners tab.**

   A Web page appears describing types of links you can make:

   • **Product Links:** These are graphic or text links to specific books, movies, or CDs you want to promote. If the search box takes up too much graphic space on your Web pages, include a simple text link that points people to specific items on Amazon.com.

   • **Banner Links:** These are banner ads you display on your site that display books or other products on Amazon.com that are related to the products you sell. For instance, if you sell baby clothes, you might recommend a book on parenting that you like.

- **Widgets:** Widgets are small-scale applications that automate the process whereby readers choose books, music, and other products from the Amazon.com catalog. You can include an Amazon.com search engine on your page, for instance. You can also include your own favorite books or music, among other things.

You can promote your friends' books and CDs, books or CDs that relate to your own goods and services, or other books and CDs you admire. By spreading the word about such materials, you can earn a few cents or perhaps a few dollars. Because I have some specific books to promote, I chose the first option, Product Links.

7. **Choose a link option and then click the Add Now link for that option.**

8. **On the next page that appears, search for the book or CD that you want to promote.**

The results of my search are shown in Figure 12-3.

9. **Click the Get HTML button to access the HTML code. Copy and paste the HTML to your Web page in order to display the cover.**

This display serves as a link to the book or CD's page on Amazon.com.

I noticed that, by default, the image opened as an *inline frame* — a container within the Web page. This seemed too complex to me, so I clicked the Customize HTML link and changed the link to a simple clickable image file rather than a frame. I pasted the HTML into my Web page, which produced the link, as shown in Figure 12-4.

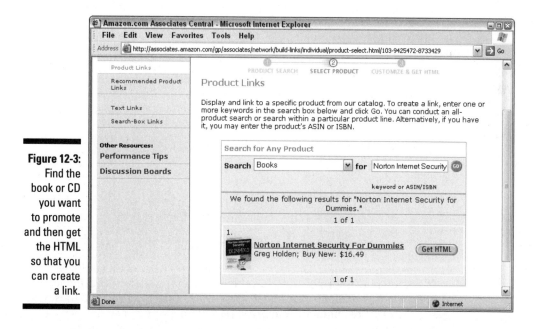

Figure 12-3:
Find the book or CD you want to promote and then get the HTML so that you can create a link.

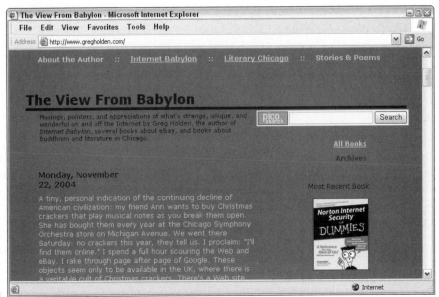

Figure 12-4:
You can turn a book cover into a clickable link that can earn you a referral fee.

Becoming a search marketer

Most people who earn affiliate sales fees by advertising Amazon.com products do so by posting links on their Web sites or blogs. A growing number of enterprising individuals are advertising by placing ads on search and content sites such as Google, Yahoo!, and MSN Search. They're taking products sold on one popular Web site and advertising on another well-traveled site.

The process works like this: You locate a product on Amazon.com that you want to sell. You become an Amazon Associate and create a link to the product on the Amazon.com Web site (see the earlier section, "Becoming an affiliate"). Rather than post the link to the product on your own Web site, you create one of those paid search ads that appear off to one side or at the top of a page full of search results. You write an ad that attracts people's attention. Some of them click the link included with the ad and go to the product page on the Amazon.com Web site. If they make a purchase as a result of clicking your ad, you earn a referral fee.

After you've signed up with Amazon.com, chosen a product to sell, and generated a link to it, sign up with Google's AdWords program (`adwords.google.com`). Start a campaign and write a short, three-line ad for the product. You identify keywords you want to associate with the ad and bid a certain amount on each one (10 cents per click is a reasonable amount). See the AdWords Help files for more instructions.

Search marketing through Google or other sites is an example of *pay-per-click* advertising: You're charged for placing an ad only when someone clicks it.

You choose keywords that cause your ad to appear in a set of search results. You place a bid on the keyword; the bid indicates how much you're willing to pay if someone clicks your ad. The higher you bid, the better placement you have in ads (but the more you pay, too).

Here's an example: Suppose you want to place an affiliate ad for an iPod Nano. This is a popular item, so you can expect to have a lot of competition from other search marketers who want to promote the same product. Suppose you have five other marketers who bid on the keywords "iPod Nano." How can you stand out from the crowd? One option is to be as specific as possible: If the other marketers bid on the keywords "iPod Nano" and you bid on "16GB iPod Nano," you distinguish yourself — and attract a more targeted audience. You'll get fewer clicks overall, but the chances are better that the people who see your ad will click it and make a purchase of the iPod Nano you're promoting. You bid 10 cents per click on these keywords. If one of your ads causes the ad to appear 1,000 times in one month and 100 people click on the ad, you pay $10 for that keyword for that month. If none of those clicks leads to a purchase, you don't earn any money, either.

Along with signing up for an account with Amazon.com and with Google, you also need to sign up at some point with an *affiliate network* — an organization that tracks how many clicks your ads have generated and issues commissions to you. Affiliate networks, such as Commission Junction and AffiliateFuel.com, consolidate payments from many different advertisers and pay you in a single check. They're most useful when you have multiple payouts from different advertisers.

Creating an aStore

If you enjoy making referrals in a particular area and find that some of the shoppers you've referred are subsequently making purchases on Amazon.com, you might want to present the items you recommend in an aStore. An *aStore* is an online store with a twist. An aStore isn't a site where you put your own merchandise up for sale; rather, you present your own selection of items from Amazon.com's merchandise on such a site.

The aStore interface helps you set up your page full of links and product images; you can then publish the page as part of your Web site. The theory is that by having a "dedicated shopping area" on your site, you'll keep visitors there longer (although if they want to investigate a link, they'll leave your site and go to Amazon's). Find out more about aStores at `affiliate-program.amazon.com/gp/associates/join/info6.html`.

You probably won't make a fortune from Amazon.com's referral fees. You earn on average 4 to 5 percent of the value of the items sold, depending on the number of items you sell. If you refer someone who purchases a book for $15, for instance, you earn about 75 cents for that purchase.

Join the marketplace

Suppose you have a pile of recently published books or CDs around (books or CDs that are being sold on Amazon.com) and you need to sell them. When you join the Amazon Marketplace, you can sell those books yourself. Suppose you purchase a book and you're so happy with it that you just feel compelled to sell it so that others can share the wisdom contained within. Here's how you sell it:

1. **Go to the Amazon.com home page (**www.amazon.com**) and click the Sell on Amazon link (under the Selling on Amazon header along the left side of the screen, about halfway down the page).**

   The Sell on Amazon.com page appears.

2. **Click one of the two Start Selling buttons, depending on whether you want to be an individual or professional seller. Individuals sell fewer than 40 items a month for $.99 per sale; professionals sell more than 40 items per month for $39.99 per month.**

3. **Choose the category you're interested in and enter the name or *ISBN* (the number on the back cover, just above the "zebra stripe" code) of the specific item you want to see; then click the Start Selling button.**

   The sales page for the item (in this case, the book) appears.

4. **Click the Sell Yours Here button on the right side of that page.**

   The Sell Your Item - Select Condition page appears.

5. **Choose an option from the Condition drop-down list to describe the condition of your item. Add some text that describes the condition if you want and then click Continue.**

   The Sell an Item - Enter Price page appears. This page includes the important information about Amazon.com's fees: You're charged 99 cents plus a 6–15 percent fee for each item you sell.

6. **Enter your price in the Price box and then click Continue.**

   Make sure that your price is at or below Amazon.com's own price.

   The Sign In page appears.

7. **Enter your Amazon.com e-mail address and password. (You can use the same password you use to make purchases or sell as an Associate.) Then click Continue.**

   The Registration page appears.

8. **Choose a credit card from the list (or enter a new card name and number) to identify you and then click Continue.**

   Another Registration page appears.

9. **Enter your nickname and a daytime phone number and then click Continue.**

   Optionally, you have the opportunity to enter checking account information so that Amazon.com can deposit purchase money into your account. You can skip this step for now.

   A Confirmation page appears.

10. **Click Submit Your Listing.**

    The Your Listing Is Complete page appears. In addition, Amazon.com sends an e-mail message confirming that your item is now up for sale.

If your item doesn't sell within 60 days, Amazon.com closes your listing, and you pay nothing. You receive an e-mail with details for relisting the item if you want.

Professional Subscription

If you have lots of items to sell, consider taking out a Professional Subscription. You have to pay a $39.99 monthly fee to be part of this Amazon.com program, but here are some big advantages:

- ✔ You don't have to pay the 99-cent fee.
- ✔ Your listings aren't closed after 60 days.

A Professional Subscription also allows you to use the powerful inventory reports to view orders, sold listings, and current open listings. You also get access to a bulk-listing tool so that you can create lots of descriptions simultaneously. You have to sell at least a few books each month to make back your subscription fee, but if you're a bookseller by trade and have a lot of inventory to unload, this is a good alternative.

You can find out more about the Professional merchant program at www.amazonservices.com/content/sell-on-amazon.htm.

WebStores

On top of everything else it does, Amazon.com is trying to be a Web hosting service as well. The WebStores program gives you the ability to run your own branded store through the site. The difference between a conventional hosting service and a WebStore is that the latter makes use of Amazon.com's own e-commerce technology. Customers pay a monthly fee of $59.95 and a 7 percent per-transaction fee. Find out more atwww.amazonservices.com/content/webstore-by-amazon.htm

Learning from Amazon's business strategy

Some of the things that Amazon.com does aren't direct sales opportunities for fledgling businesses like yours. They are, however, good examples of new ways to make money on the Web — options that don't always involve catalogs, tangible items such as books, or retail or wholesale prices.

In 2006, for instance, Amazon founder Jeff Bezos spoke on new initiatives the company was taking to promote its computing power. One service, Compute Cloud, has really taken off and has been replicated widely by Google and many other service providers. A "cloud" or online storage and work area lets businesses tap into the computing power of Amazon.com's own servers: They can use the servers for storage space and even use them to perform computations. A company that makes virtual reality

software "borrowed" Amazon.com's computers to enable its customers to quickly download its new software version, for instance.

It's all about making your business a resource that people turn to on a regular basis rather than a source of a single product or service. This wouldn't work if you're a childcare provider or a dentist — someone whose business requires personal contact. But if you help someone complete a dissertation, write essays to apply for college, provide legal advice, sell your home, or manage a condo association, the Web can help you. More and more commerce on the Web is taking the form of services that help businesses operate more efficiently. If Amazon.com and Google are putting their energy into Web-based services, you should think about doing so, too.

Letting CafePress Sell Your Creative Work

Amazon.com is among the best-known Web businesses. Although its hosting service is reliable, it might not be ideal for your needs. If you're a creative artist and you just want to sell a few examples of your work to family and friends, CafePress might be just what you need. If you already have an account with PayPal and regularly use its payment services for sales on eBay, it makes sense to open a PayPal store. If you use Microsoft products, such as Expression Web, to create your Web pages, Microsoft Small Business Center is a good option for creating an online sales catalog and storefront. It's all a matter of deciding what you need.

Creative people aren't always the best at marketing and selling their own work. Millions of amateur artists are probably out there hoping to become professionals: They have great ideas for cartoons, logos, and drawings, but the prospect of getting them printed and sold in stores is a big obstacle.

It's easy enough to start your own CafePress store. (See Figure 12-5 for an example of a CafePress store.) Follow these steps:

1. **Connect to the Internet, start up your Web browser, and go to the CafePress Free Store page (**www.cafepress.com/cp/info/sell**).**

   The Sell Online: Introduction page appears in your browser window.

2. **Click the Start Selling Now! button.**

   The Join CafePress.com! page appears. Before creating a store, you need to register with CafePress.

3. **Assign yourself a username and password (if you haven't done so already). When you're done, click Join Now.**

   The New Member Survey page appears.

4. **Fill out the survey and click Open Your Shop!**

   The Open a Shop page appears.

5. **Click Open a Basic Shop.**

   The Welcome to CafePress.com Basic Shops! page appears.

6. **Under the Shop Information heading, enter a short ID that will be included in your store's URL and enter a name for your store. Fill out the rest of the options on the page if necessary and click Submit when you're done.**

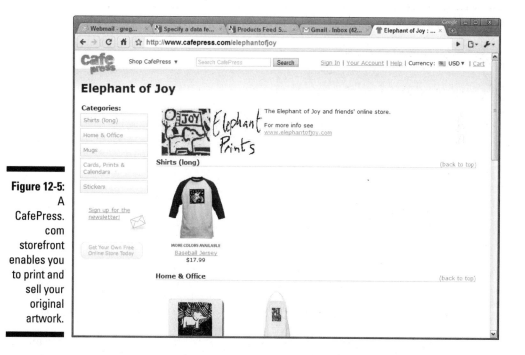

Figure 12-5:
A CafePress.com storefront enables you to print and sell your original artwork.

The Welcome to CafePress.com Basic Shops! page appears. Click the URL supplied for your new store so that you can see that although it's empty, it really exists (see Figure 12-6).

7. **Click the Build Your Shop button.**

The Products page appears.

8. **Under the Storefront Contents tab, click Add a Product.**

The Choose a Product page appears, with a set of products you can personalize and sell in your store (see Figure 12-7).

9. **Close the new browser window that opened so that you could inspect your page and return to the Welcome to CafePress.com Basic Shops! page. Click the Add These Products button at the bottom of the page.**

The Your Account page appears.

If you want to sell something other than a tote bag, license plate frame, book, or other products shown on the Choose a Product page, you'd better open a site with another Web host. But if you're just beginning with e-commerce and aren't sure what to sell, a CafePress.com store is a good starting point.

10. **Click the box that contains the type of item you want to sell and then click the Edit button.**

The Product Designer page appears.

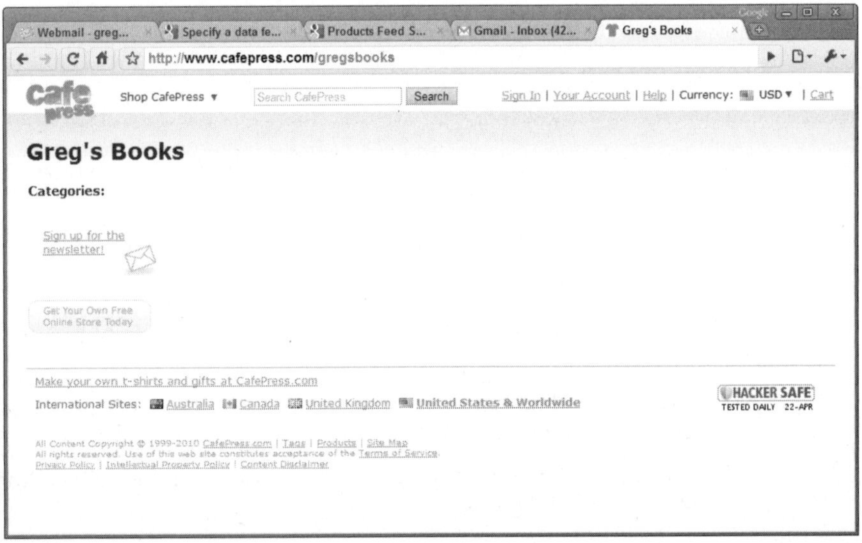

Figure 12-6:
Presto!
You've
opened your
store, which
you can
now fill with
merchan-
dise.

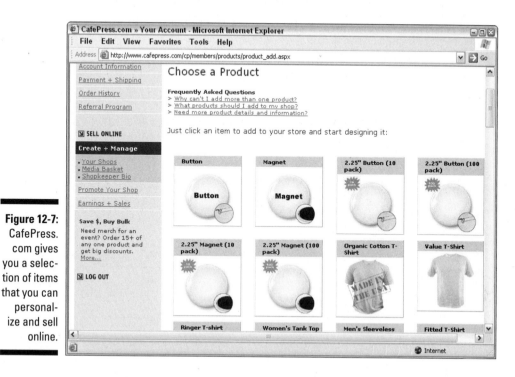

Figure 12-7:
CafePress.
com gives
you a selec-
tion of items
that you can
personal-
ize and sell
online.

11. **Click Select Image.**

    The Media Basket page appears. This page is intended as a storage
    area — a place where you can store product images so that you can add
    them later when you want to put them up for sale.

12. **Click Add Image.**

    The Upload Image page appears, with an explanation you should read
    that describes the acceptable file formats.

13. **Click Browse.**

    The Choose File dialog box appears.

14. **Select the file you want to place on the front of the object and click
    Open.**

    The path leading to the location of the image file on your computer
    appears in the Image file box.

15. **Check the I Agree to the Terms and Conditions Described Above box
    and then click Upload.**

An Uploading dialog box appears with a progress bar that describes the progress of the file transfer. When the transfer is complete, the image appears in your Media Basket.

16. Click Add image.

The image is added to the front of your product (see Figure 12-8).

17. Click Next and follow Steps 11 through 16 to add images to the back of the object and to add more objects to your online store.

Make sure that your logo or other image meets the height and other requirements for a CafePress.com store. Images must be 200 pixels in height (1 inch equals approximately 72 pixels). Find out more by clicking the Need More Image Help? link, which appears on the product design pages as you're creating your store.

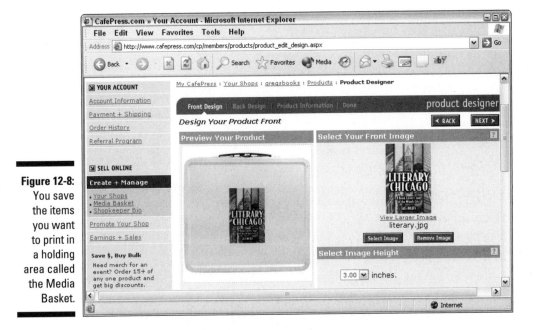

Figure 12-8:
You save the items you want to print in a holding area called the Media Basket.

Visit your new site by entering your own Web address, which takes the form `www.cafepress.com/storename` (where *storename* is the name you choose in Step 6).

CafePress.com sets a base price for each object. For instance, a set of six greeting cards has a base price of $10.99. If you charge $14.99 for the cards, CafePress.com collects the base price, but you get the $4.00 profit. You don't have to do the printing or shipping; CafePress.com handles all of that for you.

Part IV
Expanding beyond Your Own Web Site

The 5th Wave   By Rich Tennant

"For 30 years I've put a hat and coat on to make sales calls and I'm not changing now just because I'm doing it on the Web in my living room."

In this part . . .

A Web site still functions as "home base" for an online business. But these days, it's just the hub for a web of presences and storefronts. The most innovative and industrious entrepreneurs have stores in multiple locations.

When it comes to doing business online, consider using tools provided by Google to your best advantage and selling products with sites such as Craigslist and Amazon. com. Chapter 13 explains one of the best hosting and sales options for new businesspeople: online auction sites such as eBay. You no doubt already use Google several times a day, but Chapter 14 explains the basics of making Google work for you. Chapter 15 shows how to branch out to social networking sites such as Facebook and Twitter, and to your own blog, where you can brand yourself and advertise your products as well. Somebody is going to get the best, and it might as well be you.

Chapter 13

Running a Business with Online Auctions

As an online businessperson, you're concerned with establishing store-fronts where customers can find you, browse through your products and services, and make purchases. Online auction sites such as eBay and its many competitors provide you with user-friendly options for setting up store-fronts and marketing yourself and your merchandise.

eBay is now a fixture in the marketplace. More and more often, when consumers are looking to purchase rare or unusual items or simply to save money, they automatically turn to this popular auction site. For sellers of all sorts, eBay is a viable place to find customers and boost revenue.

Chances are, you've already bought or sold some items yourself on the world's most popular auction site. These days, signs show that eBay is no longer growing as fast as it once did, and sites such as Bonanzle, OnlineAuctions.com, iOffer, and others are growing in popularity. All these venues give you the chance to start from zero and have a business up and running in a matter of weeks, or perhaps even days.

Learning from the pros: My own story

I was assigned, as part of the research for a book I was writing, to attend a convention in Atlanta of the Professional eBay Sellers Alliance (PeSA). PeSA members are among the elite of the eBay merchant association. Just to get into the group, you had to have met two of three criteria: gross eBay sales income of $25,000 per month, eBay fees of $1,500 per month, or 500 positive feedbacks in the past 30 days. Today, PeSA is open to any eBay seller who has achieved PowerSeller status.

These are hard-working, enterprising, and successful individuals. But when I spoke to them and got to know them, I realized that they weren't very different from me: Other than a strong business sense and drive, most of them were normal folks with families who hadn't been selling professionally until they discovered eBay.

I left the meeting inspired not only to write my book but also to start selling on my own. I have always collected antiques and other items and I like "scrounging" for used items that are valuable. I am lucky enough to have a network of good resale shops in my area. I had already found some shoes at my local store that I knew cost $350 new. They weren't new but were in good condition and cost only a few dollars. I bought some shoes for myself and gave others to friends or relatives.

Now, I've started buying shoes to resell on eBay. At first, it felt strange to be shopping for "business" purposes at the store where I had previously shopped only for enjoyment and for my own benefit. It took me a few weeks to get over this, but it was easy to do so when I had made a few sales — of my own merchandise and some antiques sold on behalf of my mother — and realized that I was a legitimate businessperson.

Before too long, I easily achieved my initial goal of making $300 to $400 per month in sales. I decided to put into practice the most important lesson I have gained from the PowerSellers I'd met: In order to make more money on eBay, you need to increase your volume. This sounds deceptively simple. But the tendency is to start slowly — perhaps putting ten items up for sale in a week. Putting up ten items for sale three, five, or even seven days a week is much more work. But the extra time and labor does pay off: The more you can put up for sale, the more you actually sell.

To make a long story short, I became a PowerSeller in only about three months. I got a special icon next to my User ID. As a PowerSeller, I attracted more bids and more sales. After a year, I had raised my feedback rating to nearly 400. I found out a great deal about eBay and had some extra spending money besides. I got a debit card through eBay's payment service PayPal (www. paypal.com) and used the money I collected from my eBay sales to pay daily expenses as well as some bills.

There's a difference, though, between selling occasionally to make a few extra bucks and doing what thousands have already done: selling on eBay and other sites as a means of self-employment. eBay itself has estimated that as many as 450,000 individuals run a business on the auction site full time. Countless others do it on a permanent part-time basis to help boost the family income. Whatever the reason, you can't overlook online auction marketplaces as a way to get a first business off the ground. With such sites, you don't necessarily have to create a Web site, develop your own shopping cart, or become a credit card merchant: The marketplace you choose handles each of those essential tasks for you. But that doesn't mean it's easy to develop your own eBay or other online storefront. It takes hard work and commitment, combined with the important business strategies I describe in this chapter.

Running a business on eBay or another site doesn't necessarily mean you depend on that site as the sole source of your income. It might mean that you sell on that site part time for some supplementary income each month. This chapter assumes that you want to sell regularly on eBay or another marketplace and build a system for successful sales that can provide you with extra money, bill-paying money, or "fun money."

Understanding eBay Auctions

In any contest, you have to know the ground rules. Anyone who has held a garage sale knows the ground rules for making a person-to-person sale. But eBay is different, and not just because auctions are the primary format. eBay gives its members many different ways to sell, and each sales format has its own set of rules and procedures. It pays to know something about the different sales so that you can choose the right format for the item you have.

This section assumes that you have some basic knowledge of eBay and that you have at least shopped for a few items and possibly won some auctions. When it comes to putting items up for sale, eBay gets more complicated. You have the following sales options:

- **Standard auctions:** This is the most basic eBay auction: You put an item up for sale and specify a starting bid (usually, a low amount — from $1–$9.99). You don't have a reserve price, and the highest bidder at the end of the sale wins (if there is a highest bidder). Standard auctions and other auctions on eBay can last one, three, five, seven, or ten days. The ending time is precise: If you list something at 10:09 a.m. on a Sunday and you choose a seven-day format, the sale then ends at 10:09 a.m. the following Sunday.

- **Reserve auctions:** A *reserve price* is a minimum price you specify for a successful purchase. Any bids placed on the item being offered must meet or exceed the reserve price; otherwise, the sale ends without the seller's being obligated to sell the item. You know if a reserve price is present by the message `Reserve Not Yet Met` next to the current high bid. When a bid is received that exceeds the reserve, this message changes to `Reserve Met`. The reserve price is concealed until the reserve is met.

  Reserve prices aren't used as often on eBay as in the past; in its place, you can set a starting bid that represents the minimum you want to receive.

✔ **Fixed-price Buy It Now (BIN) sales:** A *BIN price* is a fixed price that the seller specifies. Fixed prices are used in all eBay Stores: The seller specifies that you can purchase the item for, say, $10.99; you click the Buy It Now button, agree to pay $10.99 plus shipping, and you instantly win the item.

✔ **Mixed auction/fixed-price sales:** BIN prices can be offered in conjunction with standard or reserve auctions. In other words, even though bidders are placing bids on the item, if someone agrees to pay the fixed price, the item is immediately sold and the sale ends. If a BIN price is offered in conjunction with a standard auction, the BIN price is available until the first bid is placed; then the BIN price disappears. If a BIN price is offered in conjunction with a reserve auction, the BIN price is available until the reserve price is met. After the reserve price is met, the BIN price disappears and the item is sold to the highest bidder.

Those are the basic types of sales. You can also sell automobiles on eBay Motors. By knowing how eBay sales work and following the rules competently, you gradually develop a good reputation on the auction site.

How you sell is important, but the question of exactly *what* you should sell is one you should resolve well before you start your eBay business. Most people begin by cleaning out their closets and other storage areas, but that inventory doesn't last more than a few weeks. Start by selling something you love, something you don't mind spending hours shopping for, photographing, describing, and eventually packing up and shipping. Sell something that has a niche market of enthusiastic collectors or other customers. Do some research on eBay to make sure that a thousand people aren't already peddling the same things you hope to make available.

Building a Good Reputation

To run a business on eBay, you need a steady flow of repeat customers. Customer loyalty comes primarily from the trust that is produced by developing a good reputation. eBay's feedback system is the best indicator of how trustworthy and responsive a seller is because past performance is a good indication of the kind of service a customer can expect in the future. Along with deciding what you want to sell and whether you want to sell on eBay on a part- or full-time basis, you need to have the development of a good reputation as one of your primary goals as well.

Feedback, feedback, feedback!

eBay's success is due in large measure to the network of trust it has established among its millions of members. The *feedback system,* through which members leave positive, negative, or neutral comments for the people with whom they conducted (or tried to conduct) transactions, is the foundation for that trust. The system rewards users who accumulate significant numbers of positive feedback comments and penalizes those who have low or negative feedback numbers. By taking advantage of the feedback system, you can realize the highest possible profit on your online sales and help get your online business off the ground.

In recent years, eBay has refined its feedback system. Buyers have the chance to leave "detailed feedback" for sellers. One way of rating a seller on eBay is the Detailed Seller Rating (DSR). This new system makes it even more important to provide good service.

There probably aren't any scientific studies of how feedback numbers affect sales, but I've heard anecdotally from sellers that their sales figures increase when their feedback levels hit a certain number. The number varies, but it appears to be in the hundreds — perhaps 300 or so. The inference is that prospective buyers place more trust in sellers who have higher feedback numbers because they have more experience and are presumably more trustworthy. Those who have a PowerSeller icon are even more trustworthy (see the section, "Striving for PowerSeller status," later in this chapter).

eBay members take feedback seriously. You'll see this after you start selling. If you don't leave feedback for your buyers after the transaction has ended, they'll start reminding you to do so. You're in control of the feedback you leave; don't feel coerced to leave comments unless you want to. Otherwise, the feedback system won't be of value. To read someone's feedback, click the number in parentheses next to his or her User ID.

Developing a schedule

One thing that can boost your reputation above all else on eBay is timeliness. If you respond to e-mail inquiries within a few hours, or at most a day or two, and if you can ship merchandise quickly, you're virtually guaranteed to have satisfied customers who leave you positive feedback (that is, as long as the product they receive is in the condition you promised). The way to achieve a timely response is to observe a work schedule.

It's tedious and time consuming to take and retake photos, edit those photos, get sales descriptions online, and do the packing and shipping that's required at the end of a sale. The only way to come up with a sufficient number of sales every week is to come up with a system. A big part of coming up with a system is developing a weekly schedule that spells out when you need to do all your eBay activities. Table 13-1 shows a possible schedule.

Table 13-1	eBay Business Schedule	
Day of Week	*First Activity*	*Second Activity (Optional)*
Sunday	Get 7-day sales online	Send end-of-sale notices
Monday	Packing	E-mails
Tuesday	Shipping	E-mails
Wednesday	Plan garage sales	Take photos
Thursday	Go to garage sales	Prepare descriptions
Friday	More sales	Prepare descriptions
Saturday	Respond to buyer inquiries	Get some sales online

You'll notice that something is conspicuously missing from this proposed schedule: a day of rest. You can certainly work in such a day on Sunday (or whatever day you prefer). If you sell on eBay part time, you can probably take much of the weekend off. But most full-time sellers (and full-time self-employed people in general) will tell you that it's difficult to find a day off, especially when it's so important to respond to customer e-mails within a day or two of their receipt. You don't have to do everything all by yourself, however. You can hire full- or part-time help, which can free time for family responsibilities.

Sunday nights are traditionally considered the best times to end eBay sales (or sales on iOffer or other sites) because that's when most potential buyers are available. But if you have an item for sale that someone really wants, any night of the week attracts buyers. And you can try starting a five-day sale on a Tuesday night so that it will end on the following Sunday night; that way, you won't have to work on Sunday.

Creating an About Me page

One of the best ways to build your reputation on eBay is to create a Web page called About Me that eBay makes available to each member free of charge. Your About Me page should describe who you are, why you collect or sell what you do, and why you're a reputable seller. You can also tell about an eBay Store, if you have one, and provide links to your current auction sales. Creating an About Me page takes only a few minutes (not much longer than filling out the Sell Your Item form to get a sale online, in fact). If you want to include a photo, take a digital image and edit it in an image-editing program, such as Paint Shop Pro or Photoshop, just as you would any other image. A photo isn't absolutely necessary, though.

Laura Milnor Iverson, the eBay seller I profile later in this chapter, has a simple About Me page, shown in Figure 13-1.

When you've decided what you want to say on your page, you need to save a digital photo if you want to include one. You then need to upload your photo to the Web server where you usually store your photos. Make note of the URL that identifies the location of the photo (for example, www.myphoto-host.com/mydirectory/photoname.jpg).

Figure 13-1:
A simple About Me page that contains links to an eBay Store and auction sales.

Follow these steps to create your About Me page:

1. **Click My eBay on the navigation bar near the top-right corner of virtually any eBay page.**

   A login page appears.

2. **Type your User ID and password and then click Sign In Securely.**

   The My eBay page appears.

3. **Click Personal Information under the My Account heading in the links on the left side of the page.**

   The My eBay Account: Personal Information page appears.

4. **Scroll down to the About Me link and click Edit.**

   The About Me page appears.

5. **Scroll to the bottom of the page and click Create My Page.**

   The Choose Page Creation Option page appears.

6. **Leave the Use Our Easy Step-By-Step Process option selected and click Continue.**

   The About Me: Enter Page Content page appears.

7. **As indicated on the page, type a heading and text for your page. Label your photo and enter the URL for the photo in the Link to Your Picture text box. You can also type links to favorite pages and your own Web page if you have one. When you're done, click Continue.**

   The Preview and Submit page appears, as shown in Figure 13-2.

8. **Choose one of three possible layouts for your page, and preview your page content in the bottom half of the page. When you're done, click Submit.**

   Your page goes online.

As with any Web page, you can change your About Me page at any time by following the preceding steps.

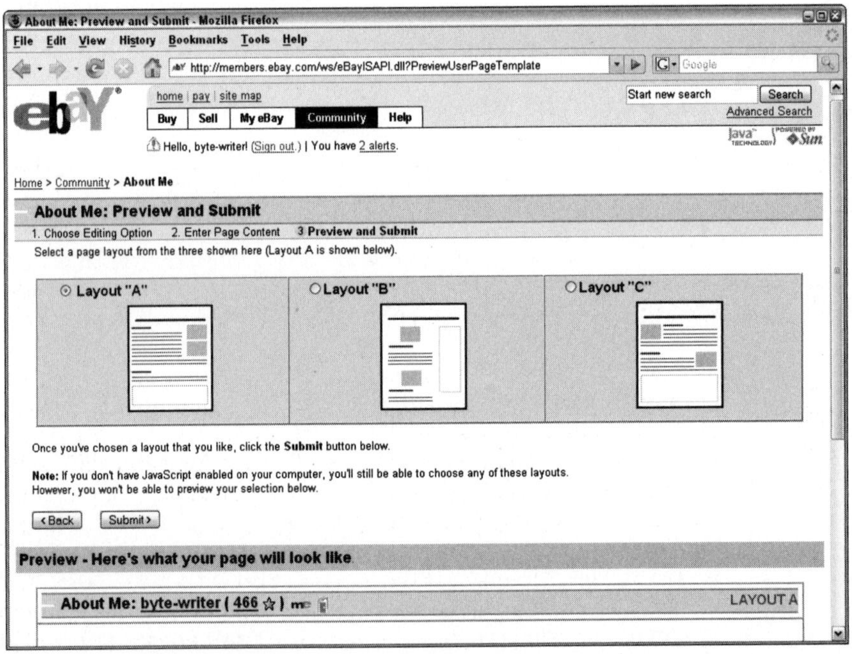

Figure 13-2:
Proofread your About Me page before you post it online!

Another way to ensure a good reputation as a seller is to participate actively in eBay's discussion boards. Pay special attention to boards that pertain to the type of merchandise you buy and sell. Responding to questions from new users and offering advice based on your experience boosts your standing within the user community.

Preparing Sales Descriptions That Sell

How do you actually go about selling on eBay or another auction-based site, or a fixed-price marketplace? The aim is similar to other forms of e-commerce: You select some merchandise, take photos, type descriptions, and put the descriptions online in a catalog. But there are some critical differences as well. You don't have to specify a fixed price on eBay; you can set a starting bid and see how much the market will bear. All sales descriptions are not created equal, however. Many sellers would argue that clear, sharp photos are the most important part of a description, and that if you show the item in its best light photographically, it practically sells itself. I'm of the opinion that a good heading and descriptions that include critical keywords are just as important as good photos. The art of creating descriptions is best discovered by inspecting other people's sales listings; the essentials are described in the sections that follow.

Details, details

The primary way of getting your sales online is eBay's Sell Your Item form. You can access this form at any time by clicking Sell on the eBay navigation bar, which appears at the top of just about any page on the eBay Web site. The Sell Your Item form is easy to use, so I don't step you through every nuance and option. In this section, however, I do point out a few features you might overlook and that can help you get more attention for your sales.

The Sell Your Item form is by no means the only way to get eBay sales online. Many full- or part-time businesspeople use special software that allows them to upload multiple images simultaneously or schedule multiple sales so that they all start and end at the same time. The auction services Vendio (`www.vendio.com`) and inkFrog (`www.inkfrog.com`) offer eBay auction-listing tools. In addition, eBay offers two programs you might find helpful:

> ✔ **Turbo Lister** (`pages.ebay.com/turbo_lister/index.html`): Turbo Lister is a free program that provides sellers with design templates they can use to add graphic interest to their sales descriptions. This is the program I use. It takes a lot of memory and is sometimes slow to run

but, as shown in Figure 13-3, Turbo Lister enables you to format auctions quickly and reuse standard elements such as your shipping or return policies.

✔ **Selling Manager (**pages.ebay.com/selling_manager/index.html**):** Selling Manager is a monthly subscription service that uses sales and management software. It gives you convenient lists that let you track what you have up for sale, which sales have ended, which items have been purchased, and what tasks you have yet to do — for instance, sending e-mails to winning bidders or relisting items that didn't sell the first time.

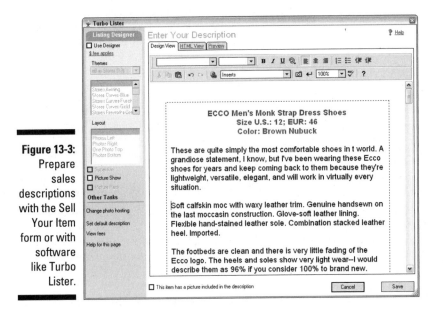

Figure 13-3:
Prepare sales descriptions with the Sell Your Item form or with software like Turbo Lister.

Choosing a second category

One of the first things you do in the Sell Your Item form is to choose a sales category in which to list your item. I highly recommend using the search box at the top of the Select Category page. Enter a keyword and click Find. You're presented with a detailed list of sales categories. The best thing about the list is that it's ranked in order of the ones that are most likely to sell items matching your desired keywords. The categories near the top of the list are the ones to choose.

I also recommend paying an extra dollar or so (when you choose a second category, your listing fee is doubled) and listing the item in a second category — especially if the second category has a percentage ranking that's almost as high as the first.

Focusing on your auction heading

The *heading* of an eBay sales description is the six or seven words that appear in a set of search results or in a set of listings in a category. In other words, this is the set of words that a potential customer initially sees when he or she is deciding whether to investigate a sale and possibly bid on it. Keep your heading short and specific. Include dates, colors, or model numbers if applicable. Try to pick one word that might attract a buyer, such as Rare, Hard-to-Find, Mint, New, or something similar.

Be sure to work keywords into your auction title — brand names or phrases that shoppers might search for on eBay. Your sale is more likely to turn up in search results with desirable brand names such as Gucci, Versace, and so on. Be as specific as you can; include sizes, colors, and original retail prices in your headings, too.

Choosing a good ending time for your sale

With eBay, the starting time isn't what counts — it's the ending time that makes a difference. The more attention you can get at the end of a sale, the more likely you are to make a profit. Most sales get attention on weekends, when the majority of shoppers aren't working. In my experience, the optimal time is to have the sale end some time on a Saturday afternoon or Sunday evening (though Wednesday evenings are also good — I'm not sure why).

Of course, bidders can come from all over the world, and what's Sunday afternoon in California is Monday morning in Australia. But don't worry too much about such distinctions: Pick an ending time that's convenient for eBay shoppers in your own country to be present — not in the middle of a workday but on the weekend.

In eBay's early days, if you wanted a sale to end at a particular time (say, 7 p.m. on a Sunday evening, when lots of bidders are available), you had to physically be present to create the description at a certain time. For instance, if you wanted such a sale to last seven days, you had to list it at precisely 7 p.m. the preceding Sunday. Now, you don't have to be physically present exactly a week, five days, three days, or one day before you want your sale to end. Instead, you can specify an ending time when you fill out the Sell Your Item form or with Turbo Lister, although you'll have to pay an extra listing fee of 10 cents for each sale you schedule.

Adding keywords

You don't have to make your auction description overly lengthy. The length isn't what counts; it's the number of keywords you include. A *keyword* is a word or phrase that describes the item you have for sale and that prospective buyers are likely to enter in their eBay searches. If your description contains a keyword that someone enters, your sale might show up in search results. And just appearing in the search results is half the battle: If a buyer can find your item, he or she can then follow through with the purchase.

The more keywords you can add to your description, the more frequently the sale is found by searchers. It's to your advantage, then, to think of all the terms that someone would use when looking for your item and add as many of those keywords to the heading as well as to the body of the description as you can. If you're selling an electric drill, for example, use keywords — such as *cordless, electric, 3/8-inch, Black & Decker,* or anything else a likely buyer might enter.

Upgrading your listings

Near the end of the Sell Your Item form, a series of items gives you the option to specify whether you want to upgrade your listings. *Upgrade,* in this case, is adding graphic highlights that are intended to help your listing stand out from those around it, either in search results or on category pages. You can choose from the options shown in Table 13-2.

Table 13-2	Listing Upgrades	
Upgrade	*Description*	*Cost*
Subtitle	You can insert another 80 characters of text to appear below the Title as buyers are searching.	$0.50
Bold	The auction title is formatted in bold type.	$2.00
Gallery Plus	Displays a larger image when users roll their mouse over the gallery thumbnail image.	$0.35
Featured First	Your auction is included (on a rotation basis) as part of eBay's Featured auctions. This is available *only* to Top-Rated Sellers.	$24.95

Note: Although it's free to register for an account on eBay and free to fill out the Sell Your Item form, eBay charges you an Insertion Fee when you actually put an item up for sale. The Insertion Fee is based on the starting price of the auction. The fee is only $.25 for a starting bid of $9.99 or less, which explains why most starting bids are less than $10. A Final Value Fee is also charged at the end of the auction, and it depends on the sale price. On a sale of $100, the Final Value Fee is 9 percent or $9; at $1,000, it is $50 because the maximum Final Value Fee is $50. For a detailed explanation of the formula used to calculate fees, see pages.ebay.com/help/sell/fees.html.

Including clear images

No matter how well written your auction's headings and description are, all your work can quickly be undone by digital images that are dark or blurry or that load too slowly because they're too large in either physical (length and width) or file size. The same principles that you use when capturing digital images for your e-commerce Web site apply to eBay images: Make sure that you have clear, even lighting (consider taking your photos outdoors); use your camera's auto-focus setting; crop your images so that they focus on the merchandise being sold; and keep the file size small by adjusting the resolution with your digital camera or your image editing software.

Some aspects to posting images along with auction descriptions are unique to eBay:

✔ **Image hosting:** If you run a business on eBay and have dozens or even hundreds of sales items online at any one time, you can potentially have hundreds of image files to upload and store on a server. If you use eBay Picture Services as your photo host, the first image for each sale is free. Each subsequent image costs 15 cents. It's worth your while to find an economical photo-hosting service, such as PixHost (www.pixhost.com) or PhotoBucket (www.photobucket.com).

✔ **Close-ups:** If what you're selling has important details, such as brand names, dates, and maker's marks, you need to have a camera that has *macro capability* — that is, the ability to get clear close-ups. Virtually all digital cameras have a macro setting, but it can be tricky to hold the camera still enough to get a clear image (you may need to mount the camera on a tripod). If you use a conventional film camera, invest in a macro lens.

✔ **Multiple images:** You never hear an eBay shopper complaining that you included too many images with your auction listings. As long as you have the time and patience as well as an affordable image host, you can include five, six, or more views of your item. (For big objects such as automobiles and other vehicles, multiple images are especially important.)

Be sure to crop and adjust the brightness and contrast of your images after you take them, using a program such as Paint Shop Pro by Corel (www.corel.com) or Adobe Photoshop Elements (www.adobe.com).

If you want to find out more about creating sales descriptions (and practically every aspect of buying or selling on eBay, for that matter) take a look at my book, *eBay PowerUser's Bible* (Wiley).

Being flexible with payment options

Payments might seem like the most nerve-racking part of a transaction on eBay. They have been, in the past; but as time goes on, eBay provides more safeguards for its customers. That doesn't mean you won't run into the occasional bidder who won't respond after winning your auction, or whose check bounces. But as a seller, you have plenty of protections: If someone doesn't respond, you can relist your item; if someone's check bounces, you don't lose your sales item because you hold on to it while the check clears.

You can enable your customers to pay with a credit card, either by using your merchant credit card account if you have one (see Chapter 7) or eBay's own PayPal payment service. (www.paypal.com) PayPal is by far the most popular option. In the case of PayPal, you're charged a nominal fee (2.2–2.9 percent of the amount plus a 30-cent fee) when a buyer transfers money electronically to your account.

Don't accept other forms of payment from buyers. Occasionally, a buyer insists on sending you cash in an envelope; you should insist, in turn, that the buyer join PayPal or use a credit card instead. COD (Collect on Delivery) is expensive and cumbersome; it makes the delivery service responsible for collecting your money, and if the buyer isn't home when the delivery people arrive, you might have to wait a long time to get paid. Western Union wire transfers are notorious for being used by scam artists — though I have used Western Union money order payments with no problem.

Providing Good Customer Service

When you sell on eBay on a regular basis, you need to develop a good reputation. One way to achieve that goal is to provide a high level of customer service to your buyers. The single best way to do *that* is to be responsive to e-mail inquiries of all sorts. This means checking your e-mail at least once a day and spending lots of time typing messages. If you take days to get back to someone who asks you about the color or the condition of an item you have for sale, it might just be too late for that person to bid. A slow response to a high bidder or buyer after the sale can make the buyer nervous and result in neutral feedback — not a complaint about fraud or dishonesty, but a note about poor service. Such feedback is considered as bad as a negative comment on eBay.

Setting terms of sale

One aspect of good customer service is getting back to people quickly and communicating clearly and with courtesy. When you receive inquiries, always thank prospective customers for approaching you and considering the sale; even if they don't end up placing bids, you'll have spread goodwill.

Another way to be good to your customers is to be clear about how you plan to ship your merchandise and how much it will cost. When you fill out the Sell Your Item form (which I discuss further in the earlier section, "Details, details"), you can specify either an actual *shipping cost* (a cost based on weight and the buyer's residence) or a *flat shipping fee* (a shipping fee you charge for all your items).

The moment you specify a shipping charge in the Sell Your Item form, you set eBay's automated Checkout system in motion. The Checkout system enables buyers to calculate their own shipping charges. The advantage to you, as the seller, is that you don't need to send your buyers a message stating how much they need to pay you.

Packing and shipping safely

One of the aspects of selling on eBay that is often overlooked (not by *buyers*) is the practice of packing and shipping. After sending out payment for something, buyers often wait on pins and needles, eagerly hoping to receive their items while dreading an unresponsive seller who refuses to ship their purchases. Besides the danger of fraud, there's the danger that the item you send will be damaged in transit.

Be sure to use sturdy boxes when you ship and that you take care to adequately cushion your merchandise within those boxes. I've received boxes from sellers who stuffed the insides with bubble wrap and newspaper, and I was happy for the trouble. If you're shipping something particularly fragile, consider double-boxing it: Put it in a box, place the box in a larger one, and put cushioning material between the two. Your customers will be pleased to receive the merchandise undamaged, and you'll get good feedback as a result.

Place a thank-you note, business card, or even a small gift inside the box with your shipment. It spreads good feelings and reminds buyers how to get in touch with you in the future.

Moving from Auctioneer to eBay Businessperson

eBay sellers don't start out saying, "I'm going to be a PowerSeller, and I'm going to sell full time on eBay for a living!" Rather, they typically start out on a whim. They find an object lying in a box, in the attic, or on a shelf, and they wonder: Will anyone pay money for this?

That's what happened to Kimberly King, a housewife living in Longmont, Colorado. Back in March 2000, she was cleaning the house when she found an old purse. She says, "I thought, 'Gee, should I sell this?' I didn't have enough stuff to hold a garage sale. I'd heard about eBay, so I thought I would see what it was like to sell something. I found out just how easy it was to set up an ID and to register. I ended up getting $20 for the purse, which was much more than I would have at a garage sale. I was hooked."

After she felt comfortable selling on eBay, things fell into place: "You start thinking, 'Let's see, that thing sold, what else do we have that we can sell?' When I really saw that I could do this on a regular basis, I thought, 'I can do this all the time; I can have some fun money.'"

Opening an eBay Store

An *eBay Store* is a Web site within eBay's own voluminous Web empire. It's a place where sellers can post items for sale at fixed prices. The great advantage of having a store is that it enables a seller to keep merchandise available for purchase for 30, 60, 90, or even an unlimited number of days at a time. It gives customers another way to buy from you, and it can significantly increase your sales in other venues or of items you sell at auction on eBay, too.

Starting an eBay Store is a big undertaking and therefore something you should do only when you already have a proven system for selling items on eBay at auction. You should also have a ready source of inventory with which you can stock your store. The problem with stores is that they cost $15.95 and up per month, depending on the package you choose, and you have to sell that much just to break even every month. For sellers who have a small profit margin, it can sometimes be a struggle to make back that monthly payment, especially in the slow post-holiday months.

CASE STUDY

Sellers reach customers on multiple sales venues

When I wrote previous editions of this book, eBay was the marketplace of choice for enterprising entrepreneurs wanting to sell antiques, consumer goods, handicrafts, and just about any other kind of merchandise. In this edition, the atmosphere is different. I have written a number of profiles of sites that either compete directly with eBay or provide a niche alternative to the auction giant. Experienced sellers no longer focus solely on eBay. Rather, eBay is just one of a number of venues for them. For some sellers who are fed up with eBay's listing and final value fees, eBay doesn't play any role at all; they sell through their own Web sites and other marketplaces.

Laura Milnor Iverson has been selling her original artwork online since 2002 through her Zen Breeze Art Gallery Web site (www.zenbreeze.com, shown in the following figure). She also sells on eBay (User ID: iversongallery) where she is currently a Top-Rated Seller. Another successful venue is her store on CafePress (http://shop.cafepress.com/zenbreeze.com). You can also find Laura on the following sites:

- Bonanzle (www.bonanzle.com/booths/ZenBreeze)
- ArtFire (www.artfire.com/users/zenbreeze)
- 1000 Markets (www.1000markets.com/users/zenbreeze)
- eCrater (http://zenbreeze.ecrater.com/)
- Etsy (www.etsy.com/shop/laurali)

"I have a bunch of basic (free) stores, linked together by using a search tag — my Web site name: zenbreeze," she says. She sells her art online full time. Her CafePress sales, in particular, enable her to buy her own calendars on the site to send to relatives overseas.

Laura has been online long enough that much of her business comes from referrals made by satisfied customers who perform "viral marketing." In other cases, when she sells a painting or print, she sends an e-mail with a link to her sales items on CafePress. This free marketing brings her more business.

Sometimes, she even gets commissions. "I often get requests from buyers to get a painting on some item or another." She marks up her artwork modestly, making a profit of only about 15 percent.

"In this economy, I find that you have to spend more time online listing on a variety of venues," she comments. "There's no single one that's going to generate enough income."

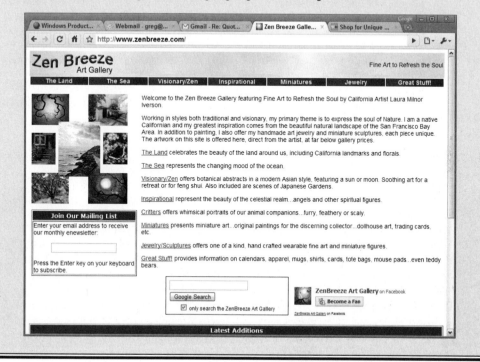

When you know what you want to sell and have good-quality inventory to offer (not just castoffs that went unsold at auction), go to the eBay Stores home page (stores.ebay.com) and click the Open a Store link to get the ball rolling. You need to decide on a name for your store and to organize your merchandise into sales categories. You also need to attend to and update your store to make it a success. But having a store can be a key step toward making an eBay business work, and if you're serious about making eBay a regular source of income, I encourage you to give the store option a try.

A 2008 article on the AuctionBytes Web site describes how eBay gets your items listed on Google and contains links to eBay tutorials on search engine optimization. You can read the article at www.auctionbytes.com/cab/abu/y208/m11/abu0227/s02.

Striving for PowerSeller status

PowerSellers are among the elite on eBay. Those members who have the coveted icon next to their names can feel justifiably proud of their accomplishments. They have met the stringent requirements for PowerSellers, which emphasize consistent sales, a high and regular number of completed sales, and excellent customer service. Moving from occasional seller to PowerSeller is a substantial change — and quite a thrill, I assure you. Requirements include

- ✔ At least 100 unique feedback results — 98 percent of which are positive
- ✔ A minimum of $1,000 of average gross monthly sales, or 100 items sold per month, for three consecutive months
- ✔ A good standing record — achieved by complying with eBay Listing Policies
- ✔ A current account — achieved by contacting bidders within three business days and upholding the eBay Community Values

In return for the hard work required to meet these standards, PowerSellers do get a number of benefits. These include discounts on eBay final value fees, merchandise with a special logo on it, customer support via telephone, a special discussion board just for PowerSellers, and more. The big benefit is that the number of bids and purchases goes up because buyers have more confidence in you.

The PowerSeller program isn't something you apply for. eBay reviews your sales statistics and invites you to join the program when you meet the requirements. You can find out more about the requirements and benefits of the PowerSeller program at http://pages.ebay.com/sellerinformation/powerseller/welcome.html.

Branching Out to Other Marketplaces

For many online sellers, an eBay store is only a starting point. They also set up storefronts on similar marketplaces. Having multiple venues lets you reach a wider customer base. Your sites can link to one another, which improves their placement on Google. You can advertise your sites on a site called EveryPlaceISell, which is run by my colleagues Ina and David Steiner. This site lets sellers collect links to all their storefronts on one convenient page. For example, Figure 13-4 shows links to no fewer than 16 venues where you can purchase photos by nature photographer Skye Ryan-Evans, who sells her work through her Web site, Rustic Moon Crafts (`www.rusticmoon crafts.com`).

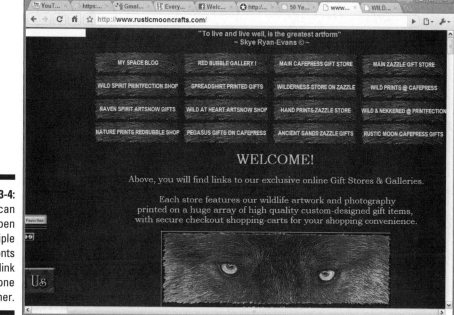

Figure 13-4:
You can open multiple storefronts and link them to one another.

Chapter 14

Taking Advantage of Google's Tools

*L*ong ago, Main Street was the place to see and be seen as well as make money as a merchant in many small towns in America. Later, the shopping mall attracted sellers of all sorts along with curious shoppers. Those marketplaces haven't gone away altogether, but these days, Google is the best-known, single online resource for businesses around.

Google started as a *search engine* — a Web site that organizes the contents of the entire Internet and made information easy to find. It turns out that the same approaches that apply to organizing content and presenting search results apply to merchants as well as their goods and services. Google now makes millions by giving online businesspeople the ability to pay for ads that steer consumers to their Web sites. The site has branched out to supply a variety of new services, including free e-mail, Web hosting, and business applications.

You owe it to yourself to pay attention to what Google has to offer and take advantage of the services that can help you. This chapter examines some, though not all, of Google's software and services. The focus is on tools that can help your business get organized and connect with customers — to get yourself *Googled,* in other words.

Spreading the Word with Google

The fact that Google has become a verb as well as a noun shows how it's become a part of mainstream culture. When consumers want to find anything online, most of them turn to Google. Conversely, when new businesspeople create their first e-commerce Web sites, they also turn to Google to help them get found by those same consumers. After you get your site online, you do *Search Engine Optimization* (SEO), the practice of optimizing your content to get the best placement in Google's search results. The sections that follow briefly summarize the basics of using Google for marketing and publicity, two of the most important ways in which Google can help small businesses.

The practice of SEO is such an important and cost-effective marketing strategy for small businesses that Chapter 11 examines it in depth.

Getting yourself listed in the Google Directory

The Holy Grail for many online businesspeople is a ranking right at the top of Google's search results — or at least on the first page of search results. I write a good deal about my brother's Web site in this book, and this isn't just because I want to give him free publicity (although I do) but also because he's done some smart things with respect to marketing his site and protecting himself legally in a field in which he could get into legal trouble: copying and restoring records and other recordings.

When you do a search for the terms "transfer LP to CD" on Google (at least, at the time I wrote this chapter) and scan the first page of search results, you find my brother's Web site (`www.lp2cdsolutions.com`) listed as number three in the first page of ten search results. (His site ranked number eight when I checked a couple of years ago; he has been improving his search placement steadily.) He has done a lot of work to get to this point. He has submitted his site to Google and other search engines, updated his site frequently, asked other sites to exchange links with him, and more.

Following any or all of these steps is a good idea, but the best two among them are the following: submitting your site for inclusion in Google's directory and exchanging links with other Web sites.

Submitting your site for inclusion

Perhaps the simplest and most practical approach all businesses can take is to add the business's URL to the Google Directory. I mention how to do this — by accessing Google's form for submitting a Web page URL to the directory (`www.google.com/addurl`) — in Chapter 13. But I don't mention one thing you should do when you fill out this form: Create your own description of your Web site. The description you type appears in Google's search results. For instance, with the lp2cdsolutions.com site, the Google search result description looks like this:

```
Transfer your LP collection (also 78, 45, 8-track, reel-
       to-reel . . .
Audio restoration and transfer to CD of recordings
       (LP, 33, 78, 45, 8-tracks, reel, cassette)"
       Drastically improve the sound of the original
       recording to . . .
```

The ellipses (. . .) are shown because the descriptions are too long to fit in the search results. Nevertheless, what does appear gets the message across. By taking the time to submit your own description instead of waiting for Google's spiders to index your site, you can control exactly what appears in the search results and in the directory as well. (A longer description you type appears in Google's directory to the Web.)

The *Google Directory* is a Yahoo!-style index to the contents of the Internet, arranged by category. Most people access the Google database of Web sites by using its well-known search page, which is also the site's home page. To find the Directory, you have to burrow into the site: Go to the home page, click More, click Even More, and when the More Google Products page appears, click Directory under the Search heading.

Exchanging links with other Web sites

Google's engine is smart enough that it doesn't necessarily give a good ranking to Web sites that have added keywords and descriptions to their Web pages. The search engine favors sites that are frequently updated and that are popular. A sign of popularity, from the search index program's point of view, is the number of links made to a page. The higher the number of links, the more valuable the page must be, and the higher the ranking Google gives it.

One of the best ways to get better visibility in search results, then, is to get other sites to link to you. How do you do it? You might automatically start thinking of programs or technological shortcuts that can create links for you on other people's Web sites. There are such tools, but the best way is to roll up your sleeves and create links the old-fashioned, time-consuming, human way: Look for sites that have products and services that complement yours, approach the owners of those sites, and ask to exchange links ("I'll publicize your site if you publicize mine.") You find some examples of such links in Chapter 11.

Link exchanges are networks of online businesspeople who are specifically looking to increase their links to other sites. Burrow into the Google Directory. Then go to this category: Computers⇨Internet⇨Web Design and Development⇨Promotion⇨Link Popularity⇨Reciprocal Links. You'll find a long list of Web sites that match you up with link partners.

Optimizing your site for better search results

For just about all online businesses, it's important to get a good ranking in Google search results. Google's exact formula for determining search result rankings is a well-kept secret. But again, you can take some simple and practical approaches to better your chances of getting placed near the top of the first page. Chapter 11 describes such strategies in more detail; I cover two other tips in the following sections.

Keeping it fresh

When you submit your site for inclusion in the Google Directory, you read the following instructional note: "Google updates its index on a regular basis, so updated or outdated link submissions are not necessary. Dead links will 'fade out' of our index on our next crawl when we update our entire index."

In other words, Google continually reindexes the Web and ignores sites that are considered dead. A *dead site* is one that hasn't been updated for a long time and that doesn't receive many (or any) visits. To avoid becoming one of these cobweb sites, update some of your content on a regular basis.

You don't have to update your whole site. If you have a blog online, you only have to make an entry every week (or better yet, every day) to keep your site fresh. Otherwise, make a commitment to change something — anything — on your site every week or so. This can be something as insignificant as the "last updated" date at the bottom of your Web page or as significant as the page title. Just add a bit of information as often as you can; this practice not only improves your search results but also keeps your visitors coming back to you on a regular basis.

Some sites (for example, Google Guide, www.googleguide.com) claim that popular Web pages are reindexed as often as they're updated. However, I don't know whether this is true. A post on Webmasterworld (www.web masterworld.com/forum10003/1015.htm) estimates that the index is updated several times a month, but Google employee Matt Cutts as been quoted as saying that the index is "incrementally updated every day (or faster)." On his blog, he reports that his own site has had more than 430 pages indexed in a day (www.mattcutts.com/blog/more-webmaster-console-goodness/). All of this means that you have another incentive to update your site as often as you can.

Building in keywords

When Google's automated indexing programs scour Web pages, they ignore common words such as *the, at, is, a, how,* and so on. What do they pay attention to? *Keywords* — nouns and verbs that individuals might enter into Google's search box when they're looking for your site.

How does your site rank? A peek behind the scenes

Google keeps its algorithm for ranking pages secret. But it's generally known that Google assigns a Web page a score called a PageRank. The PageRank is based on lots of different and complex factors. Although it dates back to December 2003 and the formulas for calculating PageRank have certainly evolved, it gives you plenty of clues for how the Google PageRank system operates. A patent application was filed by a group of Google employees with the U.S. Patent and Trademark Office. More recent comments on Google employee Matt Cutts' blog (for example, www.mattcutts.com/blog/pagerank-sculpting/) indicate that freshness of content, good organization, good use of keywords, and the speed with which pages load all play a role in calculating PageRank. Here are some tidbits from the original patent application, which are still applicable today:

✔ The history of the Web page is important. This includes the date the page was first discovered by a search engine.

✔ The frequency with which the content of the Web page changes is also important. This includes an average time between the changes, a number of changes in a time period, and a comparison of a rate of change in a current time period with a rate of change in a previous time period.

✔ The number of new pages associated with the document matters as well.

✔ The amount of content that changes as a proportion of the amount of content in the entire document matters, too.

✔ How frequently the document is associated with search queries is taken into account.

These are just a few of the 63 separate claims listed in the patent request. You can read a detailed and more recent interpretation of PageRank at www.webworkshop.net/pagerank.html. The claims all boil down to making your page worthwhile, keeping it up-to-date, and promoting as many links as you can to other Web sites and from those sites to yours.

To determine what keywords your customers are likely to enter into the Google search box when they're looking for you or your services, use a service such as Wordtracker (www.wordtracker.com), which suggests likely terms for you based on the name and content of your Web site.

Keywords do make a difference — especially if you place them in strategic locations such as the title of your page, the headings, and the first 50 or so words of text on a page. Sprinkle your Web page text with key terms and don't worry about repeating them from page to page. The more frequently they appear, the better your chances of ending up number one.

Having Google's spider programs crawling through your Web pages isn't always a good idea. Some Webmasters don't like to give all their content (such as newspaper or magazine articles) away for free. However, you can block indexing programs such as Google's from including your pages in their index. Include a simple text file named robots.txt and identify the automated program you want to block or the pages on your site that you don't want indexed. You then post this text file on your Web site. Google itself provides instructions for people who want to block indexing programs at `www.google.com/support/webmasters/bin/answer.py?answer=40362`.

Adding Google Apps to Your Business

Web site hosting and business applications are particularly important to small organizations that don't have in-house information technology (IT) staff. Google has created a set of similar services, which are called Google Apps (`www.google.com/apps/`).

You can't beat the price: The Standard version of Google Apps, which is recommended for individuals for personal use, is free, whereas the Premier Edition, which is recommended for small businesses, costs $50 for a year's license for each user account. However, Google can't know if you own a small business and you sign up for the Standard version. You can always upgrade to the Premier version later on. With Premier, you get a whopping 25GB of online storage space for your files and applications and a guarantee that your files will be available 99.9 percent of the time. With either version, you do have to pay a $10 per year fee to register a domain name, which is still pretty reasonable. If you're frustrated with login problems and slow performance of similar applications such as Microsoft's Office Live Workspace service, Google Apps might be just the ticket.

For more information on the differences between the Standard and Premier Editions of Google Apps, see the Frequently Asked Questions page (`www.google.com/apps/intl/en/business/faq.html`).

Becoming master of a domain

As do Yahoo! Small Business and other hosting services, Google gives small businesses the ability to register a domain name. Google partnered with the domain name registrars Go Daddy and eNom to offer services in the `.com`, `.net`, `.org`, `.biz`, and `.info` domains. This is a somewhat wider range of options than Office Live Workspace offers. (Office Live covers only the `.com`, `.net`, and `.org` domains, but those are the most popular ones.)

It's often a good idea to "lock down" the same domain name in many different domains; for instance, I paid an extra fee to GoDaddy to register not only gregholden.com but also gregholden.net and gregholden.org so that others couldn't purchase them.

You don't have to obtain a brand-new domain to take advantage of Google Apps. If you already own a domain, you can associate Google Apps with it. Whether you already have a domain or want to get one through Google, and whether you want the Standard or Premier edition, the initial steps are the same. The following steps illustrate how to get started with Standard edition:

1. **Go to the Standard Edition Welcome page at** www.google.com/apps/ intl/en/group/index.html/ **and click the Get Started button.**

   The Sign Up for Google Apps page appears.

2. **Click either the Administrator or End-User button.**

3. **Enter the domain you want to use with Google Apps or purchase a new one.**

   If you don't already own a domain name, you have to click the I want to Buy a Domain Name link on the right half of this page and then click Check Availability. When you have a domain, your browser displays a page stating that your domain is available, and you can register it with Google for one year for $10.

4. **Click Get Started.**

5. **Enter information about your organization and click Continue.**

6. **Create an administrator account for yourself.**

7. **Review the terms of service and click the I Accept. Continue with Setup button.**

   A page appears that asks you to verify that you own the domain.

Verifying ownership

After you obtain a domain and sign up for the service, you need to verify that you own the site. After you complete verification, one option you have is to upload a file that will serve as your Start page .

The other option is to change the CNAME record for your domain registration. If you have an existing Web site, you already know how to upload a file to it, so you should choose that option. If you don't have a Web site (for instance, if you registered your domain name but haven't created any pages for it), choose the CNAME option. The following steps assume that you already have a business Web site and want to upload a file:

1. **Create a Web page HTML file and name the file** googlehosted service.html. **You have to insert a string of characters, which Google gives you.**

2. Upload the file to your Web site. Make sure that the file is in the same directory as your home page.

3. Click the I've Completed the Steps Above button.

Google Apps offers you the chance to launch its Setup guide. If you click Skip this Guide, the Dashboard page, shown in Figure 14-1, appears.

When you first sign up for Google Apps, you go to your Dashboard page. You use this page to access all the apps for which you signed up. Simply signing up for a service isn't enough to start working on it. You need to activate it from the Dashboard.

The details on creating a Web page and uploading it to the server that hosts your site vary, depending on the type of software you use to create Web pages. Creating a Web page is as simple as opening a text editor (such as Notepad), adding the `<html>`, `<head>`, `<title>` and `<body>` tags that define a Web page, and saving the document with the `.htm` or `.html` file extension. But if you use a program such as Dreamweaver to create your Web pages, the process is even easier. Uploading the file is a matter of using a file transfer program, such as WS FTP or CuteFTP, or a Web editor that has FTP capabilities. See Chapter 5 for more details on working with Web editors.

The Dashboard page allows you to add new services (Google Apps, in other words) to your domain. You also use the Dashboard page to create new user accounts for your colleagues (see the upcoming section, "Creating user accounts)."

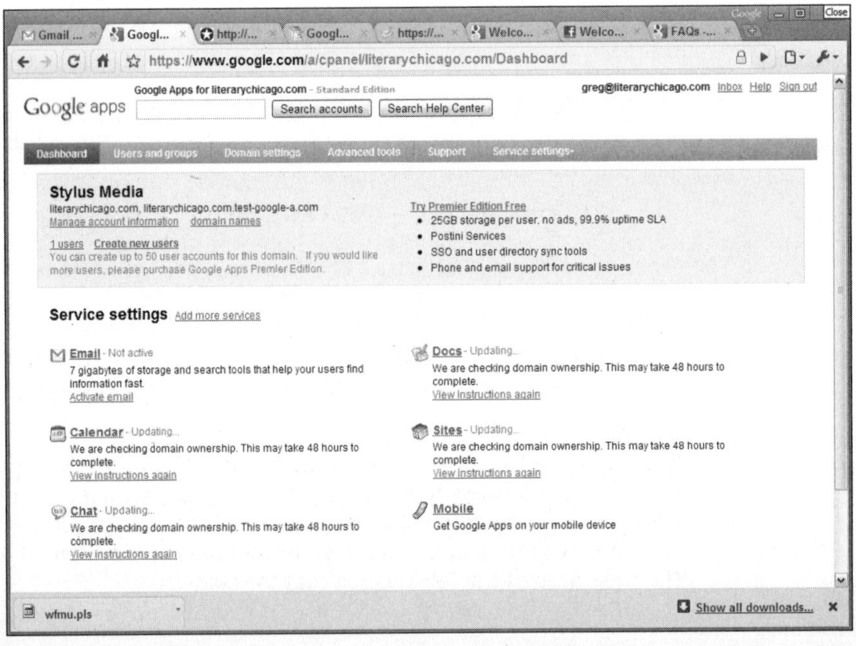

Figure 14-1:
You can add Google Apps to an existing domain you own or one you obtain through Google.

At some point, after verifying ownership and accessing your Dashboard, you'll also want to create a Start page for your Google Apps domain. The Start page is where you and your small business co-workers can check your Gmail inboxes, see shared calendars, and view links that you provide for them. Your Start page takes the form `http://partnerpage.google.com/domain`. For instance, if your domain were gregholden.com, your Start page would be `http://partnerpage.google.com/gregholden.com`.

Creating user accounts

Google Apps isn't really intended for a lone user working in isolation. If you're a one-person shop, you can obtain a Gmail account for yourself and create your Web pages through GeoCities or Office Live. Google Apps excels (to use a Microsoft pun) in giving a group of users an easy and free way to share information. To allow others into your Google Apps-powered domain, create user accounts. You have room for no fewer than 50 separate accounts in your domain in the Standard Edition of Google Apps, so there's plenty of room to grow.

To add user accounts, follow these steps:

1. **Click the Create New Users link.**

2. **On the next page (shown in Figure 14-2), enter the name of the new user and assign a username.**

   The username takes the form of *username@domainname*. You're assigned a temporary password; when the user logs in with this password, he or she can create a new one.

3. **Click Create New User to create the account.**

4. **When you're done, click the Create New Users link again and repeat Steps 2 and 3 to create accounts for everyone in your workgroup.**

   Be sure to write down the temporary password for each account you create and send it to the account holder.

   Click the User Accounts link to view the list of all the accounts in your domain and to track when users logged in most recently.

5. **Send an announcement to all users in your workgroup, telling them that the Google Apps service has been added to your domain.**

   On the Dashboard page, click the Create Email List link and assign the mailing list with its own e-mail address, such as *mailings@mydomain.com*. Then add users in your domain to a domain mailing list. When you want to communicate with everyone simultaneously, you or other users can simply send a single message to the mailing list's e-mail list, and all the members of the list receive that message.

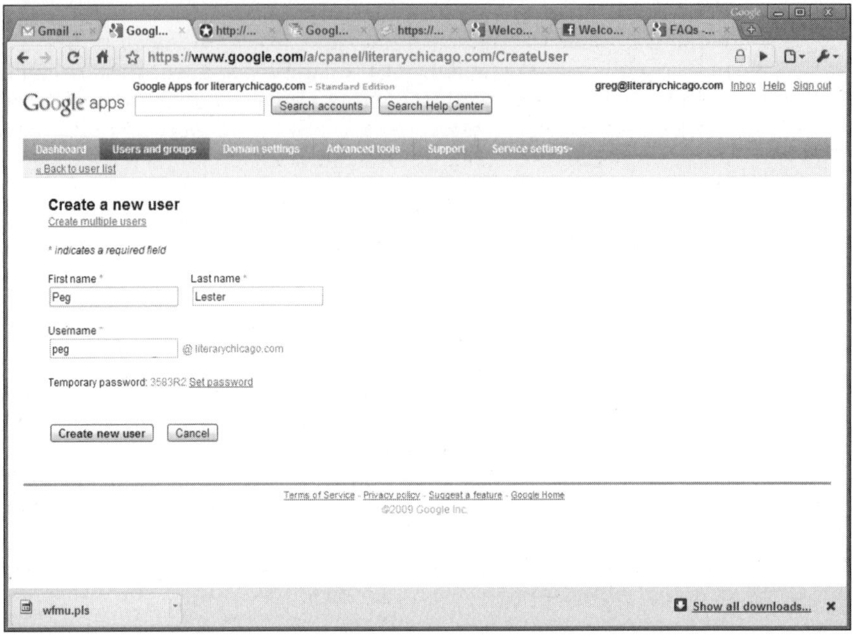

Figure 14-2:
Google Apps is primarily intended for workgroups that need to share information.

Even if you're the administrator for your domain and plan to use the administrator account, create an account for your personal use so that you can keep e-mail and other information separate.

Delivering the goods with Gmail

Aside from its search service, Google's Gmail e-mail service must be one of its most popular applications. Nearly all of my friends and many of my professional colleagues have Gmail accounts. A group I belong to distributes a mailing list with a Gmail account, too.

For a long time, Google had a policy whereby you had to be invited to have an account by someone who already has an account. Now, though, you can go to `mail.google.com/mail/help/open.html` and click the Create an Account button to get Gmail.

Many of the business services offered by Google require you to have a Google account. You can obtain one from the page given in the previous paragraph, or you can go to the Google home page, click Sign In, and click Create an Account Now under the Don't Have a Google Account? heading.

One of the best aspects of using Gmail, in fact, is the ability to create e-mail lists. Another is the fact that you get a whopping 7.3GB of storage space for your e-mail messages. (That's the space available at this writing; Google increases it periodically.) But wait, there's more: You can also redirect your e-mail from other accounts into your Gmail account so that it becomes a single point of contact for your correspondence.

Configuring e-mail for you and your co-workers is the same as activating a Start page: From the Dashboard page, click the Activate e-mail link. You have to change your mail exchange records to direct your e-mail through Google's servers if you're using Google Apps with a domain you own already. (See the warning that follows.) After you configure your e-mail, you're presented with a robust interface, as shown in Figure 14-3.

You're encouraged to follow an optional set of steps before you start using Gmail for your domain. Google requires you to have it host your domain e-mail. Chances are, if you already own a domain, you have existing e-mail service with it. If you activate your e-mail through Google, Google is your e-mail host. You may not want to do this; if you're happy with the e-mail service you already get from your existing domain host, you can skip the e-mail activation. Click Inbox to start using your e-mail without having Google function as your host.

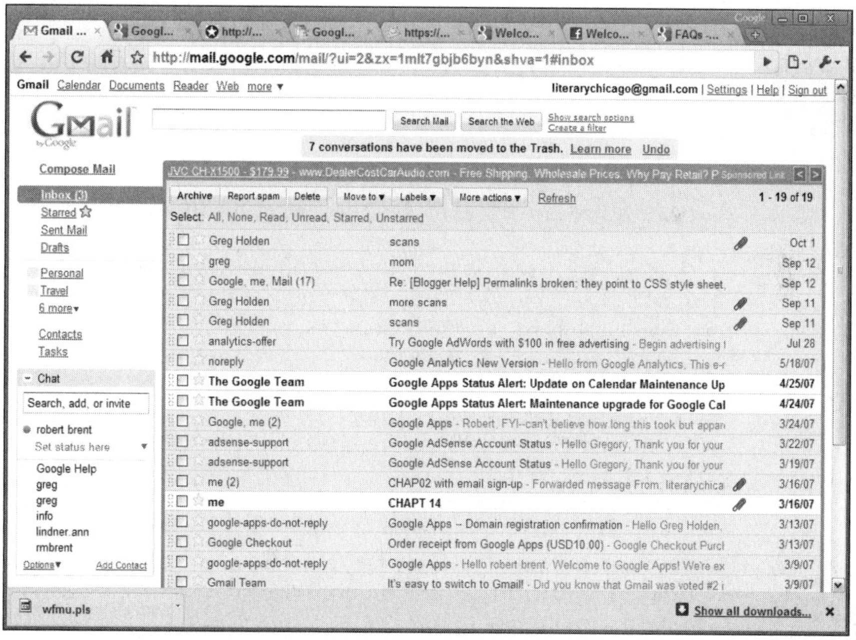

Figure 14-3:
The popular Gmail is a full-featured, Web-based e-mail client.

Staying in touch with Google Talk

Google Talk is Google's chat interface. (Don't ask me why Google didn't simply call it Google Chat.) Google Talk (`www.google.com/talk`) has two interfaces. One is a standalone chat (I mean, Google Talk) window; the other is a window that appears within the Gmail interface (see Figure 14-4). You need to download and install the chat application before you can use it. Though it's a small file and installs quickly, you may prefer to simply "reply by chat" from within your Gmail application. You don't have to activate the chat function within Gmail; it's available automatically.

To send a message, your recipient needs to be saved as a Gmail Contact (click Contacts on the left side of the Gmail window to add the individual). Then click the person's name under Contacts, click Chat, type your message in the text field, and press Enter. Your recipient has to be online at the same time in order to respond; the chat window indicates whether the person is currently online.

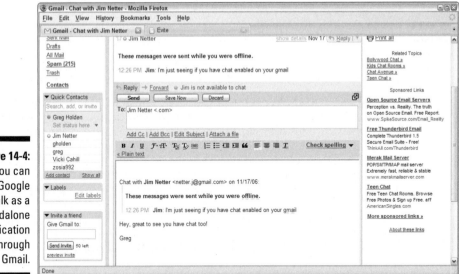

Figure 14-4:
You can use Google Talk as a standalone application or through Gmail.

Keeping track with Google Calendar

Google's Calendar application gives members of a workgroup the ability to do some advance planning and get on the same schedule with regard to upcoming meetings, deadlines, and events. The Calendar is one of the simplest Google applications to use. Just go to the Calendar page (`www.google.com/calendar`), sign in with your Google Apps account information, and you access the colorful calendar, as shown in Figure 14-5. Here's how to move around in Calendar:

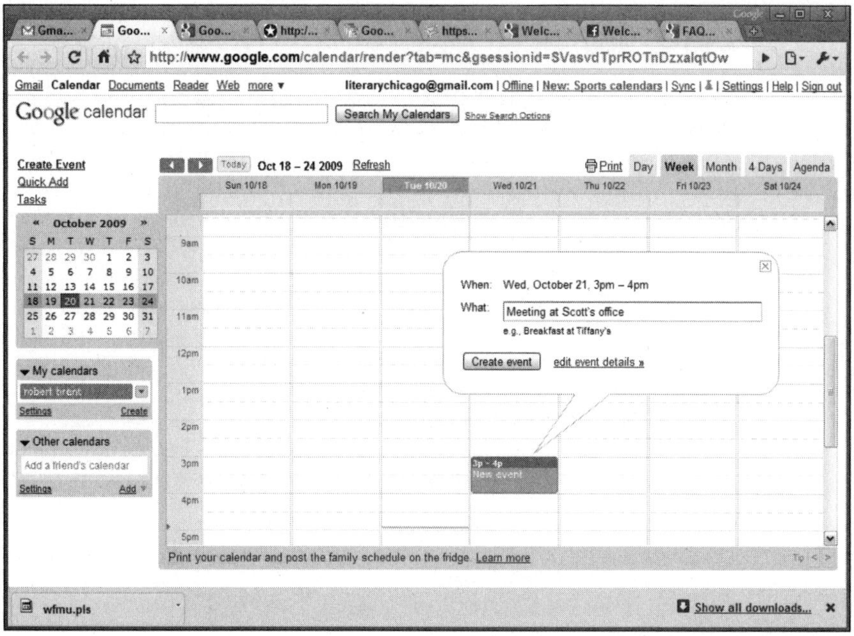

Figure 14-5:
Google
Calendar is
simple and
easy to use.

- ✔ **Move forward or back a month:** Click the left or right blue arrows.

- ✔ **Add an event:** Click the rectangle that is located at the intersection of the date and time you want. When a window pops up, type the event details in the What field. Click Create Event to add it to the calendar.

All the members of the same workgroup access the same shared calendar, so it can be used as a planning tool to keep everyone abreast of the same milestones that need to be met and meetings that can't be missed.

Creating pages with Google Sites

Google Sites, Google's Web site creation tool, includes templates and other tools for streamlining the task of weaving an interconnected web of pages. It also gives you an amazing 10GB of free storage space for images, videos, and other content you want to post online. Go to the Google Sites home page (`sites.google.com`). Click the Create New Page button to get started. A page named Create New Site appears. Here, you define the basic parameters of your new site, including its name and a basic description. Click the plus sign next to Create Page, and you are presented with several Web page templates, each with a different content arrangement, such as a series of announcements, a list, and a "file cabinet" to help you present a set of files. Type a name for your page in the Name box and click the box that lets you locate the page either in the top level of your site or as a link from your home page. Click the template you want to select it. When you're done, click Create Page.

Google Sites not only helps you create your pages but also hosts your site. When you first create the name of your site, it is added to the URL `https://sites.google.com/sites/[yoursitename]`. Type the security code at the bottom of the screen, click Create Site, and you've created the basic "shell" of your site. Now you can fill it in with content.

You don't have to sign up for Google Apps to use Google's Web page creation feature. If you have Gmail or another Google service, go to `pages.google.com`, sign in with your existing account information, and you can start creating pages.

You view your default Web page, which has an address but no real content (see Figure 14-6). Click the Edit Page button, and the page refreshes with a text cursor placed in the main content area so that you can paste or type content there .

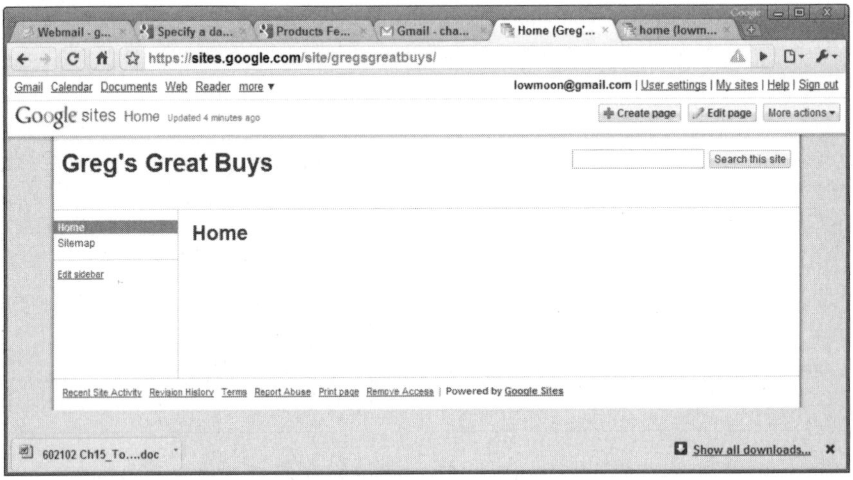

Figure 14-6:
Google Sites is a simple tool for formatting and publishing Web pages.

The toolbar buttons along the top of your page let you insert an image from your local file system, create a hyperlink, format text as bold or italic, or perform other basic functions. The drop-down lists on the left side of this toolbar let you format selected text as a heading or subheading or change text size. By default, your page has one sidebar on the left and one main content area to the right of this. You can change the arrangement or break the main content area into columns by clicking the Layout button just above the toolbar. Click Save when you're done making changes. When you save, the Create Page, Edit Page, and More Actions buttons reappear.

Click More Actions to perform common and essential Web page functions. Preview Page As Viewer gives you a chance to look your page over in a Web browser and proofread it before it goes online; this is your chance to correct typos, rewrite headings, or make other changes. After you save a page, it is posted in your hosting space on Google's servers. Publishing isn't permanent; you can always change a page after it goes online. But it's always a good idea to preview before you publish all Web content.

Adding news headlines and other gadgets

Google provides a host of applications that are designed to make navigating your desktop, and the Web, go more easily. These hosts are *gadgets:* mini-applications that can present data on one Web page that originates from another source.

To start, go to the Google Enhance Your Webpage with Free Gadgets page (www.google.com/webmasters/gadgets/foryourpage/index.html). Click the link directory under Step 1. The Google Gadgets for Your Webpage appears, as shown in Figure 14-7. This page presents some of the more common applications, which include:

Figure 14-7: Gadgets add ready-made content to your Web pages.

✔ **Google Map Search:** Specify a location, and Google publishes a map of it; it's a great way to give potential visitors directions to your office, for instance.

✔ **Google Calendar Viewer:** Put a calendar on one of your pages to let suppliers, employees, and others know about upcoming events affecting your company.

✔ **Date & Time:** This puts the current date and time on your Web page.

✔ **Google Directory Search:** This gadget places a Google search box on your page.

These are just the most obvious gadgets you might add. You'll find many others by clicking the More link in the Add a Gadget to Your Page window, searching for a gadget by name in the search box at the top of the Add a Gadget to Your Page window, or clicking one of the categories on the left side of the window.

Googling Business News and Trends

To be a smart businessperson, you need to be aware of trends and news that can affect the field in which you do business. Google can help you keep on top of the latest trends in a more targeted way than by simply scanning Google News headlines. The following sections examine options for making your site more valuable addressing current tendencies among the customers you want to reach.

Looking up newspaper and magazine articles

Often, you have to prepare reports for your company. You need to find news articles on topics related to your company's business activities. One of the most convenient clearinghouses for such information is Google News (news. google.com). You can search this part of the Google empire by entering a word or phrase in the box at the top of the Google News page and clicking Search News.

Click News Alerts in the column on the left side of the Google News home page. Your browser goes to the Your Google Alerts page, where you can enter search terms that trigger an e-mail alert to be sent to your Gmail address.

Searching through blogs

When you click the More link on the Google home page and choose Blogs from the pop-up menu that appears, your browser displays the Google Blog Search page (`blogsearch.google.com`). The Blog Search interface is quite intuitive; it resembles the main Google Web search engine. If you simply enter **Business Trends** in the search box and click Search Blogs, you turn up plenty of blogs that have Business Trends as part of their titles, for instance. You'll also find posts about business trends in the current year.

If you click Advanced Blog Search, you access a form that lets you filter results so that you get posts published within a certain date range or with a specific URL, for instance.

Working smarter with Google Analytics

This business service helps you analyze who visits your Web site so that you can determine which one of your advertising campaigns is most effective at driving you business. After you get started with tracking visits to your site, you might just find it fascinating — even addictive. I like seeing where my visitors come from, and finding what sites function as referrers to my own. To get started, follow these steps:

1. **Go to the Google Analytics home page (**`www.google.com/analytics`**) and sign in with your Google Account password.**

2. **When the Getting Started page appears, click Sign Up.**

   The New Account Signup page appears.

3. **Enter your Web site's URL and time zone and then click Continue.**

4. **Enter your contact information, including your phone number, and click Continue.**

   The Terms of Service appears.

5. **Read the Terms of Service, click Yes, and click Create New Account.**

   The Analytics: Tracking Instructions page appears, with a block of code you need to copy to any pages you want to track.

6. **Copy the code that begins with** `<script>` **and ends with** `</script>`**.**

7. **Open your Web site's home page in a Web editor or in a program such as Notepad. View the code for your home page and paste the block of Google analytics code just before the** `</body>` **tag.**

By doing so, you allow Google to run a script that tracks who comes to your Web page and run reports on where they come from.

You'll find this near the bottom of the Web page (see Figure 14-8). I've isolated the bottom of my own home page's code so that you can see where the block should go.

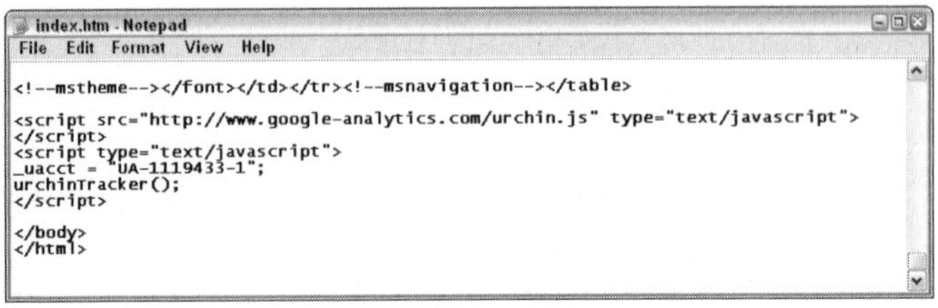

Figure 14-8:
You allow
Google to
track your
visitors and
analyze
where they
come from.

```
index.htm - Notepad
File  Edit  Format  View  Help
<!--mstheme--></font></td></tr><!--msnavigation--></table>

<script src="http://www.google-analytics.com/urchin.js" type="text/javascript">
</script>
<script type="text/javascript">
_uacct = "UA-1119433-1";
urchinTracker();
</script>

</body>
</html>
```

8. **Save your Web page file and upload it to your server.**

9. **Return to the Google Analytics page and click Continue.**

10. **When the Analytics Settings page appears, click Check Status to see whether the tracking code has been added to your page correctly.**

11. **Review your page and then click Done.**

    The Analytics Settings page reappears.

12. **Click View Reports to view the analysis of your page.**

    You'll view settings for the past several days (an example is shown in Figure 14-9); over the coming weeks, you'll view more data pertaining to your site.

This book's tech editor and others I know use site reports regularly. The Unique Visitors link, for instance, tells you how many individuals visit your blog or Web site. You can even share the information about how many visitors you've had in a given month with visitors to your site or blog; this lets them know they're part of a wider community .

One of the Analytics criteria lists the search terms that your visitors used to find your site in a given day, week, month, or year. After you determine the most popular keywords — the terms that lead individuals to your site on a regular basis — you can use those terms to your advantage. One of Google's most popular resources, AdWords, gives you a cost-effective way to take out paid search ads that steer people to your Web site. You find out more about AdWords in Chapter 11.

Figure 14-9:
Google
Analytics
lets you
chart your
traffic over
a given
period.

Selling Your Wares with Google

Not all the e-commerce sites you configure with Google offer tangible items in a sales catalog. But if you do have a catalog, whether it's online or in printed booklet form, you can take advantage of some specialized resources that can help you sell your merchandise and receive payment as well.

Google Product Search (www.google.com/products) is a search service operated by Google that scours the Internet for consumer goods. Formerly known as Froogle, Google Product Search is a popular tool for shoppers, and if you have consumer goods to sell, it pays to be included in Google's database so that you have a chance of being found, too.

As does Google's main search engine, Google Product Search uses automated programs — *spiders* — to gather content from merchant Web sites. Small, homegrown retail sites aren't necessarily indexed automatically by Product Search. You increase your chances of being included by transferring your catalog listings to the search service. You have two options:

✔ Transfer the RSS feed of your sales descriptions to a part of Google called *Google Merchant Center* — a storage area for products you list for sale.

✔ Keep your sales listed only on your own Web site but use Google Checkout to conduct electronic transactions with your buyers.

To become part of Google Merchant Center, follow these steps:

1. **Go to the Google Product Search Web site (**www.google.com/ products**) and see whether the kinds of products you sell are already carried there.**

   If they are, you may want to sell elsewhere. If your items are unique or you can sell them for less than other e-commerce sites whose catalogs are listed on Product Search, move on to Step 2.

2. **Click the Information for Merchants link.**

   The Sell with Google page appears (the direct URL is www.google. com/intl/en_us/products/submit.html). This page presents two options.

3. **To list your items on Google so that they can be indexed more easily with Product Search, click the Start a Data Feed button to get started.**

4. **The Google Merchant Center Terms of Service page appears. Choose your country from the drop-down list and click Continue.**

5. **Join Google Merchant Center by reviewing and accepting the Terms and Conditions and clicking Continue.**

6. **On the next Configure your account page, you fill out your name and personal information and provide the URL of your Web site. Click Save update.**

7. **When the new data feed page appears, type the name of your RSS data feed in the Data feed filename box. Then click Save changes.**

Google Checkout is an alternative to PayPal's popular online payment service, which lets individuals pay for items with a credit card and then transfers payment to the seller (after subtracting a fee for handling the money). Google Checkout accepts payments from buyers who use Visa, American Express, MasterCard, or Discover.

To get started, you sign up for the service, providing the URL of your Web site as well as your bank account information so that you can receive payments. You can add Google Checkout Buy Now buttons to your sales catalog pages: These direct buyers to Google Checkout to complete the transaction after making a choice. Buyers who want to use Google Checkout need to have a Google account. They then enter their credit card information as they would with any Web site.

PayPal subtracts a fee of 1.9–2.9 percent, plus a 30-cent flat fee, per transaction. Google Checkout's fees are virtually the same, at this writing at least. You'll find Google Checkout's fees at http://checkout.google.com/ seller/fees.html.

Chapter 15

Spreading the Word on Facebook, Twitter, and Blogs

*W*hen I was working on this new edition, "social networking" was the hot topic in e-commerce. That's not because of anything business-people did to promote social networking. It became popular because young people originally flocked to sites like Facebook, MySpace, and Twitter to keep up with their friends. Before long, millions were using these sites. They became part of the popular culture. Only then did they get discovered for their business and promotional promise.

But let's back up a moment. What exactly is "social networking?" If it's social rather than commercial, how can it help you and your online business? E-commerce, like more traditional kinds of business, is built on concepts such as trust, brands, and reputation. The better you can brand yourself and prove that you are either an authority in your field or someone who has desirable merchandise, the more successful you'll be. By soliciting customers on social networking sites, you go out and actively find them rather than wait for them to find your storefront.

Social networking is simply the practice of connecting with people online at venues that have been specially created for that purpose. When the venues become especially popular, they become practical places to build a brand and spread the word about yourself and your business. You can even post items for sale through a social networking site, or at the very least, advertise them online. This chapter describes business uses for two social network-ing sites — Facebook and Twitter — and one venue you create yourself and through which you can do your own social networking: an online blog.

Developing a Business Presence on Facebook

How do you find customers? Back in the early days, the way to do it was to create a Web site and then list your site on directories with names like Site of the Day. Then you sat back and hoped you would be noticed, through your merchandise or your company name. As any established businessperson will tell you, the "sit back and wait" approach just won't fly these days. You've got to go out and find customers where they hang out. Increasingly, they hang out on social networking sites like Facebook.

As you may notice, I'm not writing about other social networking sites such as Friendster and MySpace. That's partly because I don't use those sites and partly because Facebook has some features that make it especially attractive. The best is its "opt in" nature. You get content from a person or an organization only if you decide to befriend that person or indicate that you "like" an organization. You can set up two kinds of "pages" on Facebook:

- ✔ **A personal profile:** This is where you connect with family, friends, old school chums, and anyone who mutually agrees to be your Facebook "friend."

- ✔ **A community page:** This can be a page about a cause, an organization, or a business. Individuals connect to such a page by clicking a link to show they "like" it. The organization can then communicate with those who "like" it by sending out announcements.

Starting an organization page is easy, as long as you have a Facebook account. First, go to the Facebook home page (`www.facebook.com`). If you don't have an account already, fill out the form on the right side of the home page under the heading Sign Up. After you have signed up, you create a community page by going to `www.facebook.com/advertising/?pages`. When you're there, you can read some more instructions on how to set up a page.

Do some prep work first. Decide on

- ✔ The name of your page.
- ✔ The purpose of your page.
- ✔ What thumbnail image you'll post along with your page. (If you have a business logo, this is the perfect place for it. If you are selling your professional services, include a thumbnail image of yourself.)
- ✔ A short (two- to three-paragraph) description of yourself and your site ready to post.

When you're ready, click the Create community Page button. Fill out the form shown in Figure 15-1 and click Create Page.

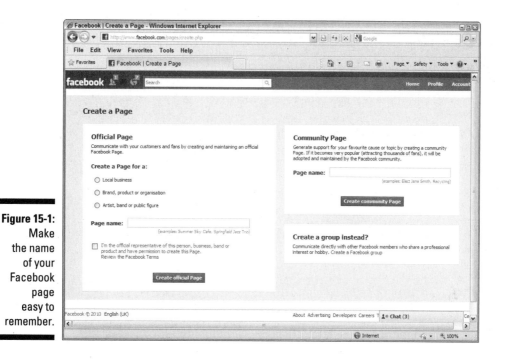

Figure 15-1:
Make
the name
of your
Facebook
page
easy to
remember.

You can also create a "group" page on Facebook. A group page is quite similar to a fan page. Fan pages are indexed on search engines, however, and are thus accessible to people who are not yet registered Facebook members. These two points make them excellent for businesses and other groups wanting to maintain ongoing relationships with interested individuals. A page on Search Engine Journal explains the differences between group and fan pages in more detail: www.searchenginejournal.com/facebook-group-vs-facebook-fan-page-whats-better/7761.

Attracting "likers" to your Facebook page

As a businessperson, your job is to encourage Facebook members to "like" you. But first, they've got to find you on Facebook. You should definitely include a link to your fan page on your Web site and as part of the signature file at the bottom of your e-mail addresses.

See Chapter 8 for more on creating and using a signature file, a cost-effective form of marketing.

There are other ways to attract fans to your page. One is shown in Figure 15-2. The venerable business 1-800-FLOWERS offers a giveaway: If you click the Become a Friend button at the top of the fan page, a "secret code" will appear that you can use to get a discount on flowers ordered from the company.

Figure 15-2:
Give visitors
a reason
to return to
your site,
such as a
game or
freebie.

As you can see in Figure 15-2, a "Secret Santa" tab is also available. Click it and you gain access to a utility that lets you send a gift to a friend. It's not necessarily a utility that will make 1-800-FLOWERS money, but that's not the point. As any Facebook user knows, members spend much of their time not posting information or commenting on their friends' news feeds, but playing games. Anything that keeps visitors on your site and gives them an incentive to return to your site makes it more likely that they'll purchase something.

Letting your customers comment

When you look at the 1-800-FLOWERS site, you immediately see another, perhaps even bigger benefit: You get to interact with individual customers and get feedback on how they deal with your site. On the Wall for the site, some leave comments about company postings, as they would about any information on Facebook; others simply indicate that they "like" a promotion or announcement. (On Facebook, "liking" is essentially a way of giving the thumbs-up gesture without actually saying anything.) Some of the comments are complaints, but the fact that they are on Facebook gives the staff person who is assigned to manage the fan page a chance to respond personally and perform some positive customer-relations work.

Other feedback on the page is enthusiastic: comments from people who are happy with the flowers they ordered and who are true "likers" of the company. Such interaction not only builds loyalty and lets customers feel empowered but also gives 1-800-FLOWERS personal comments about packages that are well received and deals that generate interest. You would have to conduct expensive and time-consuming focus groups to get the same sort of feedback.

The Info tab, which is available on Facebook community pages, allows you to put out basic information about your company and make a link to your Web site. The Shop tab, which is not typically available on Facebook pages, lets customers shop for and purchase floral arrangements. Such a utility requires a programmer to create a Facebook storefront using the Facebook application programming interface. Unless you have a programmer on hand, you can't create such a sales tab yourself — that is, unless you sign up for a Verified account with the marketplace ArtFire.

Creating a Facebook "kiosk"

An innovative and relatively new marketplace called ArtFire (www.artfire.com, profiled in Chapter 19) has developed a Facebook sales system for members who sign up for a modest subscription fee.

The Facebook kiosk is available to members who have a full-featured, "Verified" account with ArtFire. At this writing, such an account costs $12 per month.

After you create a storefront with ArtFire and list works of art or other items for sale in a catalog, you set up a fan page for your store on Facebook. Then you install the kiosk, which "grabs" your store logo and a selection of merchandise for sale and groups them in a format that those who like you will find easy to browse. You can also make purchases directly from the kiosk without ever having to log out of Facebook and go to another site.

Kharisma Ryantori, who sells handmade jewelry through an ArtFire store called Popnicute, has a fan page for her business on Facebook (see Figure 15-3). Click the tab called ArtFireKiosk near the top of this page and you can access a selection of her items for sale.

Click one of the items shown for sale in the kiosk and you will view a close-up image of the item for sale. You can select it by clicking the Add to Cart button shown in Figure 15-4. You then click another button labeled Checkout Now to complete the purchase.

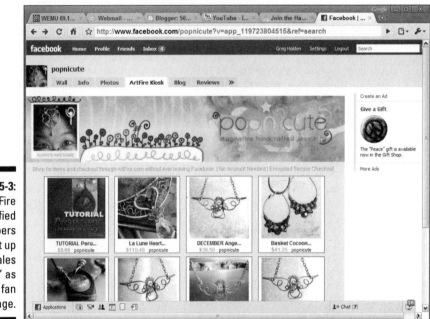

Figure 15-3:
ArtFire
verified
members
set up
a sales
"kiosk" as
part of a fan
page.

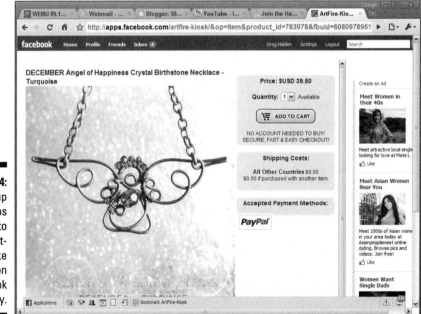

Figure 15-4:
Close-up
photos
and Add to
Cart but-
tons make
shopping on
Facebook
easy.

Building a Fan Base with Twitter

Twitter (www.twitter.com) is one of those social networking sites that you hear about and then scratch your head, saying, "What's the purpose of *that*?" At first glance, you might not think a site that lets you post 140-character messages would have a business purpose. But look around at businesses that are using Twitter, and you realize that yes, Twitter can play a huge role in keeping up with customers, building brand visibility, and promoting your own identity or that of your organization.

Although lots of individuals use Twitter for fun, celebrities like Ashton Kutcher use it to make a point about a cause or issue. Big corporations such as the following use Twitter for a variety of business-related purposes:

- **Ford Motor Company:** Through its FordCustService Twitter feed (twitter.com/FordCustService), it fields complaints, spam, and occasional useful feedback from customers.

- **Popeyes Chicken:** The company (twitter.com/popeyeschicken) jokes with customers about their food selections, announces sales, and occasionally responds with offers to personally address customer concerns with comments like this:

  ```
  sorry 'bout your experience... DM me your e-mail &
  phone# & our Mgr Guest Rels will give ya a ring.
  ```

- **Starbucks:** The coffee giant has a Twitter site called MyStarbucksIdea (twitter.com/mystarbucksidea) where the company listens to customer suggestions and implements many of them. At this writing, one Tweet boasted that 50 suggestions originally voiced via Twitter had been implemented.

- **H & R Block:** The tax preparation service (twitter.com/HRBlock) responds to customer questions, either by e-mail or phone.

Of course, one social networking forum can be used to point to another one. The Kodak CB feed (twitter.com/kodakCB) is used to publicize new posts on the Kodak Corporate Blog. The blog, in turn (1000words.kodak.com/), has links to the Kodak Web site, the Kodak Facebook page, the Kodak YouTube feed . . . get the idea?

For businesses small and large, Twitter plays a role in the overall online marketing effort. To build prominence on search engine results and word-of-mouth publicity, you need to set up a web of connections from one site to another. By chatting with your customers, even if it seems as though you are giving your knowledge away and answering questions that don't lead to immediate sales, you are building loyalty and good relations. Those benefits to others lead to sales down the road for you.

Setting up a Twitter presence

It's easy to start posting on Twitter. Here, as on Facebook, the challenge is to come up with a plan for how you will promote your business with Twitter postings (which are known as "tweets"). Before you sign up, answer a few simple questions:

- ✔ What are your business goals for being on Twitter? Who will read your Tweets?

- ✔ Do you have a cause or issue you want people to pay attention to?

- ✔ What action do you want people to take after reading a Tweet? Do you want them to visit your Web site, read your blog, or shop in your sales catalog?

- ✔ How will people find you easily? What's a one- or two-word name that you can assign to your Twitter page?

- ✔ Who will do the posting of tweets? Should this be a team effort, to keep postings flowing to Twitter on a regular basis?

- ✔ Do you have special sales or promotions you can offer?

That last part is especially important if you sell items from a catalog. Twitter denizens are used to getting special details or notices of items on sale from sites like DellOutlet (`www.twitter.com/delloutlet`). According to Business Insider (`www.businessinsider.com/henry-blodget-twitter-sells-3-million-of-computers-for-dell-2009-6`), this Twitter site generated $3 million worth of computer sales over a two-year period.

Signing up and posting

After you have a Twitter communications plan in place, you can sign up for the service and set up your Twitter feed. Go to `www.twitter.com`, click the Sign Up Now button, and fill out a simple form to create an account.

Now comes the real work: remembering to post, and updating your posts regularly. Being limited to writing only 140 characters per tweet is a relief to many. But because tweets are so short, the convention is to keep them coming at least once a day, or even several times a day.

Twitter is perfect if you have a smartphone with a keyboard and you like to type text messages. You can post on Twitter directly from your phone (at `m.twitter.com`), as long as you do some setup beforehand. You can find a help forum called Using Twitter with Your Phone at `help.twitter.com/forums/59008/entries`.

Using Your Blog for Profit . . . and Fun

You are probably familiar with blogs as online diaries whose owners record thoughts and observations and share them with anyone who cares to read them. There are millions of blogs in the world — in fact, in April 2010, the site BlogPulse (`www.blogpulse.com`) reported that there are more than 126 million blogs in the world, with more than 42,000 of them having been created the previous day.

According to a story from Technorati (`technorati.com/blogging/article/state-of-the-blogosphere-2009-introduction`), 28 percent of all people who responded to a questionnaire described themselves as "professional bloggers." Fully 17 percent reported that blogging is their primary source of income. Many blogs are just casual chatter. A few, though, make money for their creators. You, too, can use a blog to spread the word about you, your company, and what you sell, and make a few extra bucks as well.

Choosing a host with the most for your posts

One of the many nice things about blogging is that you don't have to invent the wheel. Some sites are around to set you up with a graphic look and a mechanism for posting, editing your posts, and receiving comments. Two are especially popular:

✔ WordPress (`www.wordpress.com`)

✔ Blogger (`www.blogger.com`)

Of these two, WordPress is probably the more popular at the moment because it offers more features than Blogger. For its part, Blogger (which is owned by Google) has been around a while and is free. WordPress is also free but has a Premium version that adds features such as a custom domain, extra storage, and the ability to add a feature called VideoPress to your postings. You can also buy premium themes to give your site a professional-looking design; such themes typically cost $30 to $100.

 If you are more technically minded and like to control your Web site and your blog, consider Movable Type (`www.movabletype.org`). Instead of hosting your blog on someone else's site, you post this blogging software on a server that you either own or on which you rent space. Movable Type is free for individuals but costs $395 for a five-user license.

Adding ads to your blog

The most obvious and common way to make money from a blog is to sell ads on it. This becomes practical, however, only if you are already attracting a substantial number of visitors to your blog. Advertisers aren't going to pay to place ads on a blog that has only 300 visitors a month. One that has 3,000 visitors per month has a chance of gaining some ad revenue. The most common ad sources include the following:

- ✔ **AdSense:** This service from Google allows you to choose advertisers whose products and services are related to your own content.
- ✔ **BlogAds:** This service does the "matchmaking," pairing up bloggers with advertisers and taking a fee for its work.
- ✔ **Affiliate ads:** As an affiliate, you advertise someone else's products. You sign up for a program such as the popular affiliate program run by Amazon.com. Suppose you review a book on your blog and include a link to the book's description in the Amazon.com marketplace. If someone clicks your ad to Amazon and then buys the book, you get paid an affiliate fee.

A blog is essentially a Web site in its own right — one to which you add the primary content on a regular basis. Although many blogs generate income, they also provide financial benefits because they save money for their owners. You can set one up for no money at all, as long as you have it hosted for free and are willing to take photos and write content yourself.

An October 2009 article in Technorati (`technorati.com/blogging/article/day-4-blogging-for-profit/`) reported that in a survey of active bloggers, the average income was $75,000 for those who had 100,000 or more unique visitors per month.

Asking for donations

You can simply ask people to donate to your blog. Sound crazy? It works. Add a PayPal button to your site. Visitors can then click the button and add money directly into your PayPal account. Follow these steps to add such a button:

1. **Go to the Buttons for Donations page on the PayPal Web site** (`www.paypal.com/cgi-bin/webscr?cmd=_donate-intro-outside`).

2. **Click the Create Your Button Now link.**

   A page entitled Create a PayPal payment button appears with a form to fill out.

3. **Fill out the form describing your business and the purpose of the donations. Be sure to log in so that your payments can be directed to your PayPal account. Then click the Create Button button at the bottom of the form.**

   A page appears with code that describes your button.

4. **Copy the code and paste it into the body of the Web page where you want the button to appear.**

That's all you need to do. If you don't sell merchandise, donations can be a good way of keeping your effort going.

Achieving other business benefits

Blogs give customers and potential clients a place to gather so that they can find out more about you and your company. The more time they spend with you, the greater your chances of making a sale to them. A blog also gives you a forum for developing a credible reputation. Besides that, blogs are fun. They can take on a life of their own, especially when people start posting comments and you engage in dialog with them.

Marketing yourself

Many blogs exist to give the creator a place to demonstrate his or her knowledge and expertise in a chosen field. Even if your blog isn't specifically about you, consider including some biographical information. When you do so, your visitors can find out something about your background, your knowledge of your field, and your trustworthiness. You might include the following:

- ✔ The basics about your qualifications: why you started your blog and why you went into business online
- ✔ Any certifications, honors, or titles related to your business
- ✔ Something about your business philosophy: your goals and objectives, and why you enjoy what you do

For many professionals, a blog is a place to promote and manage an image. As I wrote this, the famous golfer Tiger Woods was involved in legal controversy. He used his Web site (`web.tigerwoods.com`) to issue statements. The site includes a blog where he periodically posts about his tours and activities.

You don't have to include a photo with your blog if you want to maintain your privacy. A photo would make your blog seem more friendly and personal, however. Don't include your personal phone number or e-mail address unless you want to be especially open to your customers. Many CEOs do include e-mail addresses on their blogs and Web sites so that they can give personal attention to customer inquiries.

Selling your products instead of yourself

You don't have to get personal with your blog. Some of the most successful are roundups of software, gadgets, or other consumer goods. Some business-people advertise their products right within their blog.

Lars Hundley advertises through his Clean Air Gardening blog (`http://site.cleanairgardening.com/info`). You don't find much on the blog about Lars or his staff. Rather, you get product suggestions, gift ideas, and links to more detailed descriptions (see Figure 15-5).

Figure 15-5:
Many blogs function as advertisements for a line of products.

Part V
Keeping Your Business Legal and Fiscally Responsible

The 5th Wave   By Rich Tennant

"Ms. Lamont, how long have you been sending out bills listing charges for 'Freight,' 'Handling,' and 'Sales Tax,' as 'This,' 'That,' and 'The Other Thing'?"

In this part . . .

Before you can start raking in the big (or at least moderate) bucks on the Web, you have to get your ducks in a row. Along with the flashy parts of an online business — the ads, the Web pages, and the catalog listings — you have to add up numbers and obtain the necessary licenses.

This part addresses the aspects of doing business online that have to be covered in order to pay taxes, take deductions, and observe the law. You might think of them as necessary evils that help you avoid trouble. Chapter 16 gives you your marching orders on how to get your license, pay your taxes, and otherwise be a law-abiding citizen. Chapter 17 goes on to describe accounting tools that can help you stay on the right side of the online and offline police, as well as how to make sure you hang on to as many of your hard-earned profit dollars as possible.

Chapter 16

Keeping It All Legal

As the field of e-commerce becomes more competitive and enterprising businesspeople find new ways to produce content online, e-litigation, e-patents, e-trademarks, and other means of legal protection multiply correspondingly. The courts are increasingly called upon to resolve smaller e-squabbles and, literally, lay down the e-law.

Many of the recent legal cases in the news concern the proliferation of content on popular file-sharing sites and other Web resources. For instance, in 2009, the Illinois County Sheriff filed suit against the popular classified ad service Craigslist for alleging that the site abets prostitution through ads in the "erotic services" area of its Web site. The case was eventually dismissed. In 2006, the Chicago Lawyers' Committee for Civil Rights Under Law sued Craigslist for violating the Federal Fair Housing Act because of real estate postings that contained discriminating messages, such as "No Minorities." That suit was eventually dismissed, too.

There may be some built-in protection for sites that publish content created by others, such as YouTube. But it is clear that those who publish their own information online can be liable if they break the law. A Florida woman was awarded $11.3 million in a defamation lawsuit filed against a Louisiana woman who posted messages on the Internet calling her a "crook," a "con artist," and a "fraud." The case was seen as a warning to bloggers and other Web site owners. The point: Be sure that what you publish doesn't break the law.

In previous years, big e-commerce players, such as Microsoft and Google, were involved in patent and trademark disputes. In 2007, a company called Savvysoft ended a dispute with Microsoft when it changed the name of its

TurboExcel product to Calc4Web. Microsoft had charged that intellectual property rights associated with its trademarked Excel spreadsheet program had been violated. In summer 2004, Microsoft settled a lawsuit it filed in U.S. District Court by paying $20 million to stop a company — Lindows.com — from infringing on its trademarked name Windows.

The message for you, as a new business owner? Ignorance isn't an excuse. This area may well make you nervous because you lack experience in business law and you don't have lots of money for hiring lawyers and accountants. You don't want to be discovering for the first time about copyright law or the concept of intellectual property when you're in the midst of a dispute. In this chapter, I give you a snapshot of legal issues that you can't afford to ignore. With luck, this information can help you head off trouble before it occurs.

Note: David M. Adler of the Chicago law firm David M. Adler, Esq. & Associates, PC (www.ecommerceattorney.com), reviewed the original draft of this chapter for accuracy. Adler and his firm specialize in legal issues facing businesses that want to conduct e-commerce. Adler advises: "This chapter is a good starting point. But it cannot begin to explain all the issues in all their complexity, and [it] should be regarded as just the beginning of a discussion with a competent lawyer who will look in detail at your individual facts and situation."

Trade Names and Trademarks

A *trade name* is the name by which a business is known in the marketplace. A trade name can also be *trademarked,* which means that a business has taken the extra step of registering its trade name so that others can't use it. At the same time, it's important to realize that a trade name can be a trademark even though it hasn't been registered as such. The U.S. Patent and Trademark Office defines a trademark as "a word, phrase, symbol, or design, or a combination of words, phrases, symbols, or designs, that identifies and distinguishes the source of the goods of one party from those of others." Big corporations protect their trade names and trademarks jealously, and sometimes court battles erupt over who can legally use a name.

Although you may never get in a trademark battle and you may never trademark a name, be careful which trade name you pick and how you use it. Choose a trade name that's easy to remember so that people can associate it with your company and return to you often when they're looking for the products or services that you provide. Also, as part of taking your new business seriously and planning for success, you may want to protect your right to use your name by registering the trademark.

You can trademark any visual element that accompanies a particular tangible product or line of goods and serves to identify and distinguish it from products sold by other sources. In other words, a trademark isn't necessarily just for your business's trade name. In fact, you can trademark letters, words, names, phrases, slogans, numbers, colors, symbols, designs, or shapes. Take a look at the cover of this book. Look closely and see how many ™ or ® symbols you see. The same trademarked items are shown on the For Dummies Web site, which is shown in Figure 16-1.

Figure 16-1: You don't have to use special symbols to designate logos or phrases on your Web site, but you may want to.

You can use the ™ mark with items that may have been registered with a particular state but not with the U.S. Patent and Trademark Office. You use the ® symbol when you've registered the item with the U.S. Patent and Trademark Office.

For most small businesses, the problem with trademarks isn't so much protecting your own as it is stepping on someone else's. Research the name you want to use to make sure that you don't run into trouble.

Determining whether a trademark is up for grabs

To avoid getting sued for trademark infringement and having to change your trade name or even pay damages if you lose, conduct a trademark search before you settle on a trade name. The goal of a trademark search is to discover any potential conflicts between your trade name and someone else's. Ideally, you conduct the search before you actually use your trade name or register for an official trademark.

"If you don't have a registered trademark, your trade name becomes very difficult to protect," comments David Adler, the attorney quoted in the introduction to this chapter. "It's a good idea to do a basic search on the Internet. But keep in mind that just because you don't find a name on the Internet doesn't mean it doesn't exist. Follow that up with a trademark search. You don't want to spend all the money required to develop a brand name only to find that it isn't yours."

The following list details three ways that you can do a trademark search:

- ✔ **Search the old-fashioned, manual way by visiting one of the Patent and Trademark Depository Libraries.** They're listed online at www.uspto.gov/products/library/ptdl/index.jsp. Although time consuming, this approach doesn't cost anything.

- ✔ **Pay a professional search firm to do the research for you.** Look for professional search firms in the Yellow Pages under Trademark Consultants or Information Brokers. (You can also try SuperPages.com, www.superpages.com/yellowpages/C-Trademark+Consultants+&+Searches.) You can expect to pay $25–$50 per trademark searched. More complete searches that cover registered and unregistered marks that are similar to the one you want to use can cost several hundred dollars.

- ✔ **Conduct a search online.** You can use the Web to help you conduct a trademark search. The best place to go is TESS, the U.S. Patent and Trademark Office's federal trademark database. It's convenient and free. Just go to www.uspto.gov/ and click Search Marks.

Cyberspace goes beyond national boundaries. A trademark search in your own country may not be enough. Most industrialized countries, including the United States, have signed international treaties that enable trademark owners in one country to enforce their rights against infringement by individuals in another country. Conducting an international trademark search is difficult to do yourself, so you may want to pay someone to do the searching for you.

The consequences of failing to conduct a reasonably thorough trademark search can be severe. In part, the consequences depend on how widely you distribute the protected item — and on the Internet, you can distribute it worldwide. If you attempt to use a trademark that's been federally registered by someone else, you could go to court and be prevented from using the trademark again. You may even be liable for damages and attorney's fees. So it's best to be careful.

Protecting your trade name

The legal standard is that you get the rights to your trade name when you begin using it. You get the right to exclude others from using it when you register. But when you apply to register a trademark, you record the date of its first use. Effectively, then, the day you start using a name is when you actually obtain the rights to use it for trade.

In addition to a federal trademark law, each state has its own set of laws establishing when and how trademarks can be protected. You can obtain trademark rights in the states in which the mark is actually used, but attorney Adler says a federally registered trademark can trump such rights. It's important, then, to also file an application with the U.S. Patent and Trademark Office.

After researching your trade name against existing trademarks, you can file an application with the Patent and Trademark Office online by following these steps:

1. **Go to the Trademark Electronic Application System (TEAS) home page (**www.uspto.gov/teas/e-TEAS/index.html**, as shown in Figure 16-2).**

    This page includes links to forms and instructions on how to fill out your application online.

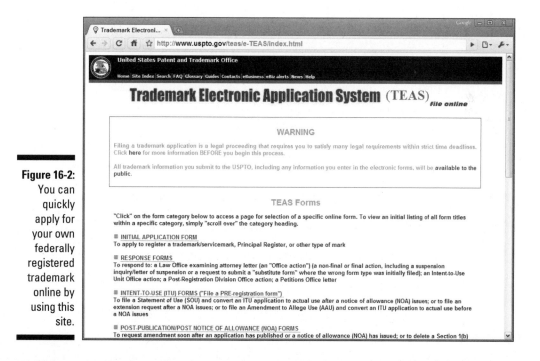

Figure 16-2: You can quickly apply for your own federally registered trademark online by using this site.

2. **Click the Initial Application Form link.**

   A page with a list of application forms appears.

3. **Click the Trademark/Servicemark Application, Principal Register link.**

   The Trademark/Service Mark Application Form Wizard page appears.

4. **Select the appropriate radio buttons and menu options (note that you're asked whether anyone else is already using the desired trademark) and then click Continue at the bottom of the page.**

   An application form page appears.

5. **Fill out the required forms in the application, including your credit card data (so that you can pay the $275 or $325 per application fee) and the electronic signature fields at the bottom of the application.**

6. **You can attach a GIF or JPEG image of a symbol or logo that you want to trademark by clicking the Attach an Image link.**

   A new page appears that lets you specify the image. Even though the image you want to trademark may be in color, the image you submit with your application must be in black-and-white form.

7. **Fill out the Applicant Information form and click Continue.**

   The Mark Information page appears.

8. **Enter the trademark in the box provided and click Continue.**

   The Goods and/or services Information page appears.

9. **Click Add Goods/Services button, enter any goods or services you provide that will be associated with your trademark, and click Continue.**

   A form entitled Correspondence Information appears.

10. **Review the correspondence information, make any corrections needed, and click Continue.**

    The Signature Information page appears.

11. **Type your signature, date, and position, and click the Validate button at the bottom of the form.**

    If you filled out all the fields correctly, a Validation screen appears. If not, you return to the original form page so that you can correct it.

12. **Print the special declaration to support the adoption of the electronic signature and retain it for your records; then click the Submit button.**

    You receive a confirmation screen if your transmission is successful. Later, you receive an e-mail acknowledgment of your submission.

Generally, each state has its own trademark laws, which apply only to trademarks that are used within a single state. Products that may be sold in more than one state (such as those sold on the Internet) can be protected under the federal Lanham Act, which provides for protection of registered trademarks. To comply with the Lanham Act, register your trademark, as I describe in the preceding steps.

Trademark registration can take 18–24 months. It's not uncommon to have an application returned. Often, an applicant receives a correspondence called an *Office Action* that either rejects part of the application or raises a question about it. If you receive such a letter, don't panic. You need to go to a lawyer who specializes in or is familiar with trademark law and who can help you respond to the correspondence. In the meantime, you can still operate your business with your trade name. You can also fill out and submit a form that communicates your intent to use a trademark, which enables you to use a trademark before it's registered.

Trademarks listed in the trademarks register last for 15 years and are renewable. You don't have to use the ™ or ® symbol when you publish your trademark, but doing so impresses upon people how seriously you take your business and its identity.

Making sure your domain name stays yours

The practice of choosing a domain name for an online business is related to the concept of trade names and trademarks. By now, with cybersquatters and other businesspeople snapping up domain names since 1994 or so, it's unlikely that your ideal name is available in the popular `.com` domain. Here are two common problems:

- ✔ Someone else has already taken the domain name related to the name of your existing business.

- ✔ The domain name you choose is close to one that already exists or to another company with a similar name. (Remember the Microsoft Windows/Lindows.com dispute that I mention early this chapter?)

If the domain name that you think is perfect for your online business is already taken, you have some options. You can contact the owner of the domain name and offer to buy it. Alternatively, you can choose a domain name with another suffix. If a dot-com name isn't available, try the old standby alternatives, `.org` (which, in theory at least, is for nonprofit organizations) and `.net` (which is for network providers).

You can also choose one of the newer *Top-Level Domains* (TLDs), a second set of domain name suffixes that were made available a few years ago, which include the following: `.biz` for businesses, `.info` for general use, and `.name` for personal names. You can find out more about the more recent TLDs at the InterNIC Web site, `www.internic.net/faqs/new-tlds.html`.

You can always get around the fact that your perfect domain name isn't available by changing the name slightly. Rather than `treesurgeon.com`, you might choose `tree-surgeon.com` or `treesurgery.com`. But be careful lest you violate someone else's trademark and get into a dispute with the holder of the other domain name. A court may order you to stop using the name and pay damages to the other domain name's owner.

On the other hand, if you've been doing business for a while and have a trademarked name, you may find that someone else owns the domain name. You can assert your rights and raise a dispute yourself. To resolve the dispute, you could go to a group such as the WIPO Arbitration and Mediation Center (`arbiter.wipo.int/center/index.html`) or ICANN, the Internet Corporation for Assigned Names and Numbers (`www.icann.org`). But first, find out more about what constitutes trademark infringement and how to enforce a trademark. Go to Nolo.com's Legal Encyclopedia (`www.nolo.com/lawcenter/ency/index.cfm`), scroll down and click the Patent, Copyright & Trademark link, click the Trademark Law link, and then click Enforcing Your Trademark Rights rather than Practicing Safe Copyright.

What's the difference between a trademark and a copyright? *Trademarks* are covered by trademark law and are distinctive words, symbols, slogans, or other things that serve to identify products or services in the marketplace. *Copyright,* on the other hand, refers to the creator's ownership of creative works, such as writing, art, software, video, or cinema (but not names, titles, or short phrases). Copyright also provides the owner with redress in case someone copies the work without the owner's permission. Copyright is a legal device that enables the creator of a work to control how the work is to be used.

Although copyright protects the way ideas, systems, and processes are embodied in the book, record, photo, or whatever, it doesn't protect the idea, system, or process itself. In other words, if Abraham Lincoln were writing the Gettysburg Address today, his exact words could be copyrighted, but the general ideas he expressed couldn't be.

Even if nobody ever called you a nerd, as a businessperson who produces goods and services of economic value, you may be the owner of intellectual property. *Intellectual property* refers to works of authorship as well as certain inventions. Because intellectual property can be owned, bought, and sold just as other types of property can, it's important that you know something about the copyright laws governing intellectual property. Having this information maximizes the value of your products and keeps you from throwing away potentially valuable assets or finding yourself at the wrong end of an expensive lawsuit.

Fair use . . . and how not to abuse it

Copyright law doesn't cover everything. One of the major limitations is the doctrine of *fair use,* which is described in Section 107 of the U.S. Copyright Act. The law states that fair use of a work is use that doesn't infringe copyright "for purposes such as criticism, comment, news reporting, teaching (including multiple copies for classroom use), scholarship, or research." You can't copy text from online magazines or newsletters and call it fair use because the text was originally news reporting.

Fair use has some big gray areas that can be traps for people who provide information on the Internet. Don't fall into one of these traps. Shooting off a quick e-mail asking someone for permission to reproduce his or her work isn't difficult. Chances are, that person will be flattered and let you make a copy as long as you give him or her credit on your site. Fair use depends entirely on the unique circumstances of each individual case, and this is an area in which, if you have any questions, you should consult with an attorney.

Copyright you can count on

These days, the controversy regarding copyright on the Web centers on the Digital Millennium Copyright Act (DMCA), which covers all forms of digital content on the Internet. Among other things, the DMCA calls for Internet radio stations to pay high royalty fees to record labels for music they play. The DMCA contains at least one provision that has implications for all online businesses: Internet service providers (ISPs) are expected to remove material from any customer Web sites that appears to constitute copyright infringement. So it pays to know something about copyright.

Everything you see on the Internet is copyrighted, whether or not a copyright notice actually appears. Copyright exists from the moment a work is fixed in a tangible medium, including a Web page. For example, plenty of art is available for the taking on the Web, but look before you grab. Unless an image on the Web is specified as being copyright free, you violate copyright law if you take it. HTML tags themselves aren't copyrighted, but the content of the HTML-formatted page is. General techniques for designing Web pages aren't copyrighted, but certain elements (such as logos) are.

 Keep in mind that it's okay to use a work for criticism, comment, news reporting, teaching, scholarship, or research. That comes under the fair use limitation. (See the nearby sidebar, "Fair use . . . and how not to abuse it," for more information.) However, I still contend that it's best to get permission or cite your source in these cases, just to be safe.

Making copyright work for you

A copyright — which protects original works of authorship — costs nothing, applies automatically, and lasts more than 50 years. When you affix a copyright notice to your newsletter or Web site, you make your readers think twice about unauthorized copying and put them on notice that you take copyright seriously. You can go a step farther and register your work with the U.S. Copyright Office.

Creating a good copyright notice

Even though any work you do is protected automatically by copyright, having some sort of notice expresses your copyright authority in a more official way. Copyright notices identify the author of a given work (such as writing or software) and then spell out the terms by which that author grants others the right (or the *license*) to copy that work to their computer and read it (or use it). The usual copyright notice is pretty simple and takes this form:

```
Copyright 2010 [Your Name] All rights reserved
```

You don't have to use the © symbol, but it does make your notice look more official. In order to create a copyright symbol that appears on a Web page, you have to enter a special series of characters in the HTML source code for your page. For example, Web browsers translate the characters `&copy;` as the copyright symbol, which is displayed as © in the Web browser window. Most Web page creation tools provide menu options for inserting special symbols such as this one.

Copyright notices can also be more informal, and a personal message can have extra impact. The graphic design company Echoed Sentiments Publishing (`www.espconcepts.com`) includes both the usual copyright notice plus a very detailed message about how others can use its design elements (`www.espconcepts.com/gratis_design_elements.html`).

Protection with digital watermarks

In traditional offset printing, a *watermark* is a faint image embedded in stationery or other paper. The watermark usually bears the name of the paper manufacturer, but it can also identify an organization for which the stationery was made.

Watermarking has its equivalent in the online world. Graphic artists sometimes use *digital watermarking* to protect images they create. This process involves adding copyright or other information about the image's owner to the digital image file. The information added may or may not be visible. (Some images have copyright information added; not visible in the body of the Web page but in the image file itself.) Other images, such as the one shown in Figure 16-3, have a watermark pasted right into the visible area, which makes it difficult for others to copy and reuse them.

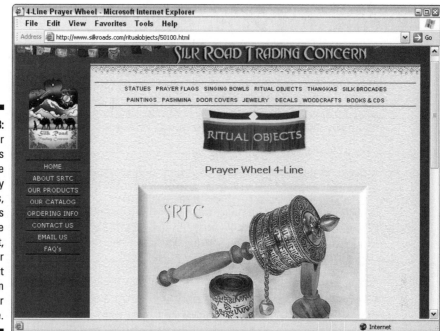

Digimarc (`www.digimarc.com`), which functions as a plug-in application with the popular graphics tools Adobe Photoshop (`www.adobe.com`) and Paint Shop Pro (`www.corel.com`), is one of the most widely used watermarking tools.

Doing the paperwork on your copyright

You have copyright over the materials you publish on the Web, but there's a difference between having a copyright and having a *registered copyright*. Registering your copyright is something I recommend for small businesses because it's inexpensive, it's easy to do, and it affords you an extra degree of protection. Having registered your copyright gives your case more weight in the event of a copyright dispute. It enables you to claim statutory damages of $150,000 if you can prove that an infringement occurred. You don't need to register, but doing so shows a court how serious you are about obtaining protection for your work.

Registering copyright is a breeze compared to the process of registering a trademark. To register your work, you can download a short application form from the U.S. Copyright Office Web site at `www.loc.gov/copyright/forms`. This form is in Adobe Acrobat PDF format, so you need Acrobat Reader to view it. (Adobe Acrobat Reader is a free application that you can download at `www.adobe.com`.) You can then send the form by snail mail, along with a check for $50 and a printed copy of the work you're protecting, to Library of Congress, Copyright Office, 101 Independence Ave., S.E., Washington, DC 20559-6000.

Licensing and Other Restrictions

Another set of legal concerns that you must be aware of when you start an online business involves any license fees or restrictions that are levied by local agencies. Some fees are specific to businesses that have incorporated, which brings up the question of whether you should consider incorporation for your own small business. (I discuss the legal concerns and pros and cons of incorporation in the upcoming section, "Deciding on a Legal Form for Your Business.")

Local regulations you should heed

Before you get too far along with your online business, make sure that you've met any local licensing requirements that apply. For example, in my county in the state of Illinois, I had to pay a $10 fee to register my sole proprietorship. In return, I received a nice certificate that made everything feel official.

Other localities may have more stringent requirements, however. Check with city, county, and state licensing and/or zoning offices. Trade associations for your profession often have a wealth of information about local regulations as well. Also, check with your local chamber of commerce. If you fail to apply for a permit or license, you may find yourself paying substantial fines.

The kinds of local regulations to which a small business may be susceptible include the following:

- ✔ **Zoning:** Your city or town government may have *zoning ordinances* that prevent you from conducting business in an area that is zoned for residential use, or it may charge you a fee to operate a business out of your home. This policy varies by community; even if your Web host resides in another state, your local government may still consider your home the location of your business. Check with your local zoning department.

- ✔ **Doing Business As:** If your business name is different from your own name, you may have to file a Doing Business As (DBA) certificate and publish a notice of the filing in the local newspaper. Check with your city or county clerk's office for more information.

- ✔ **Taxes:** Some states and cities levy taxes on small businesses, and some even levy property tax on business assets, such as office furniture and computer equipment.

Restrictions that may restrict your trade

If you're planning to sell your goods and services overseas, be aware of any trade restrictions that may apply to your business. In particular, you need to be careful if any of the following applies:

✔ You trade in foodstuffs or agricultural products.

✔ You sell software that uses some form of encryption.

✔ Your clients live in countries with which your home country has imposed trade restrictions.

Avoiding Conflicts with Your Customers

You have several ways in which you can get in legal trouble with the very people you rely on for your business success:

✔ **You fail to deliver something that a customer purchased.** The customer can seek a refund from the marketplace through which you sell (eBay, for instance). Organizations such as SquareTrade (`www.square trade.com`) have arbitration processes in place to resolve customer disputes. If you are found liable, you have to issue a refund or you'll be blocked from using the marketplace again.

✔ **You deliver late, or the merchandise isn't what you described.** The customer can complain to the marketplace and leave bad feedback for you, which damages your reputation.

✔ **You send out "spam," or unsolicited e-mail.** In severe cases, the government can go after you and arrest you. This has happened with spammers found guilty of sending out millions of unwanted e-mail messages (see `www.msnbc.msn.com/id/18955115` for an example).

✔ **You fail to safeguard your customers' personal information.** Hackers can rifle through unsecured computers and steal credit card numbers. Depending on the type of business you run, a number of government agencies can come after you for allowing identify theft to happen. See the list at `www.dfi.wa.gov/consumers/alerts/creditcard.htm`.

Offending your customers can have consequences for your business that go beyond legal trouble. People who aren't happy with you can leave comments on message boards that hurt your reputation. In some cases, disgruntled consumers sometimes go to the effort of creating Web pages such as I Hate Starbucks (`www.ihatestarbucks.com`) to voice their anger at a merchant.

Deciding on a Legal Form for Your Business

Picking a legal form for your online business enables you to describe it to city and county agencies as well as to the financial institutions you deal with.

A legal type of business is one that is recognized by taxing and licensing agencies. You have a number of options to choose from, and the choice can affect the amount of taxes you pay and your liability in case of loss. The following sections describe your alternatives.

If you're looking for more information, Eric Tyson and Jim Schell explore the legal and financial aspects of starting and operating a small business in *Small Business For Dummies,* 3rd Edition (Wiley).

Sole proprietorship

In a *sole proprietorship,* you're the only boss. You make all the decisions and get all the benefits. You take all the risk, too. This is the simplest and least expensive type of business because you can run it yourself. You don't need an accountant or lawyer to help you form the business, and you don't have to answer to partners or stockholders, either. To declare a sole proprietorship, you may have to file an application with your county clerk.

Partnership

In a *partnership,* you share the risk and profit with at least one other person. Ideally, your partners bring skills to the endeavor that complement your own contributions. One obvious advantage to a partnership is that you can discuss decisions and problems with your partners. All partners are held personally liable for losses. The rate of taxes that each partner pays is based on his or her percentage of income from the partnership.

If you decide to strike up a partnership with someone, drawing up a *Partnership Agreement* is a good idea. Although you aren't legally required to do so, such an agreement clearly spells out the duration of the partnership and the responsibilities of each person involved. Without such an agreement, the division of liabilities and assets is considered to be equal, regardless of how much more effort one person has put into the business than the other.

Advantages of a statutory business entity

A *statutory business entity* is a business whose form is created by statute, such as a corporation or a limited liability company. If sole proprietorships and partnerships are so simple to start and operate, why would you consider incorporating? After all, you almost certainly need a lawyer to help you incorporate. Plus, you have to comply with the regulations made by federal and state agencies that oversee corporations. Besides that, you may undergo a type of *double taxation:* If your corporation earns profits, those profits are taxed at the corporate rate, and any shareholders have to pay income tax at the personal rate.

Despite these downsides, you may consider incorporation for the following sorts of reasons:

- ✔ If you have employees, you can deduct any health and disability insurance premiums that you pay for them. (As a sole proprietor, you can deduct your own health insurance premiums.)
- ✔ You can raise capital by offering stock for sale.
- ✔ Transferring ownership from one shareholder to another is easier.
- ✔ The company's principals are shielded from liability in case of lawsuits.

If you offer services that may be susceptible to costly lawsuits, incorporation may be the way to go. You then have three options: a C corporation, a sub-chapter S corporation, or a limited liability corporation (LLC). The LLC is the best choice for many small businesses. But you have to designate officers, hold shareholders' meetings, and have an attorney keep the minutes of those meetings. Although it's more expensive to create, the LLC is simpler to operate and more suitable for lone entrepreneurs.

Subchapter S corporations

One benefit of forming a subchapter S corporation is liability protection. This form of incorporation enables startup businesses that encounter losses early on to offset those losses against their personal income. Subchapter S is intended for businesses with fewer than 75 shareholders. The income gained by an S corporation is subject only to personal tax, not to corporate tax.

You might designate that you're the president, your cousin Nick is the secretary, and other relatives serve as your shareholders and officers. Many corporations that are run by only one or two people have only one make-believe meeting a year; the attorney has a quick phone call to record what "happened" at the meeting and files the appropriate papers.

Sounds great, doesn't it? Before you start looking for a lawyer to get you started, consider the following:

- ✔ Incorporation typically costs several hundred dollars.
- ✔ Corporations must pay an annual tax.
- ✔ Attorneys' fees can be expensive.
- ✔ It can take weeks or months for your filing for S corporation status to be received and approved. (You need to meet your state's requirements for setting up a corporation and then file Form 2553 to elect S corporation status.)

All these facts can be daunting for a lone entrepreneur who's just starting out and has only a few customers. But my brother Mike, who owns an audio restoration business called lp2cdsolutions (www.lp2cdsolutions.com), did create an S corporation, so his liability is limited: In case of a lawsuit, assuming that no illegal conduct occurs on the part of the owner, the corporation is sued, not him personally. I recommend that you wait until you have enough income to hire an attorney and pay incorporation fees before you seriously consider incorporating, even as an S corporation.

C corporations

Many small businesses don't meet the strict requirements to become C corporations. In fact, everything about C corporations tends to be big — including profits, which are taxed at the corporate level as well as at the shareholder level — so I mention this legal designation only in passing because it's probably not for your small entrepreneurial business.

C corporations tend to be large and have lots of shareholders. To incorporate, all stockholders and shareholders must agree on the name of the company, the choice of the people who will manage it, and many other issues. The issue of double taxation in connection with C corporations means that you need to contact a tax professional if you have questions about this business entity or are thinking of creating one.

Limited liability corporations

The limited liability corporation (LLC) is a relatively new type of corporation that combines aspects of both S and C corporations. The forms required to create LLCs cost $500, and that doesn't include an attorney's fees. You also have to pay a yearly fee to maintain your LLC. And you or your attorney need to have yearly meetings at which you report on the state of the corporation. However, limited liability corporations have a number of attractive options that make them good candidates for small businesses. Benefits include the following:

- ✔ Members have limited liability for debts and obligations of the LLC.
- ✔ LLCs receive favorable tax treatment.
- ✔ The individual investors, or *members,* share income and losses.

An LLC can be a sole proprietorship, corporation, or a partnership. A similar entity, a Limited Liability Partnership (LLP), needs to be a partnership. The responsibilities of LLP members are spelled out in an *operating agreement,* an often-complex document that should be prepared by a knowledgeable attorney.

AllBusiness.com has published an article titled "How Much Does It Cost to Incorporate?" that details more costs related to incorporation. Check it out at www.allbusiness.com/legal/contracts-agreements-incorporation/2531-1.html.

Chapter 17

Online Business Accounting Tools

*W*hen times get hard economically, it's more important than ever to keep track of expenses, record financial information, and perform other fiscal functions. It's even more important to know some basic accounting procedures, especially those that relate to an online business.

Without having at least some minimal records of your day-to-day operations, you won't have any way — other than the proverbial "gut feeling" — of knowing whether your business is truly successful. Besides that, banks and taxing authorities don't put much stock in gut feelings. When the time comes to ask for a loan or pay taxes, you'll regret not having records close at hand. Even if you sell on eBay, you can't rely on the auction site to keep records for you; your records are kept on My eBay for only 60 days, and PayPal doesn't record payments by check or money order.

In this chapter, I introduce you to some simple, straightforward ways to handle your online business's financial information — and all businesspeople know that accurate record keeping is essential when revenues dwindle and expenses must be reduced. Read on to discover the most important accounting practices and to find out about software that can help you tackle the essential fiscal tasks you need to undertake to keep your new business viable.

ABCs: Accounting Basics for Commerce

The most important accounting practices for your online business are the following:

- ✔ **Deciding what type of business you are:** Will you be a sole proprietorship, partnership, or corporation? (See more about determining the legal status of your business in Chapter 16.)

- ✔ **Establishing good record keeping practices:** Record expenses and income in ways that can help you at tax time.

- ✔ **Obtaining financing when you need it:** Although getting started in an online business doesn't cost a lot, you may want to expand someday, and good accounting can help you do it.

There's nothing sexy about accounting (unless, of course, you're married to an accountant; in that case, you have a financial expert at hand and can skip this chapter!). Then again, unexpected cash shortages or other problems that can result from bad record keeping are no fun, either.

Good accounting is the key to order and good management for your business. How else can you know how you're doing? Yet, many new businesspeople are intimidated by the numbers game. Use the tool at hand — your computer — to help you overcome your fear: Start keeping those books!

Choosing an accounting method

Accepting that you have to keep track of your business's accounting is only half the battle; next, you need to decide how to do it. How and when you record your business transactions make a difference not only to your accountant but also to agencies such as the Internal Revenue Service (IRS). Even if you hire someone to keep the books for you, it's good to know what options are open to you.

You don't have to take my word for all this. Consult the Internal Revenue Service Publication 334, Tax Guide for Small Business (www.irs.gov/pub/irs-pdf/p334.pdf). Review section 2, Accounting Periods and Methods, which explains how to do everything right when tax time comes. Also check out the Accounting System section of the CCH Business Owner's Toolkit site (www.toolkit.cch.com/text/P06_1300.asp).

Cash-basis versus accrual-basis accounting

Don't be intimidated by these terms: They're simply two methods of totaling income and expenses. Exactly where and how you do the recording is up to you. You can take a piece of paper, divide it into two columns labeled *Income* and *Expenses,* and do it that way. (I describe some higher-tech tools later in this chapter.) Here are just two standard ways of deciding when to report them:

- **Cash-basis accounting:** You report income when you actually receive it and write off expenses when you pay them. This is the easy way to report income and expenses, and probably the way most new small businesses do it.

- **Accrual-basis accounting:** This method is more complicated than the cash-basis method, but if your online business maintains an inventory, you must use the accrual method. You report income when you actually receive the payment; you write down expenses *when services are rendered* (even though you may not have made the cash payment yet). For example, if a payment is due on December 1, but you send the check on December 8, you record the bill as being paid on December 1, when the payment was originally due.

Accrual-basis accounting creates a more accurate picture of a business's financial situation. If a business is experiencing cash-flow problems and is extending payments on some of its bills, cash-basis accounting provides an unduly rosy financial picture, whereas the accrual-basis method is more accurate.

Choosing an accounting period

The other choice you need to make when deciding how to keep your books is the accounting period you intend to use. Here again, you have two choices:

- **Calendar year:** The calendar year ends December 31. This is the period with which you're probably most familiar and the one most small or home-based businesses choose because it's the easiest to work with.

- **Fiscal year:** In this case, the business picks a date other than December 31 to function as the end of the fiscal year. Many large organizations pick a date that coincides with the end of their business cycle. Some pick March 31 as the end, others June 30, and still others September 30.

If you use the fiscal-year method of accounting, you must file your tax return three and a half months after the end of the fiscal year. If the fiscal year ends on June 30, for example, you must file by October 15.

Knowing what records to keep

When you run your own business, it pays to be meticulous about recording everything that pertains to your commercial activities. The more you understand what you have to record, the more accurate your records will be — and the more deductions you can take, too. Go to the office supply store and get a financial record book — a *journal* — which is set up with columns for income and expenses.

Tracking income

Receiving checks for your goods or services is the fun part of doing business, so income is probably the kind of data that you'll be happiest about recording.

You need to keep track of your company's income (or, as it is sometimes called, your *gross receipts*) carefully. Not all the income your business receives is taxable. What you receive as a result of sales (your *revenue*) is taxable, but loans that you receive aren't. Be sure to separate the two and pay tax only on the sales income. But keep good records: If you can't accurately report the source of income that you didn't pay taxes on, the IRS labels it *unreported income,* and you have to pay taxes and possibly fines and penalties on it.

Just how should you record your revenue? For each item, write down a brief, informal statement. This is a personal record that you may make on a slip of paper or even on the back of a canceled check. Be sure to include the following information:

- ✔ Amount received
- ✔ Type of payment (credit card, electronic cash, or check)
- ✔ Date of the transaction
- ✔ Name, model number, and description of the item purchased
- ✔ Name of client or customer
- ✔ Goods or services you provided in exchange for the payment

Collect all your check stubs and revenue statements in a folder labeled *Income* so that you can find them easily at tax time.

Assessing your assets

Assets are resources that your business owns, such as your office and computer equipment. *Equity* is your remaining assets after you pay your creditors.

Any equipment you have that contributes to your business activities constitutes your assets. Equipment that has a life span of more than a year is expected to help you generate income over its useful life; therefore, you must spread out (or, in other words, *expense*) the original cost of the equipment over its life span. Expensing the cost of an asset over the period of its useful life is *depreciation.* To depreciate an item, estimate how many years you're going to use it and then divide the original cost by the number of years. The result is the amount that you report in any given year. For example, if you purchase a computer that costs $3,000 and you expect to use it in your business for five years, you expense $600 of the cost each year.

Keep records of your assets that include the following information:

✔ Name, model number, and description

✔ Purchase date

✔ Purchase price, including fees

✔ Date the item went into service

✔ Amount of time the item is put to personal (as opposed to business) use

File these records in a safe location along with your other tax-related information.

Recording payments

Even a lone entrepreneur doesn't work in a vacuum. An online business owner needs to pay a Web host, an ISP, and possibly Web page designers as well as other consultants. If you take on partners or employees, things get more complicated. But in general, you need to record all payments such as these in detail as well.

Your accountant is likely to bring up the question of how you pay the people who work for you. You have two options: You can treat them either as full- or part-time employees or as independent contractors. The IRS uses a stringent series of guidelines to determine who is a contractor and who is a full-time employee. Refer to the IRS Publication 15A (`www.irs.gov/pub/irs-pdf/p15a.pdf`), which discusses the employee/independent contractor subject in detail.

Hiring independent contractors rather than salaried workers is far simpler for you: You don't have to pay benefits to independent contractors, and you don't have to withhold federal and state taxes. Just be sure to get invoices from any independent contractor who works for you. If you have full-time employees whom you pay an hourly wage, things get more complicated, and you had best consult an accountant to help you set up the salary payments.

Listing expenses

When you break down business expenses on Schedule C (Profit or Loss from Business) of your federal tax return, you need to keep track of two kinds of expenses:

✔ The first type of expenses (simply dubbed Expenses in Part II of Schedule C) includes travel, business meals, advertisements, postage, and other costs that you incur in order to *produce revenue.*

✔ The second kind of expenses (grouped under Other Expenses in Part V of Schedule C) includes instances when you're just exchanging one asset (cash) for another (a printer or modem, for example).

The difference between Expenses and Other Expenses lies in how close the relationship is between the expense and revenue produced. In the case of the Part II Expenses, your expenditure is directly related — you wouldn't take out an advertisement or take a business trip if you didn't expect it to produce revenue. In the second case, the act of spending money doesn't directly result in more revenue for you. You would purchase a modem, for instance, to help you communicate and get information online, not just to boost your bottom line. You do *hope,* though, that the equipment being purchased does *eventually* help you produce revenue.

Get a big folder and use it to hold any receipts, contracts, canceled checks, credit card statements, or invoices that represent expenses. It's also a great idea to maintain a record of expenses that includes the following information:

- ✔ Date the expense occurred
- ✔ Name of the person or company that received payment from you
- ✔ Type of expense incurred (equipment, utilities, supplies, and so on)

Recalling exactly what some receipts were for is often difficult a year or even just a month after the fact. Be sure to jot down a quick note on all canceled checks and copies of receipts to remind you what the expense involved.

Understanding the Ps and Qs of P&Ls

You're likely to hear the term *profit and loss statement* (also called a P&L) thrown around when discussing your online business with financial people. A P&L is a report that measures the operation of a business over a given period of time, such as a week, a month, or a year. The person who prepares the P&L (either you or your accountant) adds up your business revenues and subtracts the operating expenses. What's left are either the profits or the losses.

Most of the accounting programs listed later in this chapter include some way of presenting profit and loss statements and enable you to customize the statements to fit your needs.

Accounting Software for Your Business

After rummaging through piles of receipts and records stuffed into a big manila envelope, my tax preparer gently but firmly urged me to start using some accounting software so that the records could be retrieved more easily next time. Ever since, I've been happy that I took his advice. I urge you to do the same. These days, you have lots of options for software that can help you record and organize your financial information. The programs break into three general categories: simple, small-scale programs such as Owl

Simple Business Accounting; bigger, full-featured programs such as Quicken, QuickBooks, and MYOB; and online versions of the latter group. The online versions are ones that you use on the Web; you don't install any software on your computer that you have to update periodically. On the other hand, you do have to store your financial information on another Web site (not yours) when you use an online program. But all these options have one thing in common: They give you a user-friendly way to store your information and perform calculations on it. I present some examples in the rest of this section.

Full-featured software: OWL Simple Business Accounting

The well-known, commercial accounting packages, such as Quicken, QuickBooks, and MYOB, let you prepare statements and reports and even tie into a tax preparation system. Stick with these programs if you like setting up systems, such as databases, on your computer. Otherwise, go for a simpler method and hire an accountant to help you.

Whatever program you choose, make sure that you can keep accurate books and set up privacy as well as backup schemes that prevent your kids from zapping your business records.

If your business is a relatively simple sole proprietorship, you can record expenses and income by hand and add them up at tax time. Then carry them through to Schedule C or IRS Form 1040. Alternatively, you can record your entries and turn them over to a tax advisor who prepares a profit and loss statement and tells you the balance due on your tax payment.

If you're looking to save a few dollars and want an extra-simple accounting program that you can set up right now, you'll find a good option in Owl Simple Business Accounting 2 (www.owlsoftware.com/sba.htm), available for Windows XP, Vista, and 7. Mac users can try FinanceToGo by Bert Torfs (www.rocketdownload.com/query.php?q=double-entry).

Keeping It Simple: QuickBooks Simple Start

One of the big commercial accounting software programs, Intuit, has also released a free version of its popular QuickBooks software. The package is called Intuit QuickBooks Simple Start Free Edition 2010, and you can download it at http://quickbooks.intuit.com/product/accounting-software/free-accounting-software.jsp. It's a hefty download, weighing in at more than 400MB. The program works with Windows XP, Vista, or 7.

The following steps illustrate how easy it is to start keeping books with Simple Start. These instructions assume that you downloaded and installed the software from the Intuit Web site.

1. **Choose Start⇨All Programs⇨QuickBooks⇨QuickBooks Simple Start 2010 Free Edition.**

    The main QuickBooks Simple Start window opens and the Welcome to QuickBooks Simple Start 2010 Free Edition dialog box appears, as shown in Figure 17-1.

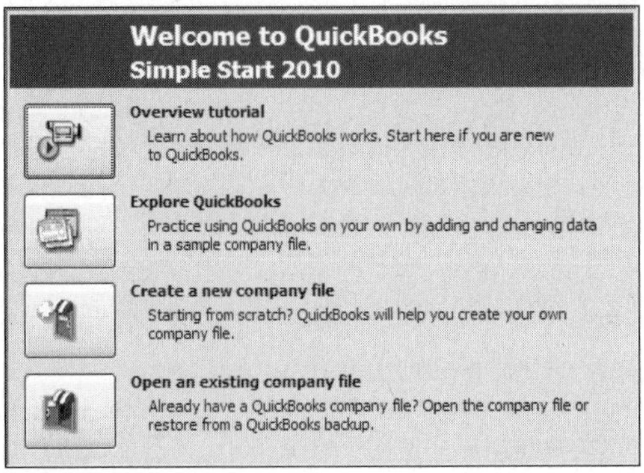

Figure 17-1:
QuickBooks
Simple Start
gets you
started with
this step-by-
step wizard.

**Welcome to QuickBooks
Simple Start 2010**

Overview tutorial
Learn about how QuickBooks works. Start here if you are new to QuickBooks.

Explore QuickBooks
Practice using QuickBooks on your own by adding and changing data in a sample company file.

Create a new company file
Starting from scratch? QuickBooks will help you create your own company file.

Open an existing company file
Already have a QuickBooks company file? Open the company file or restore from a QuickBooks backup.

TIP

Simple Start comes with extensive Help files to get you accustomed to its features. Click Overview Tutorial or Explore QuickBooks to get a jump-start on using the program.

2. **Click Create a New Company File.**

    A screen entitled Welcome to the Setup Interview appears.

3. **Click Next and then fill out the forms shown in subsequent screens to enter information about your company.**

    QuickBooks creates a "company file" that contains the information you entered. A window opens with the name of your company in the title bar (see Figure 17-2).

4. **Click any of the options in the left column to enter income, expenses, or information about your business. For instance, to enter a cash expenditure, click the Cash link next to Record Expenses.**

    The The Other Current Asset register window appears, as shown in Figure 17-3.

5. **Enter the name of the vendor.**

    Another dialog box appears that prompts you to add the vendor to your Contact List if you haven't done so already. (QuickBooks prompts you to complete steps as needed if you have forgotten to do them.)

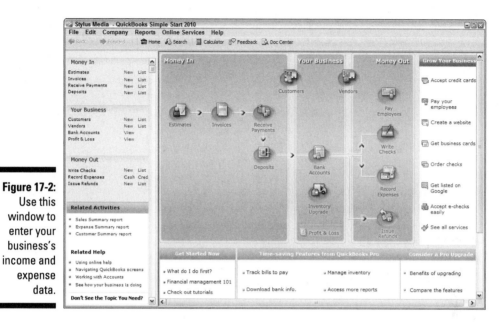

Figure 17-2:
Use this window to enter your business's income and expense data.

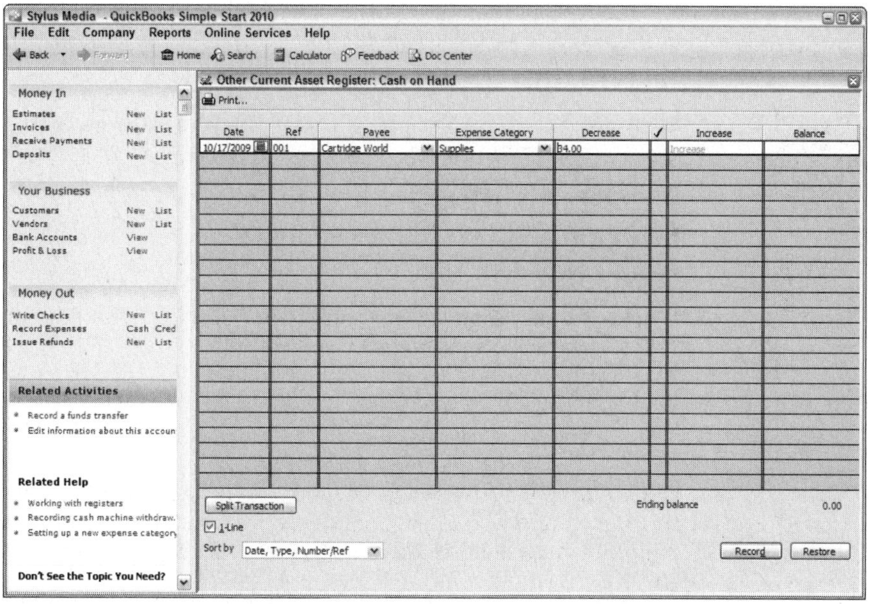

Figure 17-3:
Use this dialog box to record expenses and vendors and to track cash on hand.

6. **When you're done, click Record.**

   The expense is recorded.

7. **To record a new customer, click New next to Customer.**

   The New Customer dialog box appears.

8. **Enter the contact information for the customer, click Add New, and click OK.**

   The customer's information is added to your business file. You can now choose that customer when performing subsequent tasks.

9. **Click New next to Invoice.**

   The Create Invoices dialog box appears.

10. **Click the down arrow next to Customer and choose the name of the customer you just added.**

    The customer's name appears in the Customer box at the top of the Create Invoices dialog box.

11. **Click the down arrow next to Item and enter the type of item for which you want to bill your customer.**

    If you haven't yet defined the item, a dialog box appears, prompting you to add a description of the work and the amount.

12. **Fill out the item information as required.**

    After you define the item and choose the item from the drop-down list, the description and amount are automatically added to the invoice.

13. **Click Save & Close.**

    A dialog box appears, prompting you to set up a payment-processing method for the invoice.

14. **If you want to set up a payment-processing method, click Yes; if you don't (for instance, if you plan to receive a check and deposit it yourself), click No.**

    You return to the main program window.

15. **When you're all finished, choose File⇨Exit to exit the program until your next accounting session.**

After entering some data, you can click the Reports menu option and choose from among several reports that you can then generate and print. As shown in Figure 17-4, you can track customer activity, all expenses, all transactions, or product tax or accountant reports. When running the reports, be sure to select a reporting period within the current calendar year.

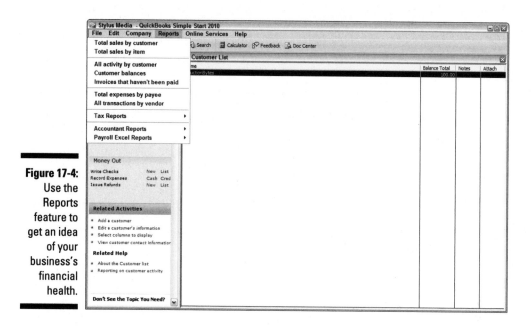

Figure 17-4:
Use the
Reports
feature to
get an idea
of your
business's
financial
health.

The Taxman Cometh: Concerns for Small Business

After you make it through the startup phase of your business, it's time to be concerned with taxes. Here, too, a little preparation upfront can save you lots of headaches down the road. But as a hardworking entrepreneur, time is your biggest obstacle.

In an American Express survey, 26 percent reported that they wait until the last minute to start preparing their taxes, and 13.9 percent said that they usually ask for an extension. Yet advance planning is truly important for taxes. In fact, Internal Revenue Code Section 6001 mandates that businesses must keep records appropriate to their trade or business. The IRS has the right to view these records if it wants to audit your business's (or your personal) tax return. If your records don't satisfy the IRS, the penalties can be serious.

Should you charge sales tax?

This is one of the most frequently asked questions I receive from readers: Should I charge sales tax for what I sell online? The short answer is that it depends on whether your state collects sales tax at all. No single regulation applies to all states equally.

If your state doesn't collect sales tax (at this writing, five states — Montana, Alaska, Delaware, New Hampshire, and Oregon — do not), you don't need to, either. However, if your state requires it, yes, you need to collect sales tax — but only from customers who live in the same state where your company has a "physical presence." A state's tax laws apply only within its own borders. If you're located in Ohio, for instance, your business is subject to Ohio sales tax regulations, but only for transactions that are completed in Ohio. If you sell to someone in, say, California, you don't need to collect sales tax from that California resident. But because tax laws change frequently, the safest thing I can tell you is to check with your own state's department of revenue to make sure.

The nature of what constitutes a "physical presence" varies. Some states define it as an office or warehouse. If you take orders only by phone or online, you don't have to collect sales tax. But again, check with your state. Also, most states require that their merchants charge sales tax on shipping and handling charges as well as the purchase price.

The U.S. president signed the Internet Tax Freedom Act Amendment Act of 2007 into law on November 1, 2007. It extends the prohibitions against new taxes on Internet access and e-commerce until November 1, 2014. But as I write this, several states have proposed state tax on Internet sales, so keep an eye on the news for new developments.

The Internet Tax Freedom Act does *not* mean that Internet sales are free from sales tax. It means only that states can't impose any new sales tax requirements on Internet merchants over and above what other merchants already have to collect in sales tax. To deal with this supposed loophole, most states charge a "use" tax in addition to a sales tax: If a resident of the state makes a purchase from another state, the transaction is still subject to use tax. But one state can't compel a merchant located in another state to collect its use tax — only merchants located within the state's own borders must do so.

Sales tax varies from state to state, city to city, and county to county. Some states tax only sales of tangible personal property, whereas others tax services as well. Not only that, but some counties and municipalities levy local taxes on sales. In my own state, Illinois, I have to report my sales tax income from my eBay sales and pay it on a monthly basis, even if it amounts to only a few dollars a month. It's important to make sure that any buyers in your own state are charged the correct sales tax and that you keep records of how much you charged. Check with your local comptroller or department of revenue to find out for sure what your requirements are.

Federal and state taxes

Although operating a business does complicate your tax return, it's something you can handle if your business is a simple one-person operation, if you're willing to expend the time, and finally, if you keep the proper business records.

If you have a sole proprietorship, you need to file IRS form Schedule C along with your regular form 1040 tax return. If your sole proprietorship has net income, you're also required to file Schedule SE to determine any Social Security and FICA taxes that are due.

State taxes vary depending on where you live. You most likely need to file sales tax and income tax. If you have employees, you also need to pay employee withholding tax. Contact a local accountant in order to find out what you have to file, or contact the state tax department yourself. Most state tax offices provide guidebooks to help you understand state tax requirements.

When you start making money for yourself independently, rather than depending on a regular paycheck from an employer, you have to start doing something you've probably never done before: You have to start estimating the tax you'll have to pay based on the income from your own business. You're then required to pay this tax on a quarterly basis, both to the IRS and to your state taxing agency. Estimating and paying quarterly taxes is an important part of meeting your tax obligations as a self-employed person.

A page full of links to state tax agencies is available at `www.tannedfeet.com/state_tax_agencies.htm`.

Deducing your business deductions

One of the benefits of starting a new business, even if the business isn't profitable in the beginning, is the opportunity to take business deductions and reduce your tax payments. Always keep receipts from any purchases or expenses associated with your business activities. Make sure that you're taking all the deductions for which you're eligible. I mention some of these deductions in the following sections.

Your home office

If you work at home (and I'm assuming that as an entrepreneur, you probably do), set aside some space for a home office. This isn't just a territorial thing. It can result in some nifty business deductions, too.

Taking a home office deduction used to be difficult because a 1993 Supreme Court decision stated that unless you met with clients, customers, or patients on a regular basis in your home office, you couldn't claim the home-office deduction. However, the 1997 tax law eliminates the client requirement and requires only that the office be used "regularly and exclusively" for business.

What you deduct depends on the amount of space in your home that's used for your business. If your office consumes 96 square feet of a house with 960 square feet of living/working space, you can deduct 10 percent of your utilities, for example. However, if you have a separate phone line or cellphone that's solely for business use, you can deduct 100 percent of that expense.

Your computer equipment

Computer equipment is probably the biggest expense related to your online business. But taking tax deductions can help offset the cost substantially. The key is showing the IRS (by reporting your income from your online business on your tax return) that you used your PC and related items, such as modems or printers, for business purposes. You track what you spend on computer equipment in the Other Expenses section, which is Part V of Schedule C in your federal tax return.

In case you're ever audited, be sure to keep some sort of record detailing all the ways in which you put your computer equipment to use for business purposes.

Other common business deductions

Many of the business-related expenses that you can deduct are listed on IRS form Schedule C. The following is a brief list of some of the deductions you can look for:

- ✔ Advertising fees
- ✔ Internet access charges
- ✔ Computer supplies
- ✔ Shipping and delivery
- ✔ Office supplies
- ✔ Utility fees that pertain to your home office

Part VI
The Part of Tens

The 5th Wave   By Rich Tennant

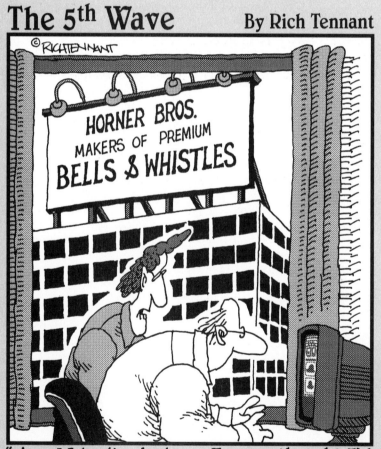

"As a Web site designer, I never thought I'd say this, but I don't think your site has enough bells and whistles."

In this part . . .

If you're like me, you have one drawer in the kitchen filled with utensils and other assorted objects that don't belong anywhere else. Strangely enough, that's the place where I can almost always find something I can use to perform the task at hand.

Part VI of this book is the Part of Tens because it's a collection of miscellaneous items arranged in sets of ten. Filled with tips, cautions, suggestions, and examples of new ways to make money online, this part presents many kinds of information that can help you plan and create your own business presence on the Internet. Both chapters will, I hope, inspire you to achieve your own business success as you read about ten must-have features for your Web site, as well as ten different e-commerce marketplaces that you can use to make money.

Chapter 18

Ten Must-Have Features
for Your Web Site

In This Chapter

▶ Finding a domain name that will help you get noticed

▶ Setting up payment systems for your online business

▶ Selling products that customers want to buy

▶ Keeping your site and product list up-to-date.

*Y*ou can put any number of snazzy features on your Web site. If you ever meet with a Web design firm, you're sure to hear about all the cool scripts, animations, and other interactive add-ons that can go on your pages. Some pizzazz isn't a bad thing, especially if you're just starting out and need to set yourself apart from the competition. Interactive features and a well-designed Web site give you an air of competence and experience, even if your online business is brand new.

But the Web site features that count toward your bottom line are the ones that attract and retain customers and induce them to return to you regularly. Along with the bells and whistles, your business home on the Web needs the essentials that shoppers expect. Make sure that your site meets the minimum daily requirements: It's easy to find and loaded with content; it contains background information about you; and it includes features that make shopping easy and secure. This Part of Tens chapter describes ten specific features that help you achieve these objectives.

Secure Some Easy-to-Remember URLs

Names are critical to the success of any business. A name becomes identified with a business, and people associate the name with its products and its level of customer service. When a small company developed a software product called Lindows, giant Microsoft sued and eventually paid $20 million to stop the infringement on its well-known, trademarked product Windows.

Write down five or six names that are short and easy to remember and that would represent your business if included in an URL. Do a domain name search and try to find the one you want. (A good place to search is Whois.net at `www.whois.net`.) Try to keep your site's potential name as short and as free of elements such as hyphens as possible. A single four- to ten-character name in between the `www.` and the `.com` sections of the URL is easy to remember.

Domain names are cheap, especially if you can lock them up for several years at a time. A name in the `.com` domain is still the most desirable type of URL suffix because it's the one that most consumers expect to see when they're trying to find your Web site's URL. Even if you can get a `.com` name, purchase domain names in other, popular domains, such as `.net` and `.org`. Also consider country-specific or state-specific domains such as `co.uk` or `il.us`. That way, you protect your URL from being poached by competitors who are trying to copy you. If your URL is easily misspelled, consider purchasing a domain name that represents a common misspelling. That way, if shoppers make a typing error, they're still directed to your site.

Provide a Convenient Payment Method

Shoppers go online for many reasons, but those reasons don't include a desire for things to be complex and time consuming. No matter how technically complex it may be to get one's computer on the Internet, shoppers still want things to be quick and seamless. At the top of the list of seamless processes is the ability to pay for merchandise purchased online.

You don't have to get a merchant account from a bank to process your own credit card payments. You don't need to get point-of-sale hardware, either. Since I've been selling on eBay, I've become quite used to the convenience and reliability of eBay's electronic payment service PayPal. You don't have to offer items for sale on eBay to use PayPal; if you have an account with PayPal, you can add PayPal "Buy" buttons to your Web pages and send your customers to PayPal to send you the money by using their credit cards. Chances are, many of your prospective customers already have accounts with PayPal if they use eBay. I did, so my purchase process was completed in less than a minute. Set up yourself as a seller with PayPal and Google Payments and then accept money orders, personal checks, and cashier's checks. If you can take the additional step of getting a shopping cart and a credit card payment system, so much the better.

Promote Security, Privacy, and Trust

Even shoppers who have been making purchases online for years may at times still feel uncertainty when they type their credit card number and click a button labeled Pay Now, Purchase, or Submit to a commercial Web site. I'm speaking from personal experience.

What promotes trust? Information and communication. Shoppers online love getting information that goes beyond what they can find in a printed catalog. Be sure to include one or more of the following details that can make shoppers feel good about pressing your Buy Now button:

- An endorsement from an organization that is supposed to promote good business practices, such as TRUSTe (`www.truste.org`)

- A privacy statement that explains how you handle customers' personal information

- Detailed product descriptions that show you're knowledgeable about a product

Another thing that promotes trust is information about who you are and why you love what you do, as described in the section "Help Your Customers Get to Know You," later in this chapter.

Choose Goods and Services That Buyers Want

How do you find out what buyers want? Try the following:

- Come right out and ask them. On your Web site, invite requests for merchandise of one sort or another.

- After a purchase, do some *upselling:* Suggest some other items your customers might be interested in.

- Visit message boards, newsgroups, and Web sites related to the item you want to sell.

- Make a weekly (remember that Saturdays and Sundays are the best days for auctions to end) search of eBay's completed auctions to see what has sold, and which types of items have fetched the highest prices.

Have a Regular Influx of New Products

With a printed catalog, changes to sales items can be major. The biggest problem is the need to physically reprint the catalog when inventory changes. One of the biggest advantages associated with having an online sales catalog is the ability to alter your product line in a matter of minutes, without having to send artwork to a printer. You can easily post new sales items online each day, as soon as you get new sales figures.

One reason to keep changing your products on a regular basis is that your larger competitors are doing so. Lands' End, which has a well-designed and popular online sales catalog (www.landsend.com), puts out new products on a regular basis and announces them in an e-mail newsletter to which loyal customers can subscribe.

Optimize Your Site for Search Engines

There's a reason that search engine optimization (SEO) is the subject of its own chapter (Chapter 11) and that so many Web site owners are immediately concerned with it. SEO is a low-cost and effective way to help your site be found by exactly the people who are looking for the content you're offering.

To do SEO, you need to leave a "trail of crumbs" for your prospective customers. Any Web site must have them. They include

- **Home page titles that will get indexed:** The more keywords you add, the better your chances that your site turns up in Google and other search results.

- **Headings that contain keywords:** Along with indexing titles, it's believed that search engines such as Google also index the main headings on Web pages.

- **Text that contains specific keywords about your site:** The first paragraph or two of text is the most important because this is most likely indexed.

In addition, you need to register your site to make sure it appears in the directories to the Web that the search engines provide. (See Chapters 11 and 14 for more information about search engines and how they work.)

Be Current with Upkeep and Improvements

Do you have a favorite blog, comic strip, or newspaper columnist that you like to visit each day? I certainly do. With luck, your customers will want to visit your site, eBay store, or other sales venue every day as well. Of course, that won't be the case unless you come up with new material on a regular basis.

I know what you're thinking: You have so many things to do that you can't possibly revisit your Web site every day and change headings or put new sales online. You have to get the kids off to school, pack up some merchandise, run to the post office, clean up the house — the list goes on and on. You can't be two places at the same time. Two people can be, though. Consider hiring a student or friend to run your site and suggest new content for you. In a five-minute phone conversation, you can tell your assistant what to do that day, and you can go on to the rest of your many responsibilities.

Personally Interact with Your Customers

Paradoxically, the personal touch counts for a lot in Internet communication. Maybe it's the lack of body language and visual clues that make shoppers and other Web surfers so hungry for attention. In any case, impersonal, mass e-mail marketing messages (in other words, *spam*) are reviled, but quick responses conveying courteous thank-yous are eagerly welcomed.

You can't send too many personal e-mail messages to your customers, even when they're making only an inquiry and not a purchase. Not long ago, I asked some questions about a heater I was thinking of buying online. I filled out the form on the company's Web site and submitted my questions. The representative of the company got right back to me.

"First of all, let me thank you for your interest in our product," the letter began. She proceeded to answer my questions and then finished with another thank-you and "If you have any further questions, please don't hesitate to ask." I didn't hesitate: I asked some more, she answered, and again said, "Don't hesitate to ask" at the end. Even if this is all "form letter" material, it makes a difference. I eventually purchased the item.

Don't be afraid to pour on the extra courtesy and provide complete answers to every question: Just tell yourself that each answer is worth an extra dollar or two in sales. It probably is.

Help Your Customers Get to Know You

Your Web site should find a way to make a personal connection with your visitors. Many site owners achieve this goal by creating a blog. Blogs, though, are more appropriate for personal Web sites. E-commerce sites can still achieve a personal touch by including an About Me or About Us page, a newsletter, or a mission statement or a history of the company.

For example, the Shiana.com Web site (www.shiana.com) contains all these links, even though its main purpose is to sell jewelry. The site's content is meant to appeal to people to help the tribe that makes the jewelry. Even if you don't have a charitable mission to tell about, offering some essential background about you, why you started your business, and what your goals are builds trust in your shoppers. Be sure to tout your experience, your background, your family, or your hobbies — anything to reassure online shoppers that you're a reputable person who is looking out for their interests.

Provide Lots of Navigation Options

Links, menus, and other navigation options aren't quite as essential as they used to be because you can establish a regular income on eBay without having any Web site at all. But even if you become a well-established eBay seller, you'll likely want a Web site at some point or another. How do you make your site well organized? Make sure that your site incorporates these essential features:

- **Navigation buttons:** Consumers who are in a hurry (in other words, almost all consumers) expect to see a row of navigation buttons along the top or one of the sides of your home page. Don't make them hunt; put them in several places on your home page — providing additional options makes them feel like they're in control.

- **A site map:** A page that leads visitors to all areas of your site can prevent them from going elsewhere if they get lost.

- **Links that actually work:** Clicking a link that's supposed to lead to a photo or a bit of information that you really want but instead produces a generic Page Not Found error message is very frustrating for site visitors.

- **Links that indicate where a customer is on the site:** Such links are helpful because, like a trail of breadcrumbs, they show how the customer got to a particular page. Here's an example:

```
Clothing > Men's > Sportswear > Shoes > Running
```

When your site grows to contain dozens of pages and several main categories, links that look like this can help people move up to a main category and find more subcategories.

Be the first to visit your Web site and test it to make sure that the forms, e-mail addresses, and other features function correctly. If someone sends you an e-mail message only to have it bounce back, you'll probably lose that customer, who might well conclude that you aren't monitoring your Web site or your business. At the very least, open your site in Microsoft Internet Explorer, Netscape Navigator, and Firefox to make sure that your text and images load correctly.

Chapter 19

Ten E-Commerce Marketplaces Worth Exploring

- ▶ Options for auctioning your creative work
- ▶ Marketplaces that let you buy and sell affordably
- ▶ Places where you can buy or sell for free

*N*ot so long ago, starting an online business primarily meant creating a Web site or selling on a marketplace such as eBay. The landscape has shifted slightly as I update the sixth edition of this book. Yes, Web sites are still important. But the notion of what constitutes a "Web site" has expanded to include a blog, a storefront on eBay, or a site hosted by any of a number of intriguing niche marketplaces.

A single Web site isn't enough. The newest entrepreneurs are focusing on branding themselves and gaining as much exposure as possible through cost-effective marketing methods. One of those is search engine optimization (SEO), the practice of optimizing a Web presence to improve your placement in search results.

By signing up with a niche marketplace, you can set up a storefront, communicate with customers, accept payments, and socialize with other sellers who deal in the same kinds of merchandise you do. You might have to pay a modest hosting fee — or you might not because many of the sites are totally free to their members. This chapter collects ten small, innovative, full-featured marketplaces that are giving the big e-commerce hosts a run for their money and presenting themselves as attractive alternatives. Consider opening storefronts in one or more venues to increase your visibility and, with luck, put some extra cash in your pocket.

The marketplaces profiled here are only ten of many. You can find more listed on AuctionBytes beneath the article about eBay alternatives at `www.auctionbytes.com/cab/cab/abu/y209/m01/abu0230/s03`. An article on SmartMoney entitled "eBay's Allure Is Going, Going, Gone" describes how eBay began losing its popularity as many sellers started exploring alternatives (`www.smartmoney.com/Spending/Rip-offs/EBay-Allure-Going-Going-Gone`).

Making Your Own Product Line: Etsy.com

If the merchandise you sell includes items you have designed or crafted yourself, consider selling them on Etsy.com. Rob Kalin, who was then a 27-year-old painter, carpenter, and photographer, started Etsy in 2005. It has since grown into a hugely successful marketplace for crafts and artwork of all kinds. In June 2008, the site announced its millionth registered user. In September 2009, Etsy reported that $16 million worth of items were sold. The site now has more than 2.6 million members and 250,000 sellers.

Etsy has been featured on Martha Stewart's TV show, and AuctionBytes editor Ina Steiner found that on a recent visit to the company's Brooklyn, New York, headquarters, the offices are decorated with many of the crafts sold on the site. (You can read her report at www.auctionbytes.com/cab/abu/y209/m04/abu0236/s02.) Selling on Etsy makes for a personal experience that brings to mind the "old days" of the Web when buyers and sellers got to know one another personally and sent out personal notes and freebies with items they sold.

Etsy, like other marketplaces, requires you to sign up for membership and gives sellers a user-friendly way to create an online storefront and list items for sale. As part of your storefront, you can describe what you make and talk about artists or craftspeople who have influenced you. You pay nothing at all for a storefront, but you are charged 20 cents per item and 3.5 percent of the final sales price of each item you sell (this does not include shipping). The 3.5 percent is much lower than eBay's final value fees, which start at 9 percent for auction items that sell for up to $50.

The Internet offers plenty of alternatives to Etsy in the field of selling arts, crafts, jewelry, and other handmade products. Etsy is just the best-known marketplace of its type. Also consider Zazzle (www.zazzle.com) and ArtFire (www.artfire.com), which I describe later in this chapter.

OnlineAuction.com

Like many online marketplaces, OnlineAuction.com (www.onlineauction.com) was founded when an antiques and collectibles dealer who started out selling on eBay became disenchanted with the site. Founder Chris Fain sold both on eBay and in brick-and-mortar businesses near Grants Pass, Oregon. When I interviewed Fain in 2008, the site had 50,000 users.

One big difference between OnlineAuction.com and other sites, including eBay, is the fee structure. At OnlineAuction.com, sellers don't pay listing fees or final value fees. They can sell as many items as they want, and in place of per-item fees, they pay annual or monthly memberships. New sellers can open a basic storefront called My OLA House for $8 per month. (The service is free to founding members.) You can also list and sell as many items as you want for $8 per month.

eCrater

Dimitar Slavov got the idea for eCrater when he ordered a book from Amazon.com. He found the Amazon site difficult to navigate. Because he is a programmer, he decided to create his own online marketplace, one that would be marked by simplicity. eCrater (`www.ecrater.com`) charges no fees for buying or selling items. You are charged only if you want to have your store featured on the site and given premium placement.

Also, sellers are allowed to host their own Web sites on the site. Through a process called "URL masking," you use your own Web address, not eCrater's, which makes it seem as though you operate a completely independent site rather than one that is part of eCrater. Sellers also get access to an administrative tool that allows them to manage their online stores. All products are advertised on Google, and Google Checkout, as well as PayPal, is accepted as a form of online payment.

See Chapter 7 for more on Google Checkout, PayPal, and other payment options.

iOffer

If you are looking for a truly different buying and selling experience, check out iOffer (`www.ioffer.com`). This site turns two basic principles of online auctions on their heads. First, there's the idea that the seller either sets a starting price, a reserve price, or a fixed price for the sale. Instead, iOffer puts buyers in charge by giving them a system through which they make an offer and then bargain with the seller until a price is agreed on.

Second, there's the notion that auction sales end at a fixed time. On eBay, this encourages buyers to wait until the last minute, or even the last second or two, to place a bid. On iOffer, there is no fixed ending time. It's free to set up a store, and sellers are charged fees only when they sell an item. Fees tend to be lower than on eBay; for items that sell for $10 to $24.99, the fee is $1.25, for instance.

WorthPoint/GoAntiques

Knowledge sells. That maxim applies on the Web, where shoppers are used to digging around for specifications and all the information they can find about items they seek. WorthPoint (www.worthpoint.com), which recently purchased the venerable online auction site GoAntiques, makes knowledge a big asset for anyone who wants to sell online.

Don't know what that antique lamp with the clock in the middle of the woman's stomach is worth? You can look up similar items on WorthPoint's database and get a good idea. Or, you can ask an expert called a "Worthologist," who is there to answer questions and provide advice just for registered sellers. You have to be a member to gain access to this wealth of information. Memberships start at $9.99 per month, which enables you to look up 25 items from the "Worthopedia" database each month.

Chatting It Up on Bonanzle

If you want to forget about the suspense of auction sales and simply offer merchandise at a fixed price, just as in a garage sale, take a look at Bonanzle (www.bonanzle.com). Lots of entrepreneurs have already taken a look. Bonanzle was only launched in June 2008, but by August 2009, it had 100,000 registered users. The most popular areas on the site are collectibles, shoes, books, records, and jewelry.

At a garage sale, buyers are apt to haggle and chat with sellers, and the same applies at Bonanzle. If you like some social networking along with your selling, this is the place for you. Sellers offer their merchandise in a sales "booth," which is the equivalent of a store on other sites. Each booth has a chat window incorporated into it. The seller can use it to say "Hi" or engage buyers in conversation. Bonanzle also has discussion boards, just as other sites do. But the fact that chat goes on in the midst of sales descriptions sets Bonanzle apart.

The interaction extends to management as well. Customers can add to a "wish list" of features they want to see on the site — a list reviewed and addressed by founder Bill Harding himself. He often responds personally to such requests.

HighWire

HighWire Commerce (formerly BuyItSellIt.com) (www.highwire.com) is more than an auction or fixed-price sales marketplace. It's a free e-commerce hosting service. It costs nothing at all to create a storefront that includes a shopping cart and the ability to accept payments from PayPal and Google Payments. For just $4.95 per month, you gain the ability to customize your site and add your own domain name. (Otherwise, your storefront's domain name takes the form `www.mystorefrontname.mybisi.com`.)

Thomas Salas, coowner of the auction service provider InkFrog, which purchased BISI in 2008, says many users pay the $4.95 fee. It includes 25MB of storage space for files and the ability to add Flash animations and other features to a site. The emphasis here is on features that make a full-featured e-commerce site run, including bulk uploading of multiple items; the ability to offer sales coupons; a customer account manager; and a customizable checkout process.

ArtFire

I've mentioned ArtFire (`www.artfire.com`) in several chapters of this book because I like the site's features. Many are available for free: ArtFire is a place where artisans can sell their handmade jewelry and other handcrafts. Here, as on other sites mentioned earlier in this chapter, sellers don't have to pay to set up a storefront or list items for sale. They don't even have to pay when they sell.

For absolutely nothing, you can list 12 items at a time. You get access to a long list of features that includes free Web hosting, a personalized URL, a shopping cart, payment processing, listing of items on Google Base, and more. For a $12 per month Verified Account, you can list an unlimited number of items, with up to ten photos per product, and many more features such as the ability to sell through your blog or on Facebook.

Webstore.com

Julio Pereda, who founded Webstore.com (`www.webstore.com`), likes to think of his site as being the Robin Hood of online marketplaces. Webstore focuses on the "Daily Deal," the practice of listing one item per day and making it available at a deep discount for a limited amount of time. It's an approach that has worked well on sites like Woot.com and on home shopping networks on television.

For sellers and buyers alike, the big advantage of Webstore.com is that no fees are charged, period. It's absolutely free to buy and sell. The site makes money from display ads posted on the side of many pages. Even though it's free, Webstore.com offers some nice features: Sellers can design their stores by using customizable templates, and buyers can shop for items in their local area if they want to pick up something in person.

Taking a Personal Approach: Wensy.com

Remember the days when every neighborhood had a corner store? You personally knew the people who ran the store, and they greeted you by name when you came in the door. For the most part, those days are gone. But in the online world, you occasionally find a site that is run by a true "lone entrepreneur," a do-it-yourselfer who doesn't have help and doesn't have to report to anyone else.

That's the story with Wensy.com (www.wensy.com), a site created and managed by Darren Bock, a man who has a day job as director of a hospital intensive care unit. In his spare time, after taking care of heart patients, he relaxes by responding to messages and managing his site. While he manages a staff of 71 during the day, his Web site staff is just one: himself. (He occasionally pays programmers to make technical changes.) The 6,000-plus registered users don't pay a penny in fees to either list items or sell them. Bock does include some ads on the site and gets donations from some users. But he's in it for the personal contact with his user community. He checks e-mails every 12 hours and responds personally to all of them. "It's a lot of fun," he told me.

Index